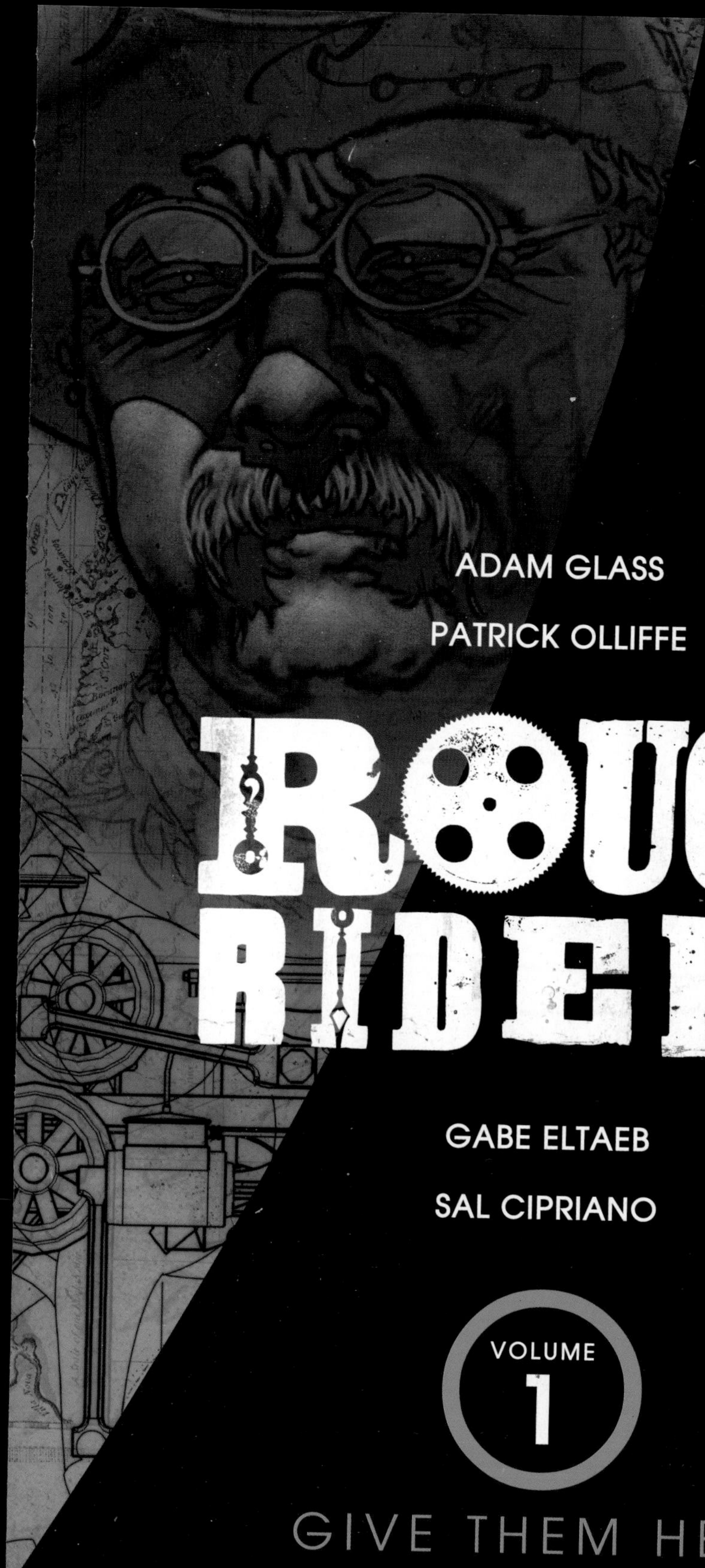

ADAM GLASS

PATRICK OLLIFFE

ROUGH RIDERS™

GABE ELTAEB

SAL CIPRIANO

VOLUME 1

GIVE THEM HELL

AFTERSHOCK™

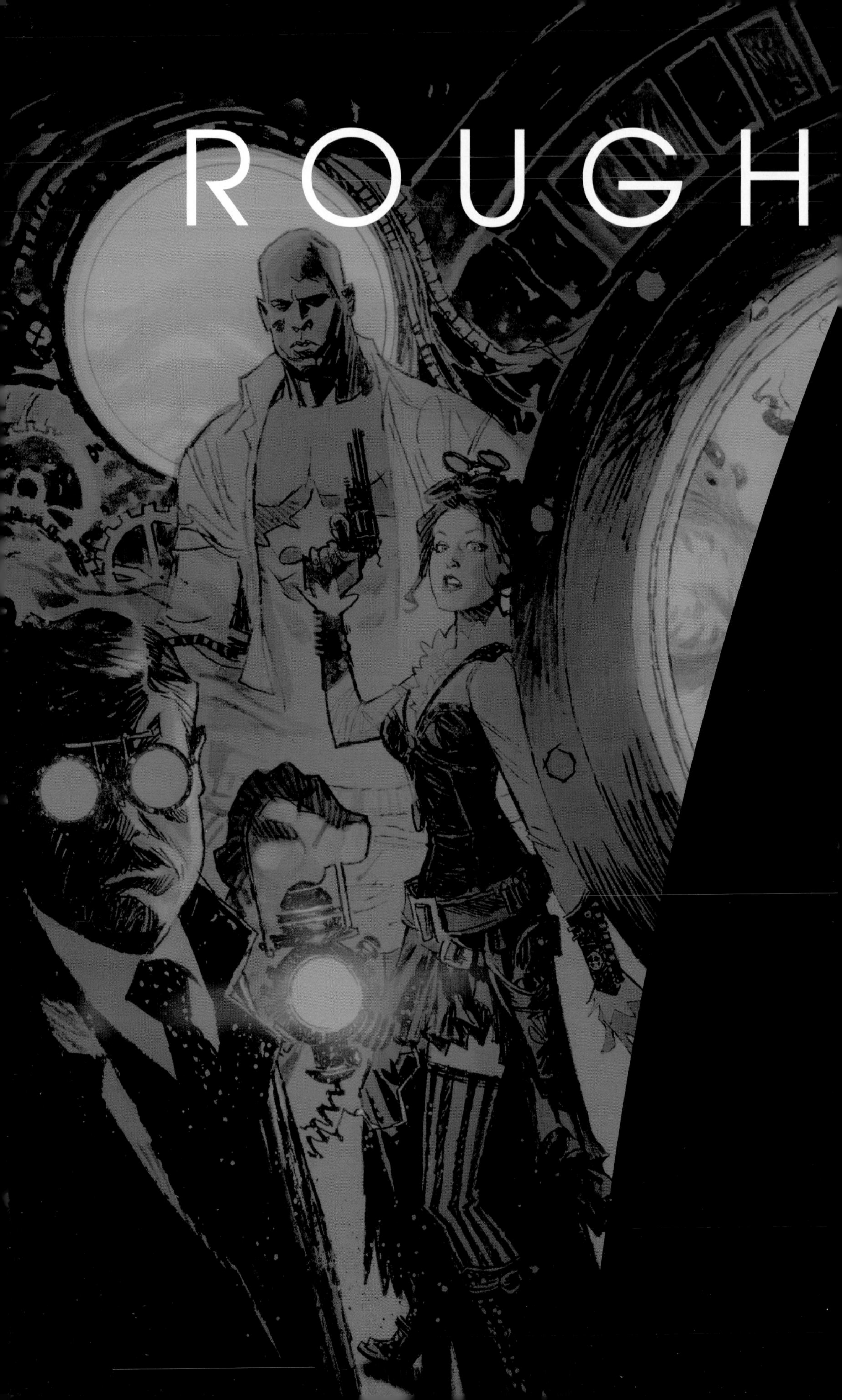
ROUGH

RIDERS

VOLUME 1

GIVE THEM HELL

ADAM GLASS creator & writer

PATRICK OLLIFFE artist

GABE ELTAEB colorist   **SAL CIPRIANO** letterer

PATRICK OLLIFFE & **GABE ELTAEB** cover

PATRICK OLLIFFE & **GABE ELTAEB** original series covers

FRANCESCO FRANCAVILLA, NICK PITARRA, ANDREW ROBINSON, HOYT SILVA & **BRIAN STELFREEZE** variant covers

TOM MULLER logo designer   **JOHN J. HILL** book designer

MIKE MARTS editor

AFTERSHOCK

MIKE MARTS - Editor-in-Chief   •   **JOE PRUETT** - Publisher   •   **LEE KRAMER** - President
JAWAD QURESHI - SVP, Investor Relations   •   **JON KRAMER** - Chief Executive Officer
MIKE ZAGARI - SVP Digital/Creative   •   **JAY BEHLING** - Chief Financial Officer   •   **MICHAEL RICHTER** - Chief Creative Officer
STEPHAN NILSON - Publishing Operations Manager   •   **LISA Y. WU** - Social Media Coordinator

AfterShock Trade Dress and Interior Design by **JOHN J. HILL**
AfterShock Logo Design by **COMICRAFT**
Proofreading by **J. HARBORE** & **DOCTOR Z.**
Publicity: contact **AARON MARION** (aaron@fifteenminutes.com) &
RYAN CROY (ryan@fifteenminutes.com) at **15 MINUTES**

ROUGH RIDERS VOLUME 1: GIVE THEM HELL Published by AfterShock Comics, LLC, 15300 Ventura Boulevard
Suite 507, Sherman Oaks, CA 91403. Copyright © 2016 by Adam Glass. Rough Riders ™ (including all prominent characters featured
herein), its logo and all character likeness are trademarks of Adam Glass, unless otherwise noted. All rights reserved. AfterShock Comics
and its logos are trademarks of AfterShock Comics, LLC. No part of this publication may be reproduced or transmitted, in any form or by
any means (except for short excerpts for review purposes) without the expressed written permission of AfterShock Comics, LLC. All names,
characters, events and locales in this publication are entirely fictional. Any resemblance to actual persons (living or dead), events or places,
without satiric intent, is coincidental. Originally published as Rough Riders #1-7. PRINTED IN KOREA.
First Printing: November 2016. 10 9 8 7 6 5 4 3 2 1

AFTERSHOCKCOMICS.COM   Follow us on social media 🐦 📷 f

INTRODUCTION

I'll skip the shitty, poor, fatherless childhood and get right to the hero of my youth: ENCYCLOPEDIA BRITANNICA. If you're under FORTY, you're now thinking, "What is an Encyclopedia Britannica?" Before the INTERNET, you had to go to this place called a "LIBRARY." And look things up. (Yes, I'm that condescending.) But what the Encyclopedia did was give you what would have taken you months to research and put it all in a single book—in alphabetical order. So, every month there would come a new letter; First was "A" (and everything that ever had to do with anything that ever started with that letter: people, places, things). Then next month would come "B," then "C," then "D," etc...and I would rip through these books, learning everything I could. Until one day, I turned the page and there he was—a man in a tuxedo, hair all tousled, struggling to get out of a bunch of shackles and handcuffs. His name was HOUDINI, and I was instantly HOOKED and wanted to know more about him. So I dove in and began to learn everything I could about him, and soon after I found a picture of Houdini standing on a ship deck with a man, a big bushy mustache hung over his top lip, a look of danger hidden behind his spectacles. He was one part gentleman, one part cowboy. He was PRESIDENT THEODORE ROOSEVELT.

These two men were my gateway drugs into becoming a history freak, and I've never looked back. Having already been a comic book fan, I could not believe the real-life super heroes I was finding in our own past. Of course, I quickly learned that many of these historical characters served as the very foundation for the heroes that I'd come to love. History is so cool, but most people don't realize that, because if it's not taught right, it can be a snooze fest. But history has it all: war, love, hate, death, despair, hope, heartbreak, etc...it has the greatest stories ever told. And they're REAL.

So I thought, why not take all these great historical characters and team them up, showing them with their warts and all. And the result has been a dream gig for sure. One I'm not sure I will ever be able to replicate. But you're only as good as the team you have around you—and I have one of the best, starting with our artist, Patrick Olliffe. Whenever I send a suggestion to Pat, he always comes back with something even better. Our colorist, Gabe Eltaeb, is a maestro with a paintbrush, and Sal Cipriano, our letterer, somehow turns my chicken scratch into something legible and entertaining. My publisher AfterShock Comics, who allows dreamers to dream and whose support I will always be thankful for. And, finally, my family—Mia, Josephine and Aidan—there is none of this without you.

With that, I hope you all enjoy reading the first adventure of the Rough Riders, because we had a blast making it. And like Theodore Roosevelt used to say, remember to always "Dare mighty things."

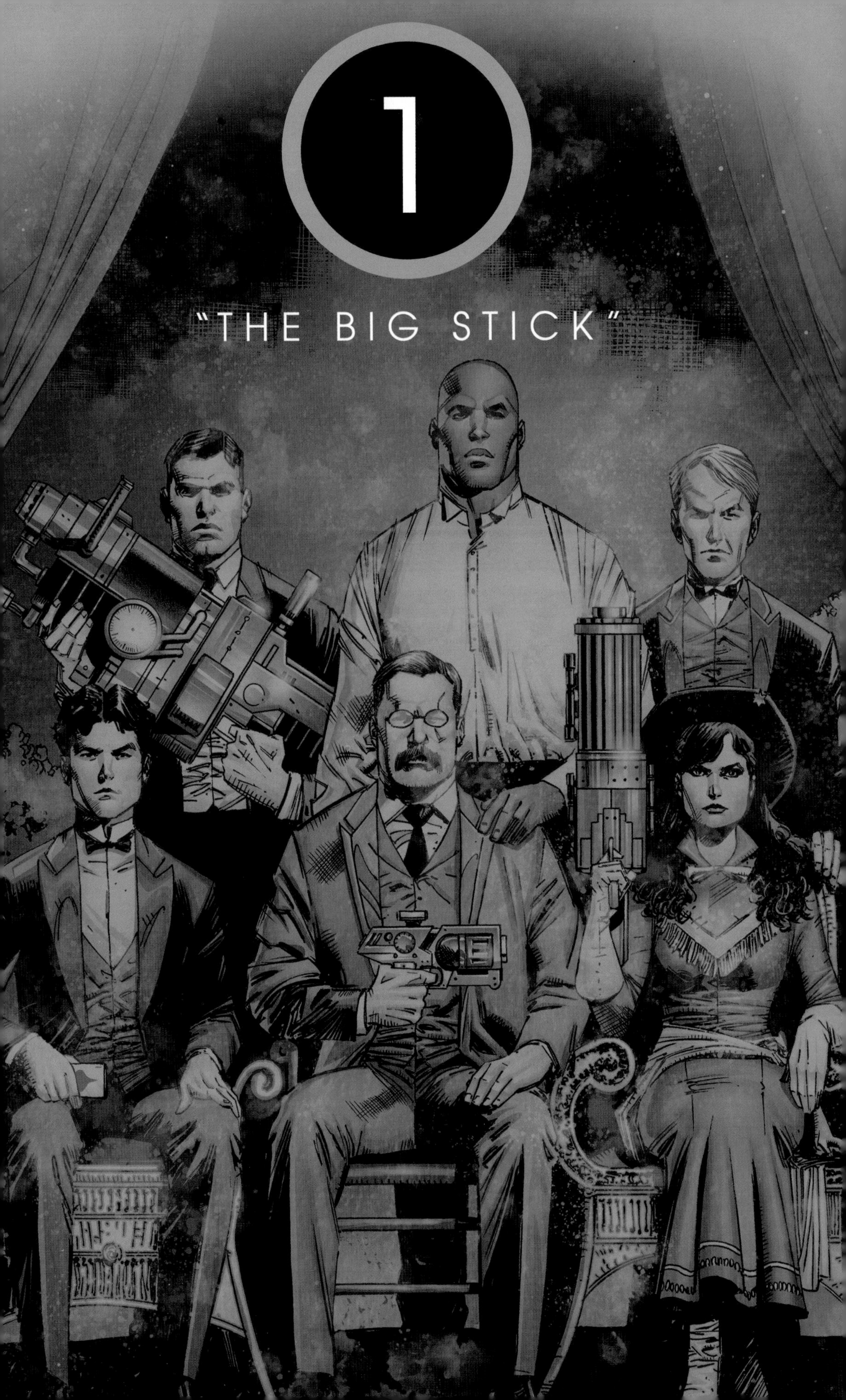
1
"THE BIG STICK"

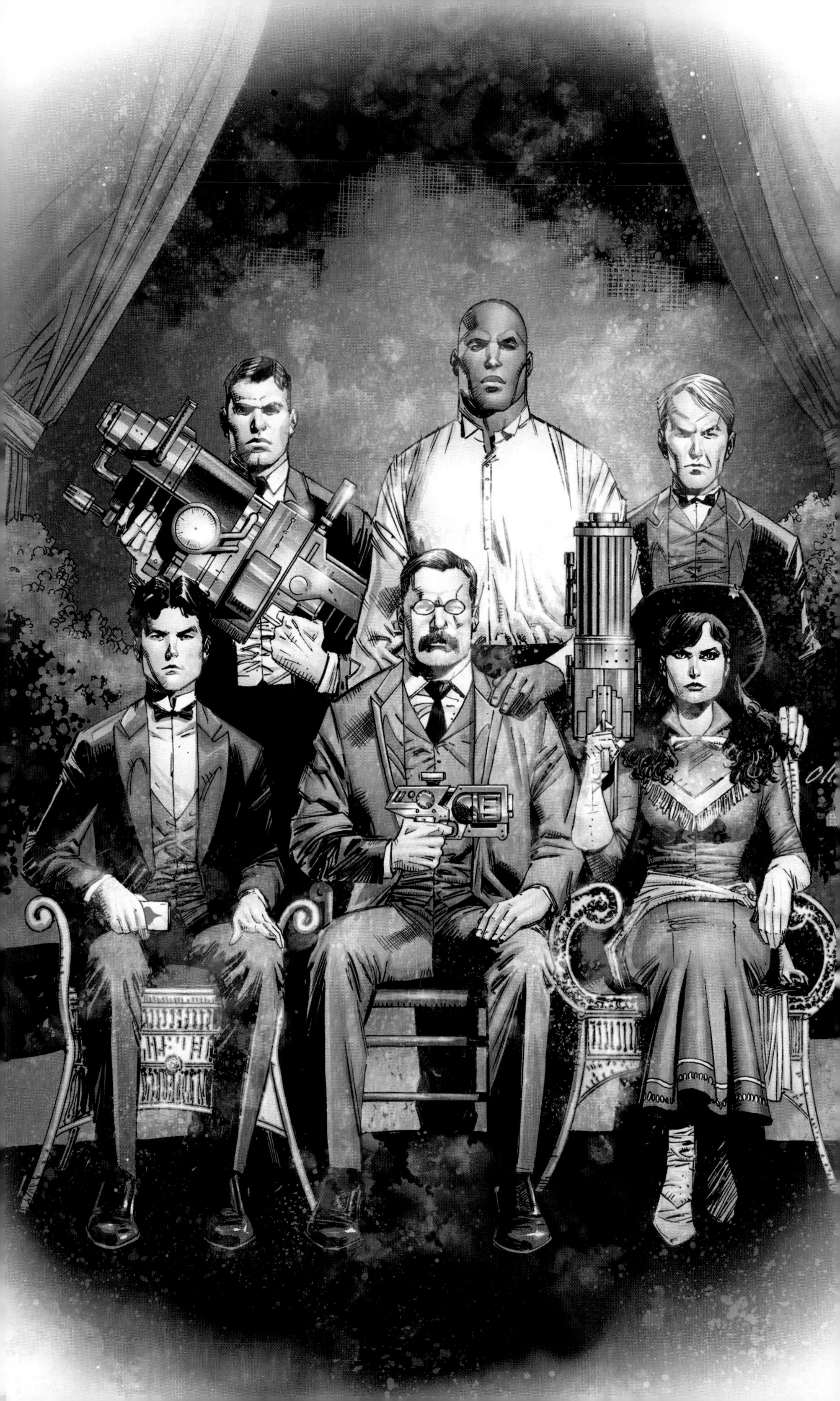

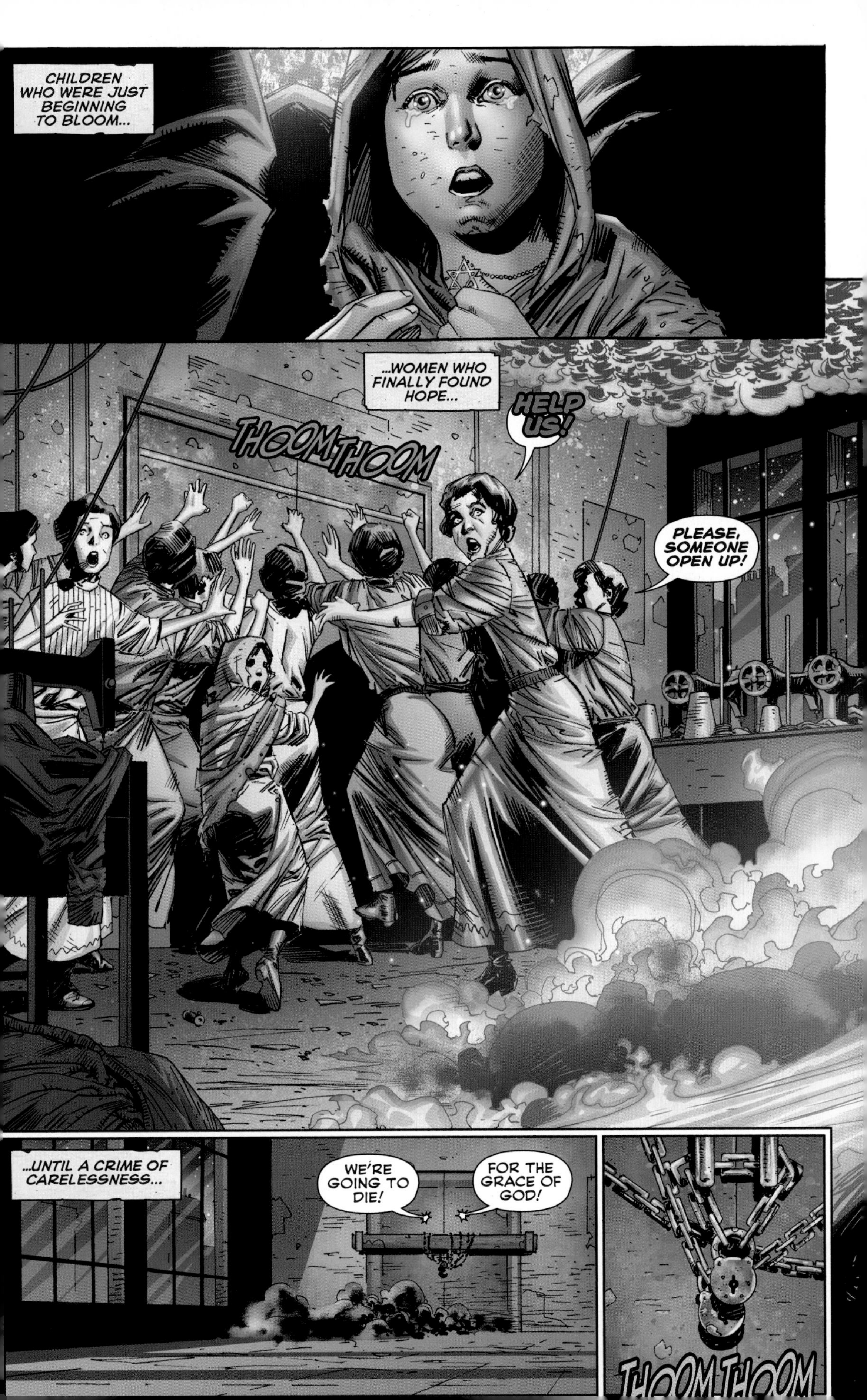

CHILDREN WHO WERE JUST BEGINNING TO BLOOM...
...WOMEN WHO FINALLY FOUND HOPE...
HELP US!
THOOM THOOM
PLEASE, SOMEONE OPEN UP!
...UNTIL A CRIME OF CARELESSNESS...
WE'RE GOING TO DIE!
FOR THE GRACE OF GOD!
THOOM THOOM

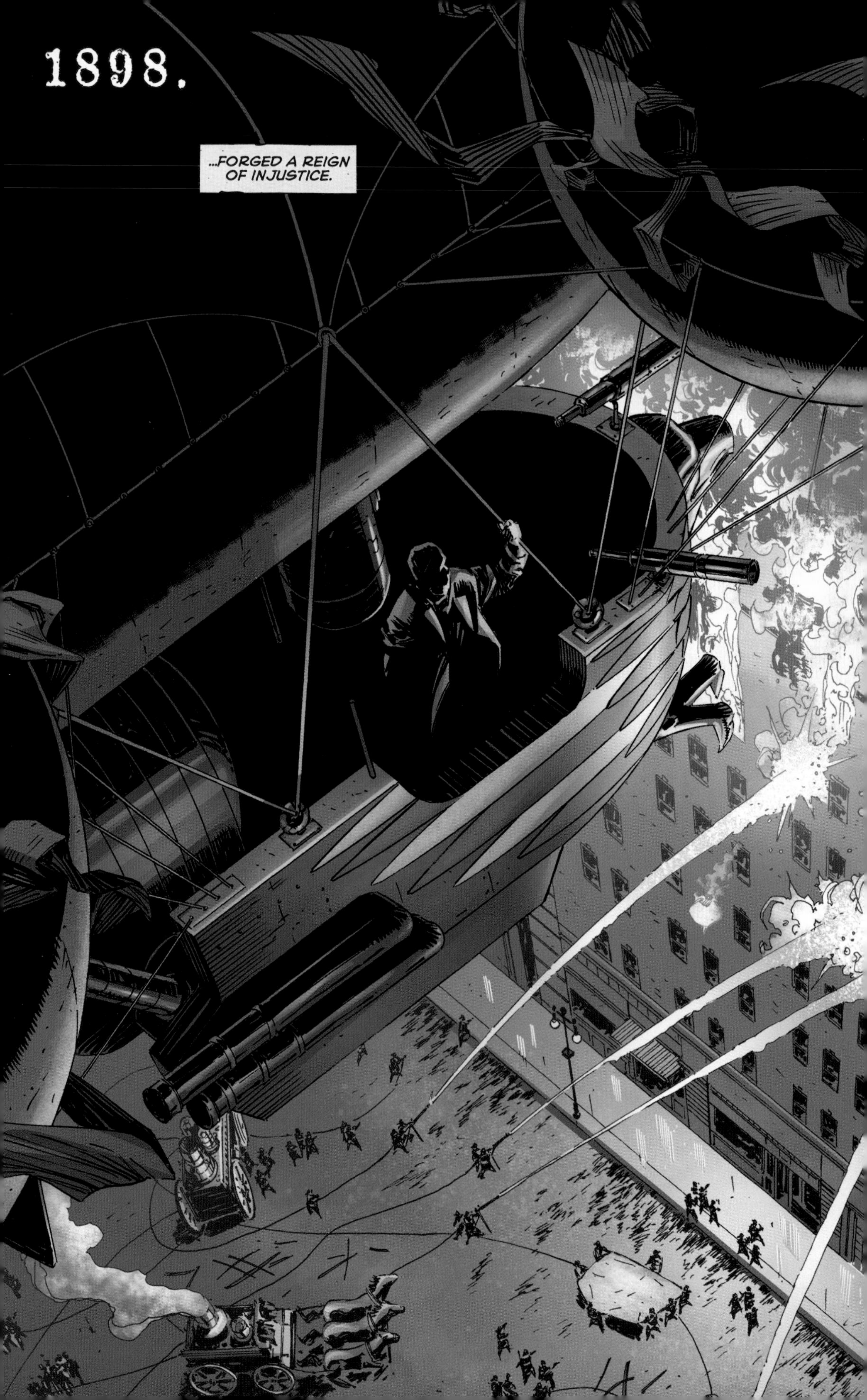
1898.
...FORGED A REIGN OF INJUSTICE.

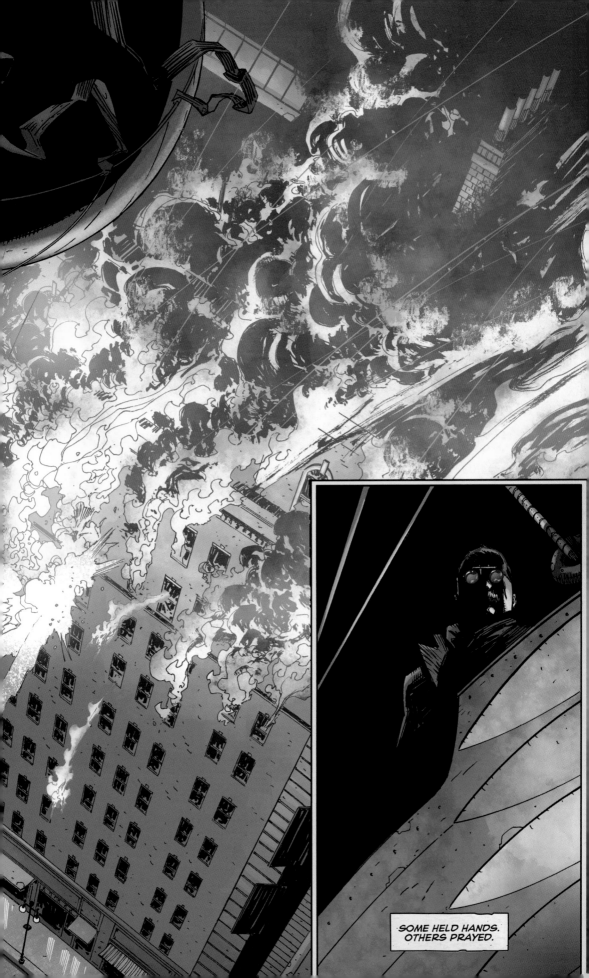

SOME HELD HANDS.
OTHERS PRAYED.

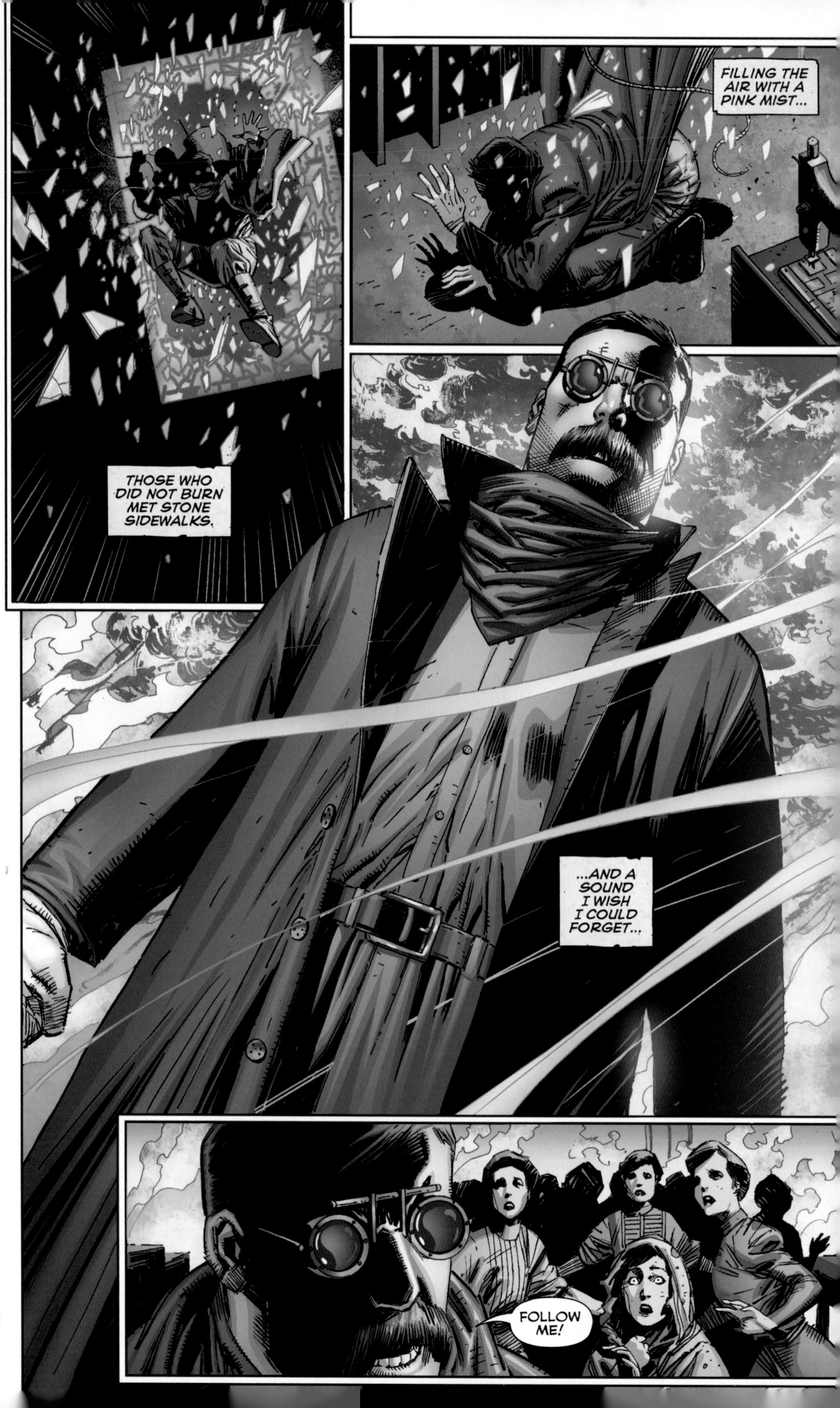
THOSE WHO DID NOT BURN MET STONE SIDEWALKS.
FILLING THE AIR WITH A PINK MIST...
...AND A SOUND I WISH I COULD FORGET...
FOLLOW ME!

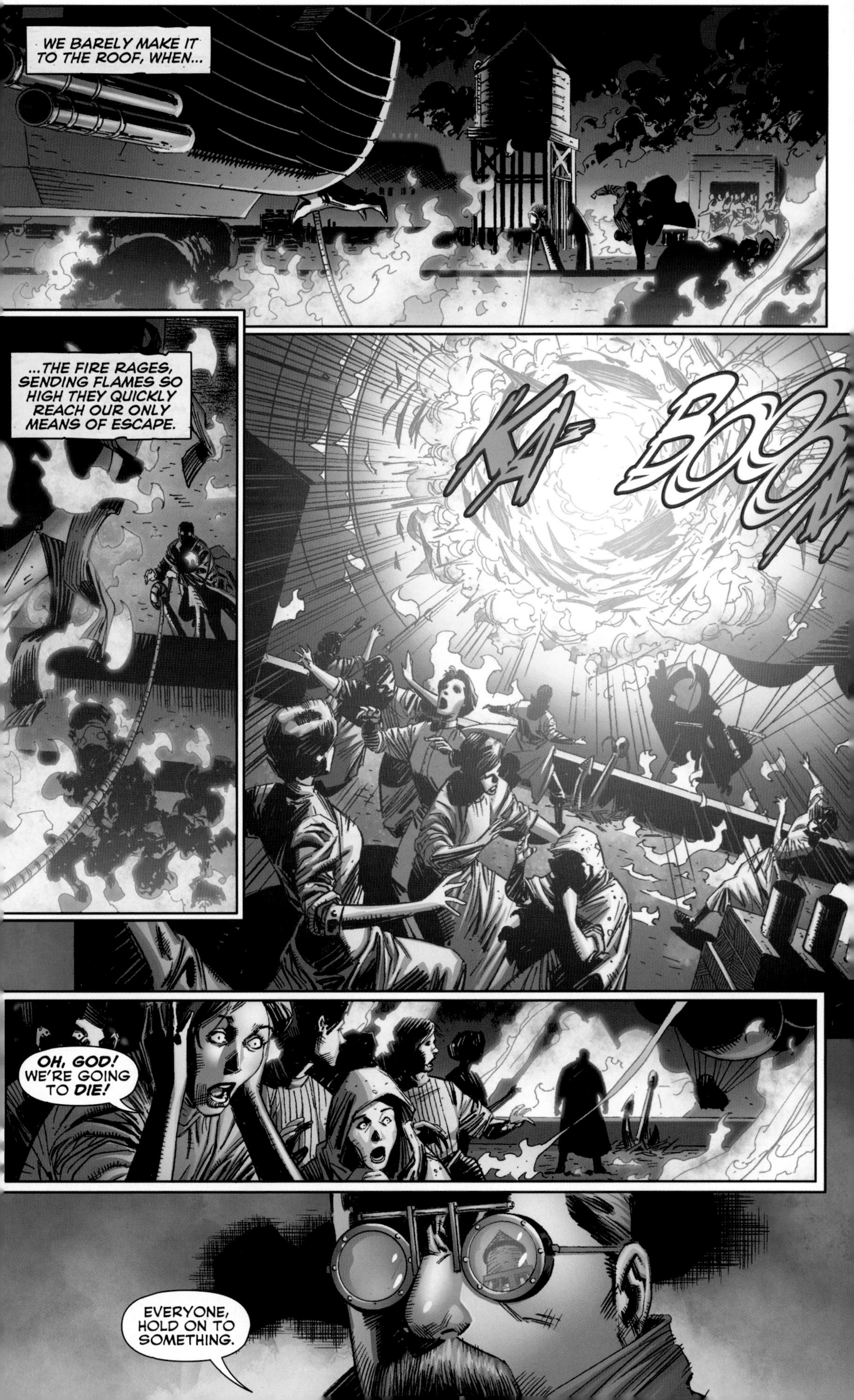

WE BARELY MAKE IT TO THE ROOF, WHEN...
...THE FIRE RAGES, SENDING FLAMES SO HIGH THEY QUICKLY REACH OUR ONLY MEANS OF ESCAPE.
KA-BOOM
OH, GOD! WE'RE GOING TO DIE!
EVERYONE, HOLD ON TO SOMETHING.

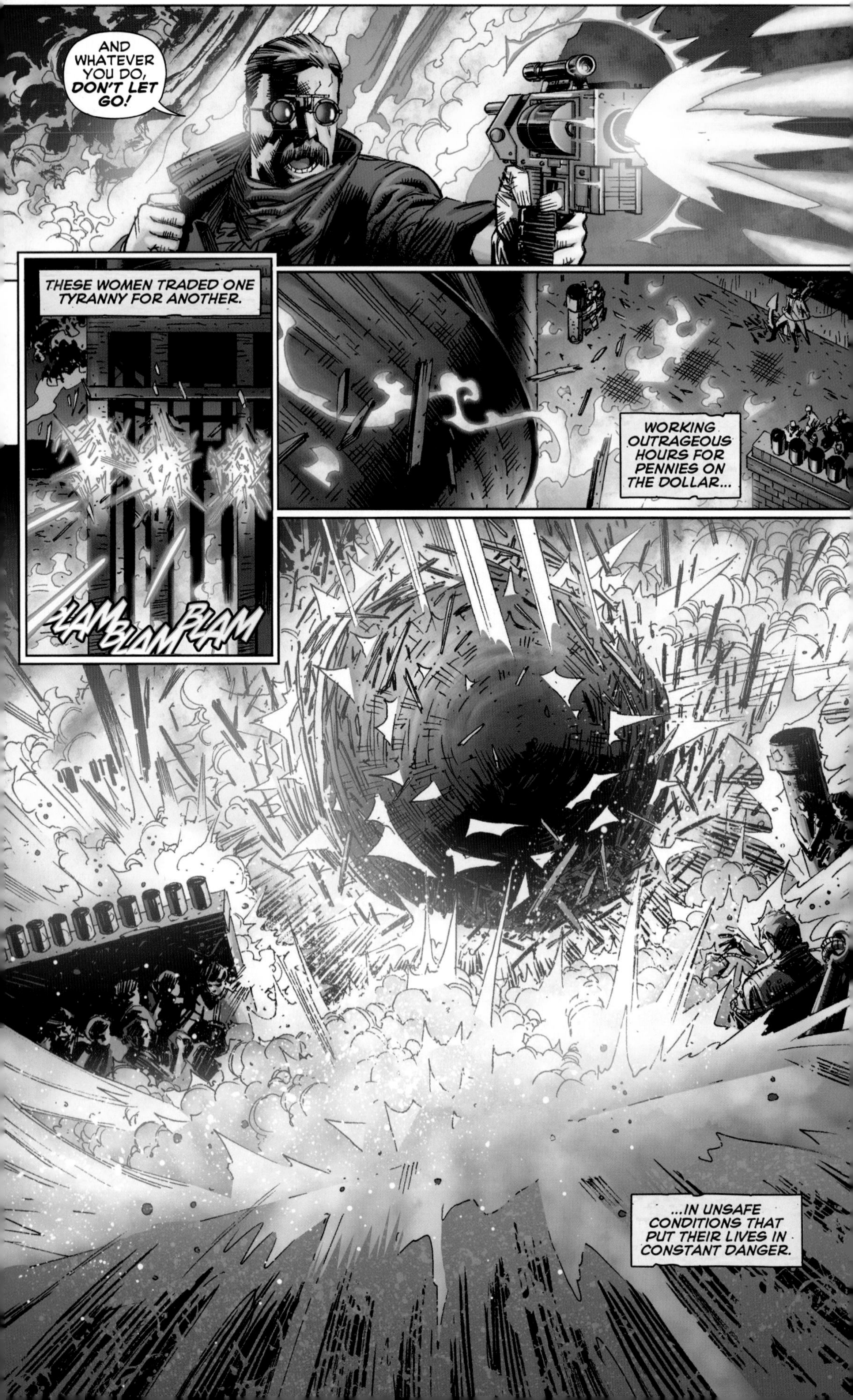
AND WHATEVER YOU DO, DON'T LET GO!
THESE WOMEN TRADED ONE TYRANNY FOR ANOTHER.
BLAM BLAM BLAM
WORKING OUTRAGEOUS HOURS FOR PENNIES ON THE DOLLAR...
...IN UNSAFE CONDITIONS THAT PUT THEIR LIVES IN CONSTANT DANGER.

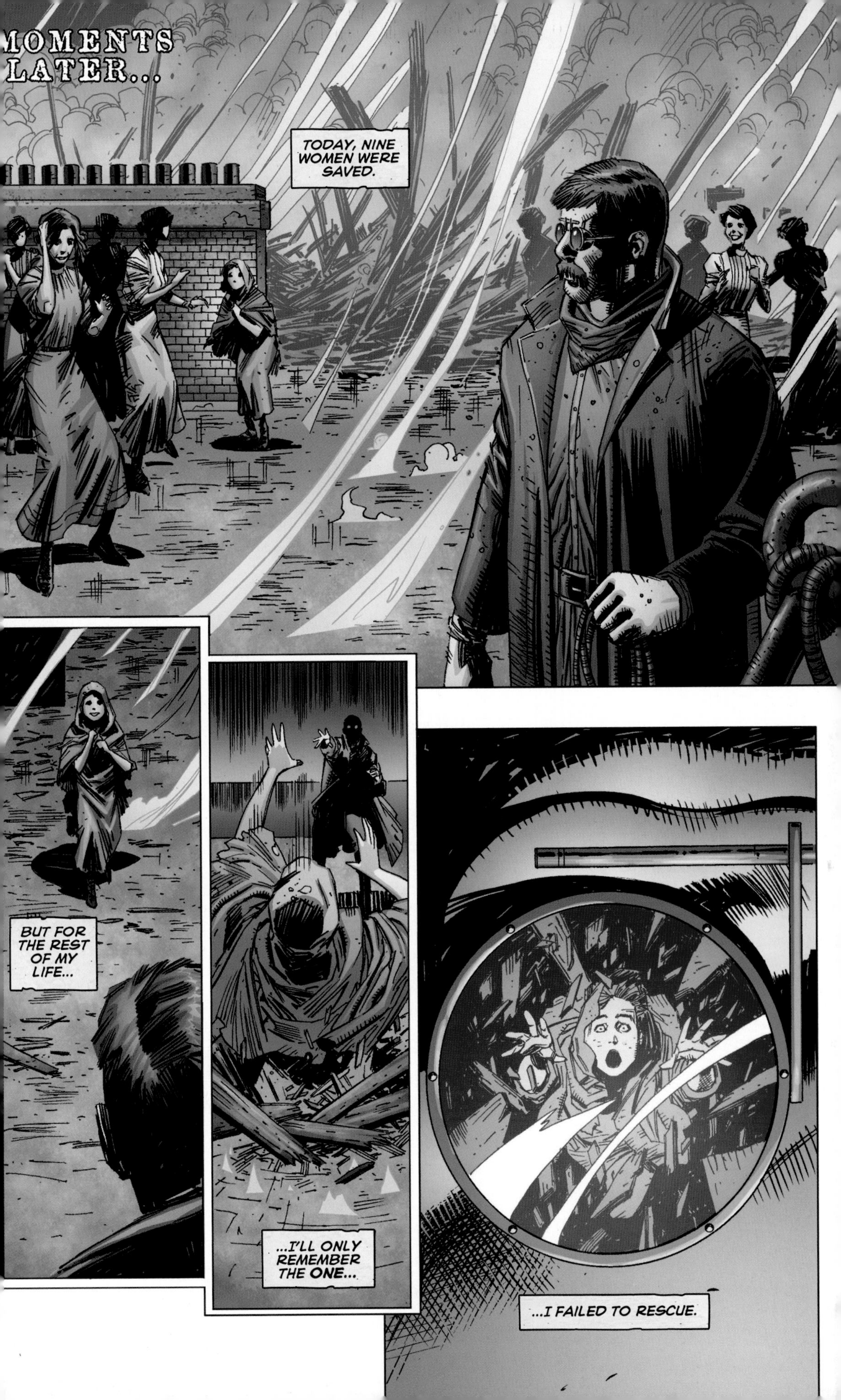

MOMENTS LATER...
TODAY, NINE WOMEN WERE SAVED.
BUT FOR THE REST OF MY LIFE...
...I'LL ONLY REMEMBER THE ONE...
...I FAILED TO RESCUE.

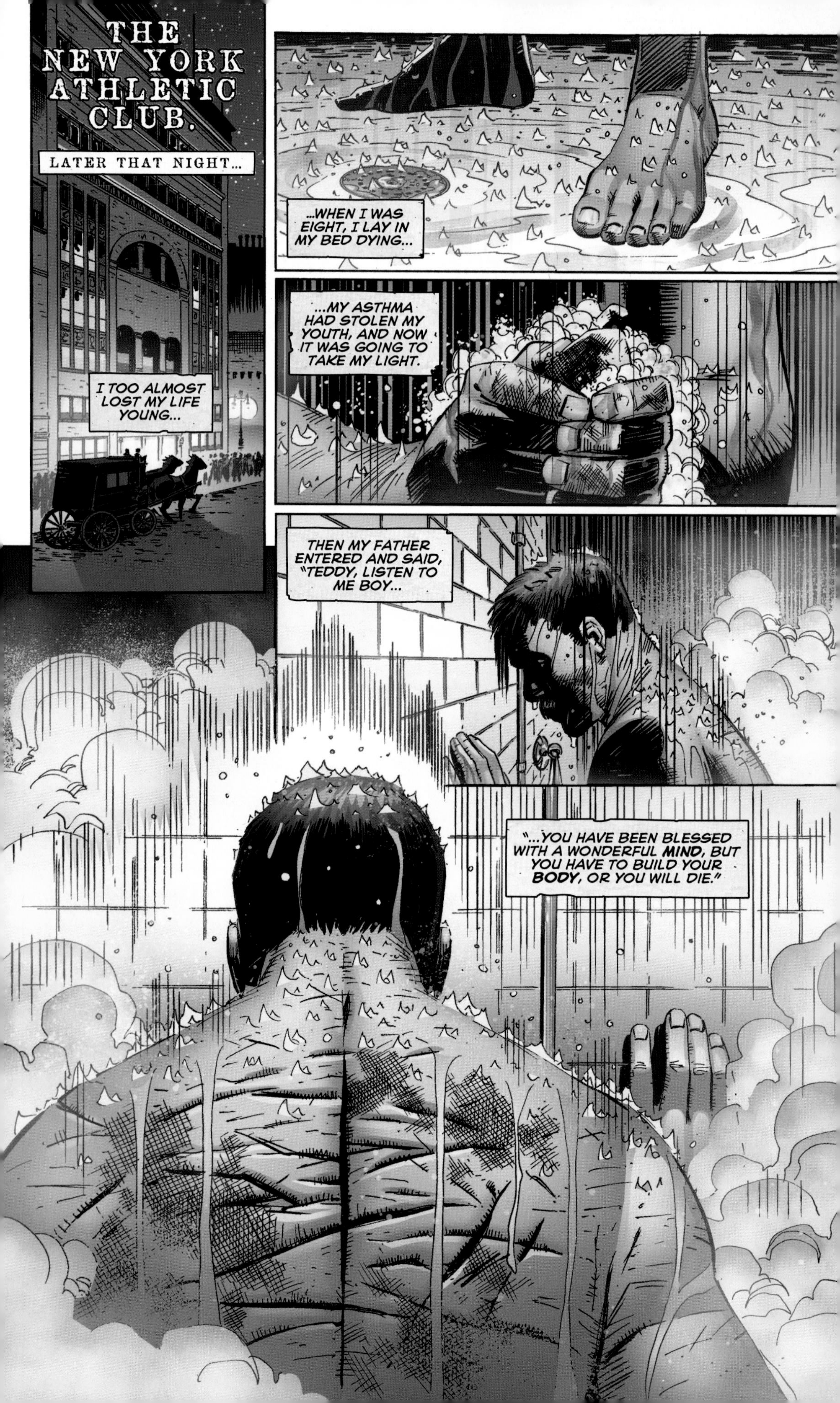
THE NEW YORK ATHLETIC CLUB.
LATER THAT NIGHT...
I TOO ALMOST LOST MY LIFE YOUNG...
...WHEN I WAS EIGHT, I LAY IN MY BED DYING...
...MY ASTHMA HAD STOLEN MY YOUTH, AND NOW IT WAS GOING TO TAKE MY LIGHT.
THEN MY FATHER ENTERED AND SAID, "TEDDY, LISTEN TO ME BOY...
"...YOU HAVE BEEN BLESSED WITH A WONDERFUL MIND, BUT YOU HAVE TO BUILD YOUR BODY, OR YOU WILL DIE."

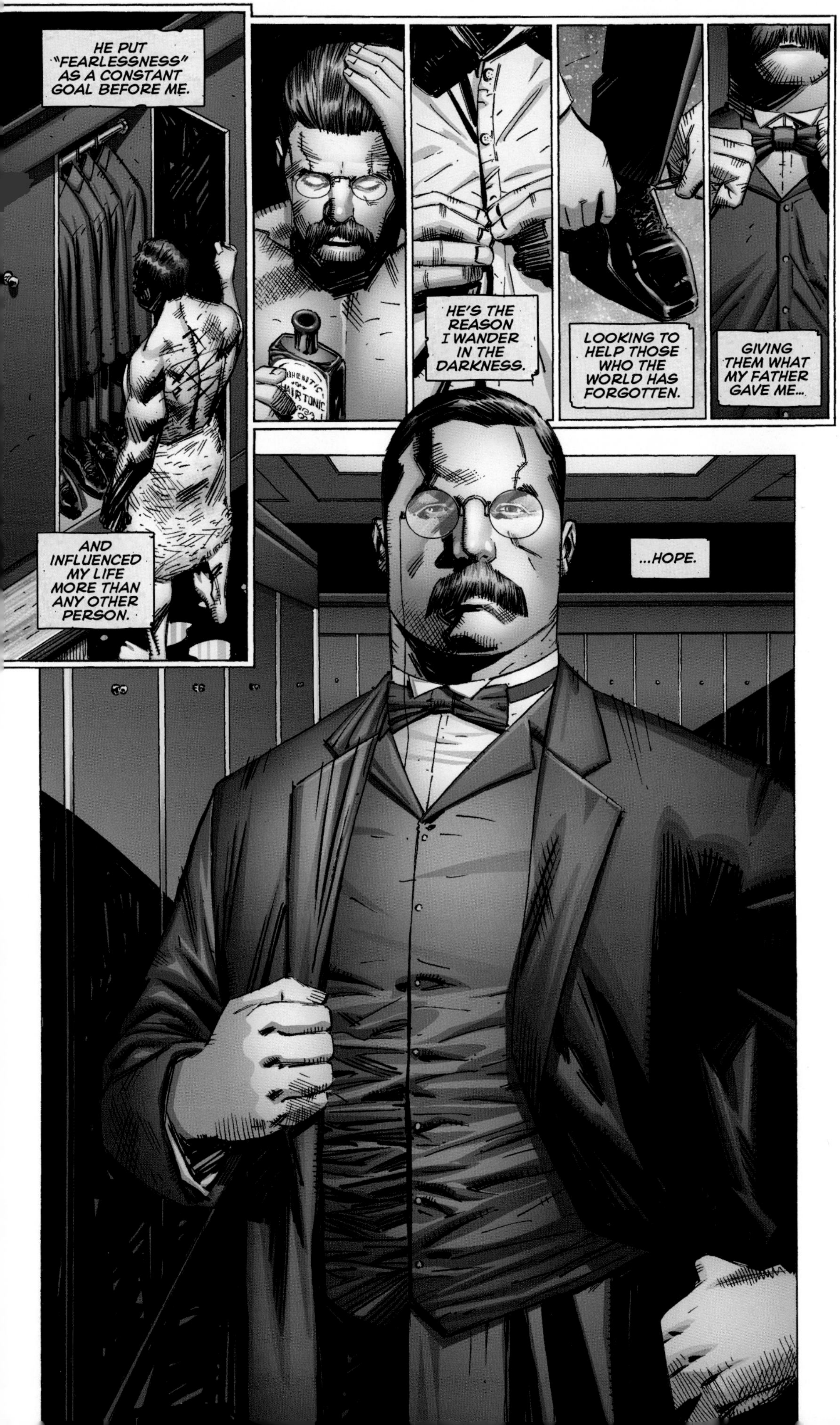
HE PUT "FEARLESSNESS" AS A CONSTANT GOAL BEFORE ME.
AND INFLUENCED MY LIFE MORE THAN ANY OTHER PERSON.
HE'S THE REASON I WANDER IN THE DARKNESS.
LOOKING TO HELP THOSE WHO THE WORLD HAS FORGOTTEN.
GIVING THEM WHAT MY FATHER GAVE ME...
...HOPE.

TEDDY, WE SURE MISS YOU DOWN AT TAMMANY HALL.

YOU'RE A TERRIFIC LIAR, MAYOR VAN WYCK. WHICH MEANS YOU'LL PROBABLY BE *GOVERNOR* IN NO TIME.

ONLY CHANCE OF THAT IS IF *YOU* DON'T RUN, OLD CHAP.

THE ONLY RUNNING I DO THESE DAYS IS CHASING MY NAMESAKES AROUND.

THEN YOU ARE TRULY BLESSED.

SO MY WIFE KEEPS TELLING ME.

TAMMANY HALL IS A DEN OF INIQUITY.

AND VAN WYCK ITS PUPPET.

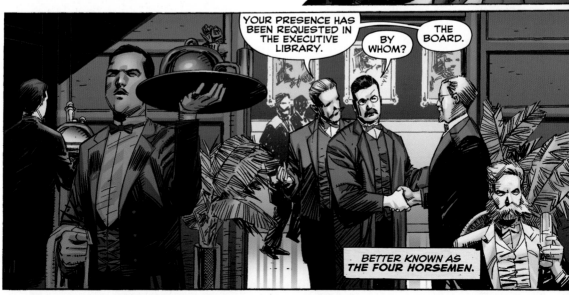

YOUR PRESENCE HAS BEEN REQUESTED IN THE EXECUTIVE LIBRARY.

BY WHOM?

THE BOARD.

BETTER KNOWN AS *THE FOUR HORSEMEN.*

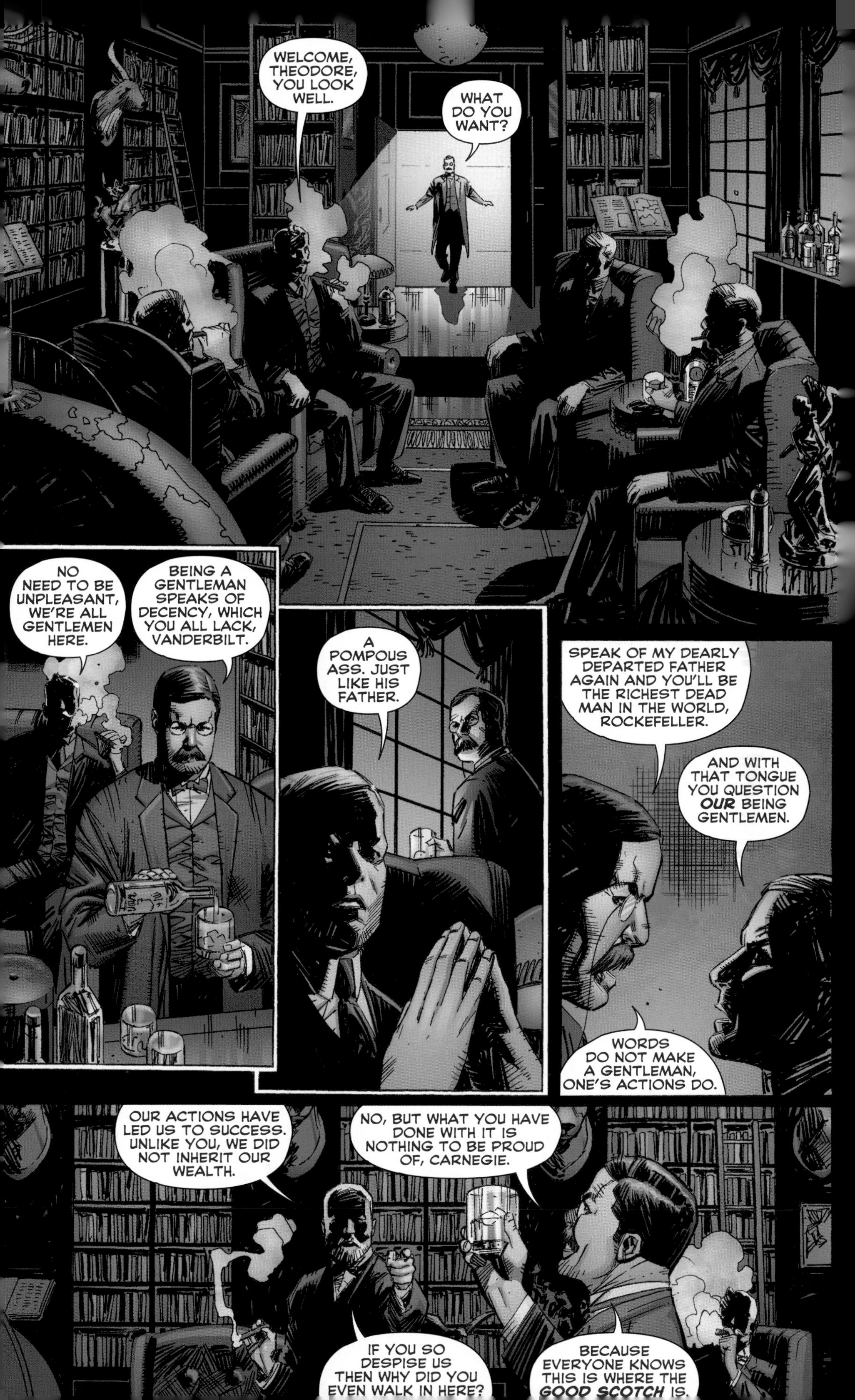
WELCOME, THEODORE, YOU LOOK WELL.
WHAT DO YOU WANT?
NO NEED TO BE UNPLEASANT, WE'RE ALL GENTLEMEN HERE.
BEING A GENTLEMAN SPEAKS OF DECENCY, WHICH YOU ALL LACK, VANDERBILT.
A POMPOUS ASS. JUST LIKE HIS FATHER.
SPEAK OF MY DEARLY DEPARTED FATHER AGAIN AND YOU'LL BE THE RICHEST DEAD MAN IN THE WORLD, ROCKEFELLER.
AND WITH THAT TONGUE YOU QUESTION *OUR* BEING GENTLEMEN.
WORDS DO NOT MAKE A GENTLEMAN, ONE'S ACTIONS DO.
OUR ACTIONS HAVE LED US TO SUCCESS. UNLIKE YOU, WE DID NOT INHERIT OUR WEALTH.
NO, BUT WHAT YOU HAVE DONE WITH IT IS NOTHING TO BE PROUD OF, CARNEGIE.
IF YOU SO DESPISE US THEN WHY DID YOU EVEN WALK IN HERE?
BECAUSE EVERYONE KNOWS THIS IS WHERE THE ***GOOD SCOTCH*** IS.

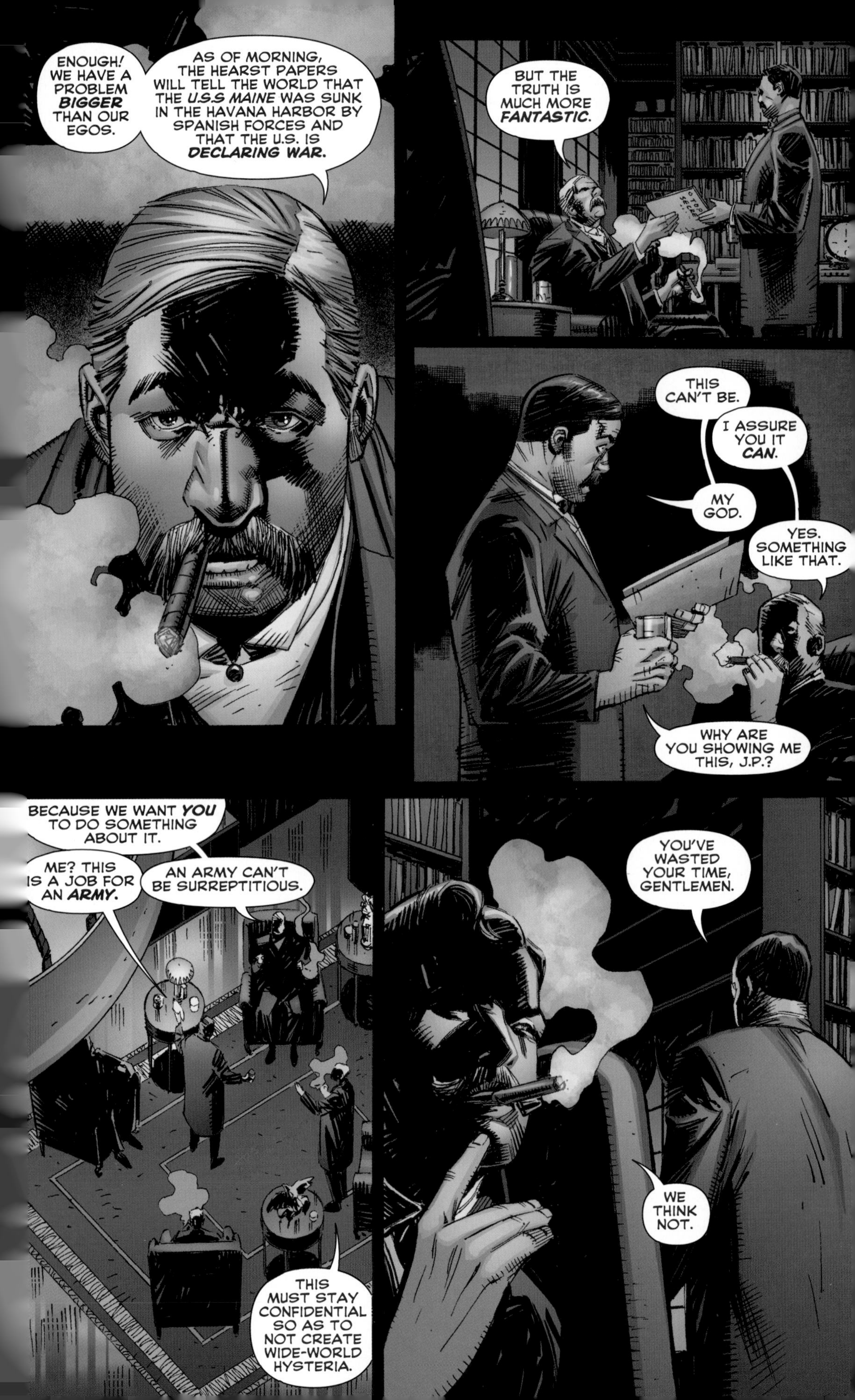
ENOUGH! WE HAVE A PROBLEM BIGGER THAN OUR EGOS.
AS OF MORNING, THE HEARST PAPERS WILL TELL THE WORLD THAT THE U.S.S MAINE WAS SUNK IN THE HAVANA HARBOR BY SPANISH FORCES AND THAT THE U.S. IS DECLARING WAR.
BUT THE TRUTH IS MUCH MORE FANTASTIC.
THIS CAN'T BE.
I ASSURE YOU IT CAN.
MY GOD.
YES. SOMETHING LIKE THAT.
WHY ARE YOU SHOWING ME THIS, J.P.?
BECAUSE WE WANT YOU TO DO SOMETHING ABOUT IT.
ME? THIS IS A JOB FOR AN ARMY.
AN ARMY CAN'T BE SURREPTITIOUS.
THIS MUST STAY CONFIDENTIAL SO AS TO NOT CREATE WIDE-WORLD HYSTERIA.
YOU'VE WASTED YOUR TIME, GENTLEMEN.
WE THINK NOT.

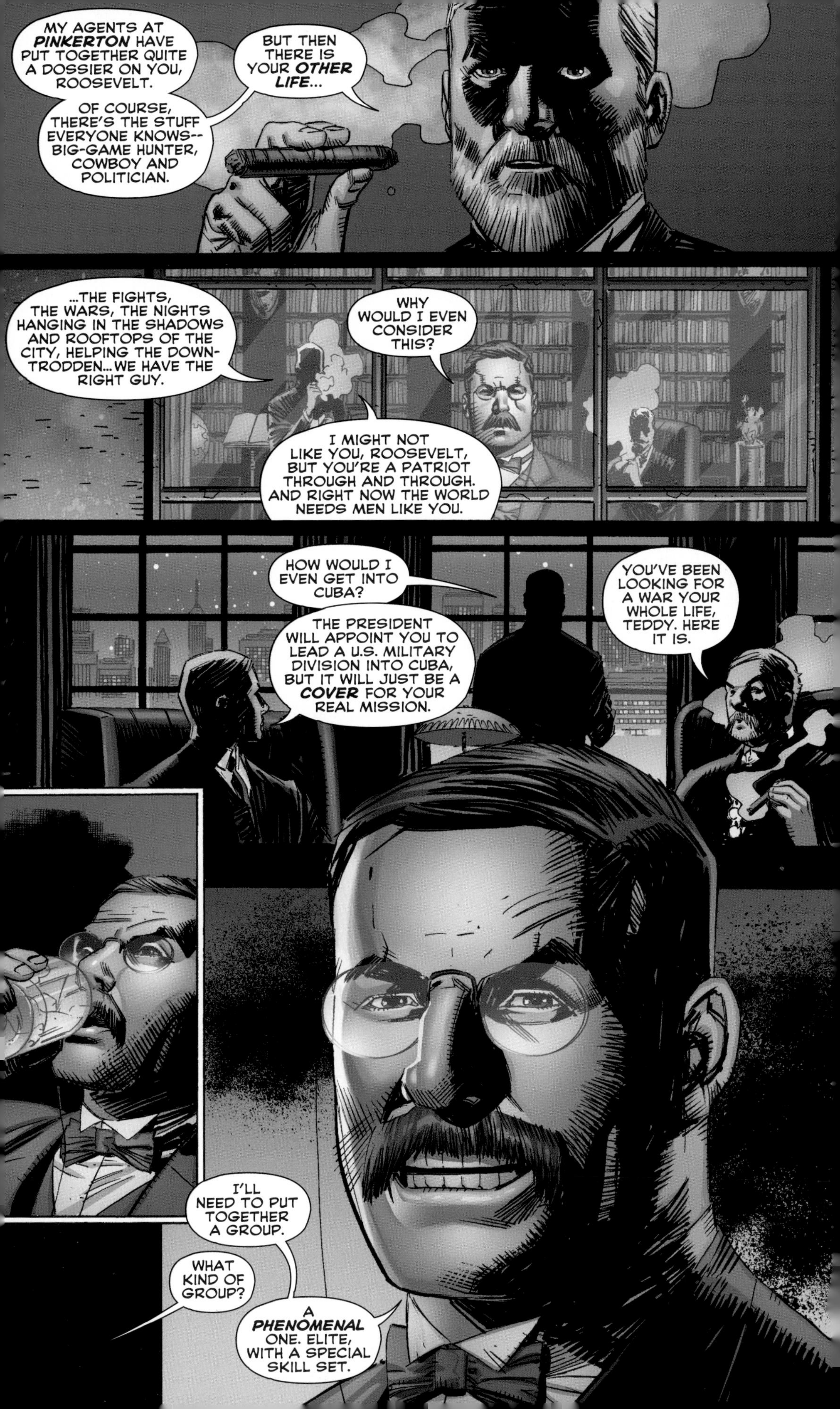

MY AGENTS AT PINKERTON HAVE PUT TOGETHER QUITE A DOSSIER ON YOU, ROOSEVELT.
OF COURSE, THERE'S THE STUFF EVERYONE KNOWS-- BIG-GAME HUNTER, COWBOY AND POLITICIAN.
BUT THEN THERE IS YOUR OTHER LIFE...
...THE FIGHTS, THE WARS, THE NIGHTS HANGING IN THE SHADOWS AND ROOFTOPS OF THE CITY, HELPING THE DOWN-TRODDEN...WE HAVE THE RIGHT GUY.
WHY WOULD I EVEN CONSIDER THIS?
I MIGHT NOT LIKE YOU, ROOSEVELT, BUT YOU'RE A PATRIOT THROUGH AND THROUGH. AND RIGHT NOW THE WORLD NEEDS MEN LIKE YOU.
HOW WOULD I EVEN GET INTO CUBA?
THE PRESIDENT WILL APPOINT YOU TO LEAD A U.S. MILITARY DIVISION INTO CUBA, BUT IT WILL JUST BE A COVER FOR YOUR REAL MISSION.
YOU'VE BEEN LOOKING FOR A WAR YOUR WHOLE LIFE, TEDDY. HERE IT IS.
I'LL NEED TO PUT TOGETHER A GROUP.
WHAT KIND OF GROUP?
A PHENOMENAL ONE. ELITE, WITH A SPECIAL SKILL SET.

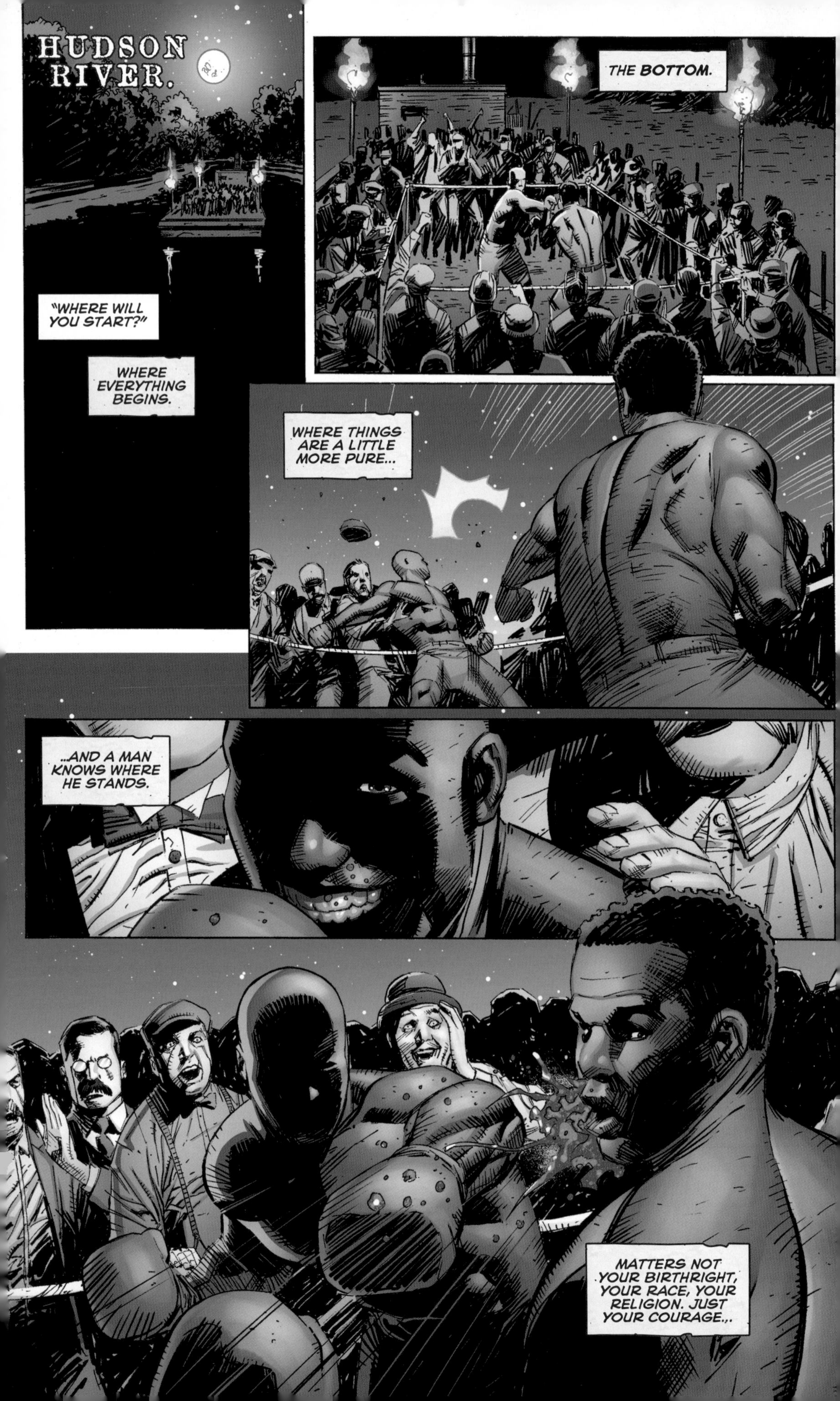
HUDSON RIVER.
THE BOTTOM.
"WHERE WILL YOU START?"
WHERE EVERYTHING BEGINS.
WHERE THINGS ARE A LITTLE MORE PURE...
...AND A MAN KNOWS WHERE HE STANDS.
MATTERS NOT YOUR BIRTHRIGHT, YOUR RACE, YOUR RELIGION. JUST YOUR COURAGE...

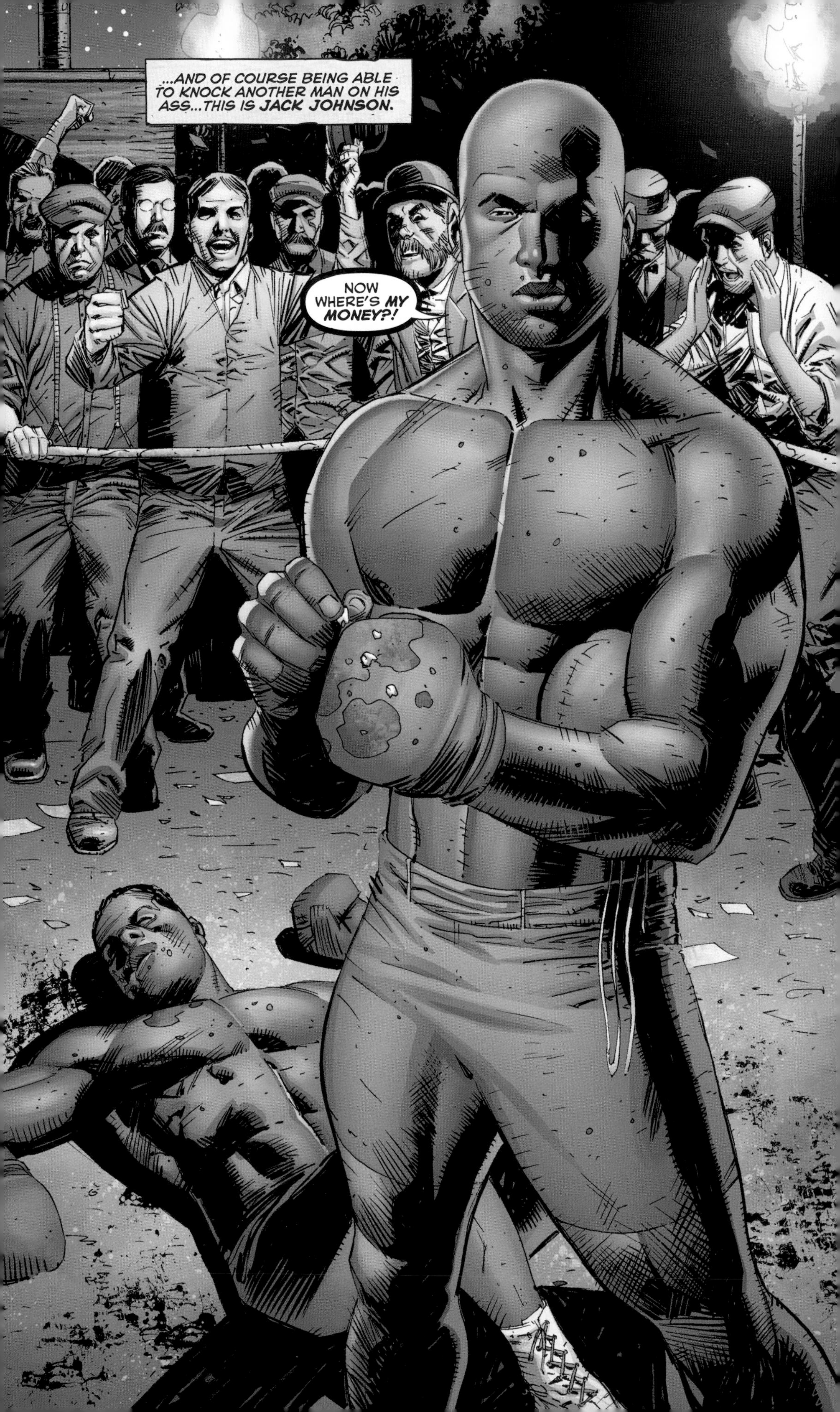
...AND OF COURSE BEING ABLE TO KNOCK ANOTHER MAN ON HIS ASS...THIS IS JACK JOHNSON.
NOW WHERE'S MY MONEY?!

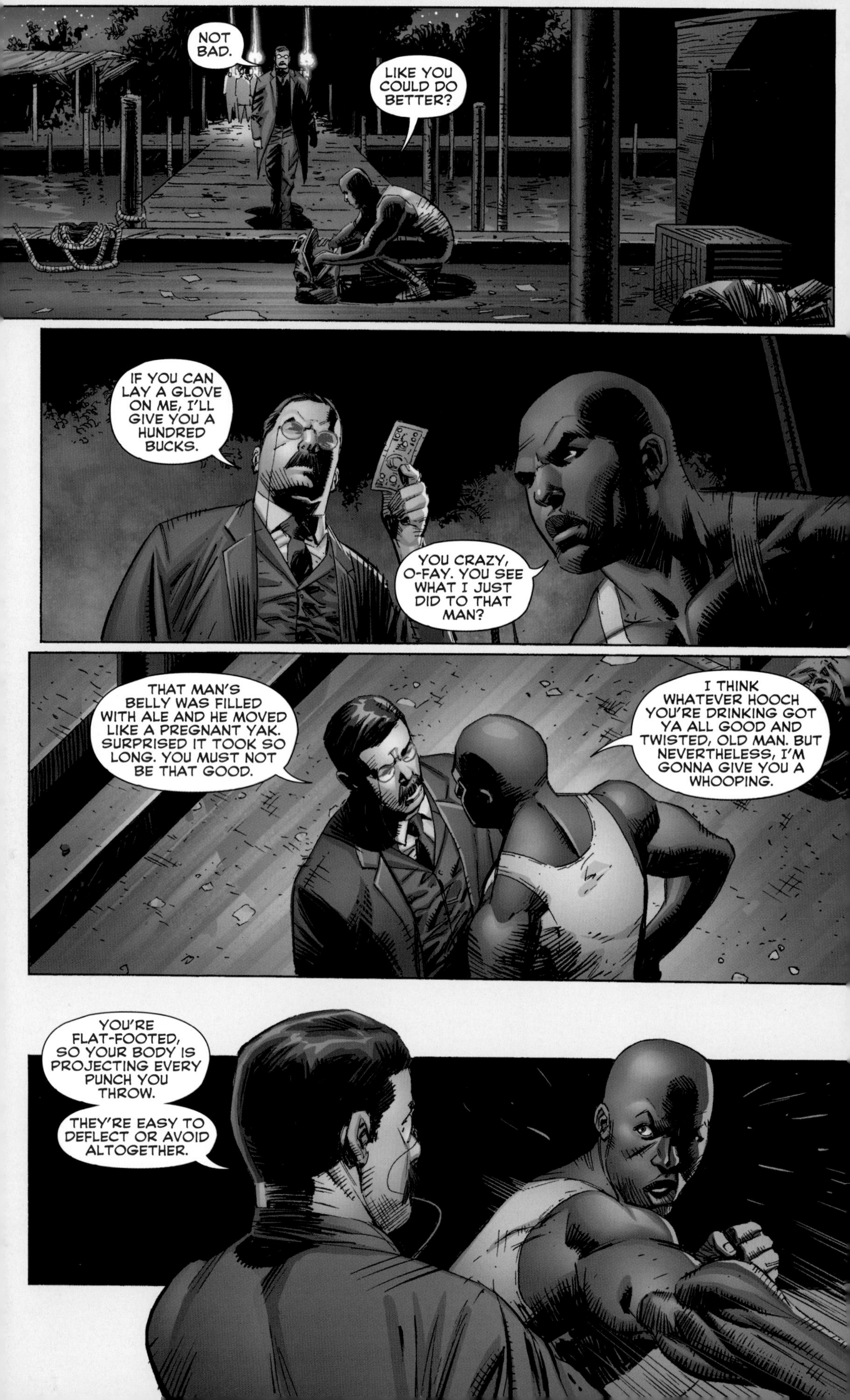
NOT BAD.
LIKE YOU COULD DO BETTER?
IF YOU CAN LAY A GLOVE ON ME, I'LL GIVE YOU A HUNDRED BUCKS.
YOU CRAZY, O-FAY. YOU SEE WHAT I JUST DID TO THAT MAN?
THAT MAN'S BELLY WAS FILLED WITH ALE AND HE MOVED LIKE A PREGNANT YAK. SURPRISED IT TOOK SO LONG. YOU MUST NOT BE THAT GOOD.
I THINK WHATEVER HOOCH YOU'RE DRINKING GOT YA ALL GOOD AND TWISTED, OLD MAN. BUT NEVERTHELESS, I'M GONNA GIVE YOU A WHOOPING.
YOU'RE FLAT-FOOTED, SO YOUR BODY IS PROJECTING EVERY PUNCH YOU THROW.
THEY'RE EASY TO DEFLECT OR AVOID ALTOGETHER.

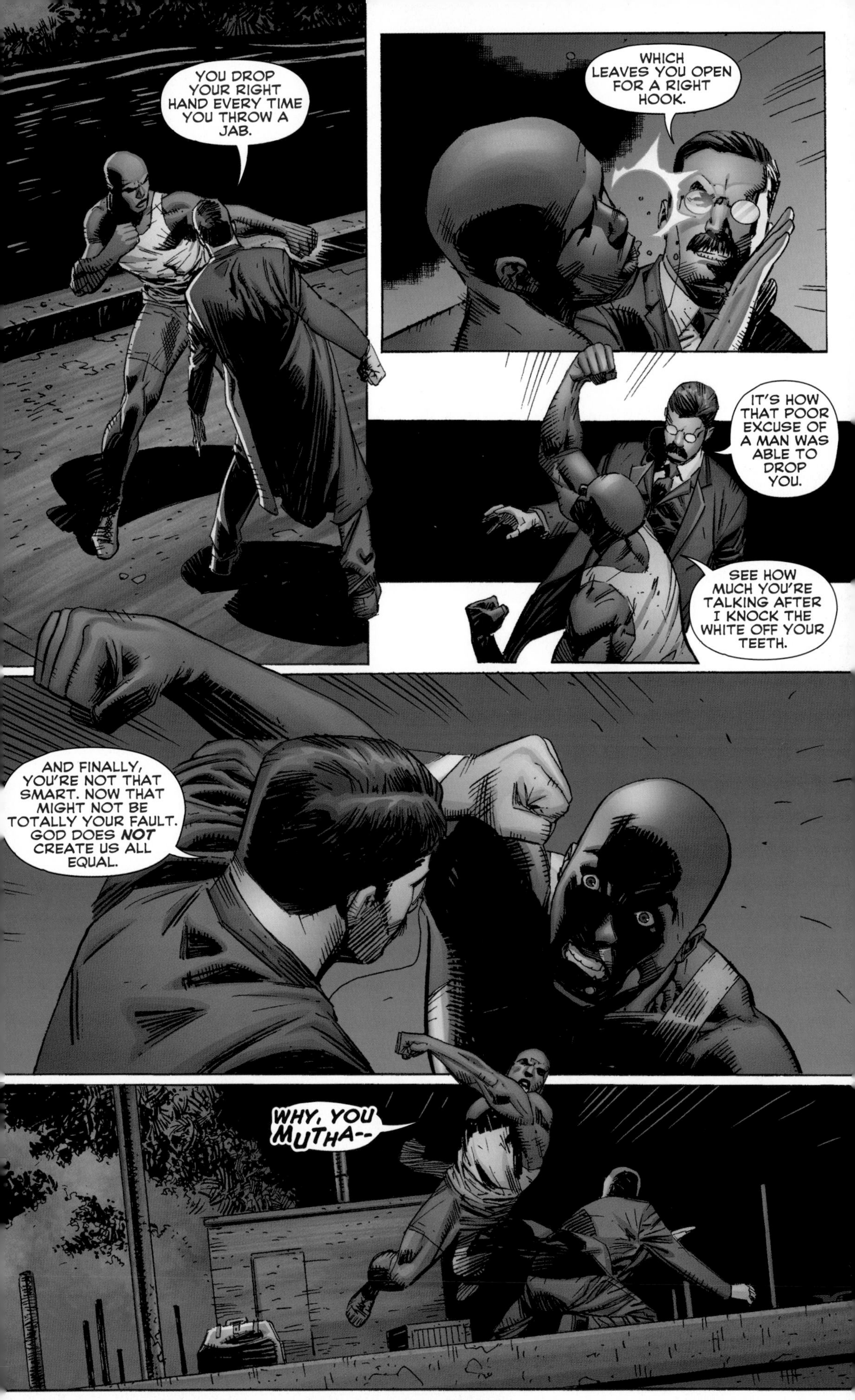
YOU DROP YOUR RIGHT HAND EVERY TIME YOU THROW A JAB.
WHICH LEAVES YOU OPEN FOR A RIGHT HOOK.
IT'S HOW THAT POOR EXCUSE OF A MAN WAS ABLE TO DROP YOU.
SEE HOW MUCH YOU'RE TALKING AFTER I KNOCK THE WHITE OFF YOUR TEETH.
AND FINALLY, YOU'RE NOT THAT SMART. NOW THAT MIGHT NOT BE TOTALLY YOUR FAULT. GOD DOES NOT CREATE US ALL EQUAL.
WHY, YOU MUTHA--

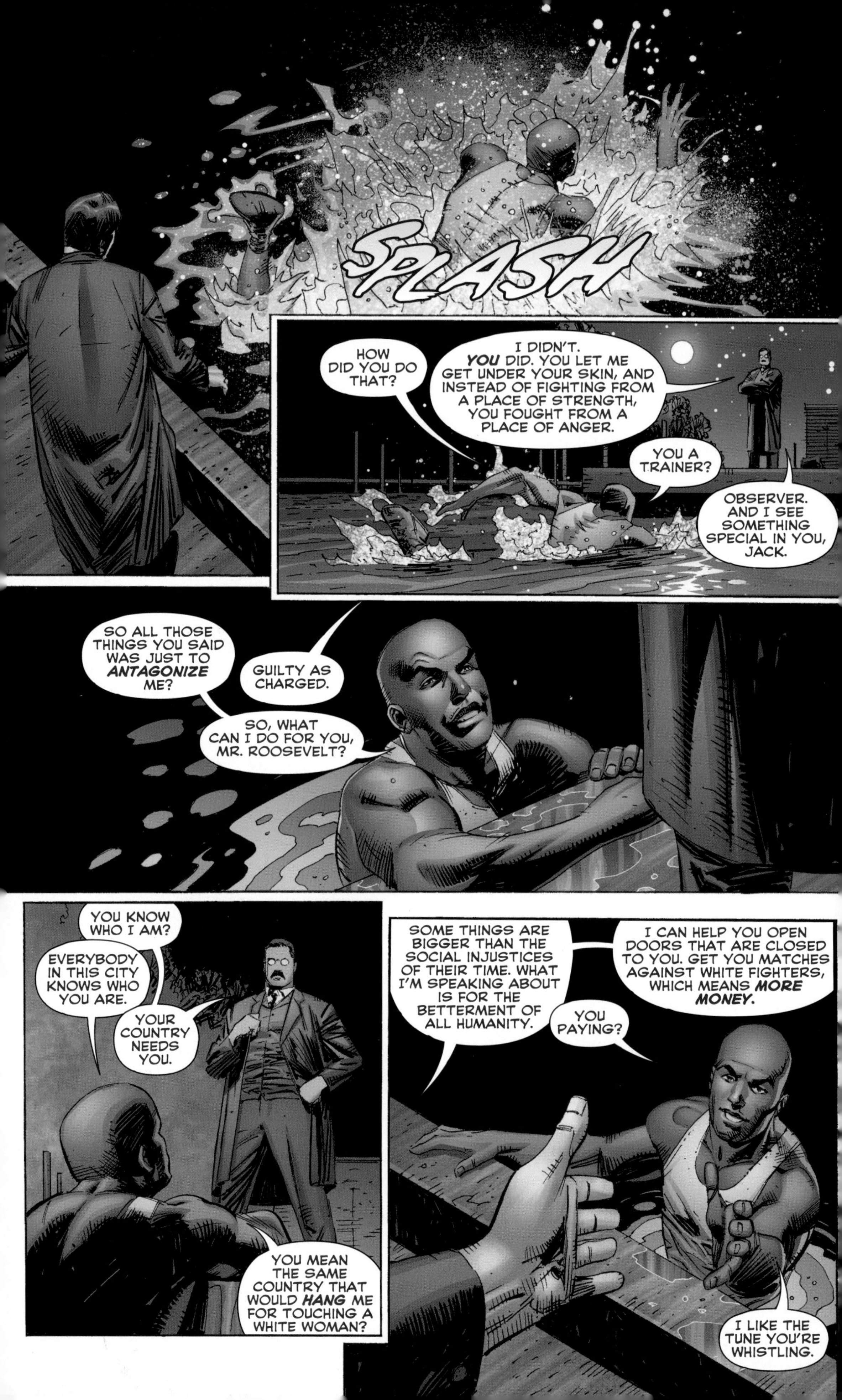
SPLASH
HOW DID YOU DO THAT?
I DIDN'T. YOU DID. YOU LET ME GET UNDER YOUR SKIN, AND INSTEAD OF FIGHTING FROM A PLACE OF STRENGTH, YOU FOUGHT FROM A PLACE OF ANGER.
YOU A TRAINER?
OBSERVER. AND I SEE SOMETHING SPECIAL IN YOU, JACK.
SO ALL THOSE THINGS YOU SAID WAS JUST TO ANTAGONIZE ME?
GUILTY AS CHARGED.
SO, WHAT CAN I DO FOR YOU, MR. ROOSEVELT?
YOU KNOW WHO I AM?
EVERYBODY IN THIS CITY KNOWS WHO YOU ARE.
YOUR COUNTRY NEEDS YOU.
YOU MEAN THE SAME COUNTRY THAT WOULD HANG ME FOR TOUCHING A WHITE WOMAN?
SOME THINGS ARE BIGGER THAN THE SOCIAL INJUSTICES OF THEIR TIME. WHAT I'M SPEAKING ABOUT IS FOR THE BETTERMENT OF ALL HUMANITY.
YOU PAYING?
I CAN HELP YOU OPEN DOORS THAT ARE CLOSED TO YOU. GET YOU MATCHES AGAINST WHITE FIGHTERS, WHICH MEANS MORE MONEY.
I LIKE THE TUNE YOU'RE WHISTLING.

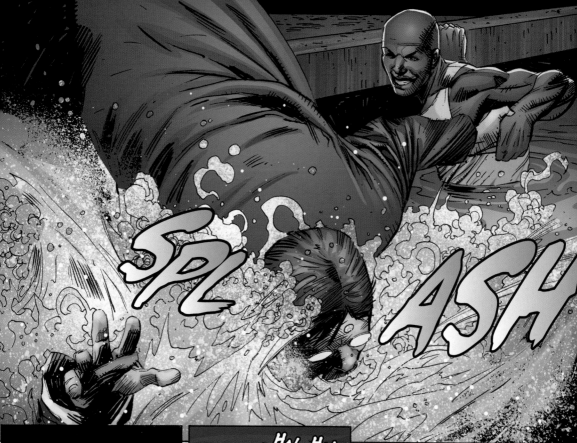

SPLASH

WHAT WAS *THAT* FOR?

I DON'T LIKE GETTING WET.

HA! HA! HA! HA! HA! HA! HA!

SO, WHAT'S NEXT?

YOU LIKE *MAGIC?*

YEAH, WHY?

THERE'S SOMEONE IN CONEY ISLAND THAT WE NEED TO SEE NEXT.

HE CALLS HIMSELF THE KING OF CARDS. OTHERS CALL HIM "THE GREAT...

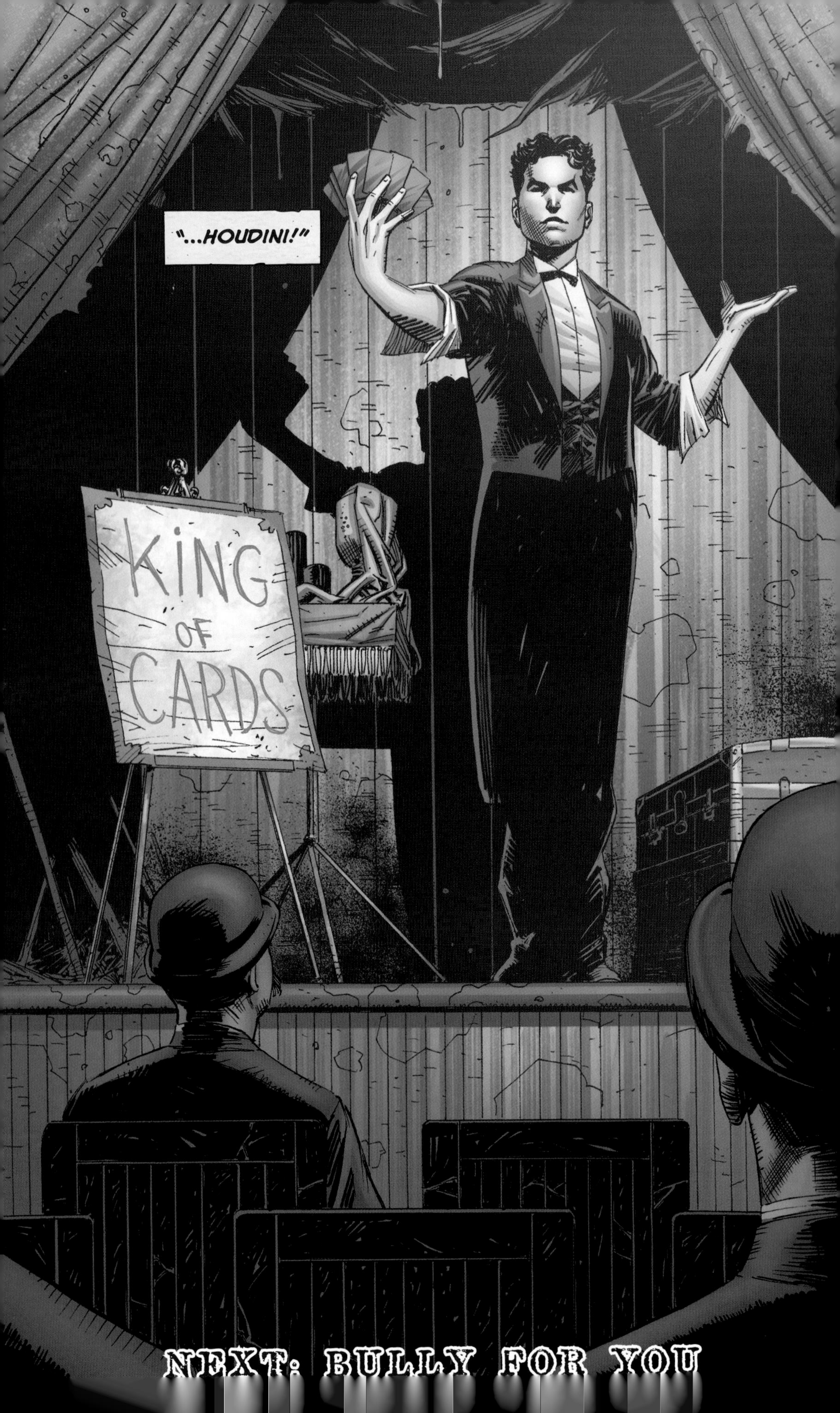
"...HOUDINI!"
KING OF CARDS
NEXT: BULLY FOR YOU

"BULLY FOR YOU"

2

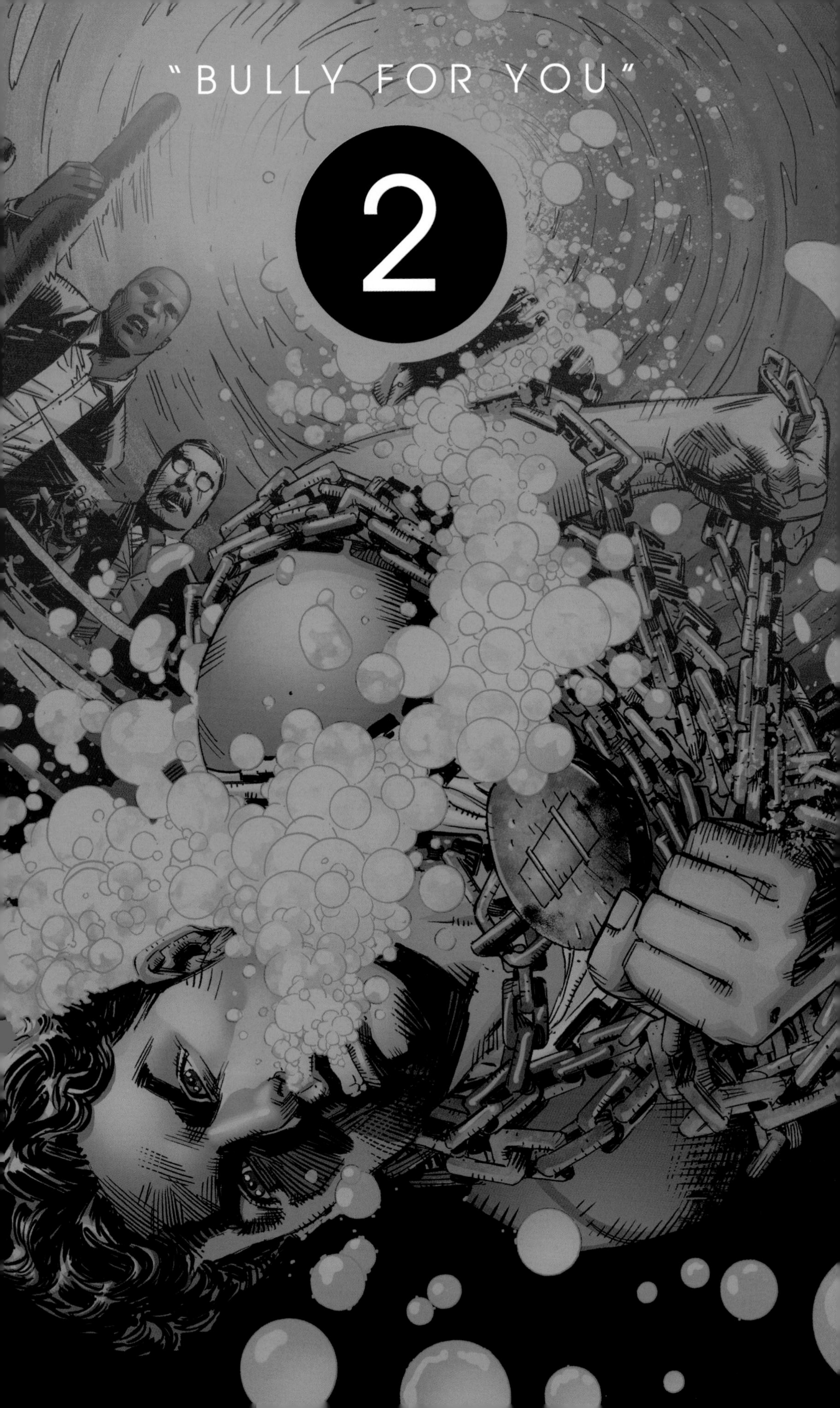

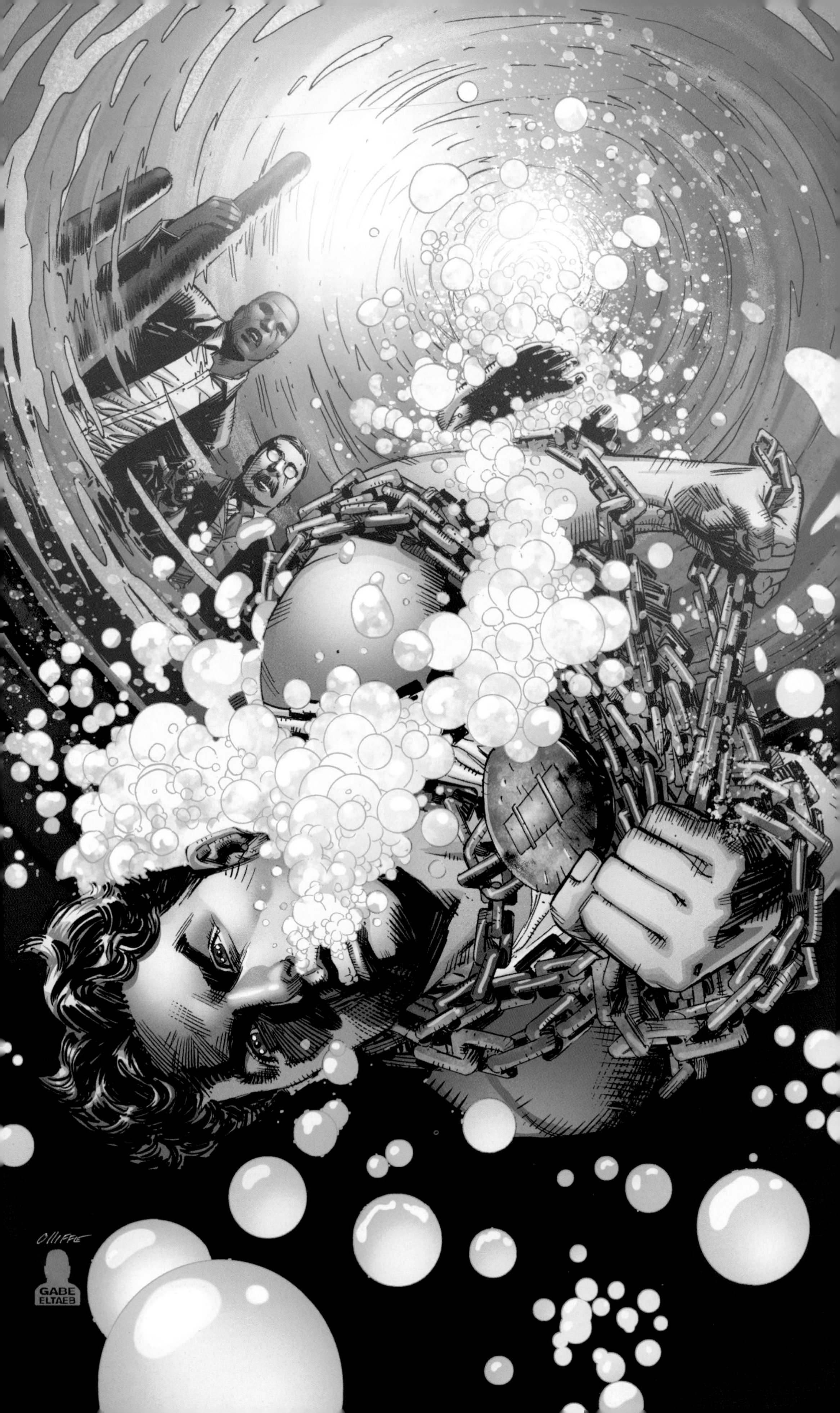
GABE
ELTAEB

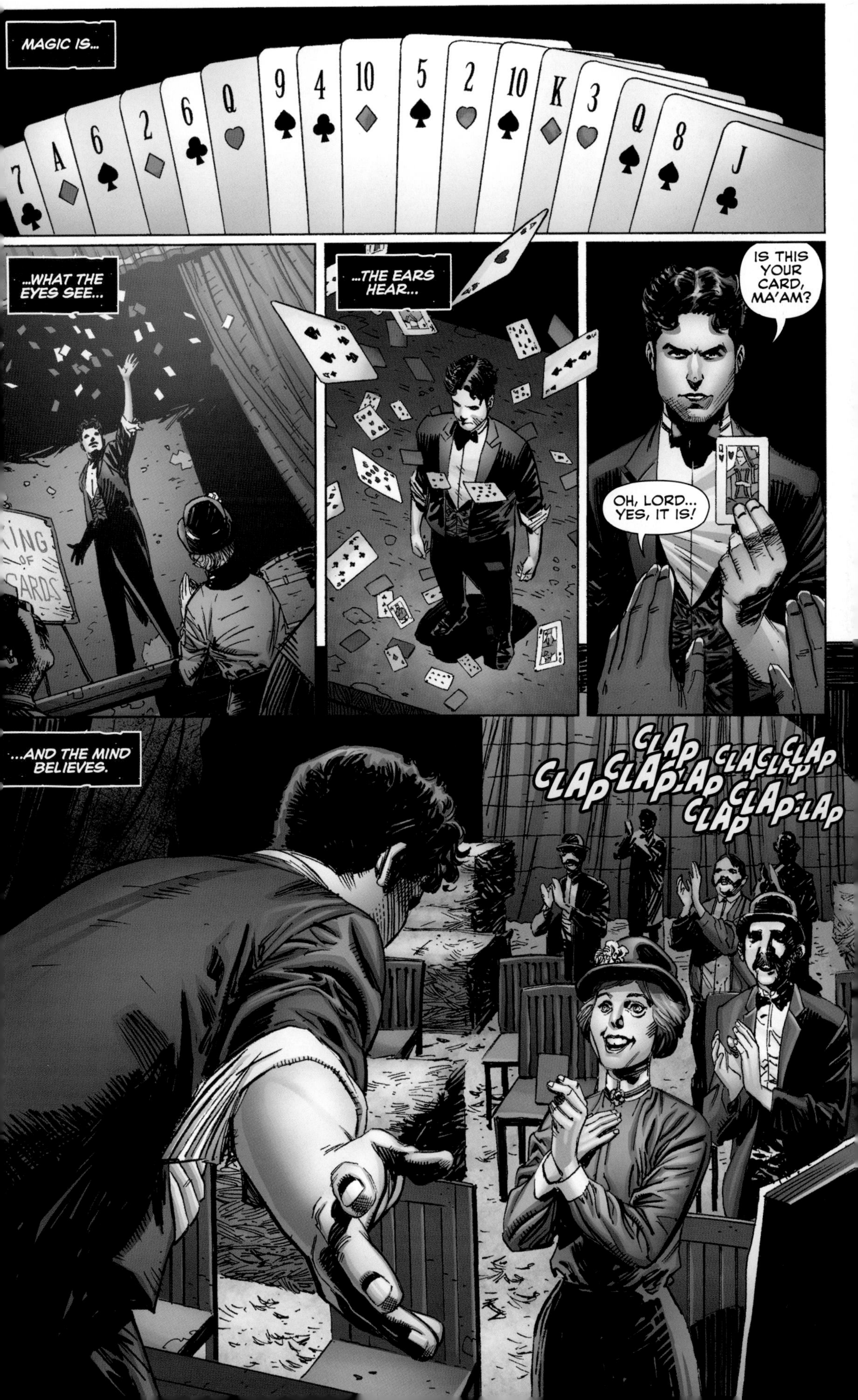
MAGIC IS...
...WHAT THE EYES SEE...
KING OF CARDS
...THE EARS HEAR...
IS THIS YOUR CARD, MA'AM?
OH, LORD... YES, IT IS!
...AND THE MIND BELIEVES.
CLAP CLAP CLAP-LAP CLAP CLAP CLAP CLAP CLAP CLAP-LAP

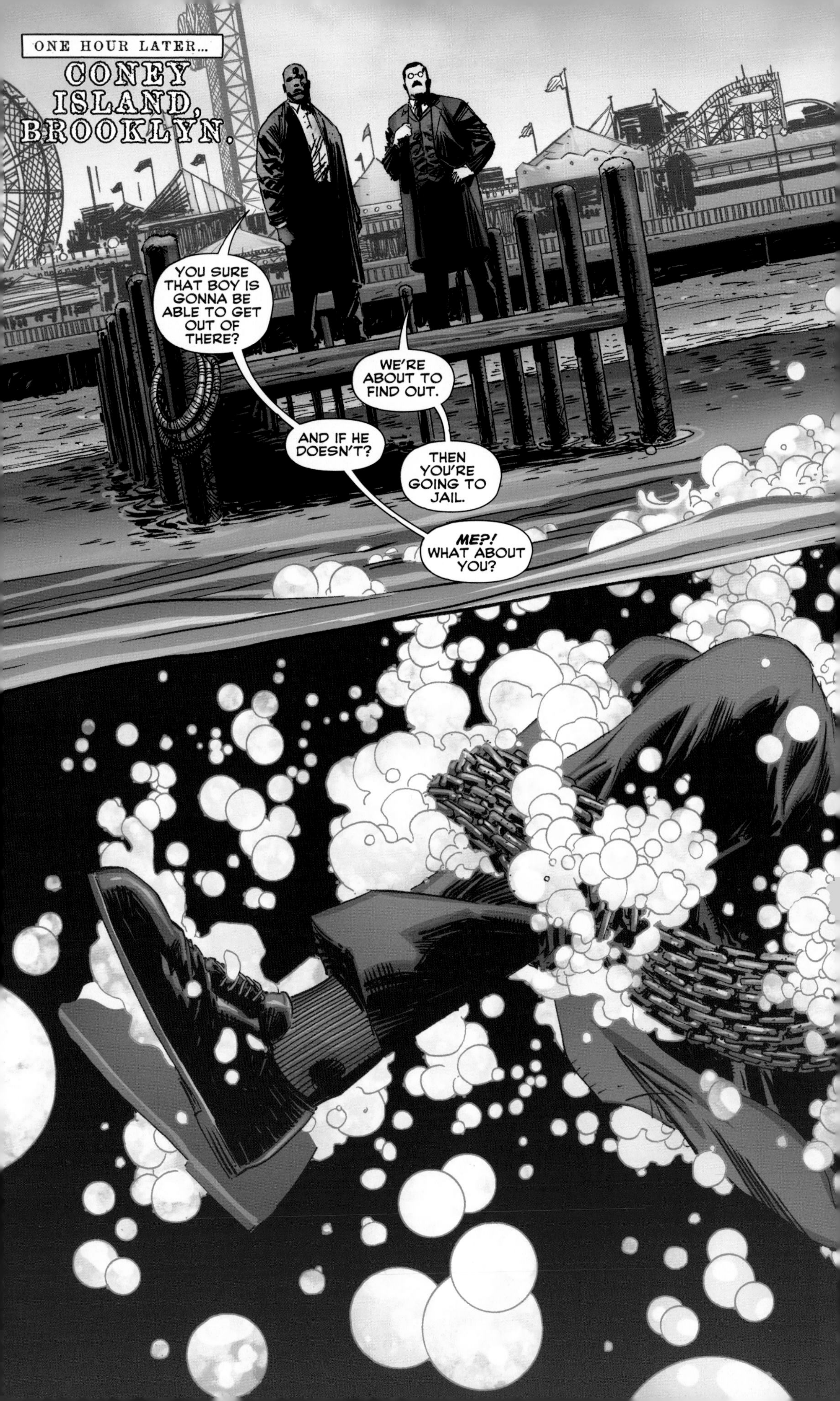
ONE HOUR LATER...
CONEY ISLAND, BROOKLYN.
YOU SURE THAT BOY IS GONNA BE ABLE TO GET OUT OF THERE?
WE'RE ABOUT TO FIND OUT.
AND IF HE DOESN'T?
THEN YOU'RE GOING TO JAIL.
ME?! WHAT ABOUT YOU?

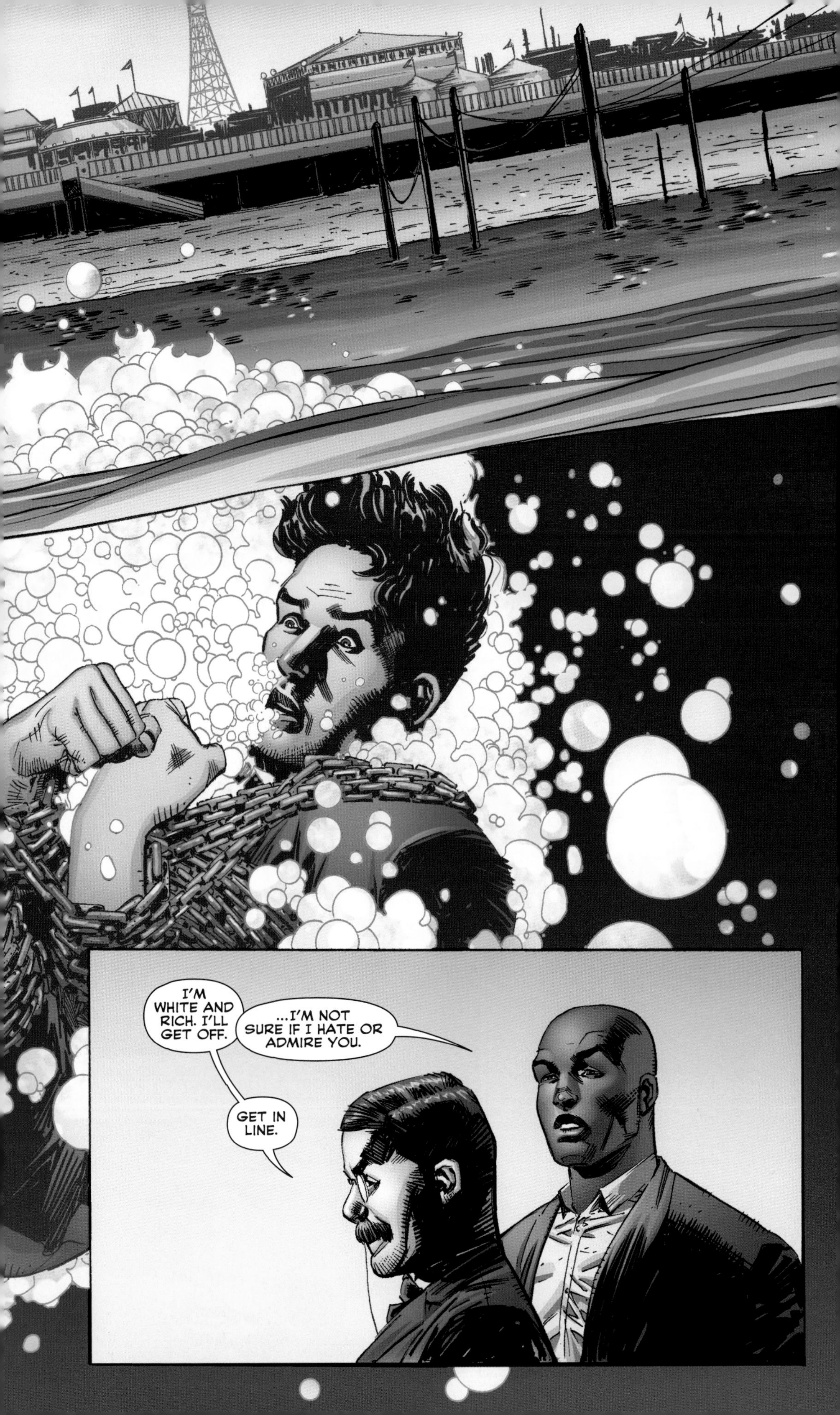
I'M WHITE AND RICH. I'LL GET OFF.
...I'M NOT SURE IF I HATE OR ADMIRE YOU.
GET IN LINE.

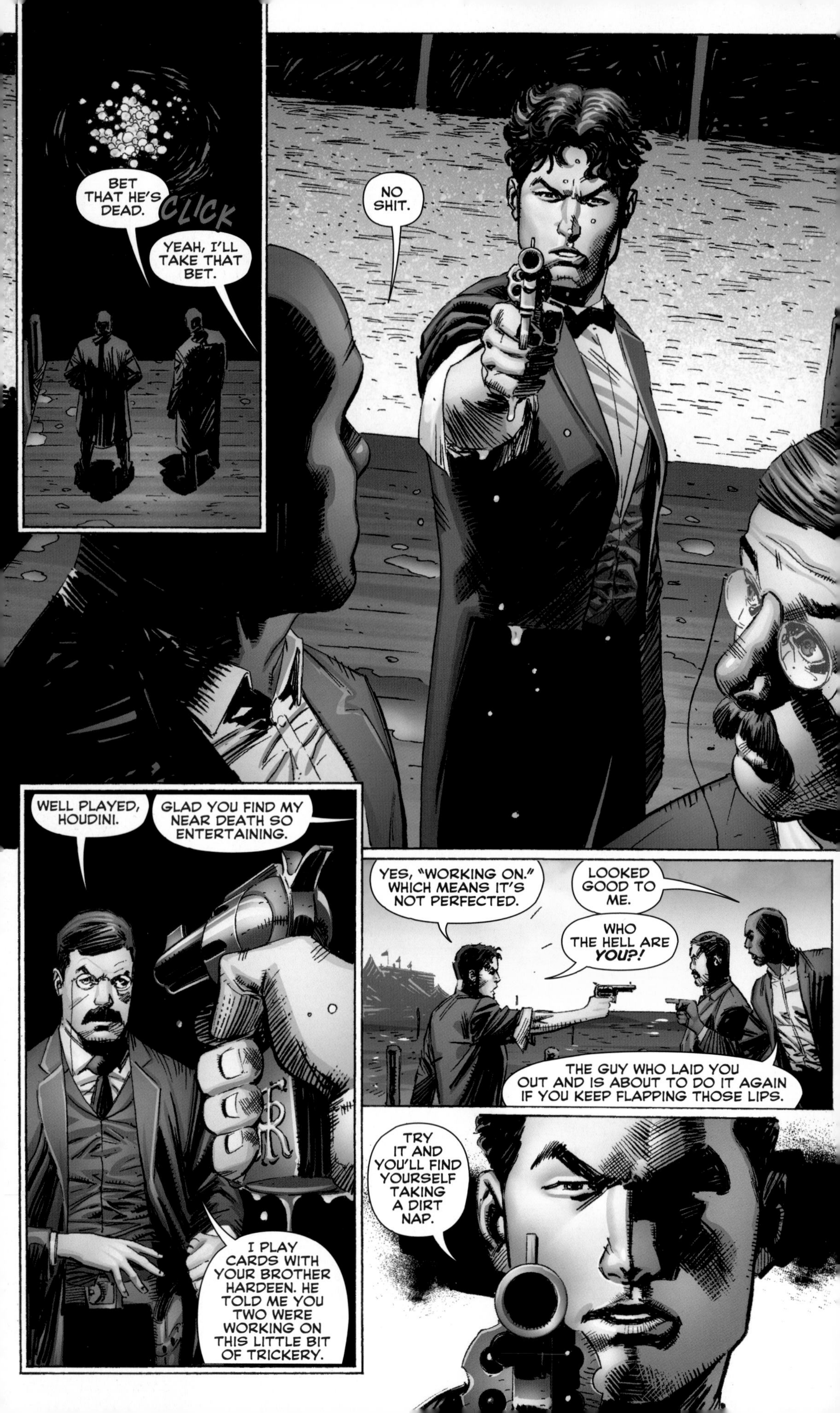
BET THAT HE'S DEAD.
CLICK
YEAH, I'LL TAKE THAT BET.
NO SHIT.
WELL PLAYED, HOUDINI.
GLAD YOU FIND MY NEAR DEATH SO ENTERTAINING.
I PLAY CARDS WITH YOUR BROTHER HARDEEN. HE TOLD ME YOU TWO WERE WORKING ON THIS LITTLE BIT OF TRICKERY.
YES, "WORKING ON." WHICH MEANS IT'S NOT PERFECTED.
LOOKED GOOD TO ME.
WHO THE HELL ARE *YOU?!*
THE GUY WHO LAID YOU OUT AND IS ABOUT TO DO IT AGAIN IF YOU KEEP FLAPPING THOSE LIPS.
TRY IT AND YOU'LL FIND YOURSELF TAKING A DIRT NAP.

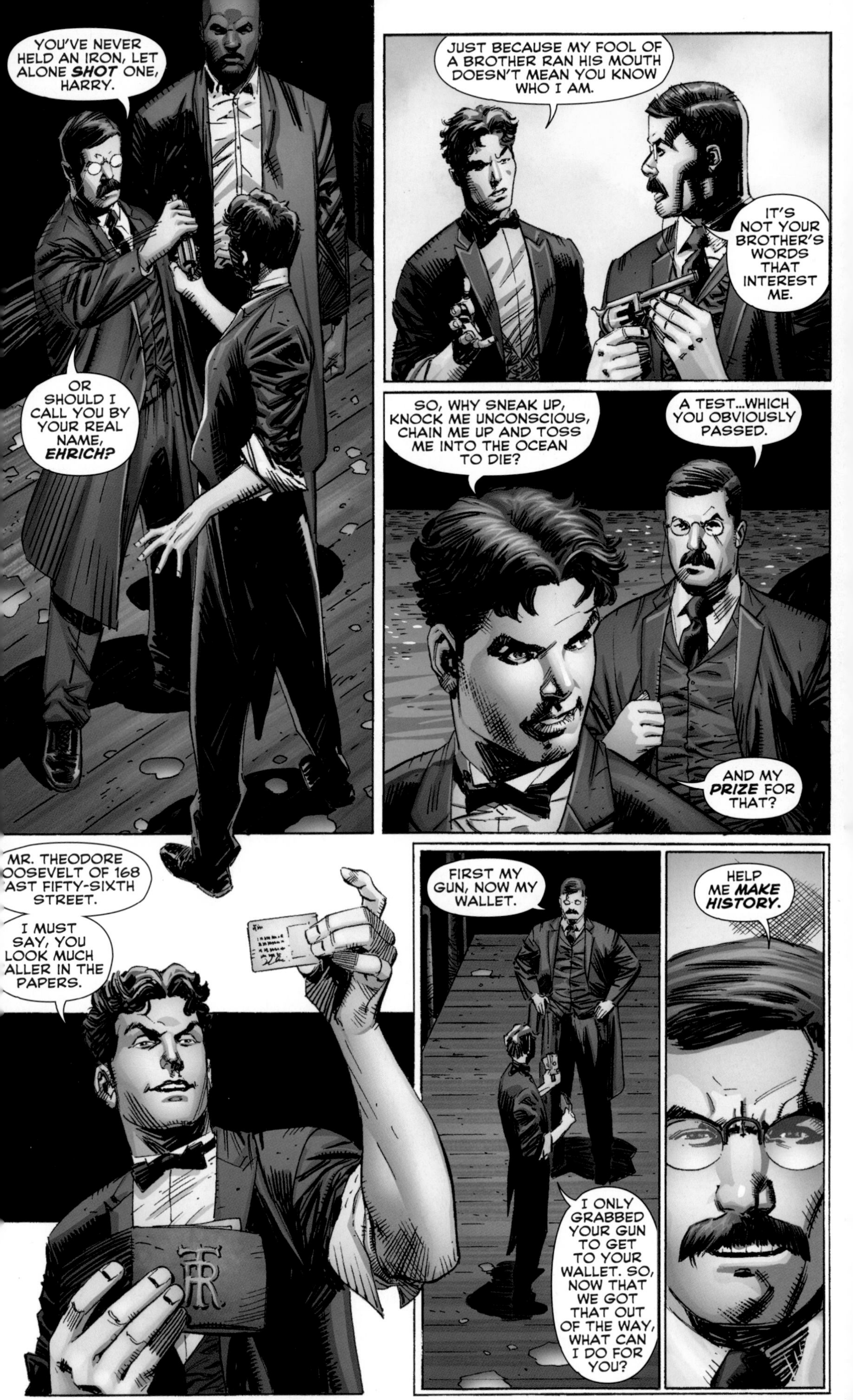
YOU'VE NEVER HELD AN IRON, LET ALONE SHOT ONE, HARRY.
OR SHOULD I CALL YOU BY YOUR REAL NAME, EHRICH?
JUST BECAUSE MY FOOL OF A BROTHER RAN HIS MOUTH DOESN'T MEAN YOU KNOW WHO I AM.
IT'S NOT YOUR BROTHER'S WORDS THAT INTEREST ME.
SO, WHY SNEAK UP, KNOCK ME UNCONSCIOUS, CHAIN ME UP AND TOSS ME INTO THE OCEAN TO DIE?
A TEST...WHICH YOU OBVIOUSLY PASSED.
AND MY PRIZE FOR THAT?
MR. THEODORE OOSEVELT OF 168 AST FIFTY-SIXTH STREET.
I MUST SAY, YOU LOOK MUCH ALLER IN THE PAPERS.
FIRST MY GUN, NOW MY WALLET.
I ONLY GRABBED YOUR GUN TO GET TO YOUR WALLET. SO, NOW THAT WE GOT THAT OUT OF THE WAY, WHAT CAN I DO FOR YOU?
HELP ME MAKE HISTORY.

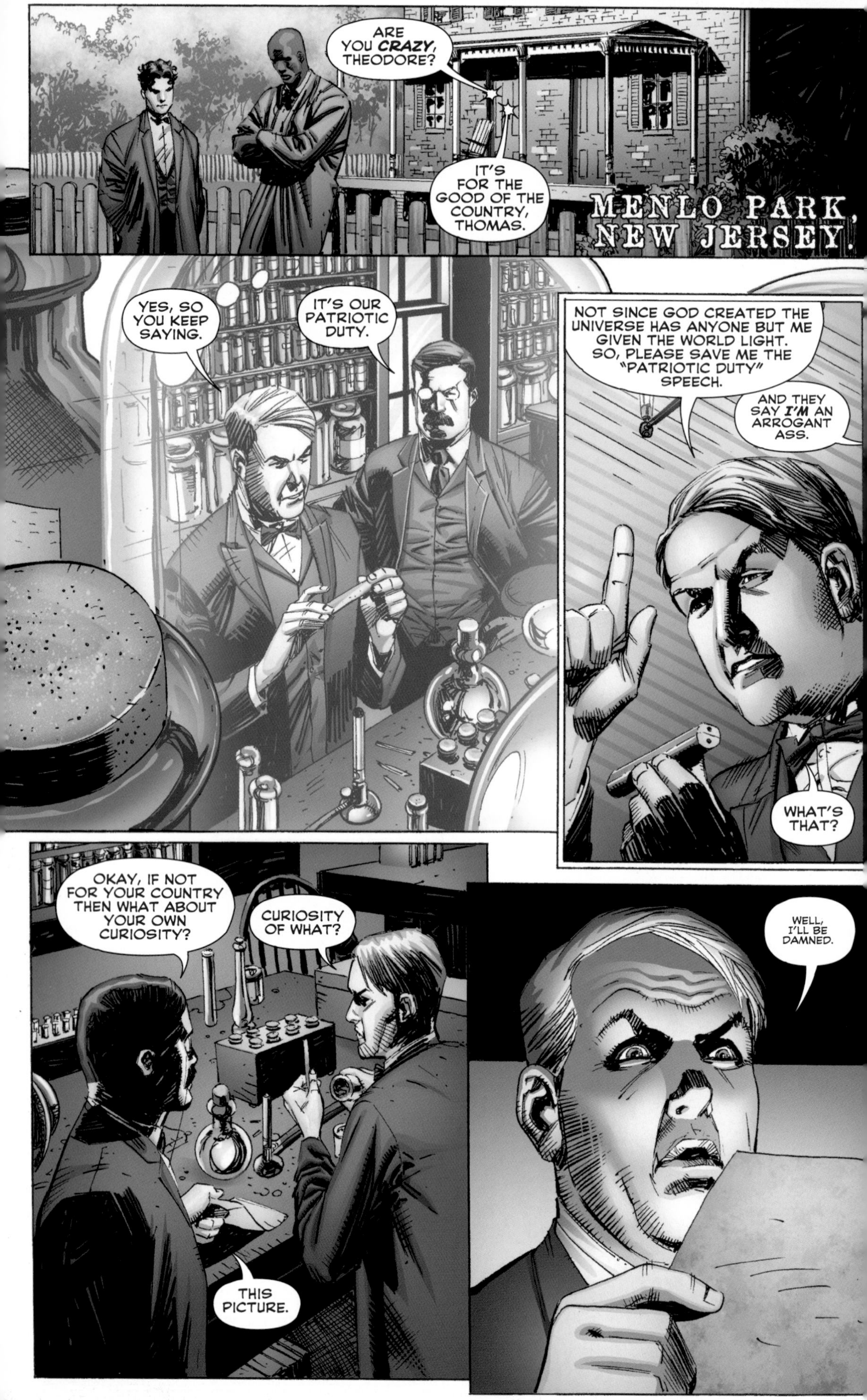
ARE YOU *CRAZY*, THEODORE?
IT'S FOR THE GOOD OF THE COUNTRY, THOMAS.
MENLO PARK, NEW JERSEY.
YES, SO YOU KEEP SAYING.
IT'S OUR PATRIOTIC DUTY.
NOT SINCE GOD CREATED THE UNIVERSE HAS ANYONE BUT ME GIVEN THE WORLD LIGHT. SO, PLEASE SAVE ME THE "PATRIOTIC DUTY" SPEECH.
AND THEY SAY *I'M* AN ARROGANT ASS.
WHAT'S THAT?
OKAY, IF NOT FOR YOUR COUNTRY THEN WHAT ABOUT YOUR OWN CURIOSITY?
CURIOSITY OF WHAT?
THIS PICTURE.
WELL, I'LL BE DAMNED.

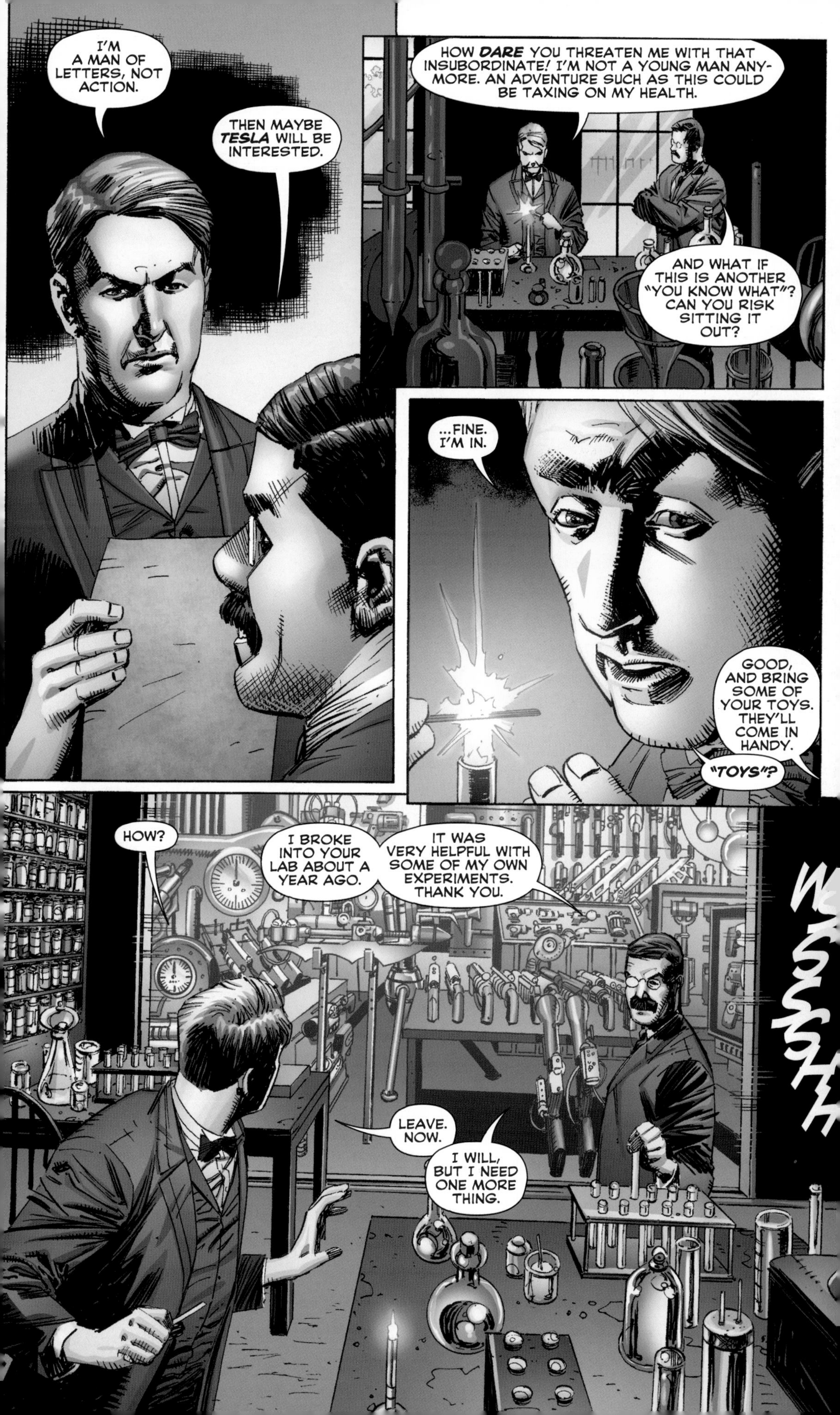
I'M A MAN OF LETTERS, NOT ACTION.
THEN MAYBE TESLA WILL BE INTERESTED.
HOW DARE YOU THREATEN ME WITH THAT INSUBORDINATE! I'M NOT A YOUNG MAN ANYMORE. AN ADVENTURE SUCH AS THIS COULD BE TAXING ON MY HEALTH.
AND WHAT IF THIS IS ANOTHER "YOU KNOW WHAT"? CAN YOU RISK SITTING IT OUT?
...FINE. I'M IN.
GOOD, AND BRING SOME OF YOUR TOYS. THEY'LL COME IN HANDY.
"TOYS"?
HOW?
I BROKE INTO YOUR LAB ABOUT A YEAR AGO.
IT WAS VERY HELPFUL WITH SOME OF MY OWN EXPERIMENTS. THANK YOU.
LEAVE. NOW.
I WILL, BUT I NEED ONE MORE THING.

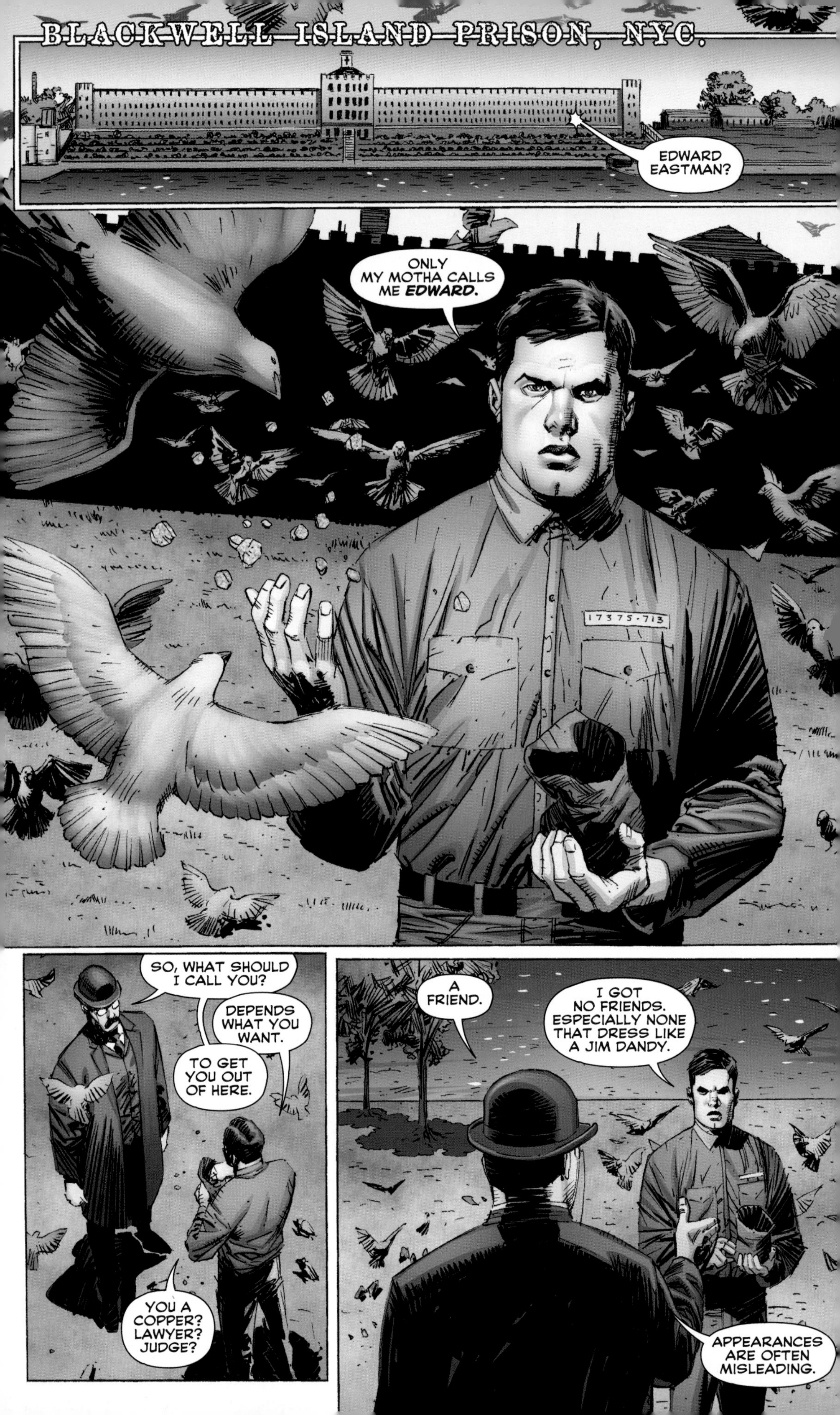
BLACKWELL ISLAND PRISON, NYC.
EDWARD EASTMAN?
ONLY MY MOTHA CALLS ME *EDWARD.*
17375-713
SO, WHAT SHOULD I CALL YOU?
DEPENDS WHAT YOU WANT.
TO GET YOU OUT OF HERE.
YOU A COPPER? LAWYER? JUDGE?
A FRIEND.
I GOT NO FRIENDS. ESPECIALLY NONE THAT DRESS LIKE A JIM DANDY.
APPEARANCES ARE OFTEN MISLEADING.

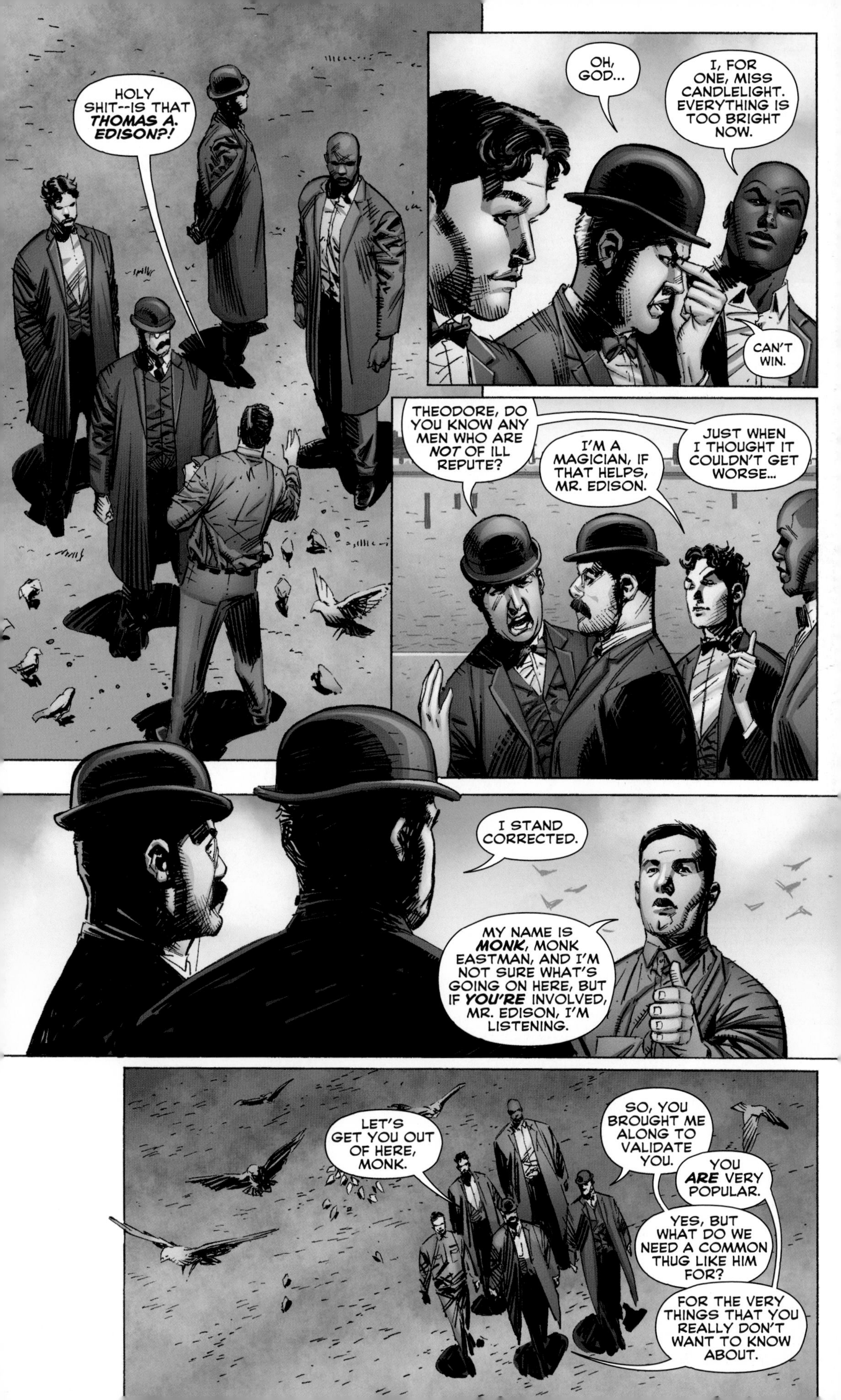
HOLY SHIT--IS THAT THOMAS A. EDISON?!
OH, GOD...
I, FOR ONE, MISS CANDLELIGHT. EVERYTHING IS TOO BRIGHT NOW.
CAN'T WIN.
THEODORE, DO YOU KNOW ANY MEN WHO ARE NOT OF ILL REPUTE?
JUST WHEN I THOUGHT IT COULDN'T GET WORSE...
I'M A MAGICIAN, IF THAT HELPS, MR. EDISON.
I STAND CORRECTED.
MY NAME IS MONK, MONK EASTMAN, AND I'M NOT SURE WHAT'S GOING ON HERE, BUT IF YOU'RE INVOLVED, MR. EDISON, I'M LISTENING.
LET'S GET YOU OUT OF HERE, MONK.
SO, YOU BROUGHT ME ALONG TO VALIDATE YOU.
YOU ARE VERY POPULAR.
YES, BUT WHAT DO WE NEED A COMMON THUG LIKE HIM FOR?
FOR THE VERY THINGS THAT YOU REALLY DON'T WANT TO KNOW ABOUT.

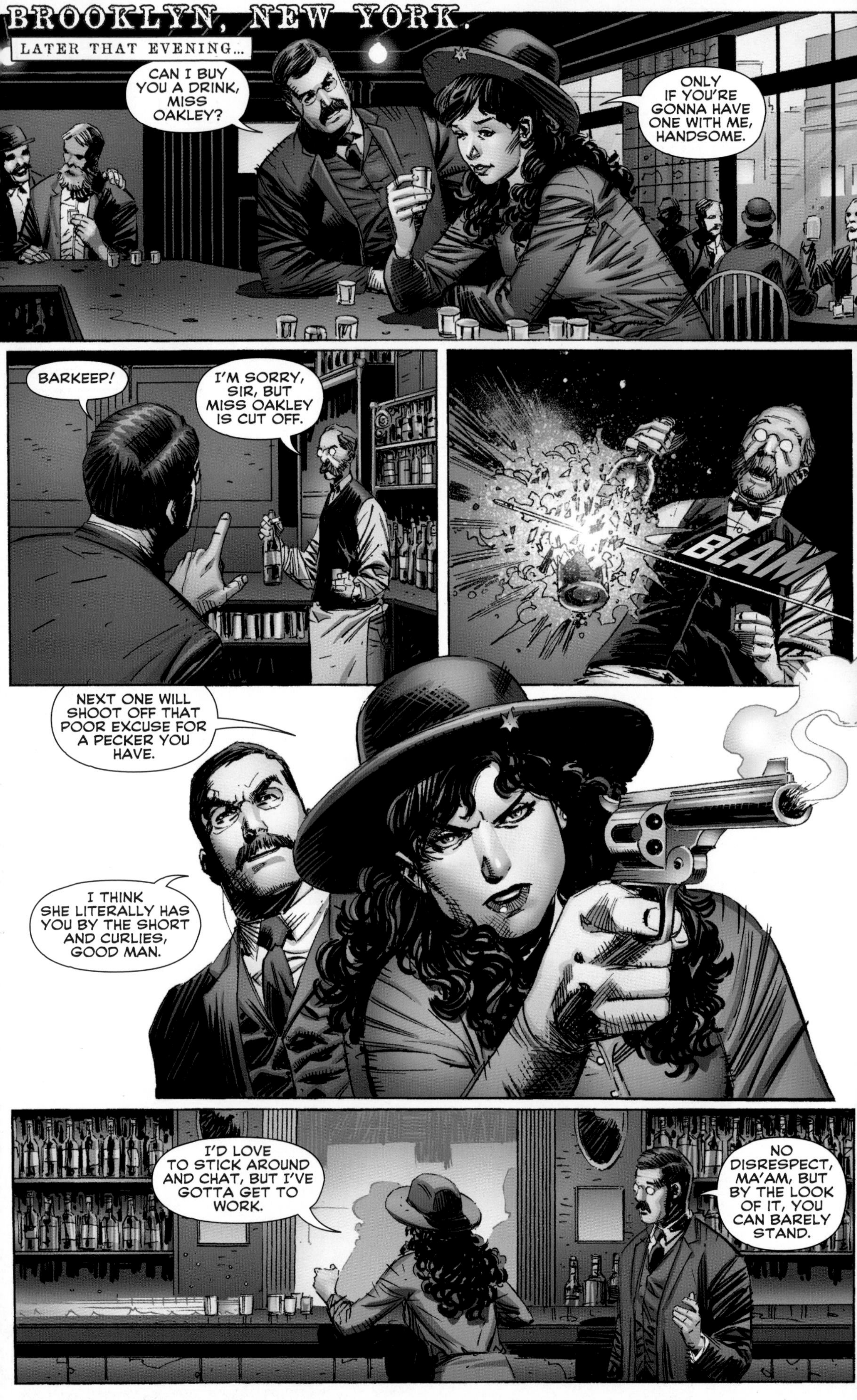
BROOKLYN, NEW YORK.
LATER THAT EVENING...
CAN I BUY YOU A DRINK, MISS OAKLEY?
ONLY IF YOU'RE GONNA HAVE ONE WITH ME, HANDSOME.
BARKEEP!
I'M SORRY, SIR, BUT MISS OAKLEY IS CUT OFF.
BLAM
NEXT ONE WILL SHOOT OFF THAT POOR EXCUSE FOR A PECKER YOU HAVE.
I THINK SHE LITERALLY HAS YOU BY THE SHORT AND CURLIES, GOOD MAN.
I'D LOVE TO STICK AROUND AND CHAT, BUT I'VE GOTTA GET TO WORK.
NO DISRESPECT, MA'AM, BUT BY THE LOOK OF IT, YOU CAN BARELY STAND.

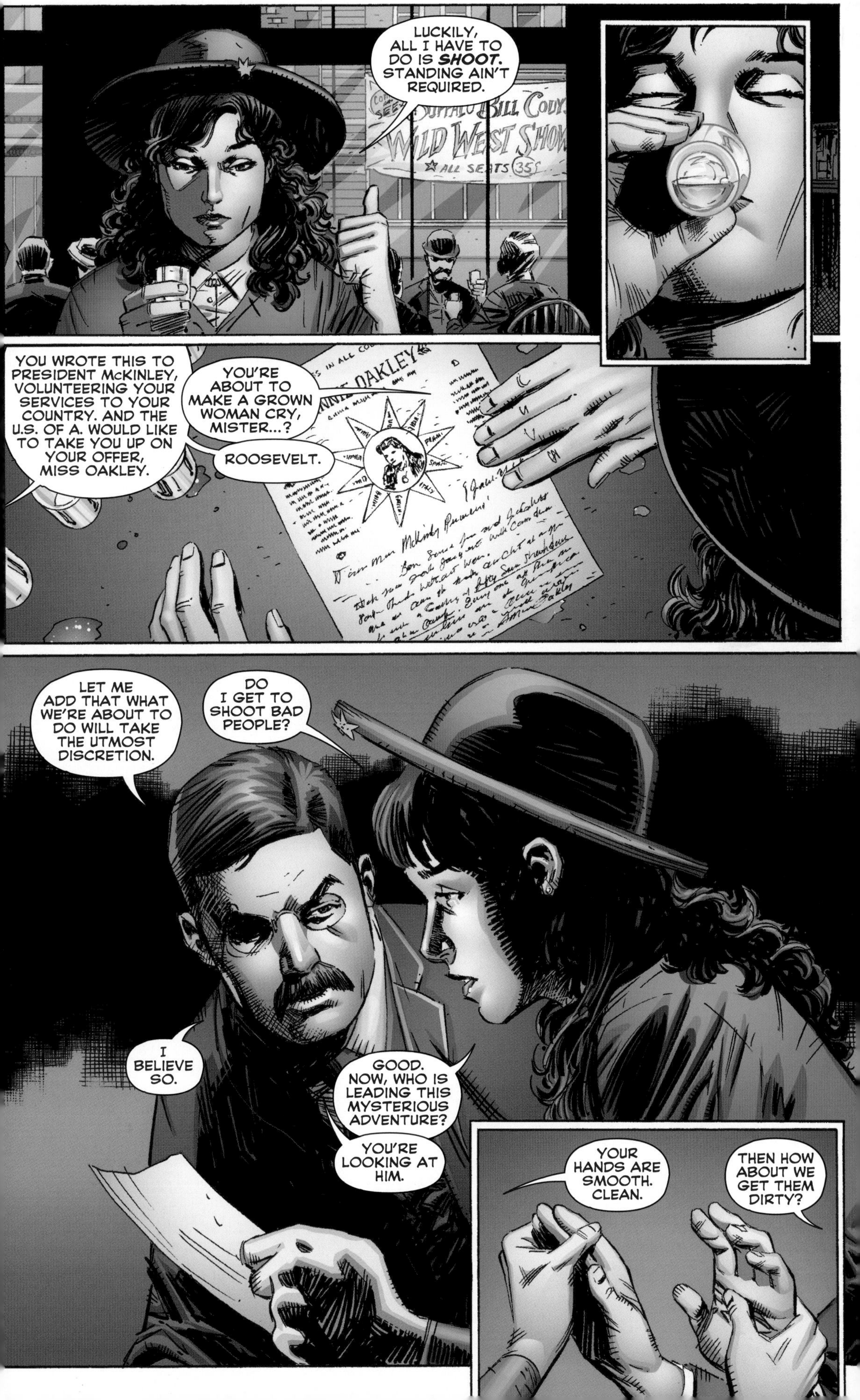
LUCKILY, ALL I HAVE TO DO IS SHOOT. STANDING AIN'T REQUIRED.
COME SEE BUFFALO BILL CODY'S WILD WEST SHOW ALL SEATS 35¢
YOU WROTE THIS TO PRESIDENT McKINLEY, VOLUNTEERING YOUR SERVICES TO YOUR COUNTRY. AND THE U.S. OF A. WOULD LIKE TO TAKE YOU UP ON YOUR OFFER, MISS OAKLEY.
YOU'RE ABOUT TO MAKE A GROWN WOMAN CRY, MISTER...?
ROOSEVELT.
LET ME ADD THAT WHAT WE'RE ABOUT TO DO WILL TAKE THE UTMOST DISCRETION.
DO I GET TO SHOOT BAD PEOPLE?
I BELIEVE SO.
GOOD. NOW, WHO IS LEADING THIS MYSTERIOUS ADVENTURE?
YOU'RE LOOKING AT HIM.
YOUR HANDS ARE SMOOTH. CLEAN.
THEN HOW ABOUT WE GET THEM DIRTY?

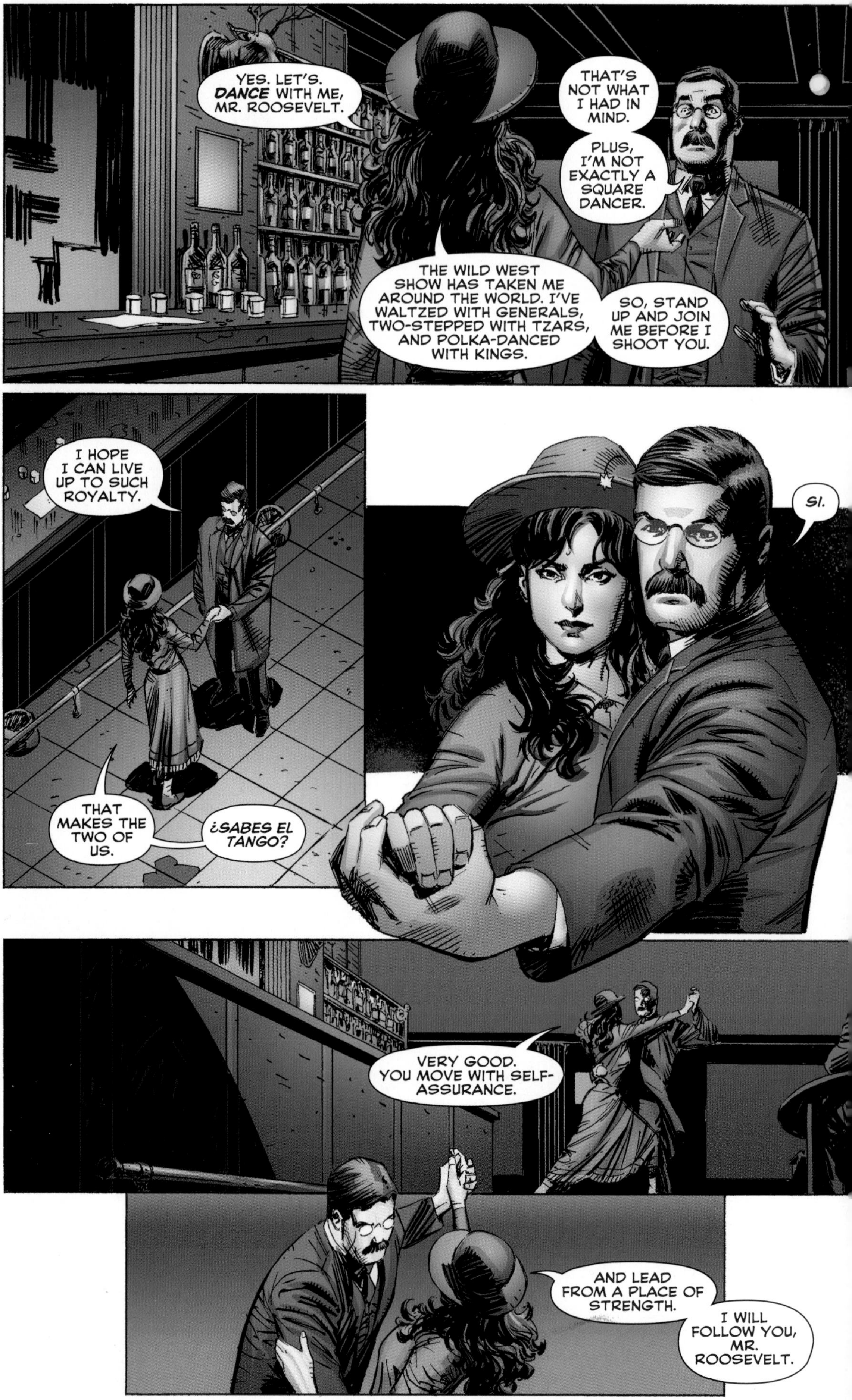

YES. LET'S. **DANCE** WITH ME, MR. ROOSEVELT.
THAT'S NOT WHAT I HAD IN MIND.
PLUS, I'M NOT EXACTLY A SQUARE DANCER.
THE WILD WEST SHOW HAS TAKEN ME AROUND THE WORLD. I'VE WALTZED WITH GENERALS, TWO-STEPPED WITH TZARS, AND POLKA-DANCED WITH KINGS.
SO, STAND UP AND JOIN ME BEFORE I SHOOT YOU.
I HOPE I CAN LIVE UP TO SUCH ROYALTY.
THAT MAKES THE TWO OF US.
¿SABES EL TANGO?
SI.
VERY GOOD. YOU MOVE WITH SELF-ASSURANCE.
AND LEAD FROM A PLACE OF STRENGTH.
I WILL FOLLOW YOU, MR. ROOSEVELT.

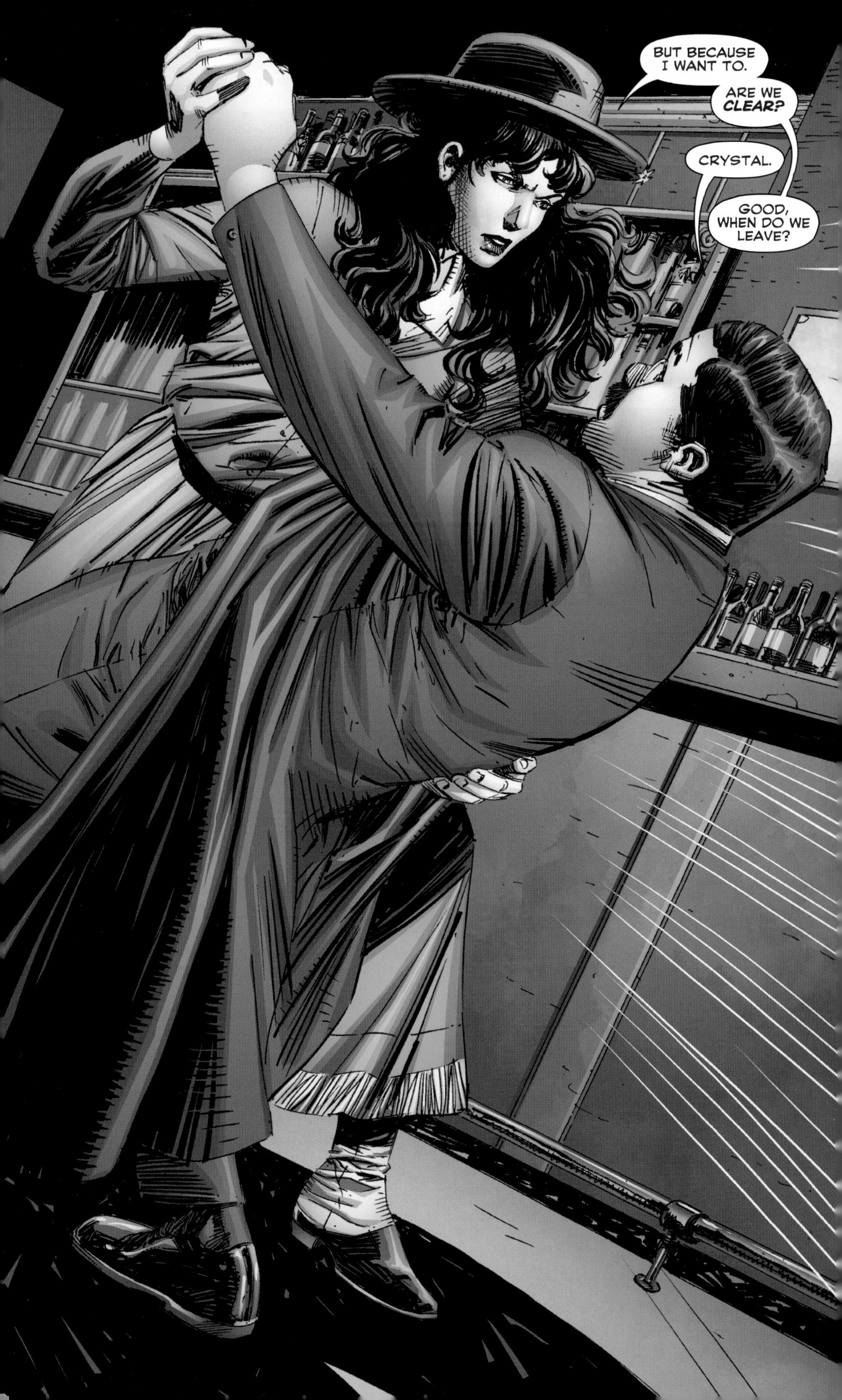

BUT BECAUSE I WANT TO.
ARE WE **CLEAR?**
CRYSTAL.
GOOD, WHEN DO WE LEAVE?

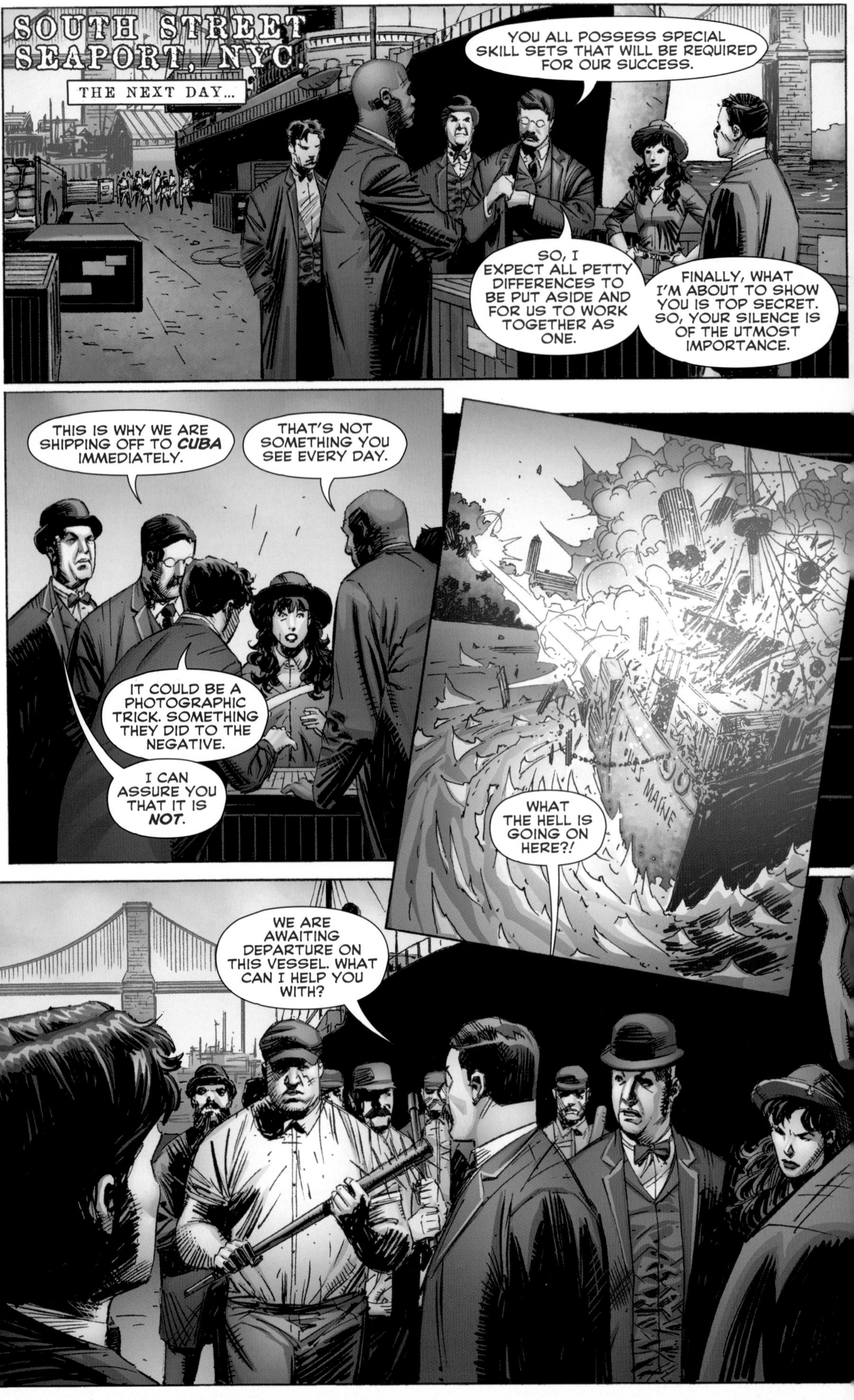

SOUTH STREET SEAPORT, NYC.
THE NEXT DAY...
YOU ALL POSSESS SPECIAL SKILL SETS THAT WILL BE REQUIRED FOR OUR SUCCESS.
SO, I EXPECT ALL PETTY DIFFERENCES TO BE PUT ASIDE AND FOR US TO WORK TOGETHER AS ONE.
FINALLY, WHAT I'M ABOUT TO SHOW YOU IS TOP SECRET. SO, YOUR SILENCE IS OF THE UTMOST IMPORTANCE.
THIS IS WHY WE ARE SHIPPING OFF TO *CUBA* IMMEDIATELY.
THAT'S NOT SOMETHING YOU SEE EVERY DAY.
IT COULD BE A PHOTOGRAPHIC TRICK. SOMETHING THEY DID TO THE NEGATIVE.
I CAN ASSURE YOU THAT IT IS ***NOT***.
MAINE
WHAT THE HELL IS GOING ON HERE?!
WE ARE AWAITING DEPARTURE ON THIS VESSEL. WHAT CAN I HELP YOU WITH?

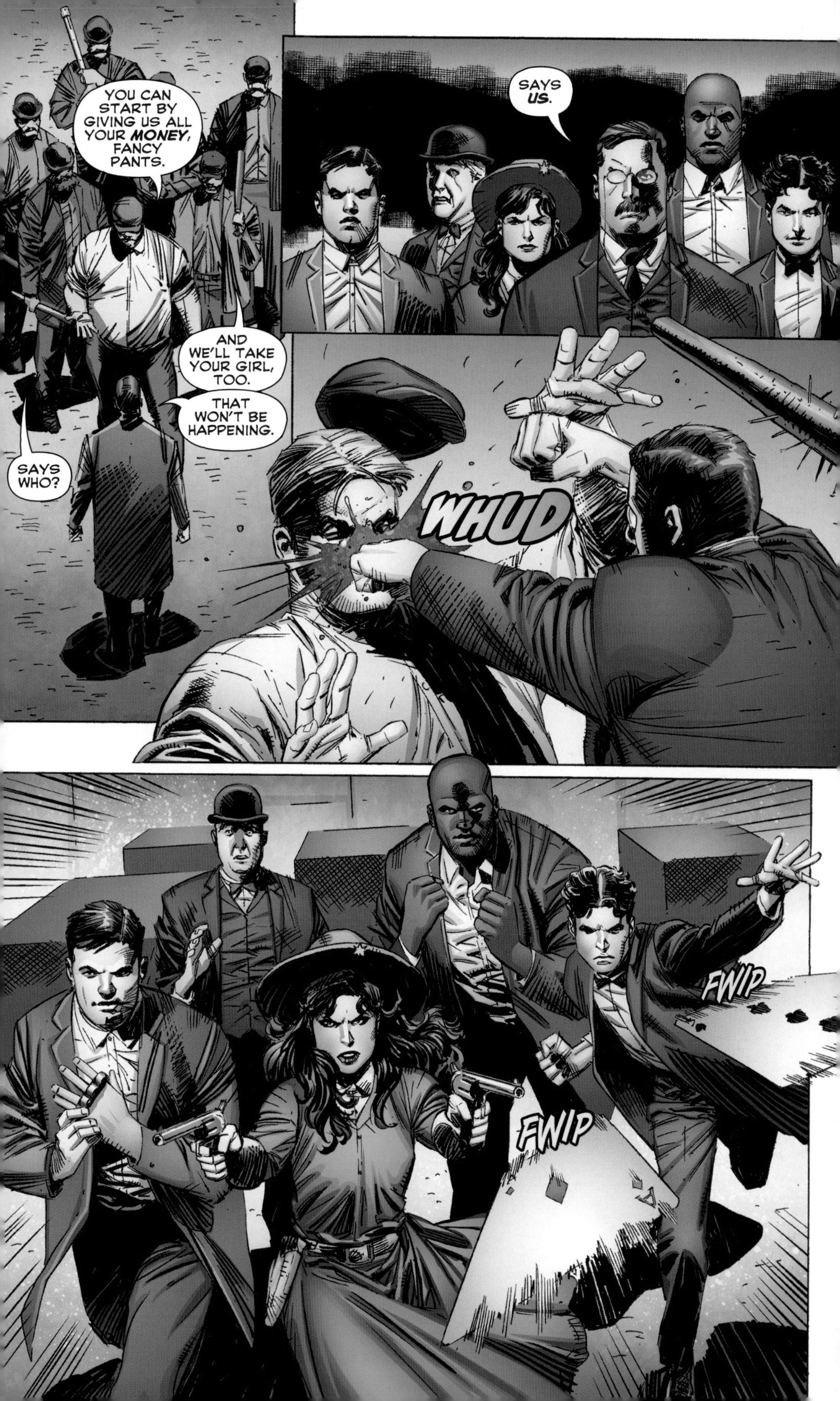
YOU CAN START BY GIVING US ALL YOUR *MONEY*, FANCY PANTS.
AND WE'LL TAKE YOUR GIRL, TOO.
THAT WON'T BE HAPPENING.
SAYS WHO?
SAYS *US*.
WHUD
FWIP
FWIP

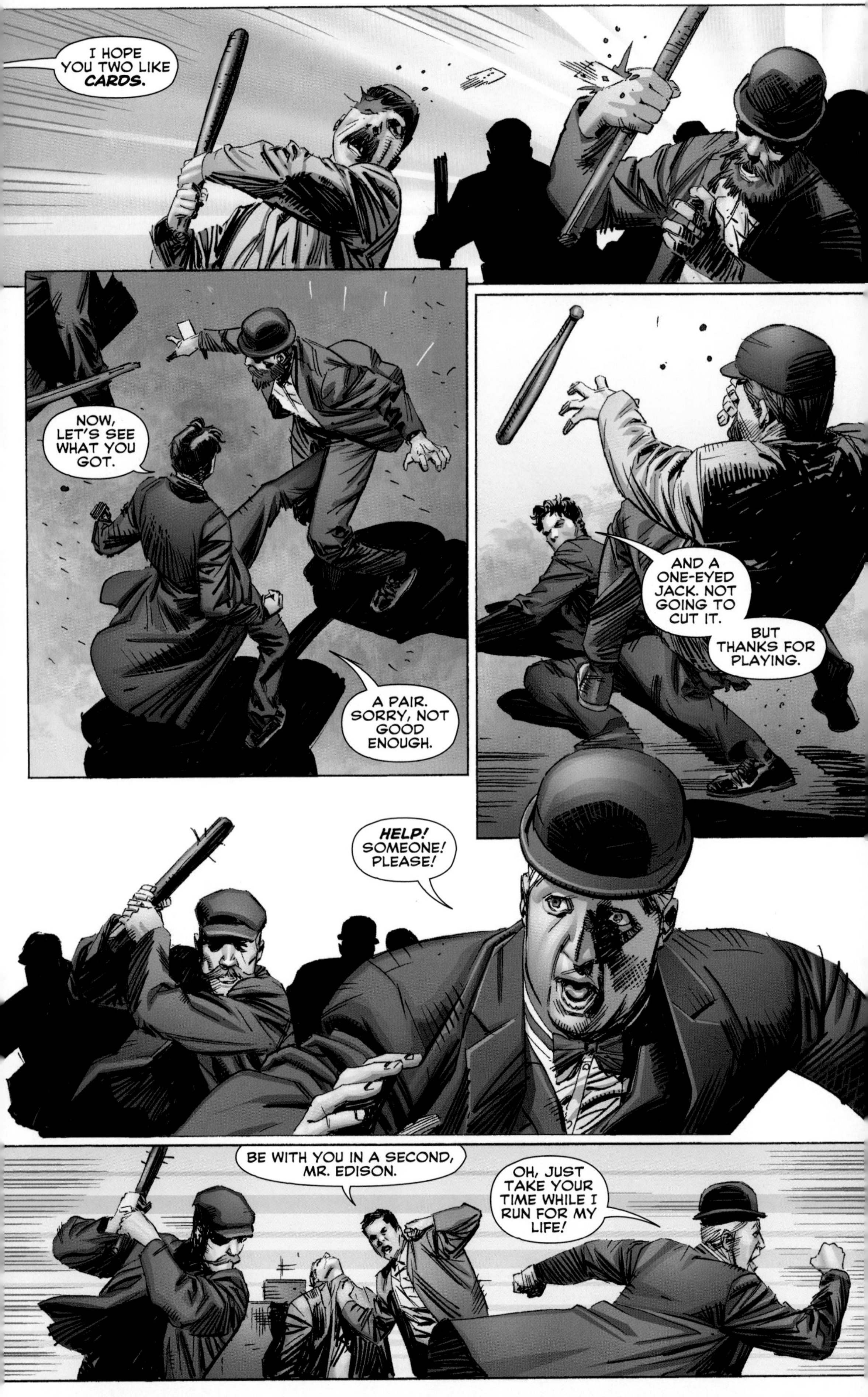
I HOPE YOU TWO LIKE *CARDS.*
NOW, LET'S SEE WHAT YOU GOT.
A PAIR. SORRY, NOT GOOD ENOUGH.
AND A ONE-EYED JACK. NOT GOING TO CUT IT.
BUT THANKS FOR PLAYING.
HELP! SOMEONE! PLEASE!
BE WITH YOU IN A SECOND, MR. EDISON.
OH, JUST TAKE YOUR TIME WHILE I RUN FOR MY LIFE!

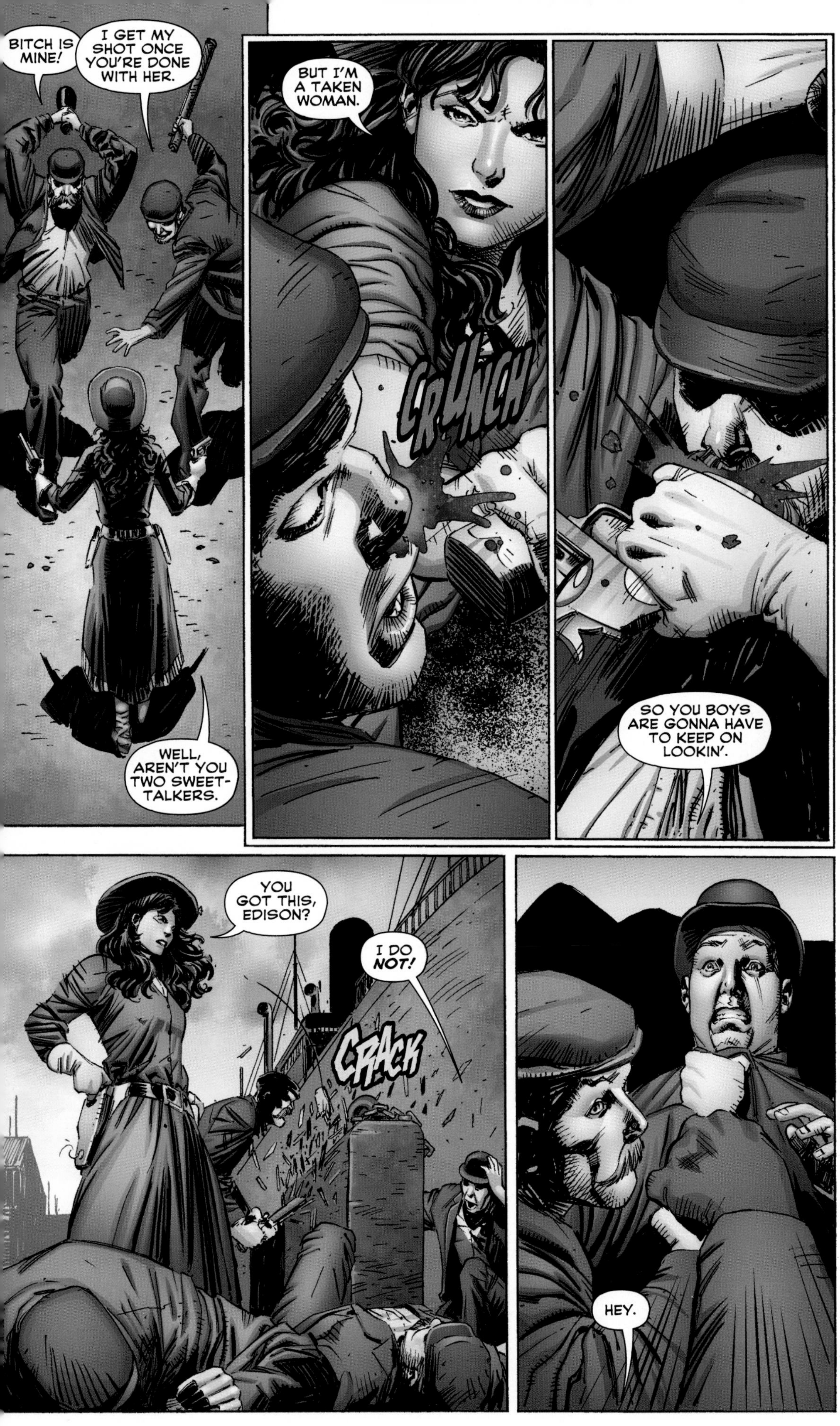
BITCH IS MINE!
I GET MY SHOT ONCE YOU'RE DONE WITH HER.
WELL, AREN'T YOU TWO SWEET-TALKERS.
BUT I'M A TAKEN WOMAN.
CRUNCH
SO YOU BOYS ARE GONNA HAVE TO KEEP ON LOOKIN'.
YOU GOT THIS, EDISON?
I DO NOT!
CRACK
HEY.

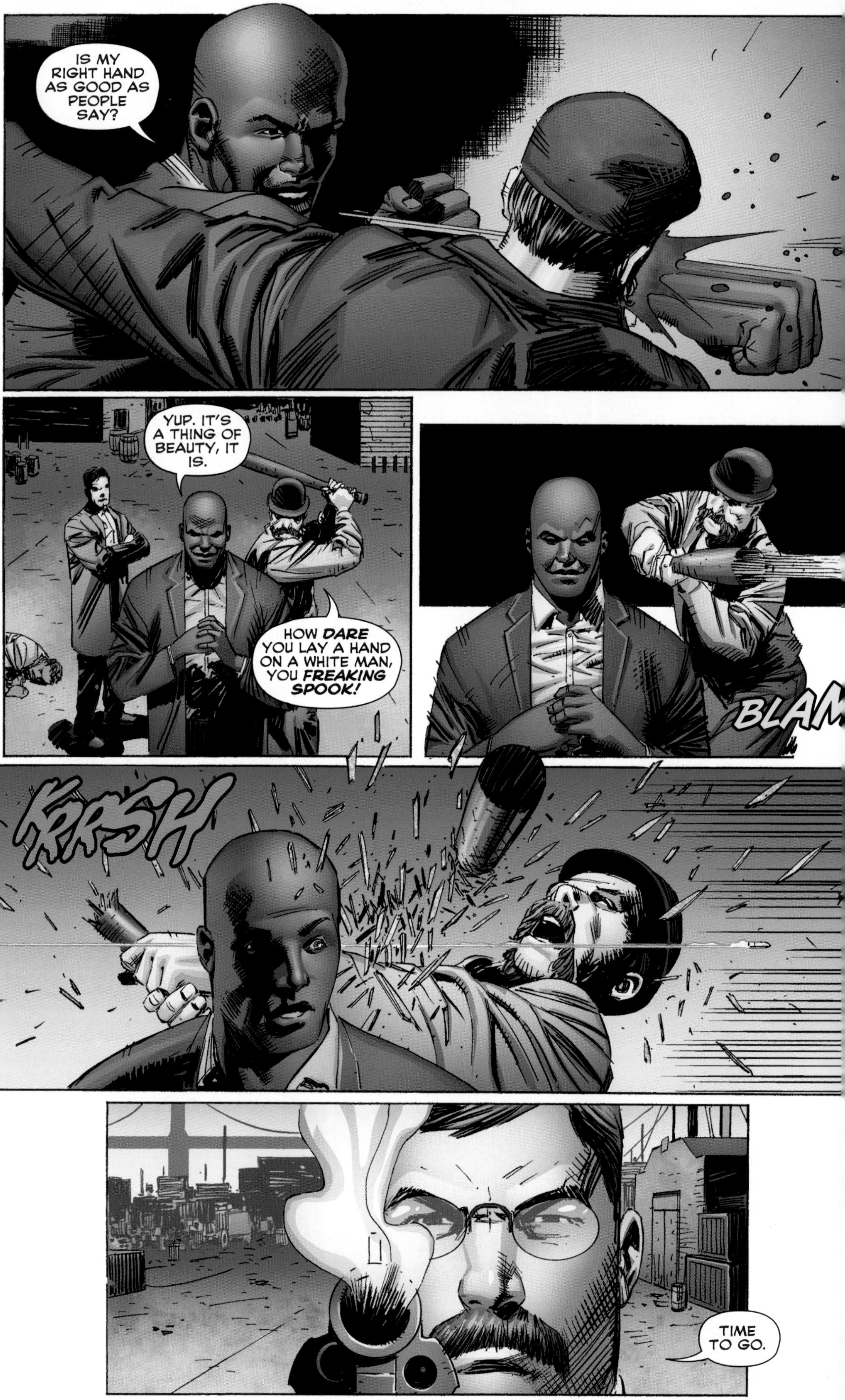
IS MY RIGHT HAND AS GOOD AS PEOPLE SAY?
YUP. IT'S A THING OF BEAUTY, IT IS.
HOW DARE YOU LAY A HAND ON A WHITE MAN, YOU FREAKING SPOOK!
BLAM
KRSH
TIME TO GO.

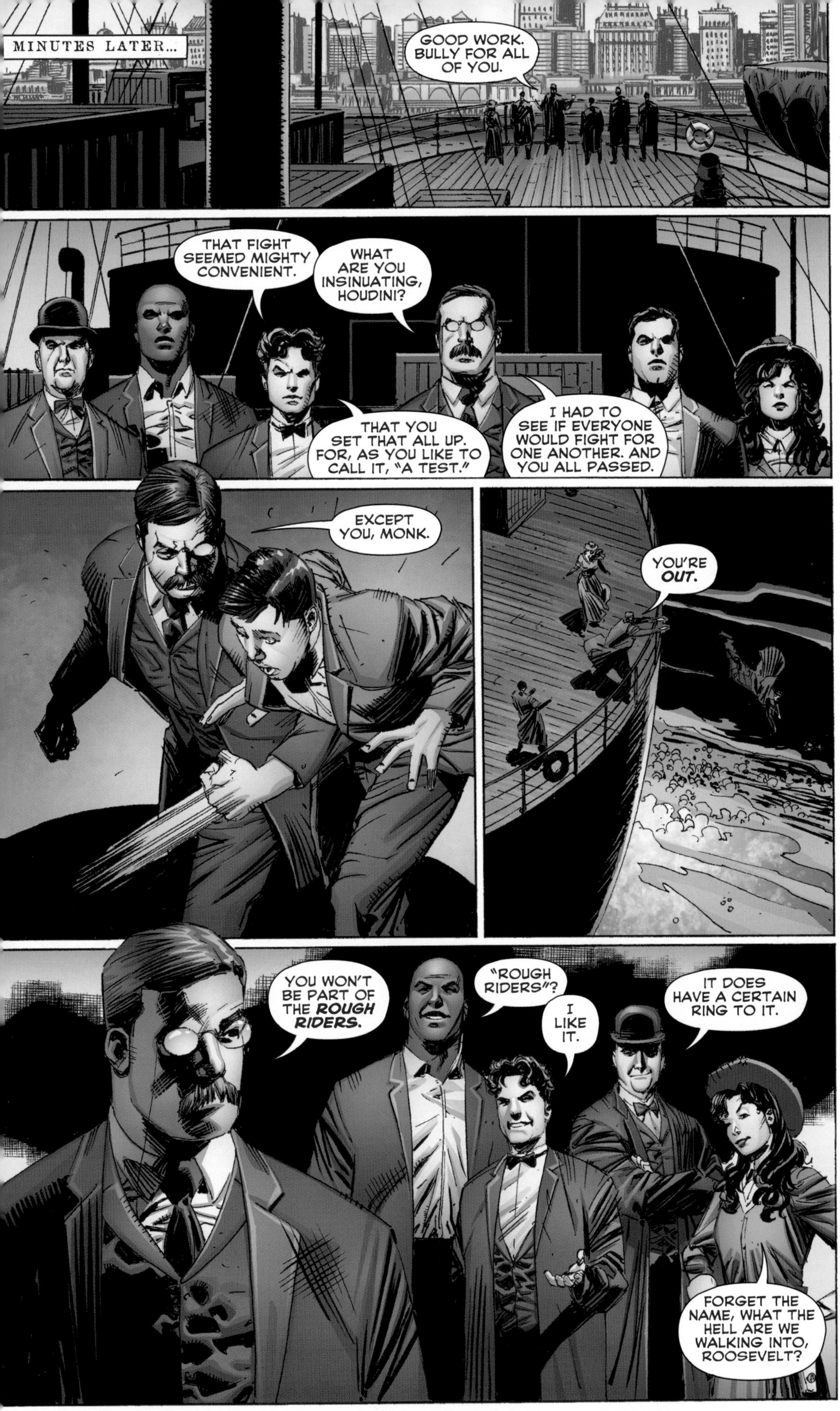
MINUTES LATER...
GOOD WORK. BULLY FOR ALL OF YOU.
THAT FIGHT SEEMED MIGHTY CONVENIENT.
WHAT ARE YOU INSINUATING, HOUDINI?
THAT YOU SET THAT ALL UP. FOR, AS YOU LIKE TO CALL IT, "A TEST."
I HAD TO SEE IF EVERYONE WOULD FIGHT FOR ONE ANOTHER. AND YOU ALL PASSED.
EXCEPT YOU, MONK.
YOU'RE OUT.
YOU WON'T BE PART OF THE ROUGH RIDERS.
"ROUGH RIDERS"?
I LIKE IT.
IT DOES HAVE A CERTAIN RING TO IT.
FORGET THE NAME, WHAT THE HELL ARE WE WALKING INTO, ROOSEVELT?

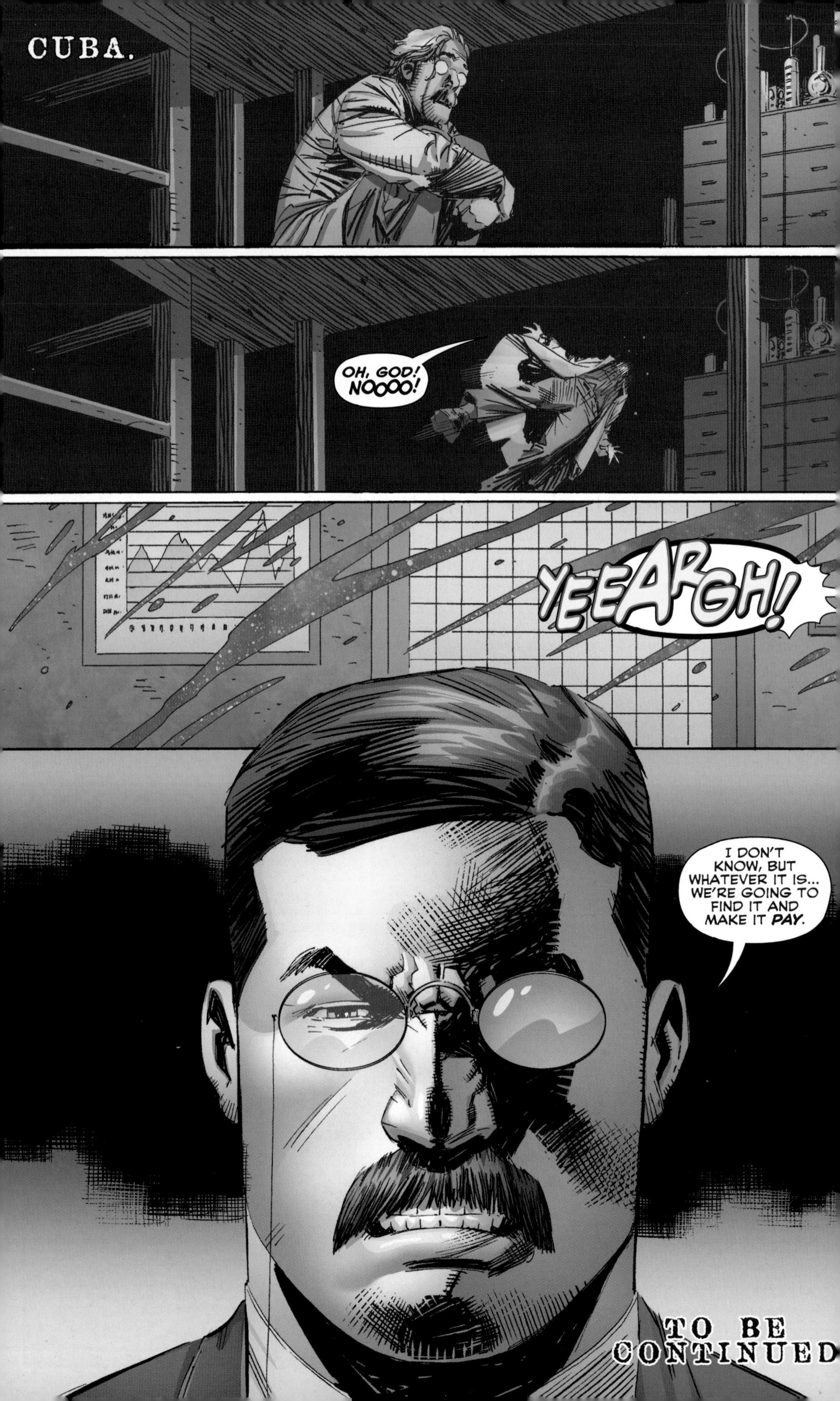
CUBA.
OH, GOD! NOOOO!
YEEARGH!
I DON'T KNOW, BUT WHATEVER IT IS... WE'RE GOING TO FIND IT AND MAKE IT PAY.
TO BE CONTINUED

"GIVE THEM HELL"

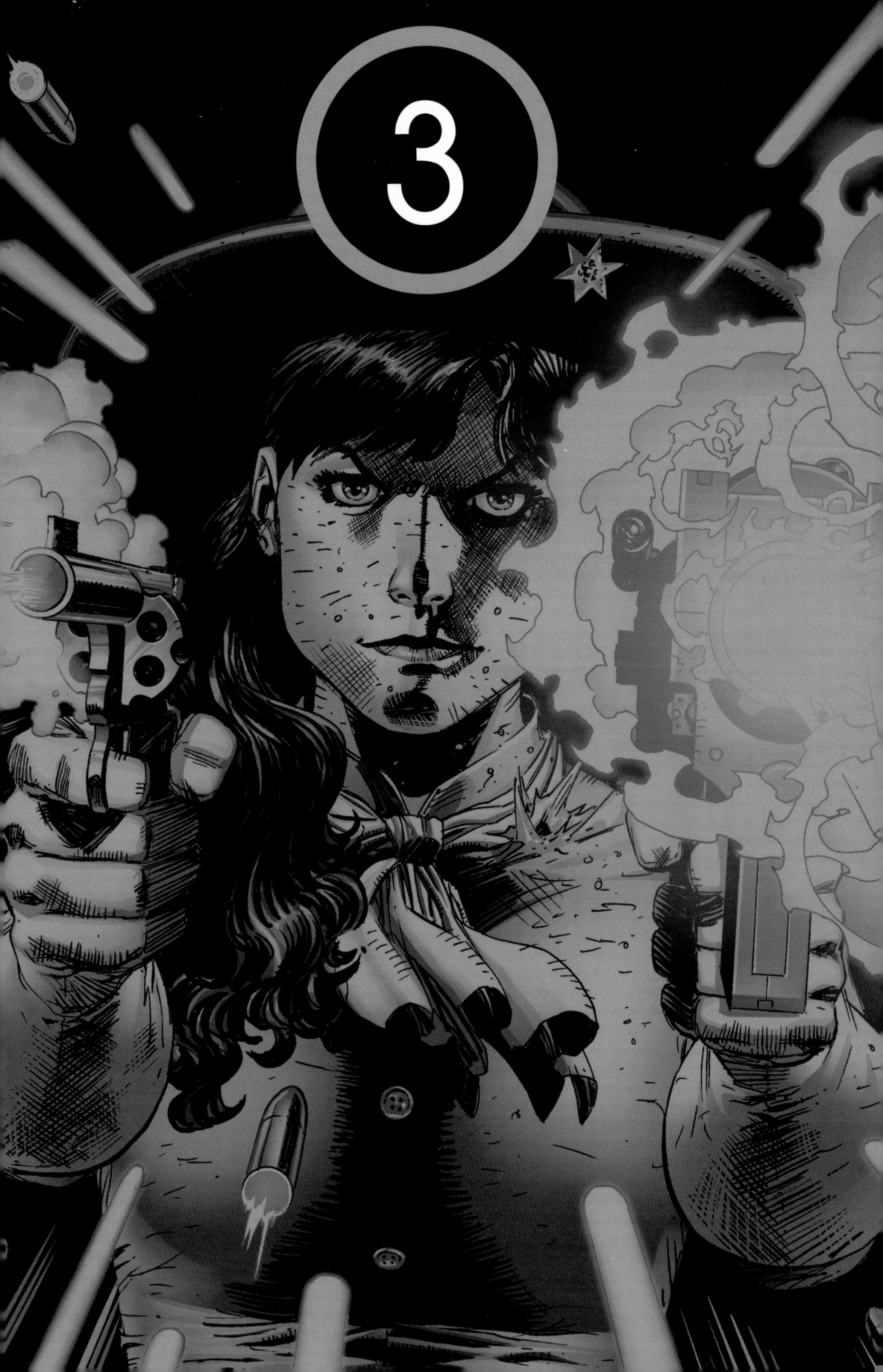

3

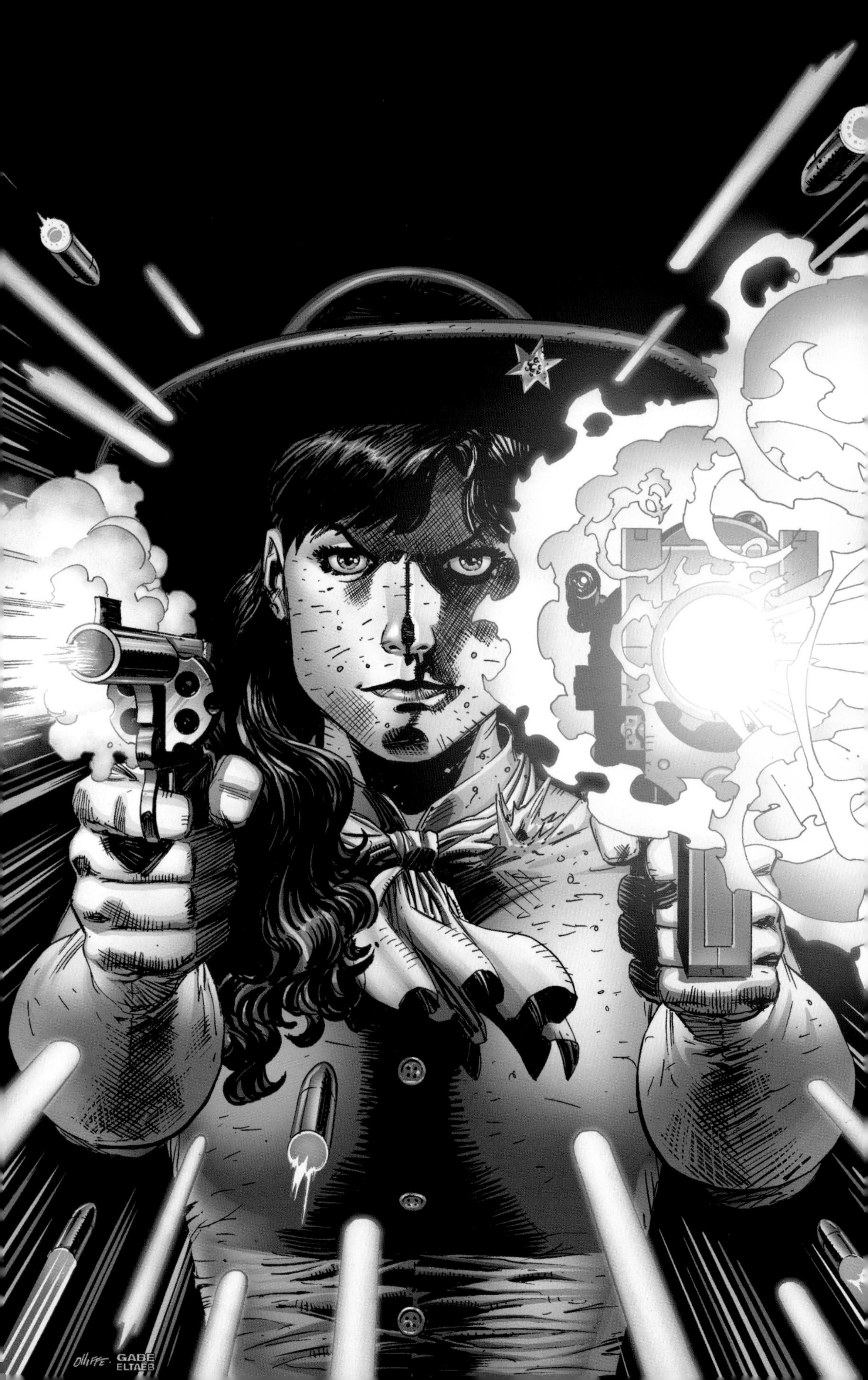

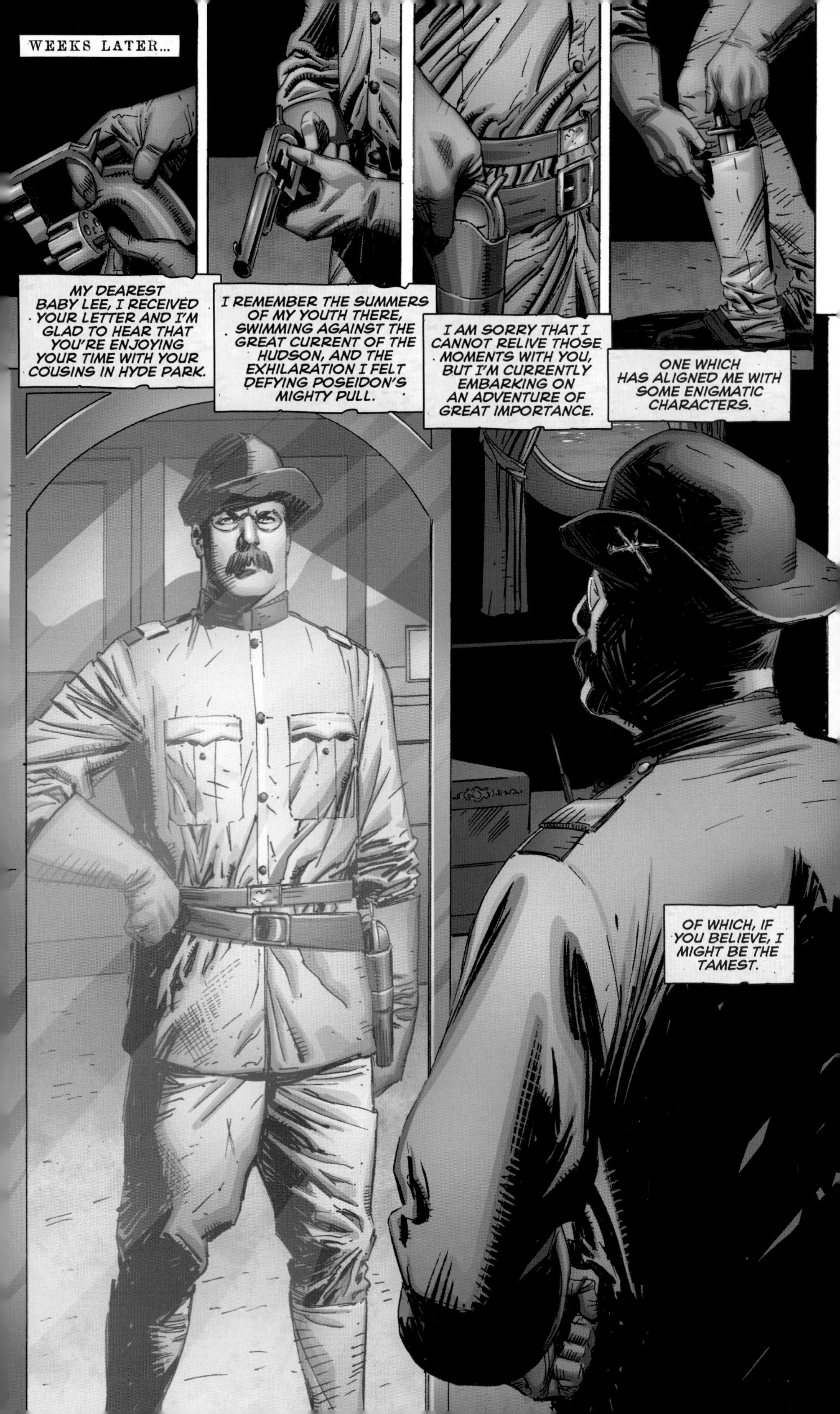
WEEKS LATER...
MY DEAREST BABY LEE, I RECEIVED YOUR LETTER AND I'M GLAD TO HEAR THAT YOU'RE ENJOYING YOUR TIME WITH YOUR COUSINS IN HYDE PARK.
I REMEMBER THE SUMMERS OF MY YOUTH THERE, SWIMMING AGAINST THE GREAT CURRENT OF THE HUDSON, AND THE EXHILARATION I FELT DEFYING POSEIDON'S MIGHTY PULL.
I AM SORRY THAT I CANNOT RELIVE THOSE MOMENTS WITH YOU, BUT I'M CURRENTLY EMBARKING ON AN ADVENTURE OF GREAT IMPORTANCE.
ONE WHICH HAS ALIGNED ME WITH SOME ENIGMATIC CHARACTERS.
OF WHICH, IF YOU BELIEVE, I MIGHT BE THE TAMEST.

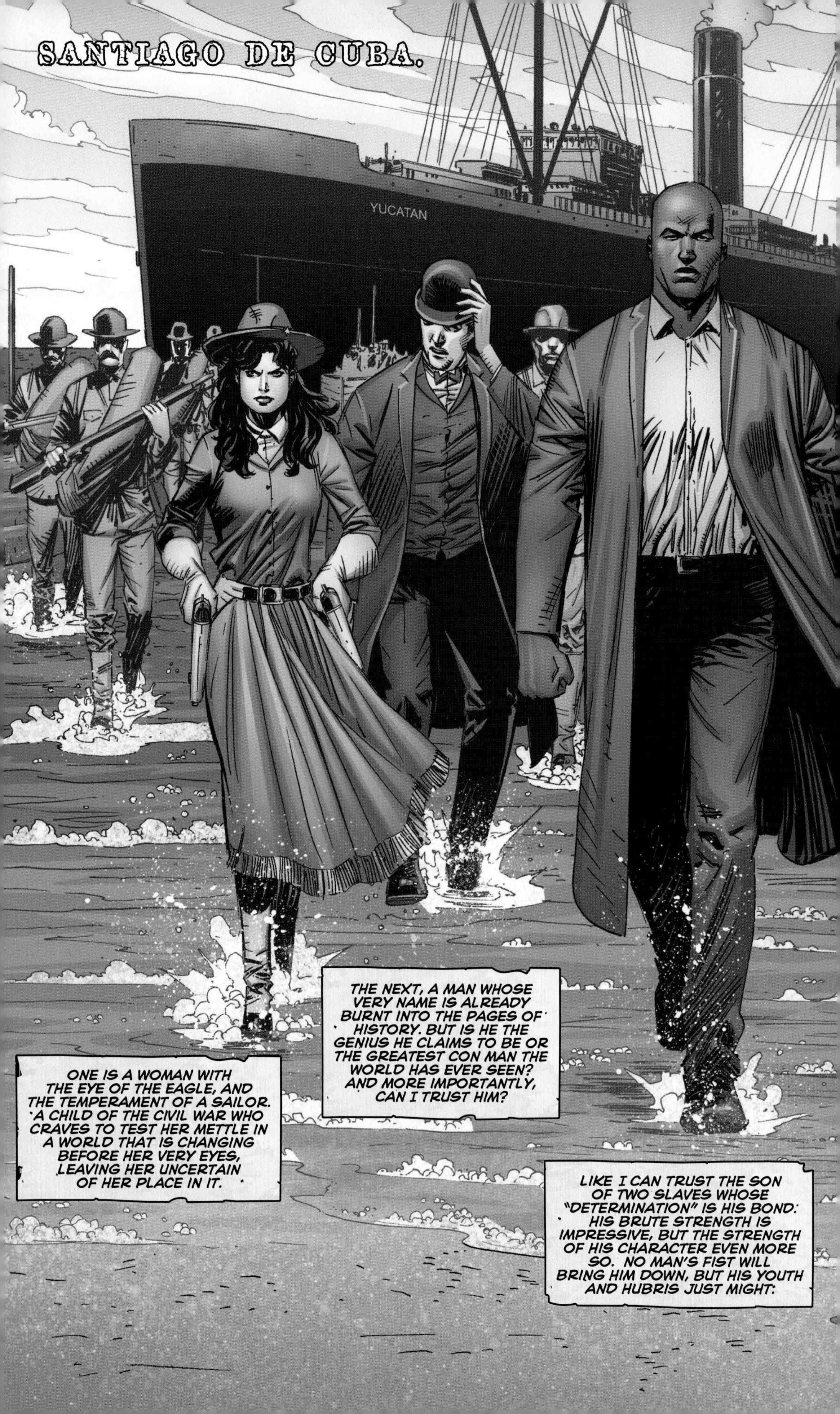

SANTIAGO DE CUBA.
YUCATAN
ONE IS A WOMAN WITH THE EYE OF THE EAGLE, AND THE TEMPERAMENT OF A SAILOR. A CHILD OF THE CIVIL WAR WHO CRAVES TO TEST HER METTLE IN A WORLD THAT IS CHANGING BEFORE HER VERY EYES, LEAVING HER UNCERTAIN OF HER PLACE IN IT.
THE NEXT, A MAN WHOSE VERY NAME IS ALREADY BURNT INTO THE PAGES OF HISTORY. BUT IS HE THE GENIUS HE CLAIMS TO BE OR THE GREATEST CON MAN THE WORLD HAS EVER SEEN? AND MORE IMPORTANTLY, CAN I TRUST HIM?
LIKE I CAN TRUST THE SON OF TWO SLAVES WHOSE "DETERMINATION" IS HIS BOND. HIS BRUTE STRENGTH IS IMPRESSIVE, BUT THE STRENGTH OF HIS CHARACTER EVEN MORE SO. NO MAN'S FIST WILL BRING HIM DOWN, BUT HIS YOUTH AND HUBRIS JUST MIGHT.

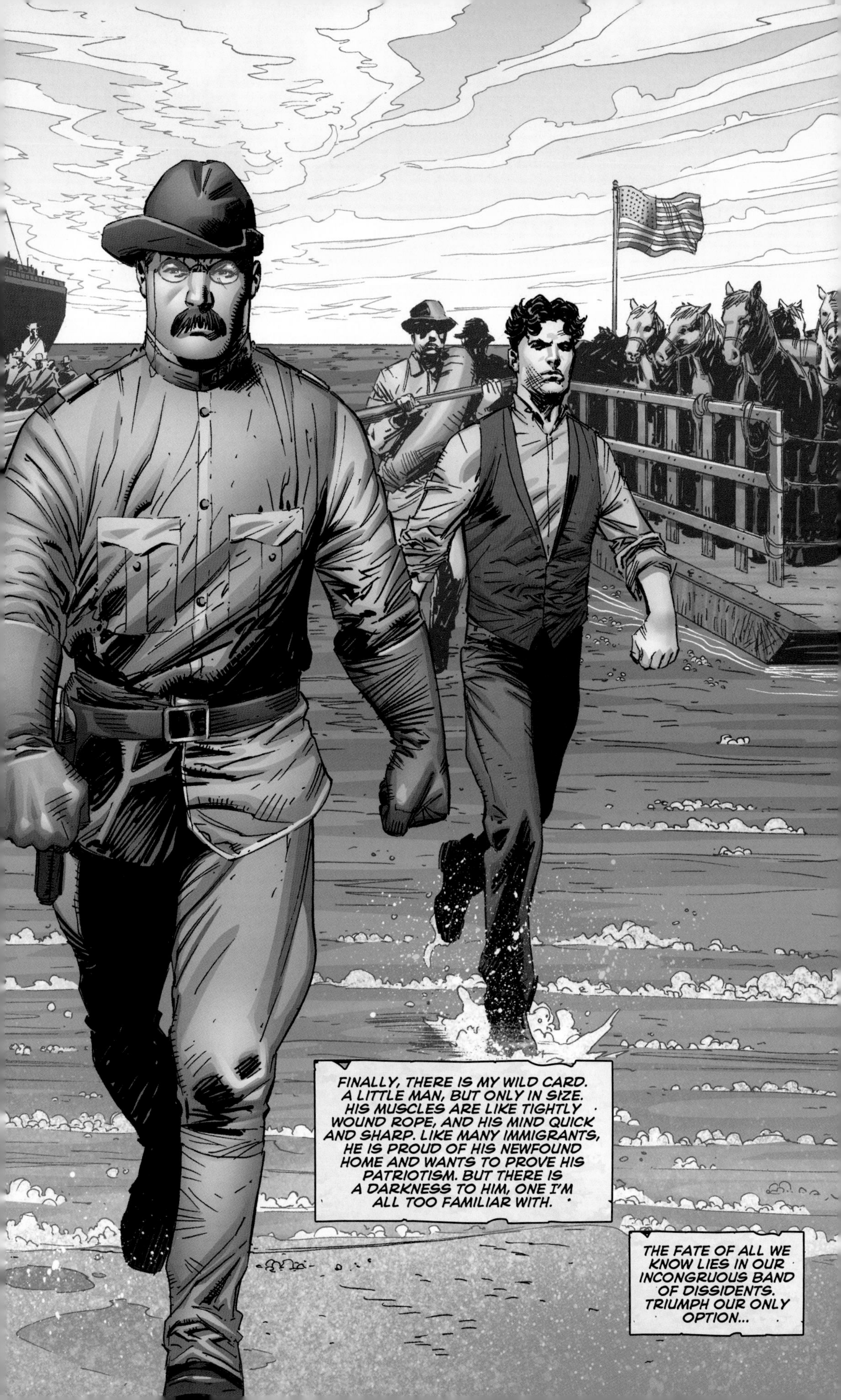

FINALLY, THERE IS MY WILD CARD. A LITTLE MAN, BUT ONLY IN SIZE. HIS MUSCLES ARE LIKE TIGHTLY WOUND ROPE, AND HIS MIND QUICK AND SHARP. LIKE MANY IMMIGRANTS, HE IS PROUD OF HIS NEWFOUND HOME AND WANTS TO PROVE HIS PATRIOTISM. BUT THERE IS A DARKNESS TO HIM, ONE I'M ALL TOO FAMILIAR WITH.
THE FATE OF ALL WE KNOW LIES IN OUR INCONGRUOUS BAND OF DISSIDENTS. TRIUMPH OUR ONLY OPTION...

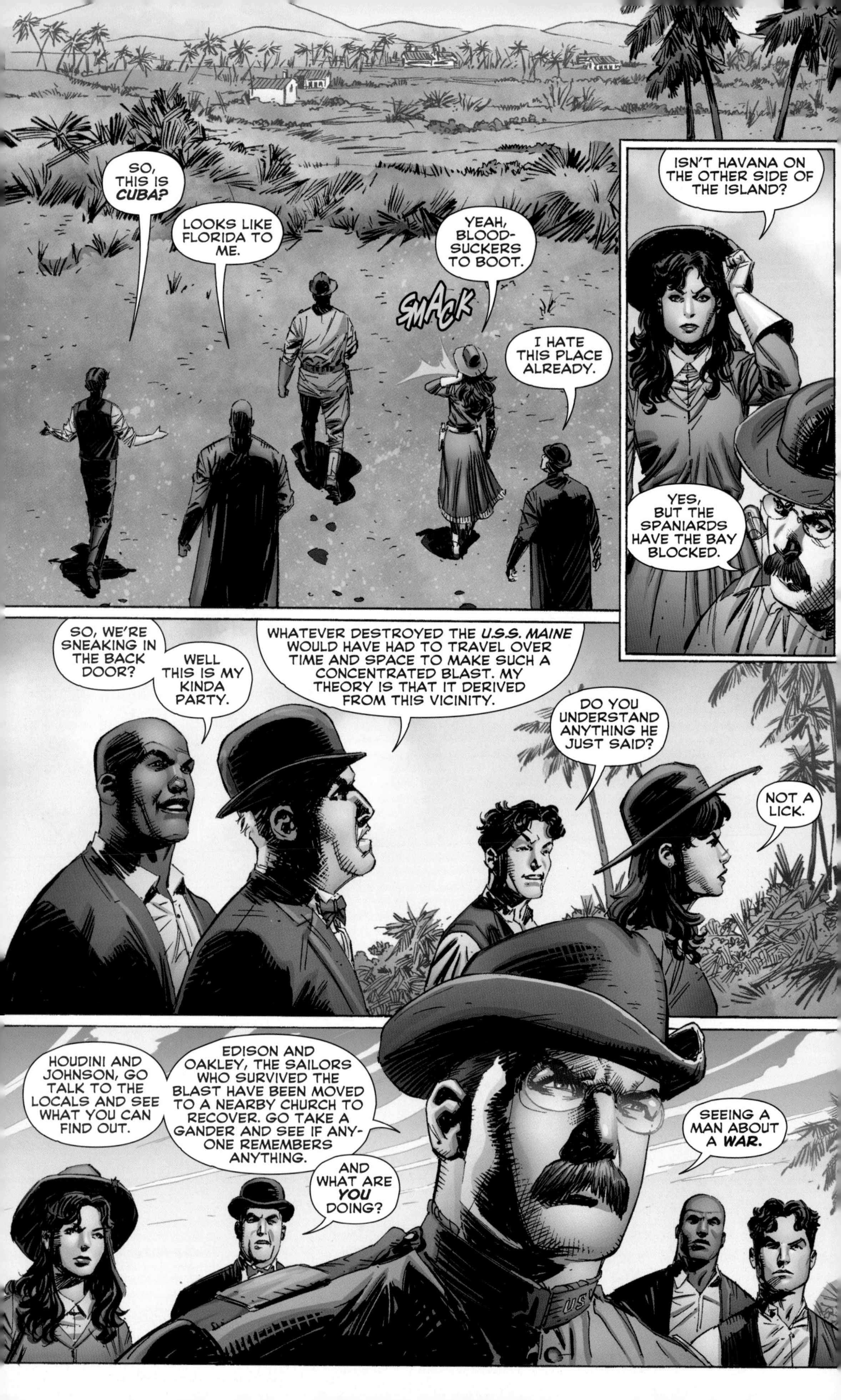

SO, THIS IS CUBA?
LOOKS LIKE FLORIDA TO ME.
YEAH, BLOOD-SUCKERS TO BOOT.
SMACK
I HATE THIS PLACE ALREADY.
ISN'T HAVANA ON THE OTHER SIDE OF THE ISLAND?
YES, BUT THE SPANIARDS HAVE THE BAY BLOCKED.
SO, WE'RE SNEAKING IN THE BACK DOOR?
WELL THIS IS MY KINDA PARTY.
WHATEVER DESTROYED THE U.S.S. MAINE WOULD HAVE HAD TO TRAVEL OVER TIME AND SPACE TO MAKE SUCH A CONCENTRATED BLAST. MY THEORY IS THAT IT DERIVED FROM THIS VICINITY.
DO YOU UNDERSTAND ANYTHING HE JUST SAID?
NOT A LICK.
HOUDINI AND JOHNSON, GO TALK TO THE LOCALS AND SEE WHAT YOU CAN FIND OUT.
EDISON AND OAKLEY, THE SAILORS WHO SURVIVED THE BLAST HAVE BEEN MOVED TO A NEARBY CHURCH TO RECOVER. GO TAKE A GANDER AND SEE IF ANY-ONE REMEMBERS ANYTHING.
AND WHAT ARE YOU DOING?
SEEING A MAN ABOUT A WAR.

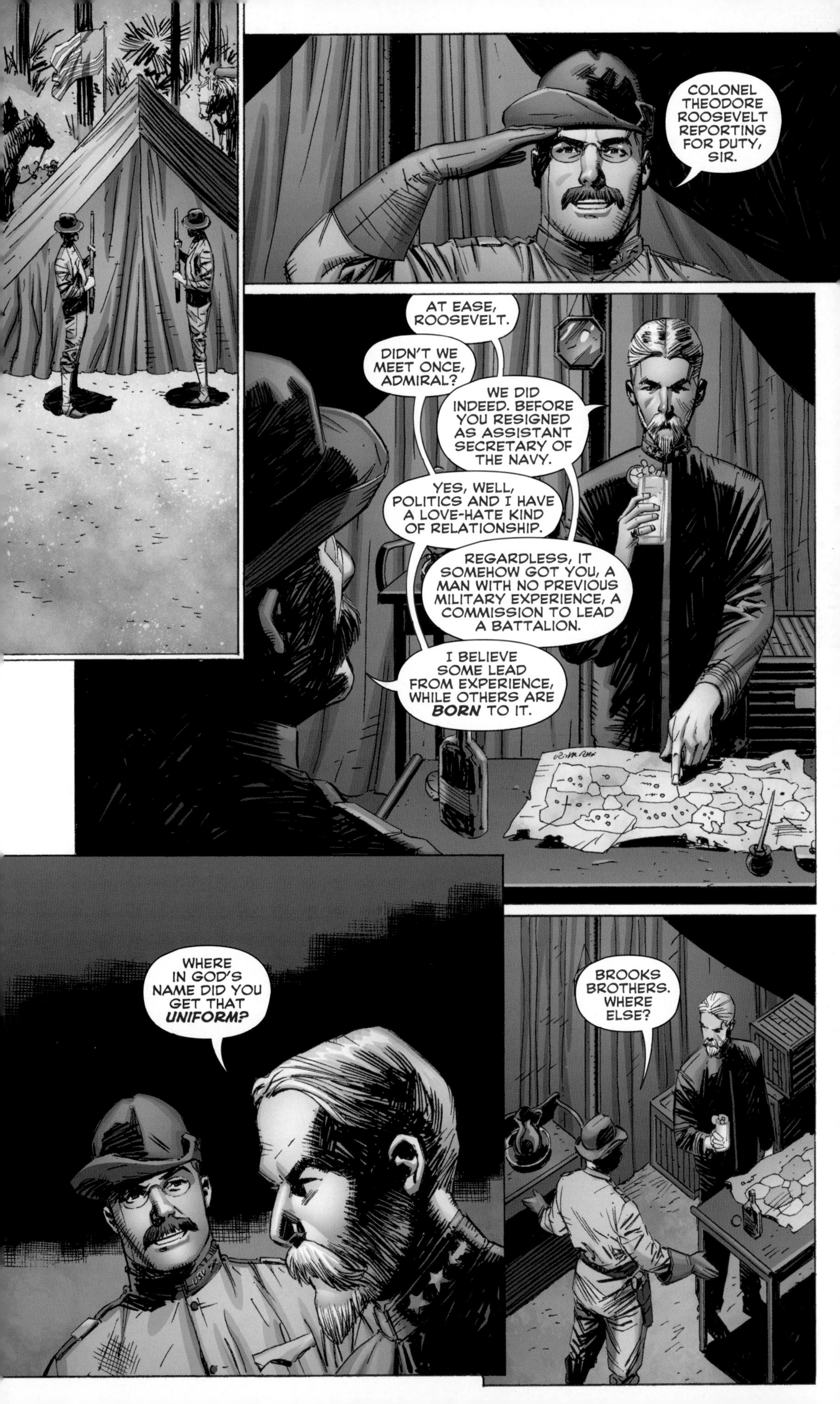
COLONEL THEODORE ROOSEVELT REPORTING FOR DUTY, SIR.
AT EASE, ROOSEVELT.
DIDN'T WE MEET ONCE, ADMIRAL?
WE DID INDEED. BEFORE YOU RESIGNED AS ASSISTANT SECRETARY OF THE NAVY.
YES, WELL, POLITICS AND I HAVE A LOVE-HATE KIND OF RELATIONSHIP.
REGARDLESS, IT SOMEHOW GOT YOU, A MAN WITH NO PREVIOUS MILITARY EXPERIENCE, A COMMISSION TO LEAD A BATTALION.
I BELIEVE SOME LEAD FROM EXPERIENCE, WHILE OTHERS ARE ***BORN*** TO IT.
WHERE IN GOD'S NAME DID YOU GET THAT ***UNIFORM?***
BROOKS BROTHERS. WHERE ELSE?

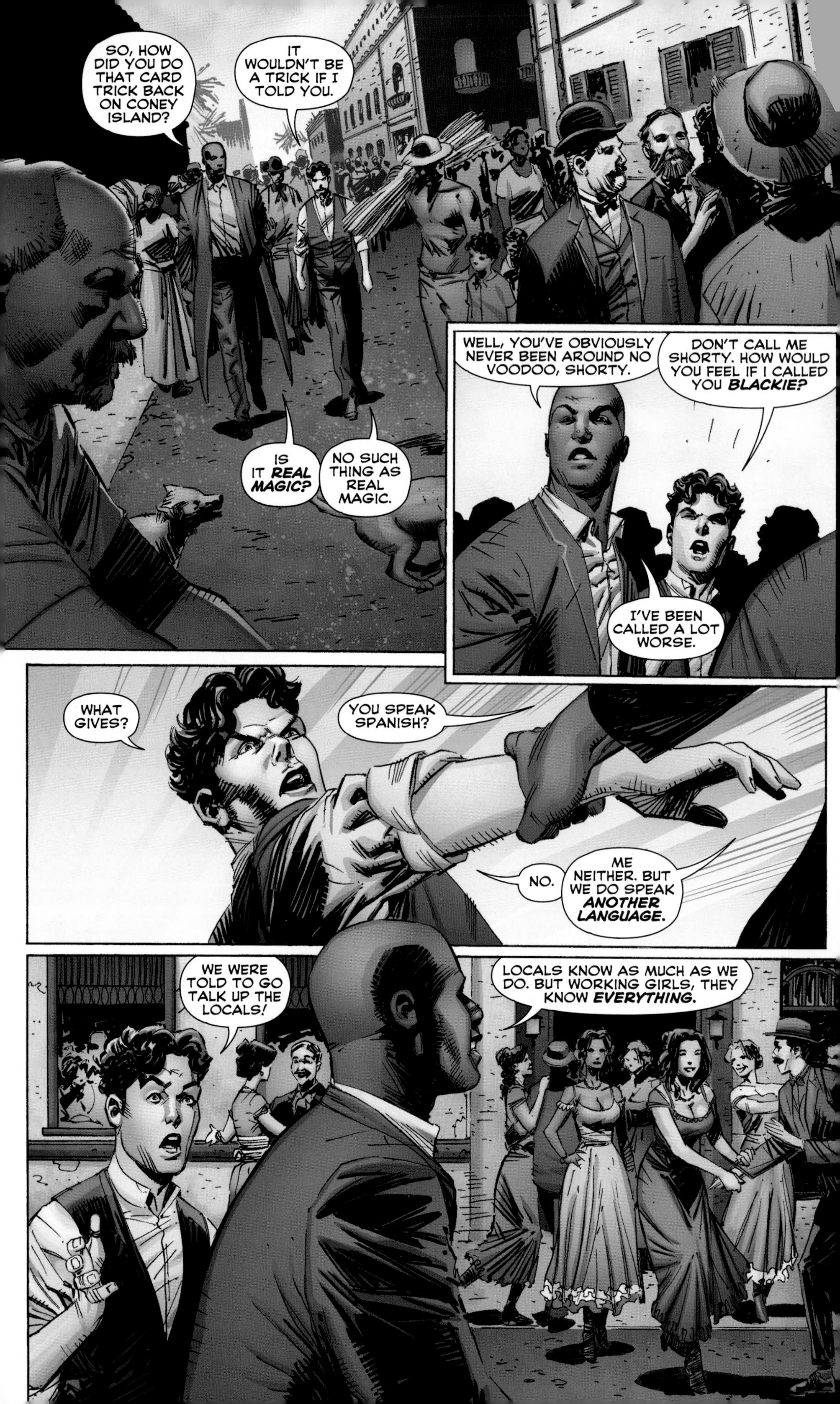
SO, HOW DID YOU DO THAT CARD TRICK BACK ON CONEY ISLAND?
IT WOULDN'T BE A TRICK IF I TOLD YOU.
IS IT REAL MAGIC?
NO SUCH THING AS REAL MAGIC.
WELL, YOU'VE OBVIOUSLY NEVER BEEN AROUND NO VOODOO, SHORTY.
DON'T CALL ME SHORTY. HOW WOULD YOU FEEL IF I CALLED YOU BLACKIE?
I'VE BEEN CALLED A LOT WORSE.
WHAT GIVES?
YOU SPEAK SPANISH?
NO.
ME NEITHER. BUT WE DO SPEAK ANOTHER LANGUAGE.
WE WERE TOLD TO GO TALK UP THE LOCALS!
LOCALS KNOW AS MUCH AS WE DO. BUT WORKING GIRLS, THEY KNOW EVERYTHING.

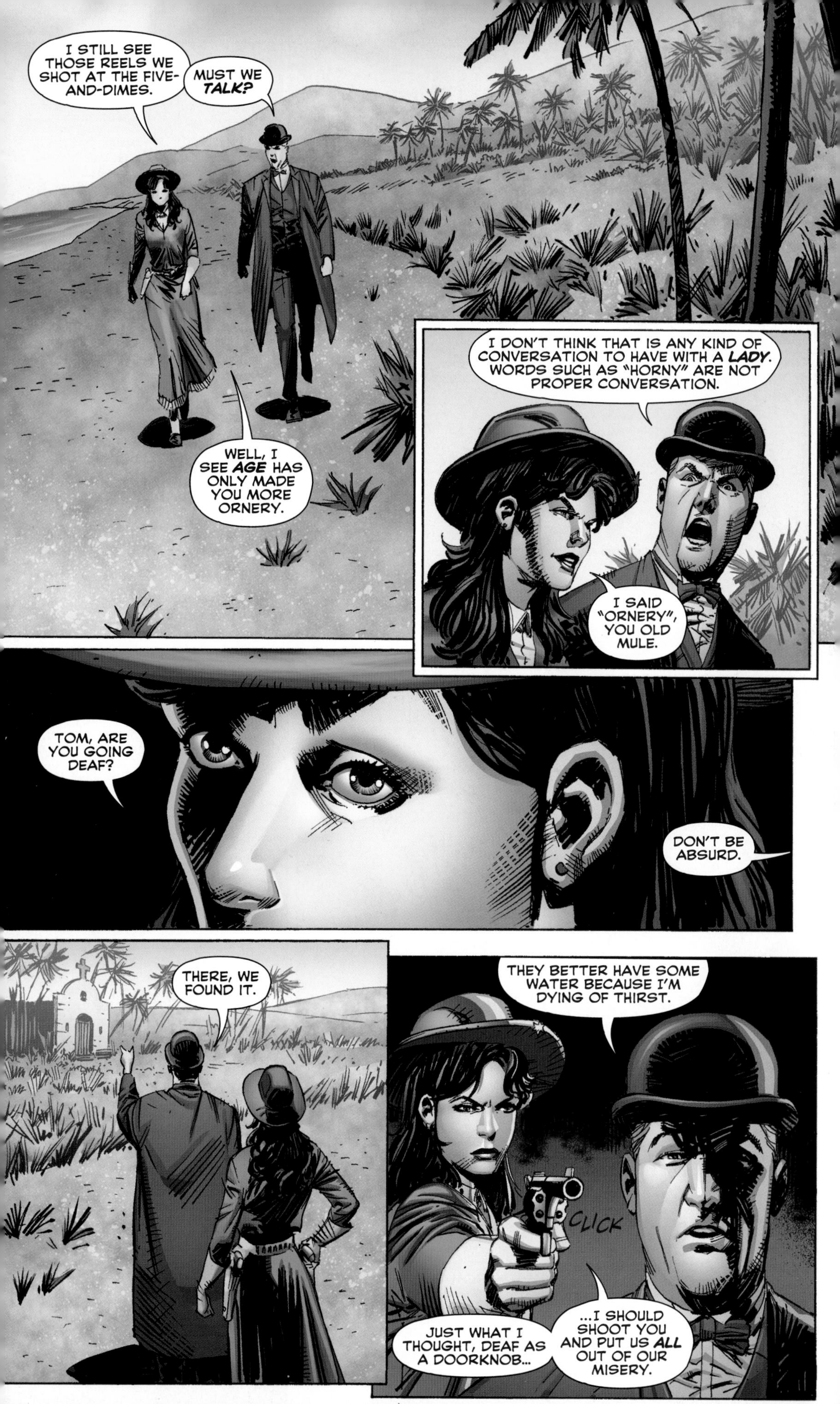
I STILL SEE THOSE REELS WE SHOT AT THE FIVE-AND-DIMES.
MUST WE *TALK?*
WELL, I SEE ***AGE*** HAS ONLY MADE YOU MORE ORNERY.
I DON'T THINK THAT IS ANY KIND OF CONVERSATION TO HAVE WITH A ***LADY***. WORDS SUCH AS "HORNY" ARE NOT PROPER CONVERSATION.
I SAID "ORNERY", YOU OLD MULE.
TOM, ARE YOU GOING DEAF?
DON'T BE ABSURD.
THERE, WE FOUND IT.
THEY BETTER HAVE SOME WATER BECAUSE I'M DYING OF THIRST.
CLICK
JUST WHAT I THOUGHT, DEAF AS A DOORKNOB...
...I SHOULD SHOOT YOU AND PUT US *ALL* OUT OF OUR MISERY.

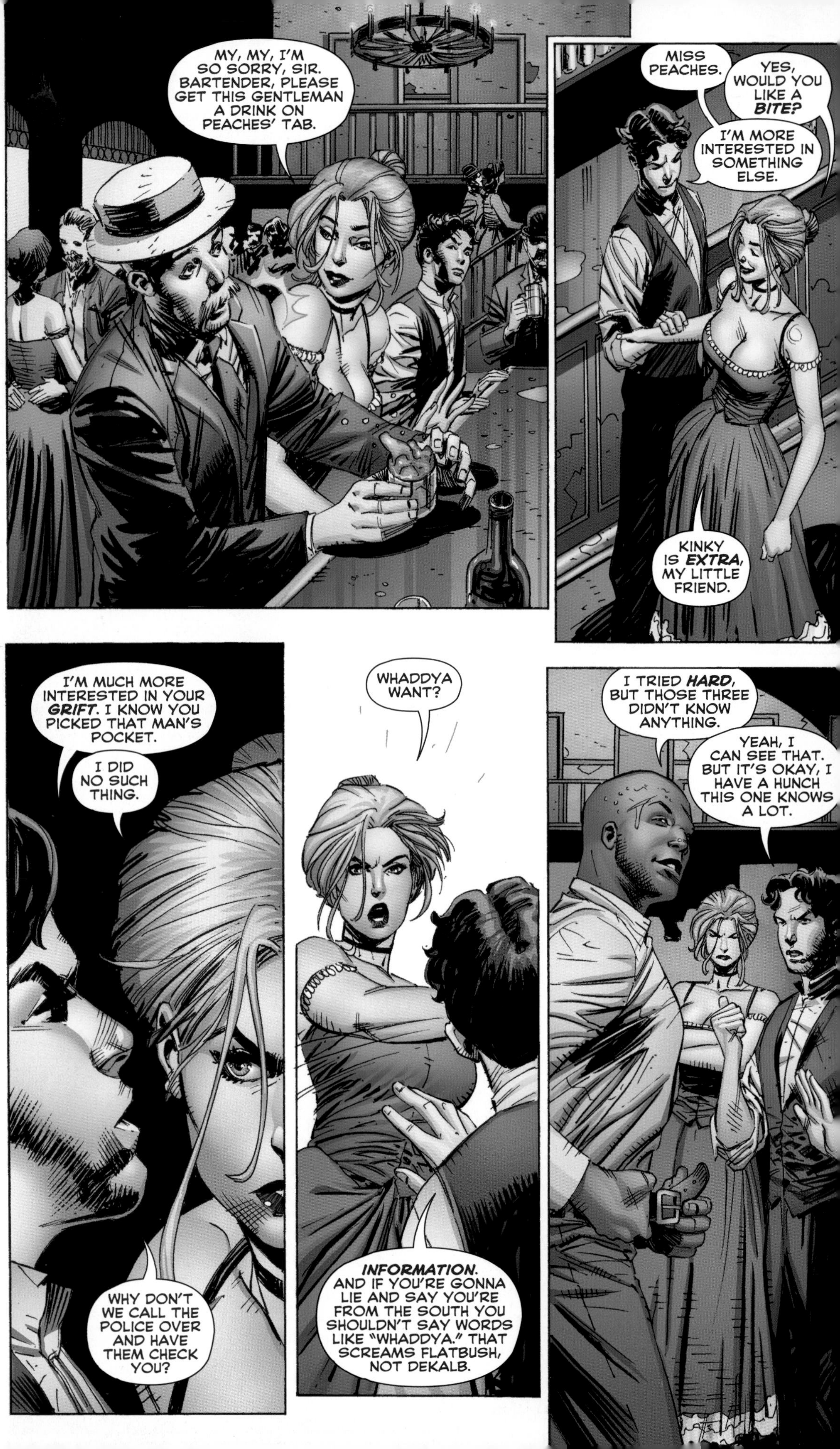
MY, MY, I'M SO SORRY, SIR. BARTENDER, PLEASE GET THIS GENTLEMAN A DRINK ON PEACHES' TAB.
MISS PEACHES.
YES, WOULD YOU LIKE A *BITE?*
I'M MORE INTERESTED IN SOMETHING ELSE.
KINKY IS *EXTRA*, MY LITTLE FRIEND.
I'M MUCH MORE INTERESTED IN YOUR *GRIFT*. I KNOW YOU PICKED THAT MAN'S POCKET.
I DID NO SUCH THING.
WHY DON'T WE CALL THE POLICE OVER AND HAVE THEM CHECK YOU?
WHADDYA WANT?
INFORMATION. AND IF YOU'RE GONNA LIE AND SAY YOU'RE FROM THE SOUTH YOU SHOULDN'T SAY WORDS LIKE "WHADDYA." THAT SCREAMS FLATBUSH, NOT DEKALB.
I TRIED *HARD*, BUT THOSE THREE DIDN'T KNOW ANYTHING.
YEAH, I CAN SEE THAT. BUT IT'S OKAY, I HAVE A HUNCH THIS ONE KNOWS A LOT.

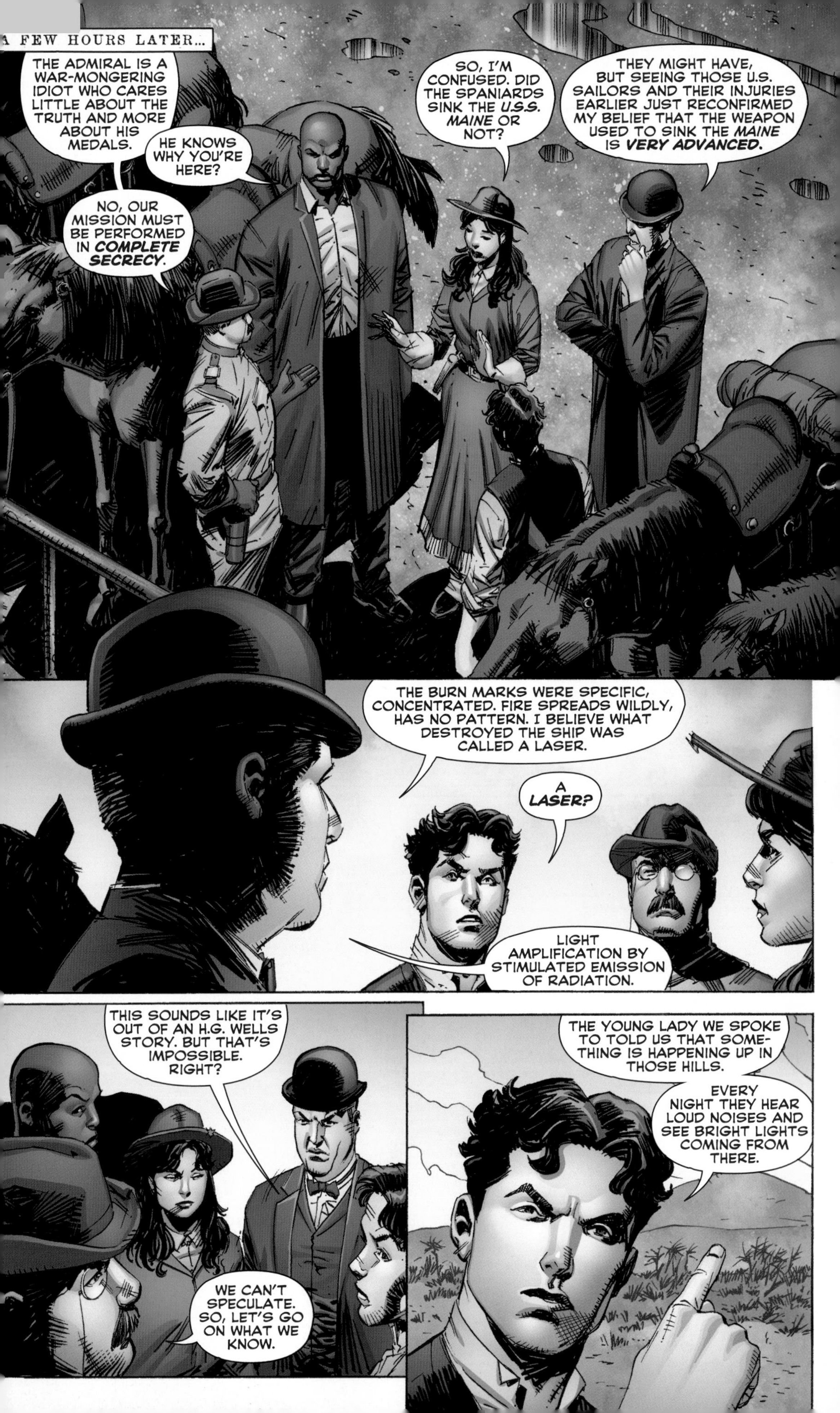
A FEW HOURS LATER...
THE ADMIRAL IS A WAR-MONGERING IDIOT WHO CARES LITTLE ABOUT THE TRUTH AND MORE ABOUT HIS MEDALS.
HE KNOWS WHY YOU'RE HERE?
NO, OUR MISSION MUST BE PERFORMED IN COMPLETE SECRECY.
SO, I'M CONFUSED. DID THE SPANIARDS SINK THE U.S.S. MAINE OR NOT?
THEY MIGHT HAVE, BUT SEEING THOSE U.S. SAILORS AND THEIR INJURIES EARLIER JUST RECONFIRMED MY BELIEF THAT THE WEAPON USED TO SINK THE MAINE IS VERY ADVANCED.
THE BURN MARKS WERE SPECIFIC, CONCENTRATED. FIRE SPREADS WILDLY, HAS NO PATTERN. I BELIEVE WHAT DESTROYED THE SHIP WAS CALLED A LASER.
A LASER?
LIGHT AMPLIFICATION BY STIMULATED EMISSION OF RADIATION.
THIS SOUNDS LIKE IT'S OUT OF AN H.G. WELLS STORY. BUT THAT'S IMPOSSIBLE. RIGHT?
WE CAN'T SPECULATE. SO, LET'S GO ON WHAT WE KNOW.
THE YOUNG LADY WE SPOKE TO TOLD US THAT SOMETHING IS HAPPENING UP IN THOSE HILLS.
EVERY NIGHT THEY HEAR LOUD NOISES AND SEE BRIGHT LIGHTS COMING FROM THERE.

THEN I THINK YOU TWO WILL HAVE TO PAY THE TOP OF THAT MOUNTAIN A VISIT TONIGHT.

JUST *RECON*. GET IN, TAKE A LOOK AROUND AND GET OUT.

AND WHAT THE HELL AM *I* DOING?

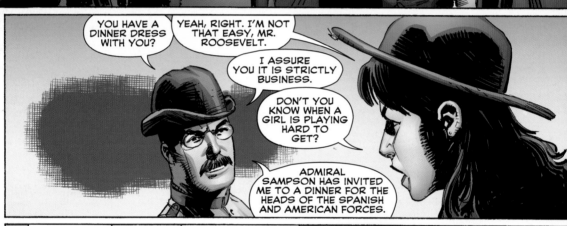

YOU HAVE A DINNER DRESS WITH YOU?

YEAH, RIGHT. I'M NOT THAT EASY, MR. ROOSEVELT.

I ASSURE YOU IT IS STRICTLY BUSINESS.

DON'T YOU KNOW WHEN A GIRL IS PLAYING HARD TO GET?

ADMIRAL SAMPSON HAS INVITED ME TO A DINNER FOR THE HEADS OF THE SPANISH AND AMERICAN FORCES.

WAIT, YOU'RE SITTING WITH THE *ENEMY*?

A SOCIAL COURTESY, IN HONOR OF THE ART OF WAR.

WHITE PEOPLE ARE *CRAZY*.

EDISON, FIND THE HIGHEST POINT HERE, PULL OUT ONE OF YOUR CONTRAPTIONS AND SEE WHAT THIS LIGHT SHOW IS ALL ABOUT.

WHAT IF IT'S ANOTHER LITTLE BIG-HORN?

CROSS THAT BRIDGE WHEN WE GET THERE.

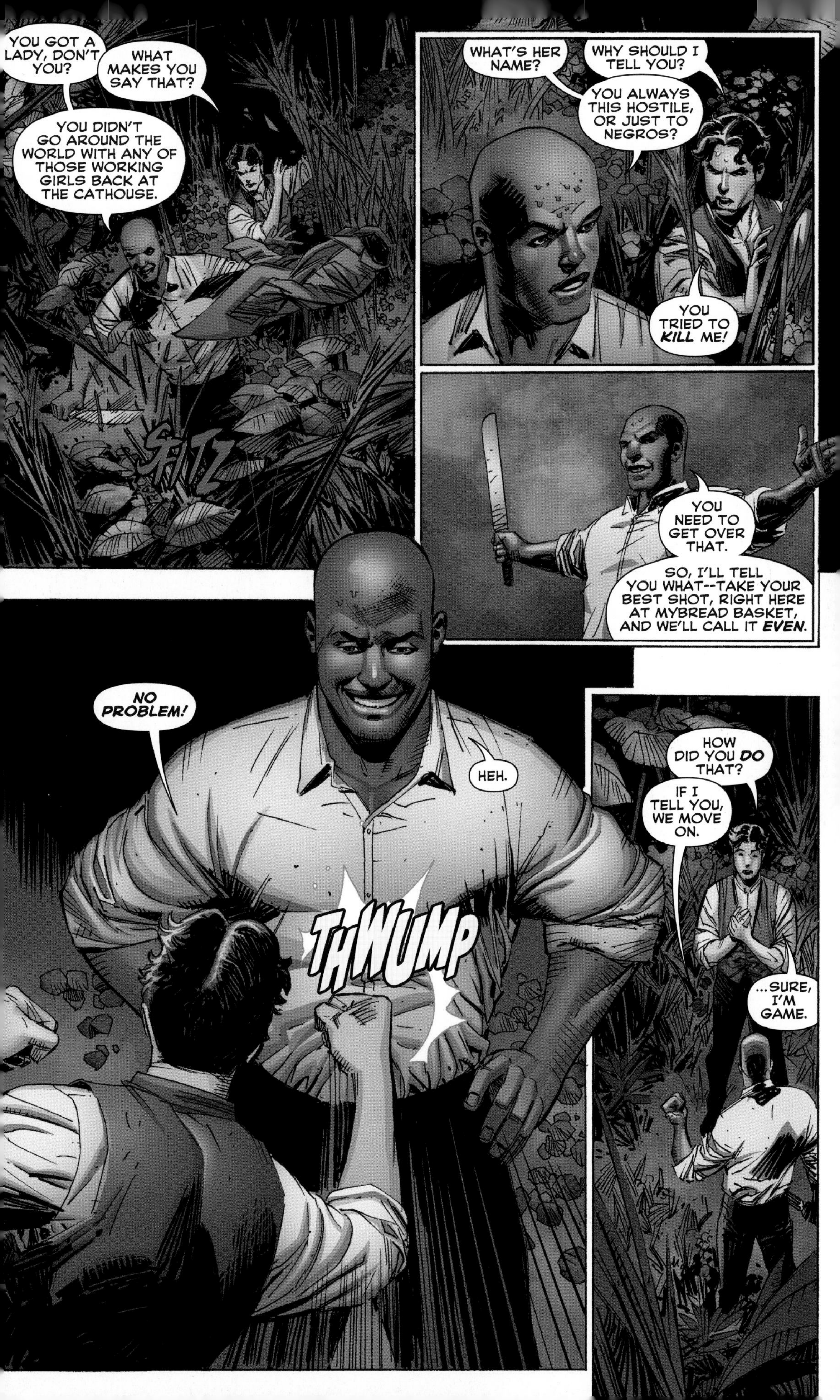

YOU GOT A LADY, DON'T YOU?
WHAT MAKES YOU SAY THAT?
YOU DIDN'T GO AROUND THE WORLD WITH ANY OF THOSE WORKING GIRLS BACK AT THE CATHOUSE.
SFITZ
WHAT'S HER NAME?
WHY SHOULD I TELL YOU?
YOU ALWAYS THIS HOSTILE, OR JUST TO NEGROS?
YOU TRIED TO KILL ME!
YOU NEED TO GET OVER THAT.
SO, I'LL TELL YOU WHAT--TAKE YOUR BEST SHOT, RIGHT HERE AT MYBREAD BASKET, AND WE'LL CALL IT EVEN.
NO PROBLEM!
HEH.
THWUMP
HOW DID YOU DO THAT?
IF I TELL YOU, WE MOVE ON.
...SURE, I'M GAME.

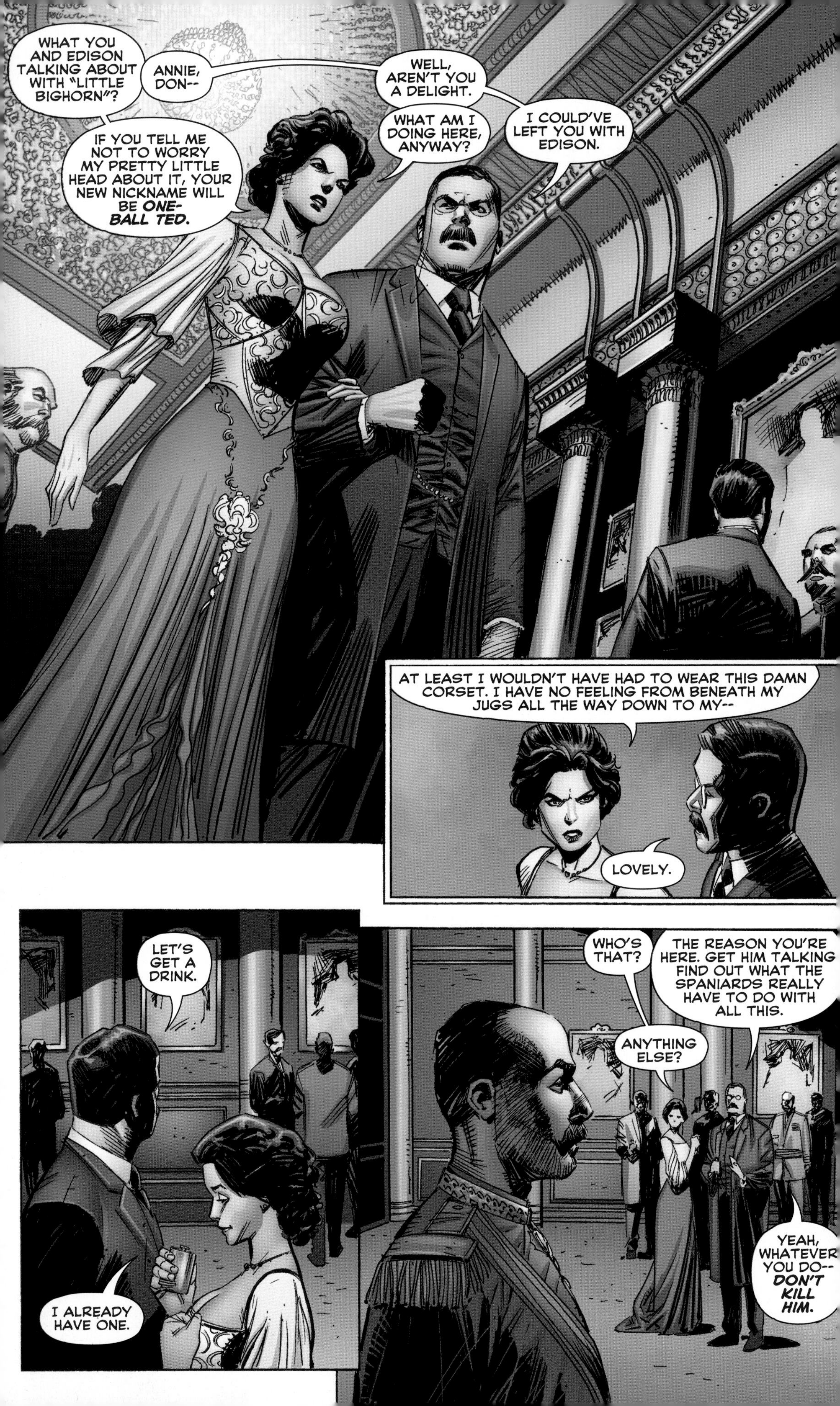
WHAT YOU AND EDISON TALKING ABOUT WITH "LITTLE BIGHORN"?
ANNIE, DON--
WELL, AREN'T YOU A DELIGHT.
IF YOU TELL ME NOT TO WORRY MY PRETTY LITTLE HEAD ABOUT IT, YOUR NEW NICKNAME WILL BE *ONE-BALL TED.*
WHAT AM I DOING HERE, ANYWAY?
I COULD'VE LEFT YOU WITH EDISON.
AT LEAST I WOULDN'T HAVE HAD TO WEAR THIS DAMN CORSET. I HAVE NO FEELING FROM BENEATH MY JUGS ALL THE WAY DOWN TO MY--
LOVELY.
LET'S GET A DRINK.
I ALREADY HAVE ONE.
WHO'S THAT?
THE REASON YOU'RE HERE. GET HIM TALKING FIND OUT WHAT THE SPANIARDS REALLY HAVE TO DO WITH ALL THIS.
ANYTHING ELSE?
YEAH, WHATEVER YOU DO-- *DON'T KILL HIM.*

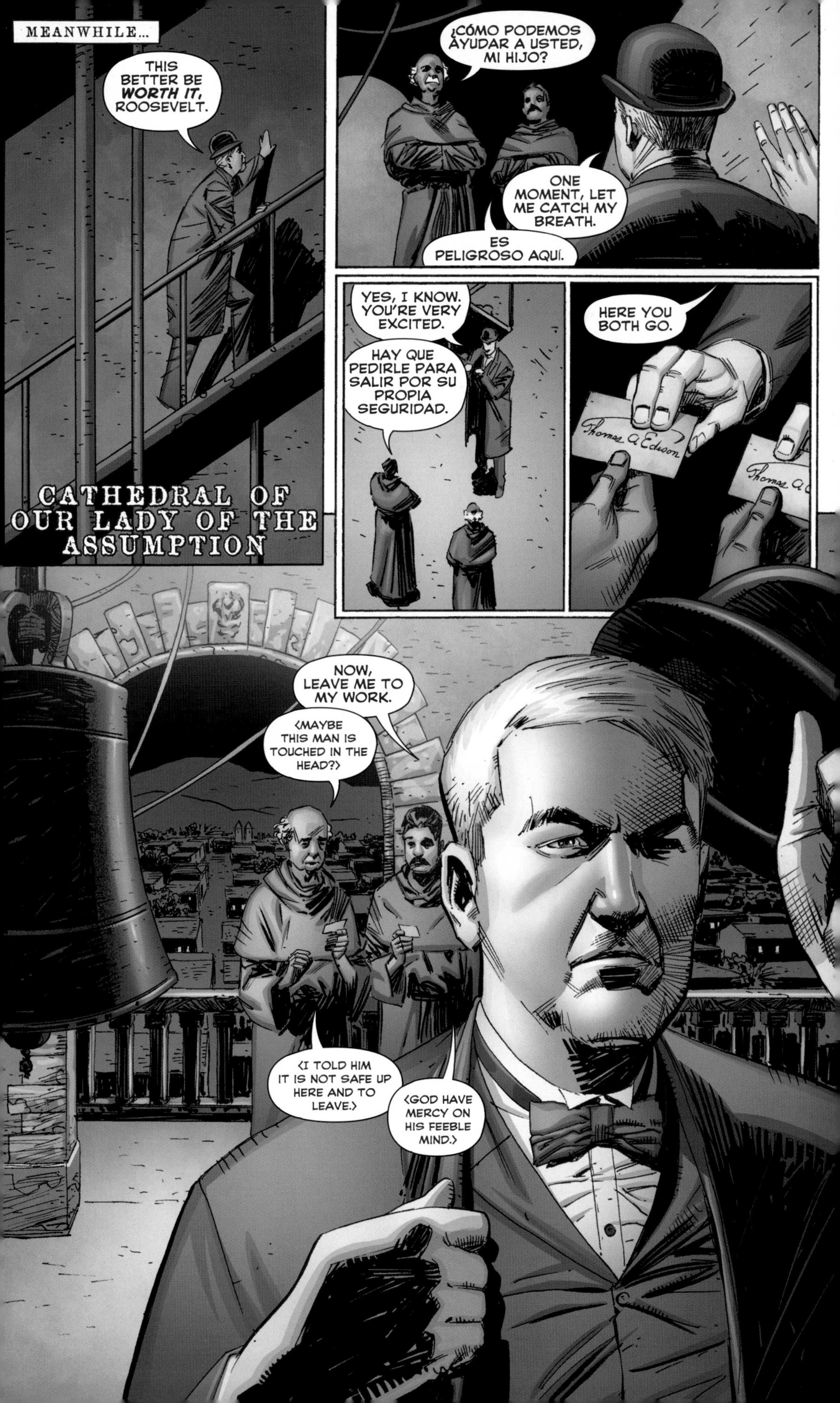
MEANWHILE...
THIS BETTER BE WORTH IT, ROOSEVELT.
CATHEDRAL OF OUR LADY OF THE ASSUMPTION
¿CÓMO PODEMOS AYUDAR A USTED, MI HIJO?
ONE MOMENT, LET ME CATCH MY BREATH.
ES PELIGROSO AQUÍ.
YES, I KNOW. YOU'RE VERY EXCITED.
HAY QUE PEDIRLE PARA SALIR POR SU PROPIA SEGURIDAD.
HERE YOU BOTH GO.
Thomas A Edison
NOW, LEAVE ME TO MY WORK.
<MAYBE THIS MAN IS TOUCHED IN THE HEAD?>
<I TOLD HIM IT IS NOT SAFE UP HERE AND TO LEAVE.>
<GOD HAVE MERCY ON HIS FEEBLE MIND.>

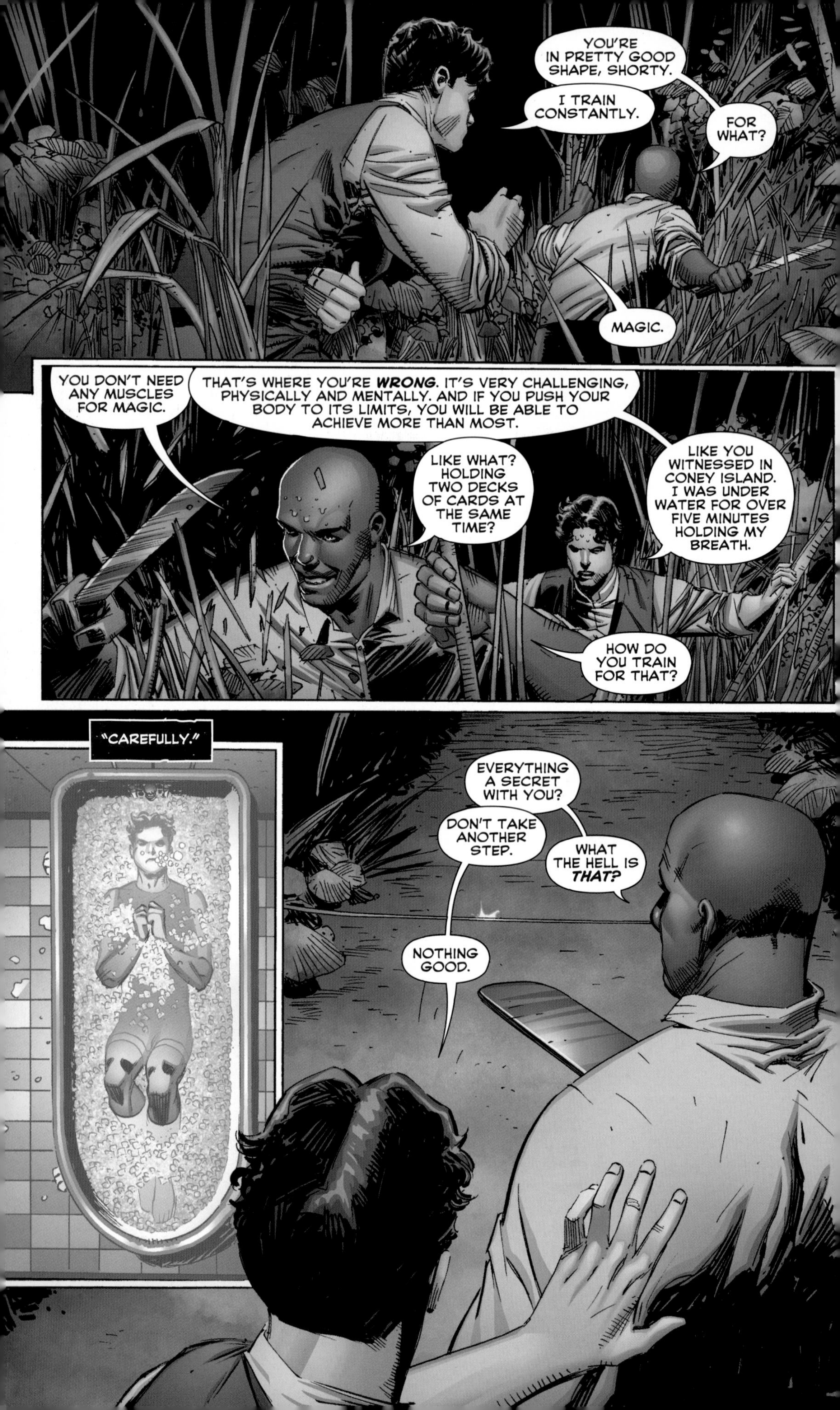
YOU'RE IN PRETTY GOOD SHAPE, SHORTY.
I TRAIN CONSTANTLY.
FOR WHAT?
MAGIC.
YOU DON'T NEED ANY MUSCLES FOR MAGIC.
THAT'S WHERE YOU'RE WRONG. IT'S VERY CHALLENGING, PHYSICALLY AND MENTALLY. AND IF YOU PUSH YOUR BODY TO ITS LIMITS, YOU WILL BE ABLE TO ACHIEVE MORE THAN MOST.
LIKE WHAT? HOLDING TWO DECKS OF CARDS AT THE SAME TIME?
LIKE YOU WITNESSED IN CONEY ISLAND. I WAS UNDER WATER FOR OVER FIVE MINUTES HOLDING MY BREATH.
HOW DO YOU TRAIN FOR THAT?
"CAREFULLY."
EVERYTHING A SECRET WITH YOU?
DON'T TAKE ANOTHER STEP.
WHAT THE HELL IS THAT?
NOTHING GOOD.

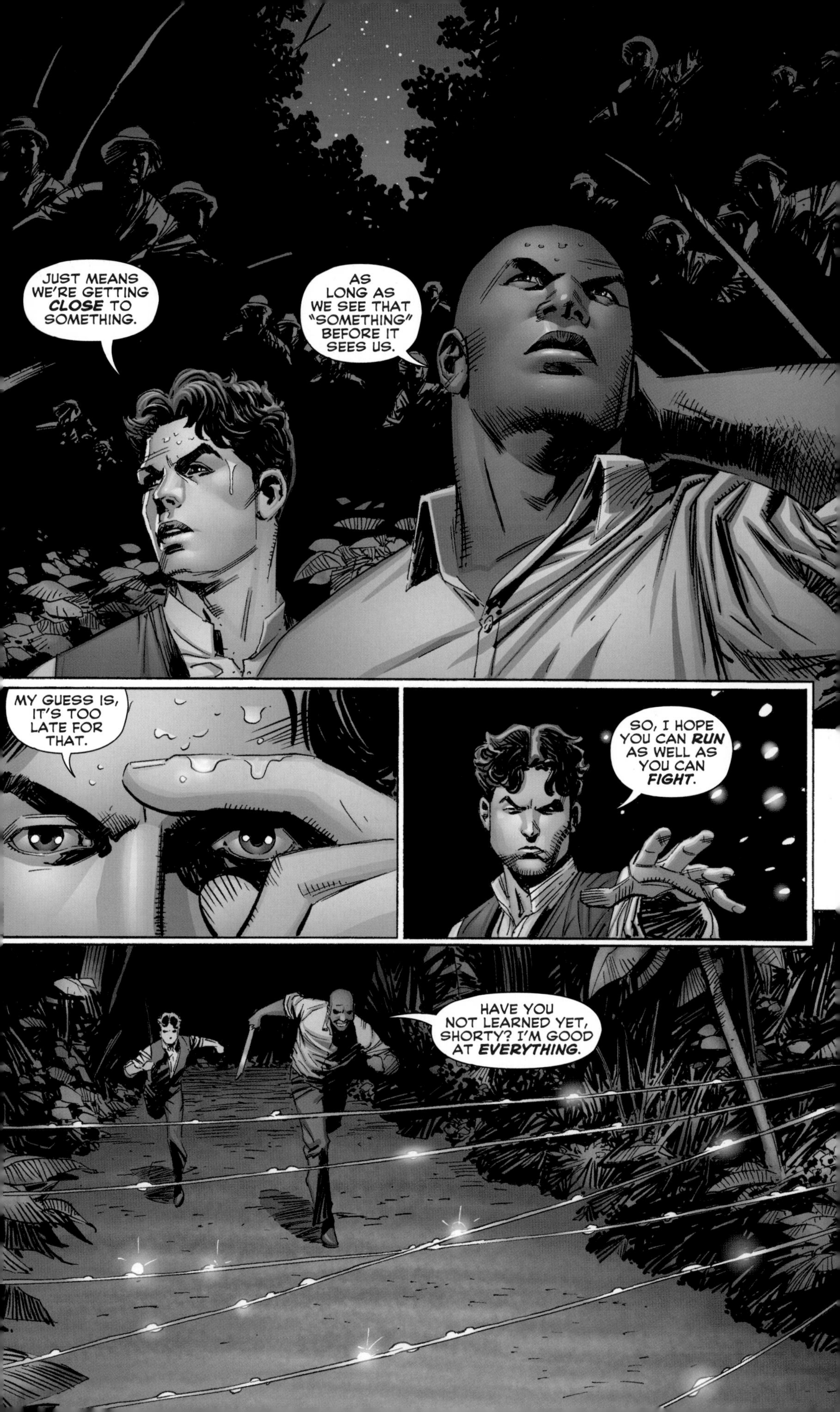
JUST MEANS WE'RE GETTING CLOSE TO SOMETHING.
AS LONG AS WE SEE THAT "SOMETHING" BEFORE IT SEES US.
MY GUESS IS, IT'S TOO LATE FOR THAT.
SO, I HOPE YOU CAN RUN AS WELL AS YOU CAN FIGHT.
HAVE YOU NOT LEARNED YET, SHORTY? I'M GOOD AT EVERYTHING.

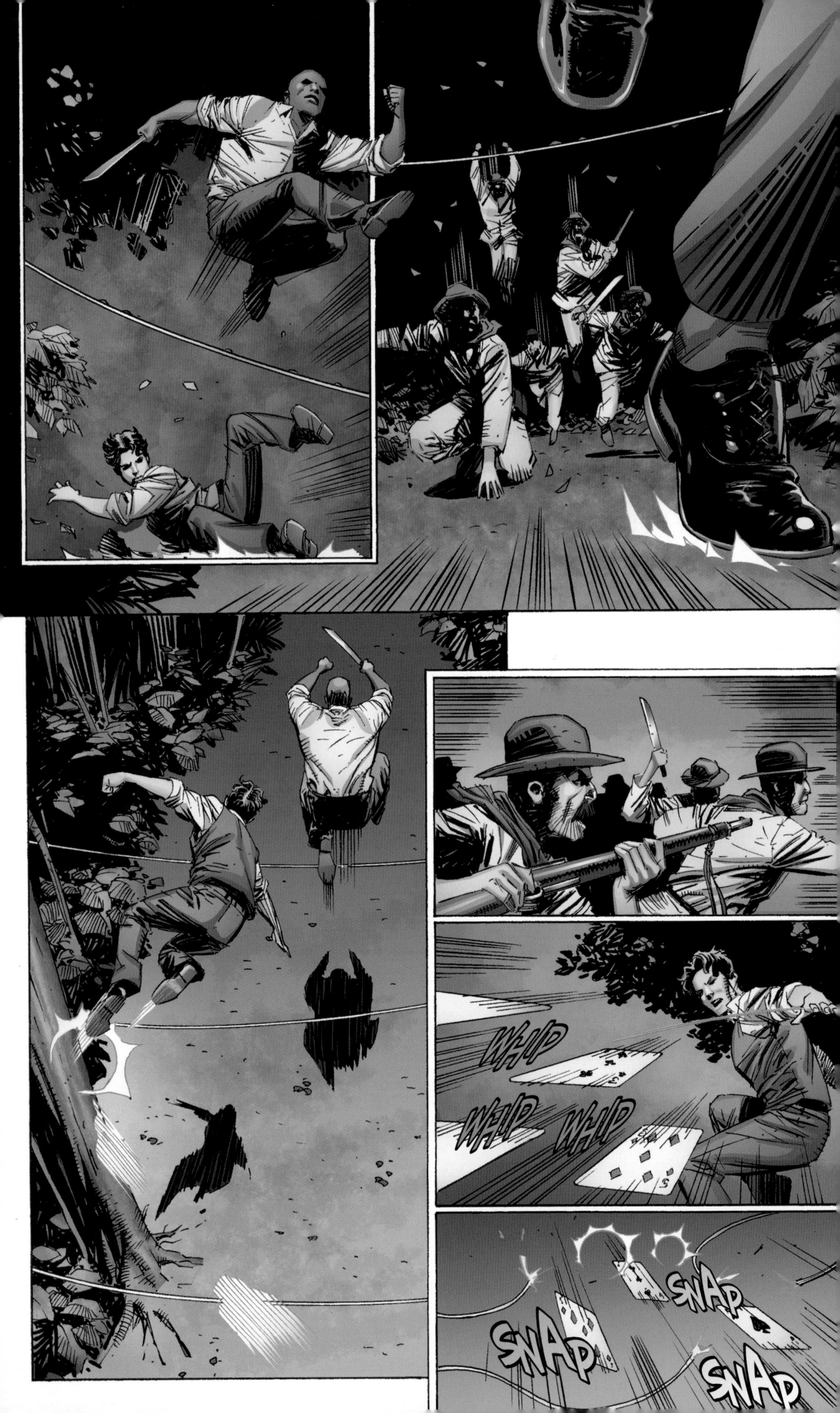
WHIP
WHIP
WHIP
SNAP
SNAP
SNAP

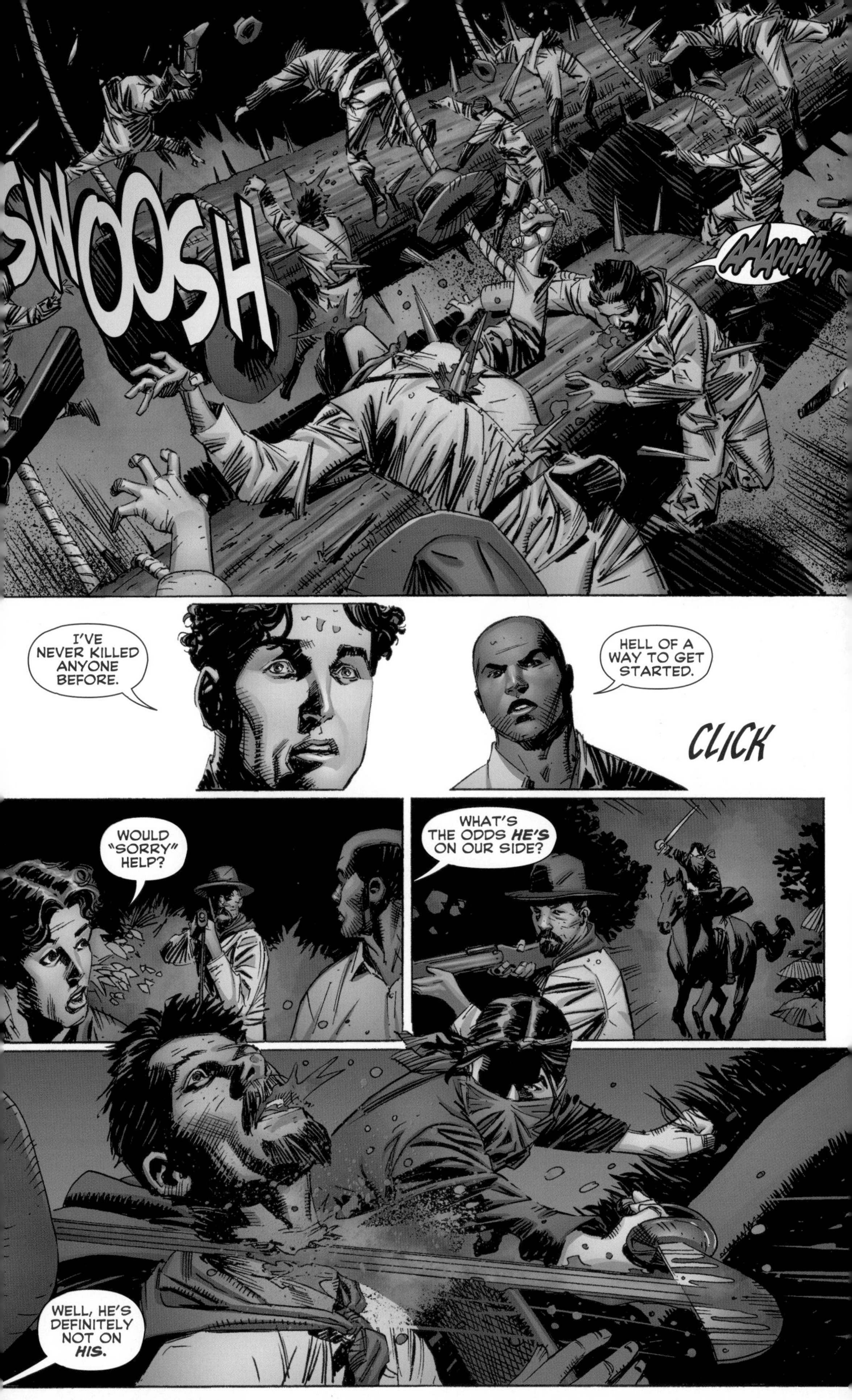
SWOOSH
AAAHHHH!
I'VE NEVER KILLED ANYONE BEFORE.
HELL OF A WAY TO GET STARTED.
CLICK
WOULD "SORRY" HELP?
WHAT'S THE ODDS HE'S ON OUR SIDE?
WELL, HE'S DEFINITELY NOT ON HIS.

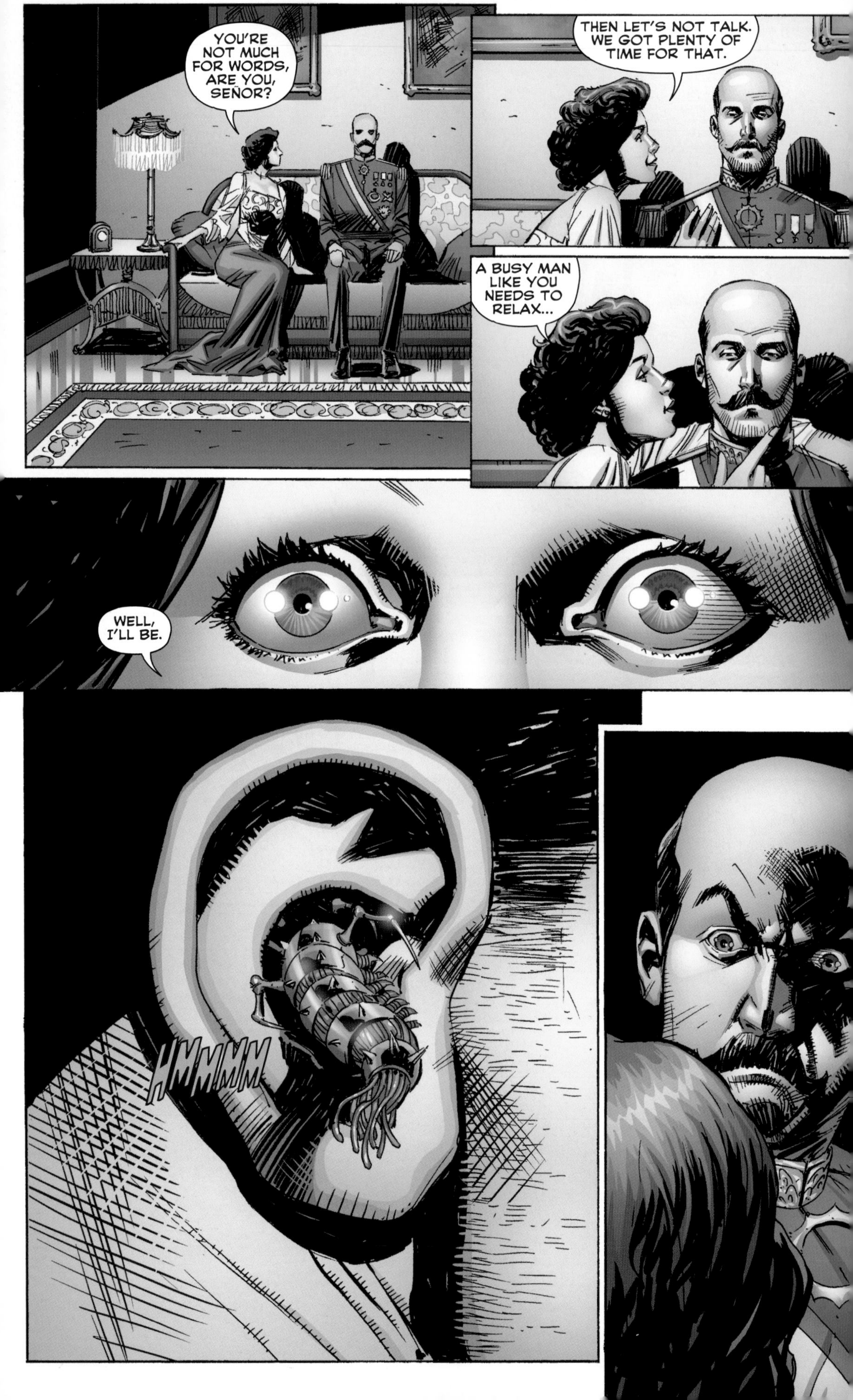
YOU'RE NOT MUCH FOR WORDS, ARE YOU, SEÑOR?
THEN LET'S NOT TALK. WE GOT PLENTY OF TIME FOR THAT.
A BUSY MAN LIKE YOU NEEDS TO RELAX...
WELL, I'LL BE.
HMMMM

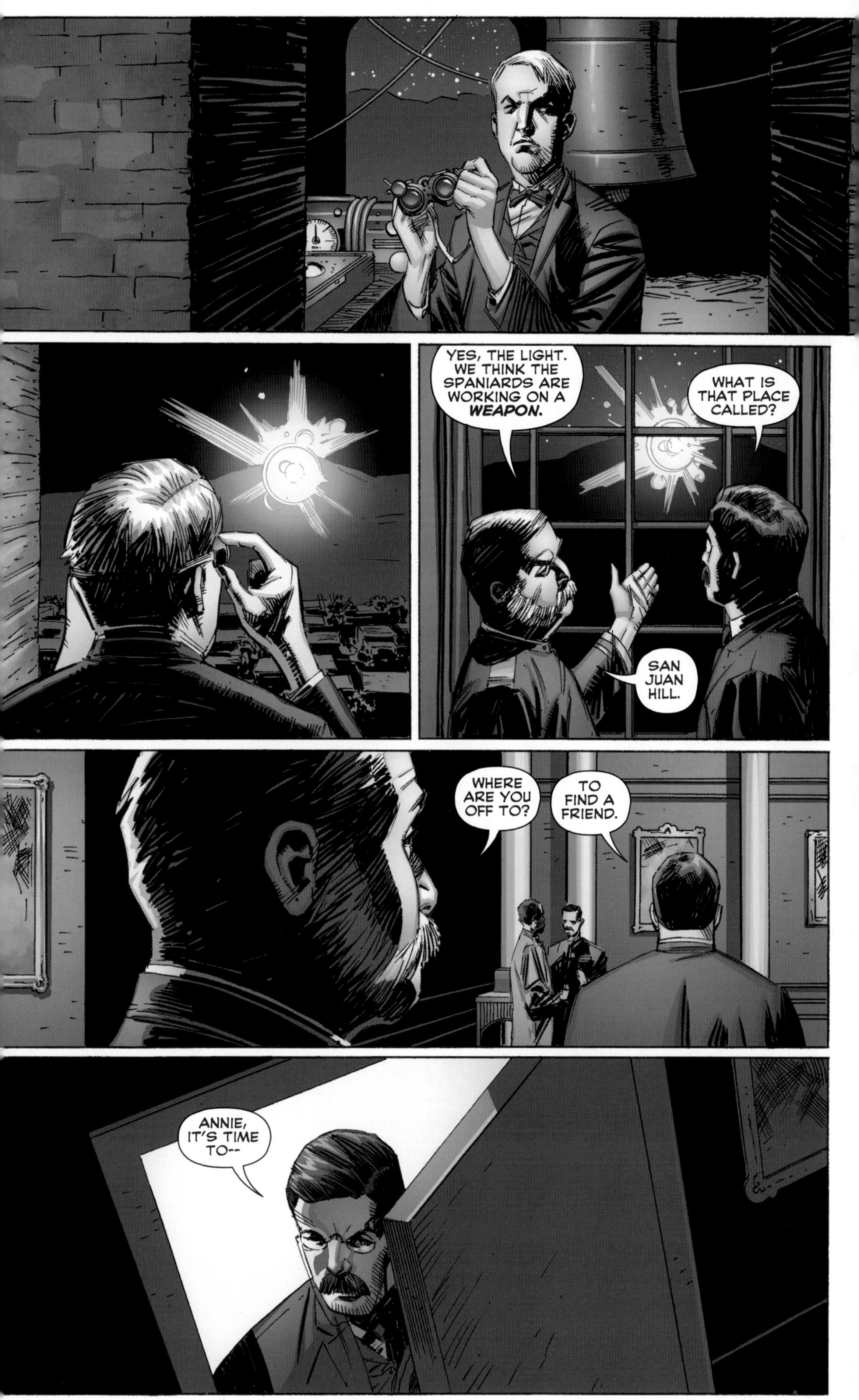
YES, THE LIGHT. WE THINK THE SPANIARDS ARE WORKING ON A **WEAPON.**
WHAT IS THAT PLACE CALLED?
SAN JUAN HILL.
WHERE ARE YOU OFF TO?
TO FIND A FRIEND.
ANNIE, IT'S TIME TO--

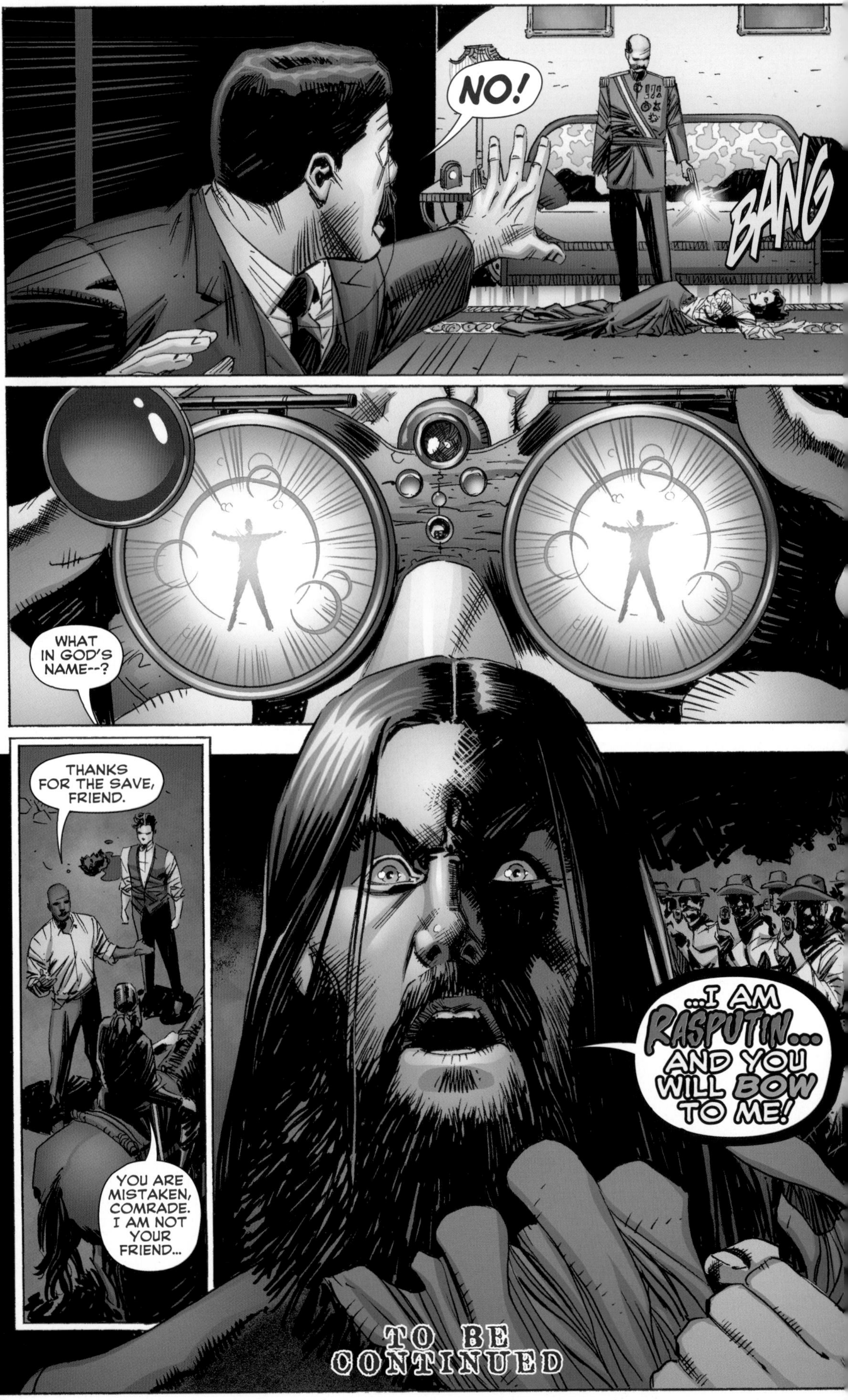
NO!
BANG
WHAT IN GOD'S NAME--?
THANKS FOR THE SAVE, FRIEND.
YOU ARE MISTAKEN, COMRADE. I AM NOT YOUR FRIEND...
...I AM RASPUTIN... AND YOU WILL BOW TO ME!
TO BE CONTINUED

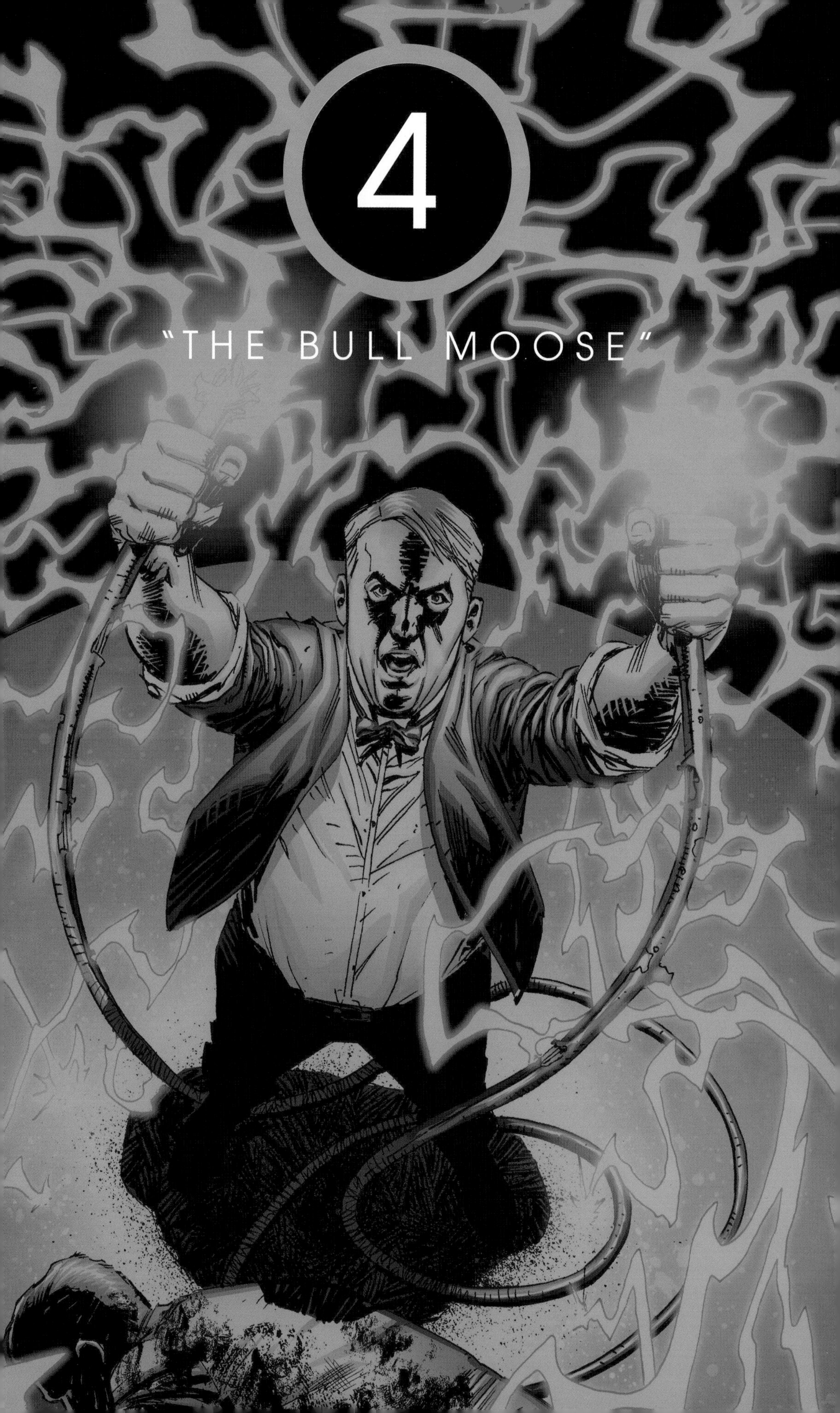
4
"THE BULL MOOSE"

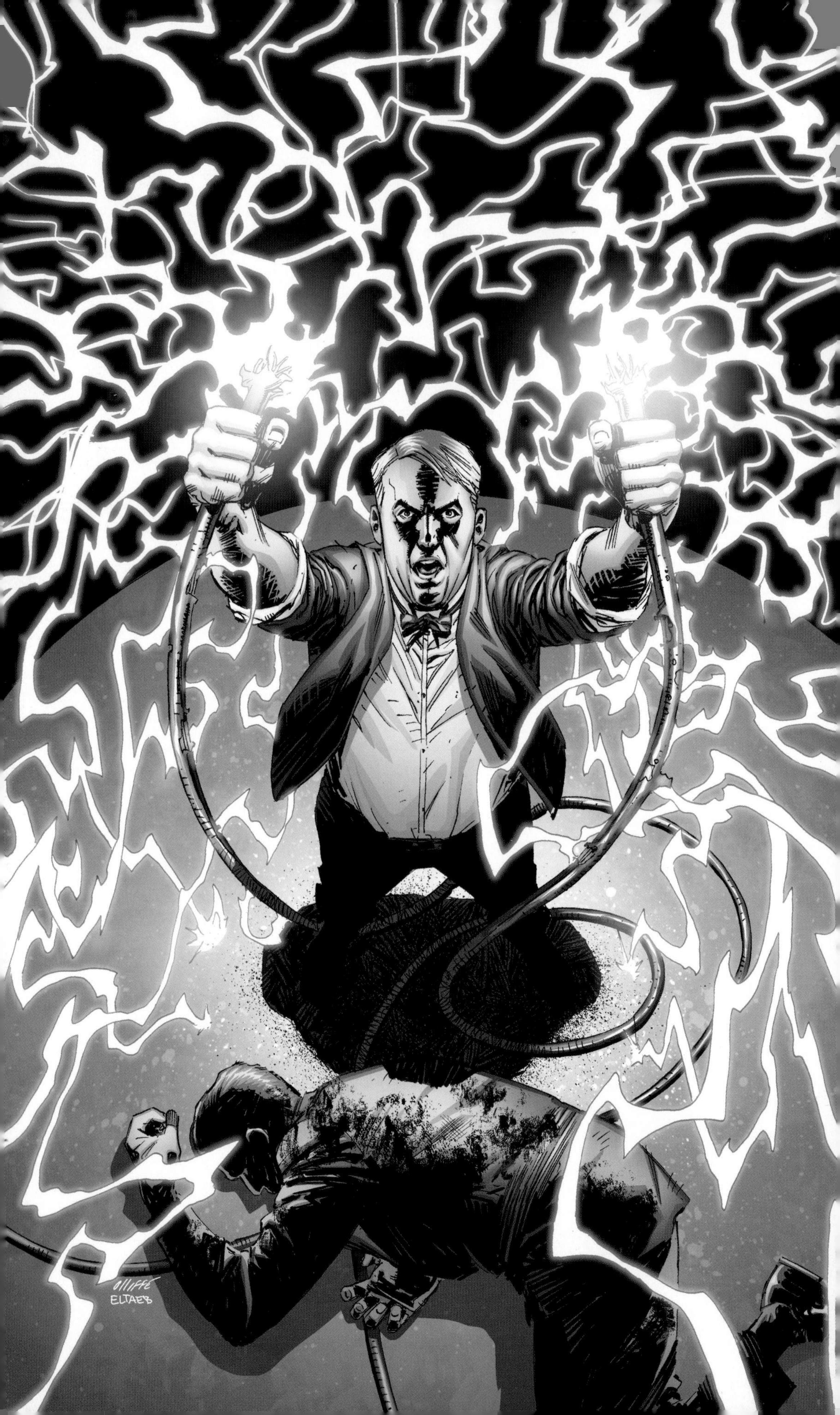

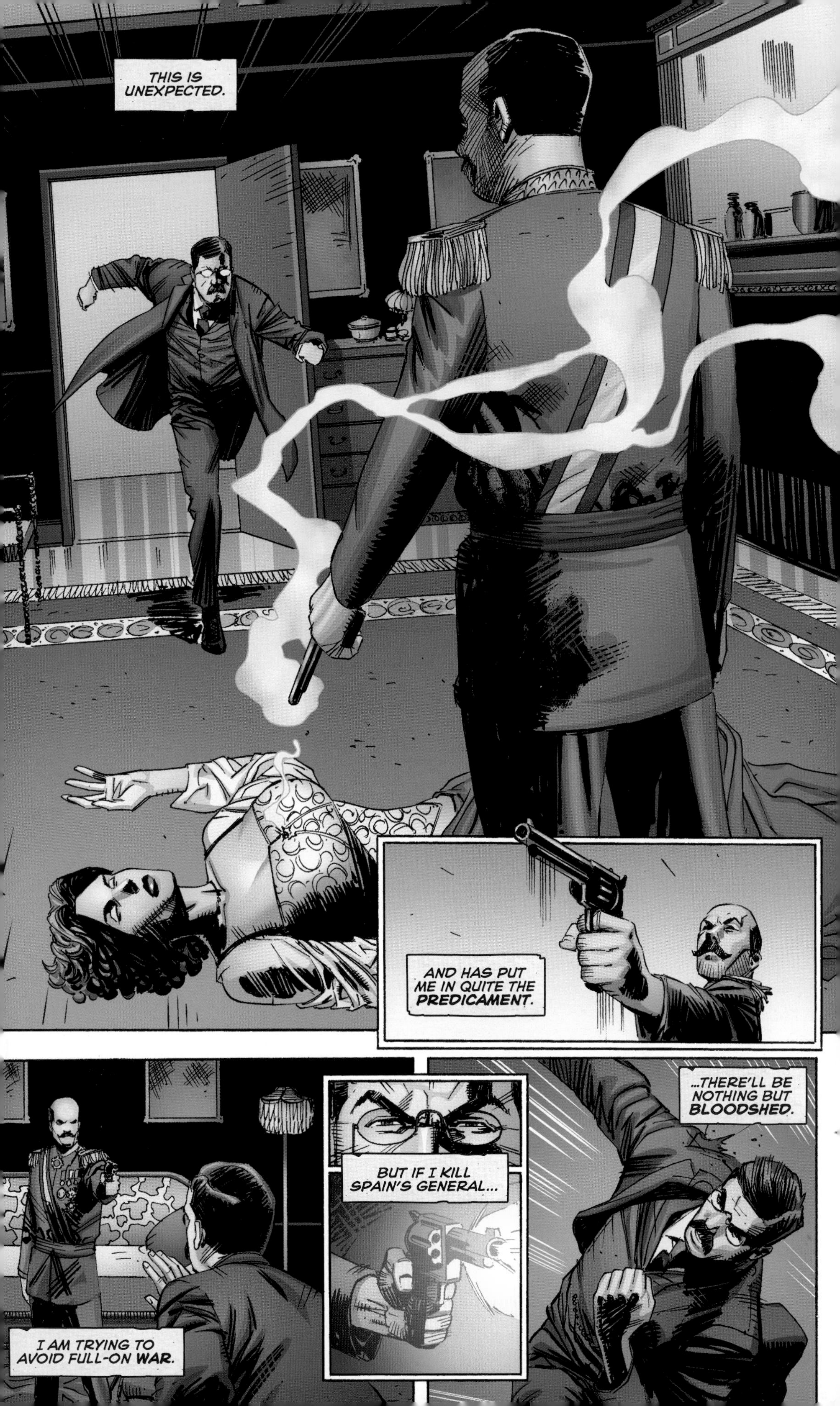
THIS IS UNEXPECTED.
AND HAS PUT ME IN QUITE THE PREDICAMENT.
I AM TRYING TO AVOID FULL-ON WAR.
BUT IF I KILL SPAIN'S GENERAL...
...THERE'LL BE NOTHING BUT BLOODSHED.

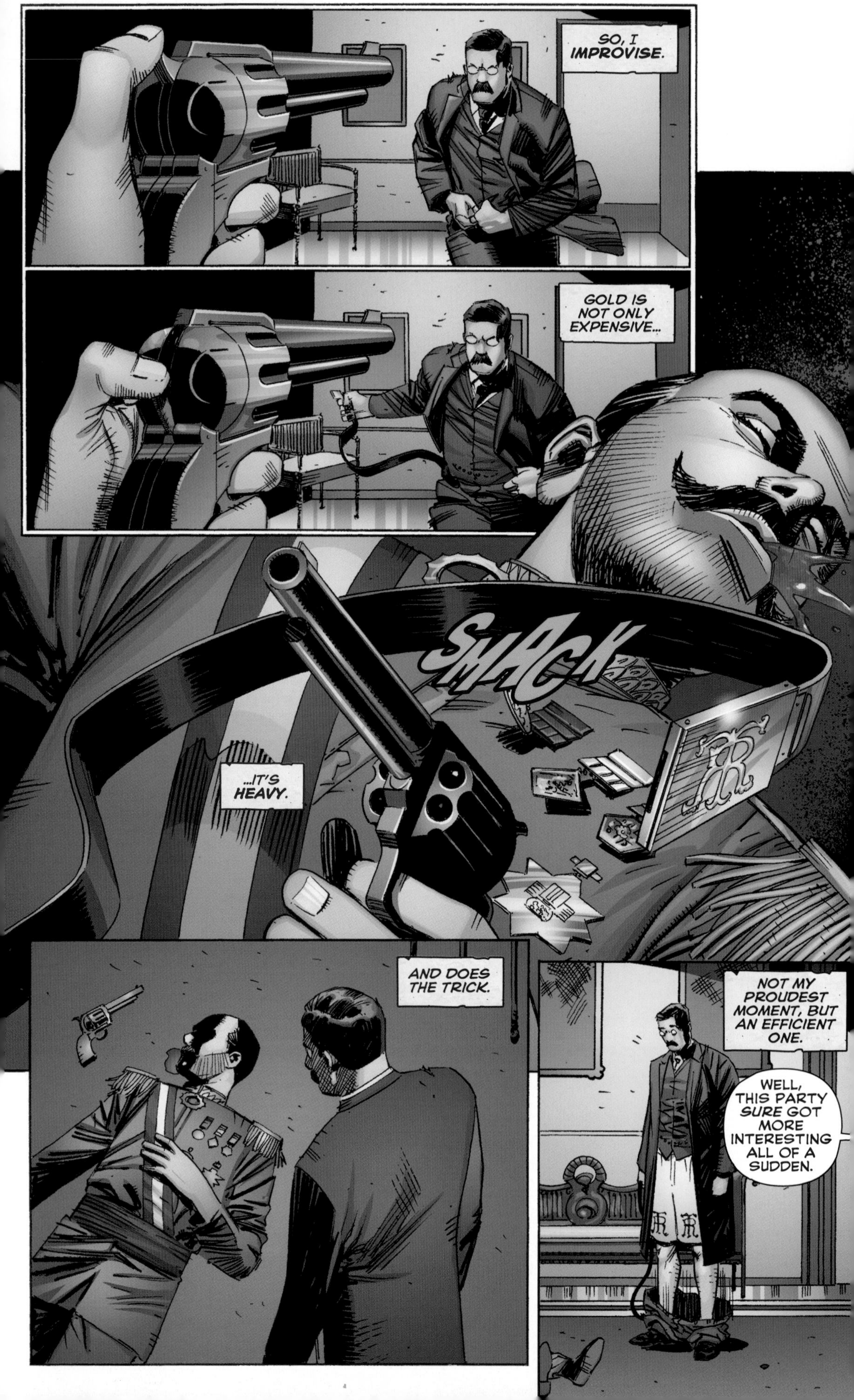
SO, I IMPROVISE.
GOLD IS NOT ONLY EXPENSIVE...
SMACK
...IT'S HEAVY.
AND DOES THE TRICK.
NOT MY PROUDEST MOMENT, BUT AN EFFICIENT ONE.
WELL, THIS PARTY SURE GOT MORE INTERESTING ALL OF A SUDDEN.

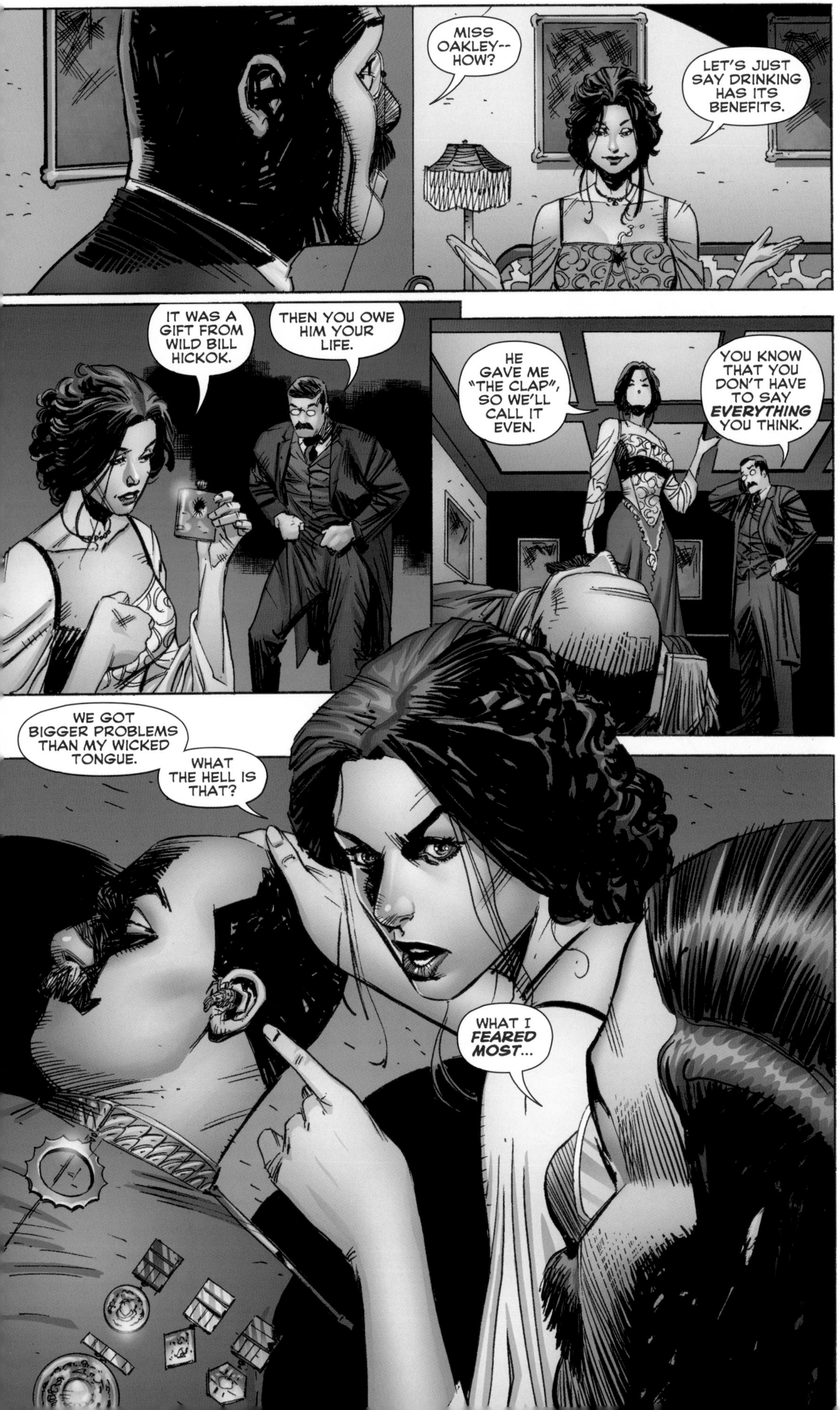

MISS OAKLEY-- HOW?
LET'S JUST SAY DRINKING HAS ITS BENEFITS.
IT WAS A GIFT FROM WILD BILL HICKOK.
THEN YOU OWE HIM YOUR LIFE.
HE GAVE ME "THE CLAP", SO WE'LL CALL IT EVEN.
YOU KNOW THAT YOU DON'T HAVE TO SAY *EVERYTHING* YOU THINK.
WE GOT BIGGER PROBLEMS THAN MY WICKED TONGUE.
WHAT THE HELL IS THAT?
WHAT I *FEARED MOST*...

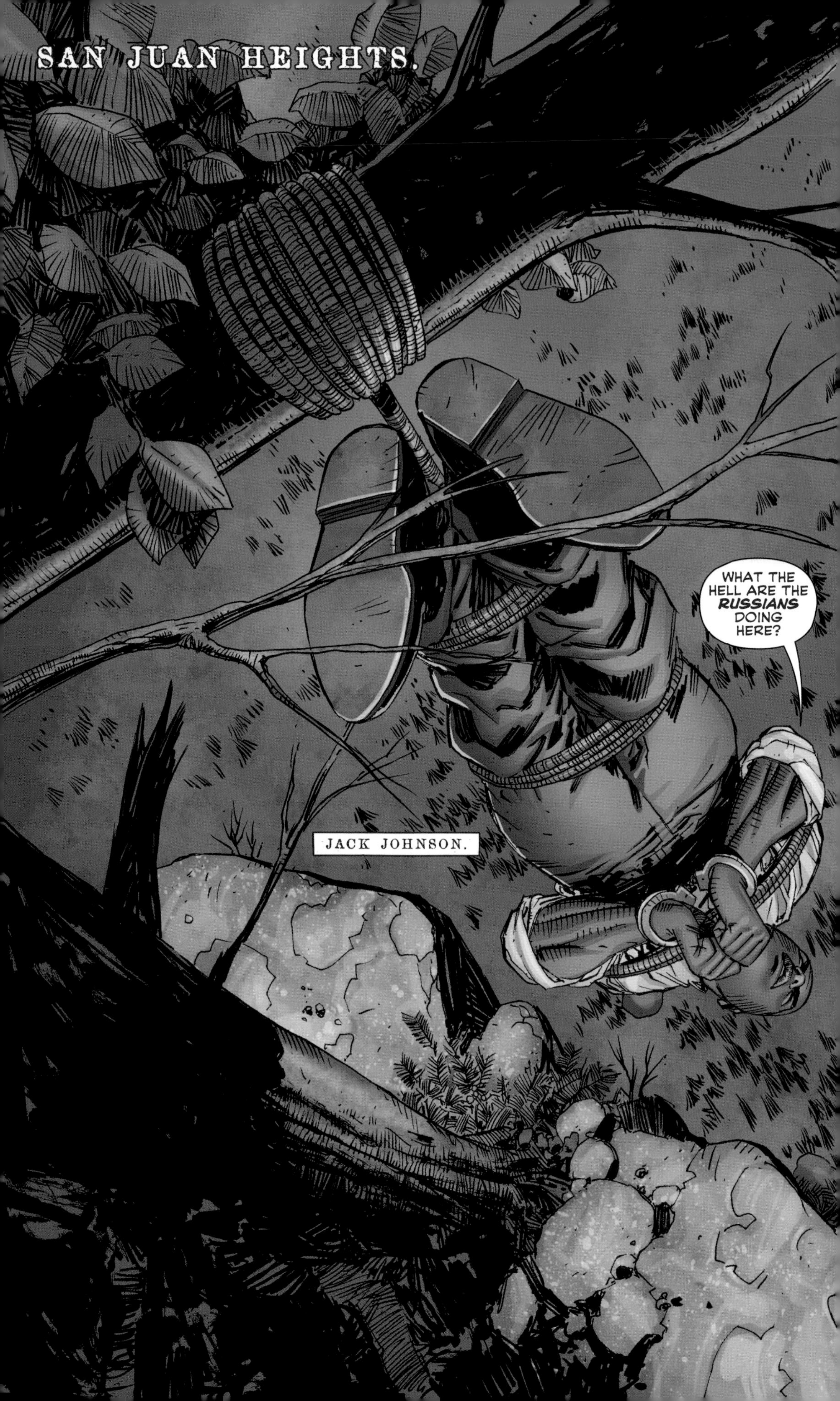
SAN JUAN HEIGHTS.
WHAT THE HELL ARE THE *RUSSIANS* DOING HERE?
JACK JOHNSON.

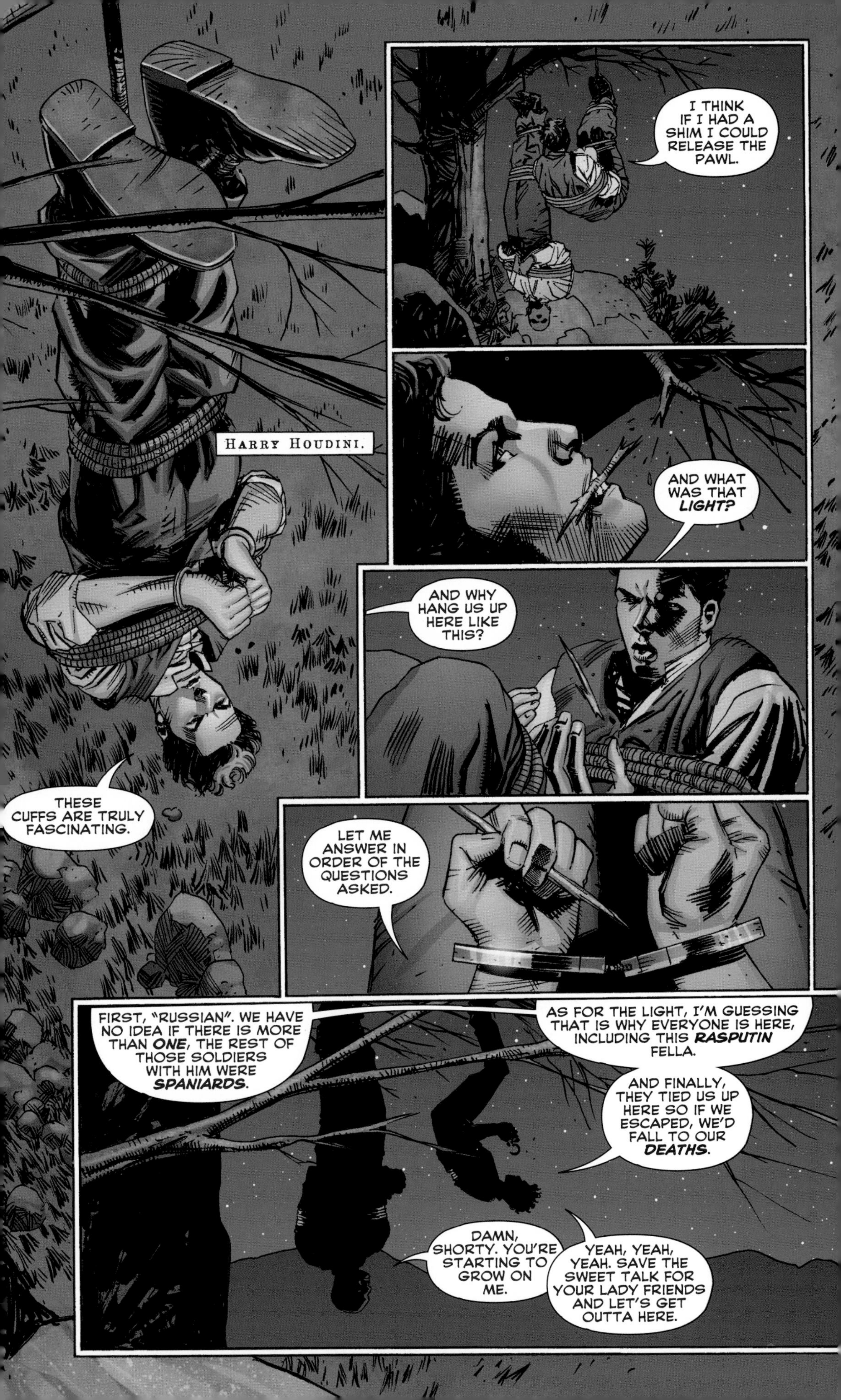
HARRY HOUDINI.
THESE CUFFS ARE TRULY FASCINATING.
I THINK IF I HAD A SHIM I COULD RELEASE THE PAWL.
AND WHAT WAS THAT LIGHT?
AND WHY HANG US UP HERE LIKE THIS?
LET ME ANSWER IN ORDER OF THE QUESTIONS ASKED.
FIRST, "RUSSIAN". WE HAVE NO IDEA IF THERE IS MORE THAN ONE, THE REST OF THOSE SOLDIERS WITH HIM WERE SPANIARDS.
AS FOR THE LIGHT, I'M GUESSING THAT IS WHY EVERYONE IS HERE, INCLUDING THIS RASPUTIN FELLA.
AND FINALLY, THEY TIED US UP HERE SO IF WE ESCAPED, WE'D FALL TO OUR DEATHS.
DAMN, SHORTY. YOU'RE STARTING TO GROW ON ME.
YEAH, YEAH, YEAH. SAVE THE SWEET TALK FOR YOUR LADY FRIENDS AND LET'S GET OUTTA HERE.

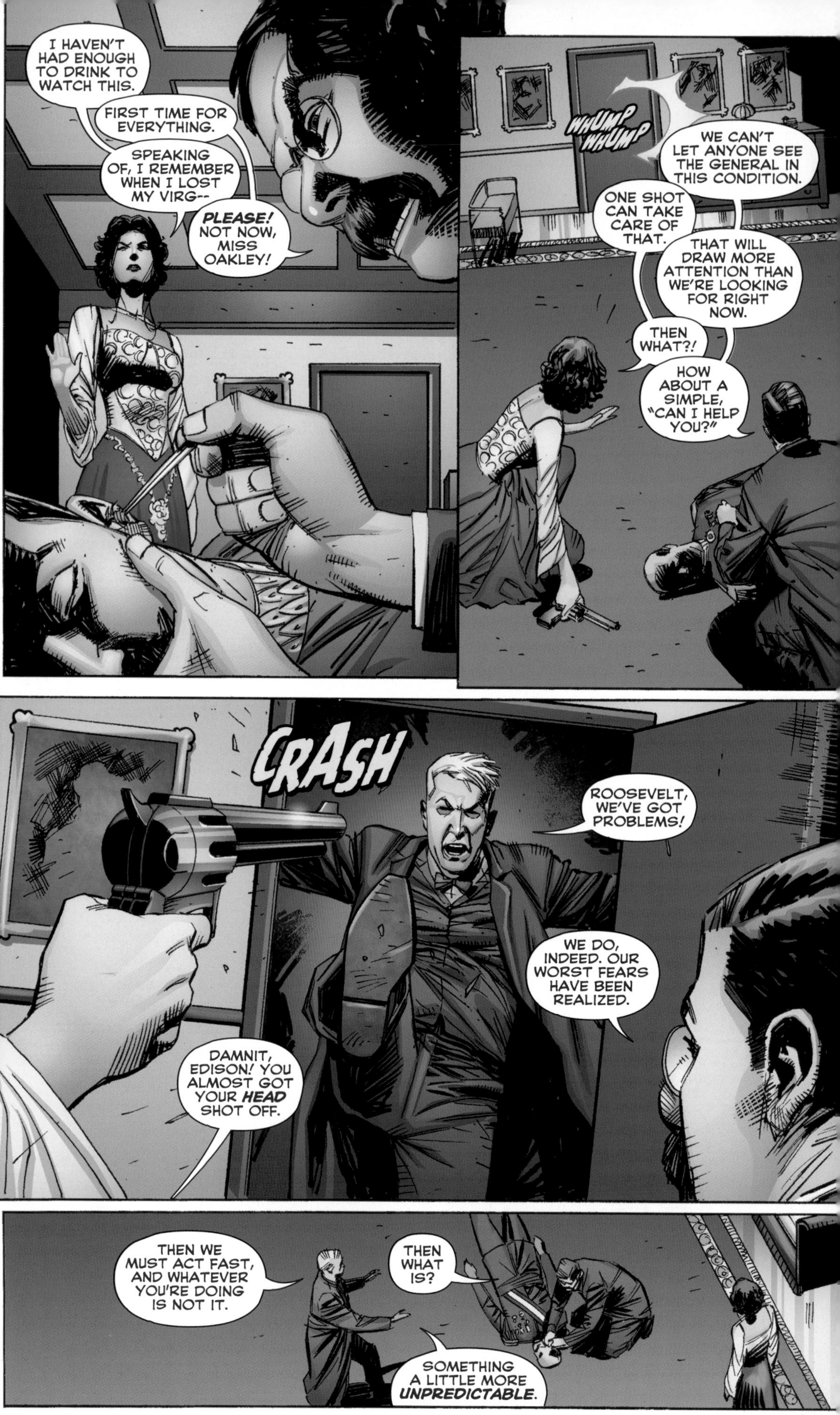

I HAVEN'T HAD ENOUGH TO DRINK TO WATCH THIS.
FIRST TIME FOR EVERYTHING.
SPEAKING OF, I REMEMBER WHEN I LOST MY VIRG--
PLEASE! NOT NOW, MISS OAKLEY!
WHUMP WHUMP
WE CAN'T LET ANYONE SEE THE GENERAL IN THIS CONDITION.
ONE SHOT CAN TAKE CARE OF THAT.
THAT WILL DRAW MORE ATTENTION THAN WE'RE LOOKING FOR RIGHT NOW.
THEN WHAT?!
HOW ABOUT A SIMPLE, "CAN I HELP YOU?"
CRASH
ROOSEVELT, WE'VE GOT PROBLEMS!
WE DO, INDEED. OUR WORST FEARS HAVE BEEN REALIZED.
DAMNIT, EDISON! YOU ALMOST GOT YOUR HEAD SHOT OFF.
THEN WE MUST ACT FAST, AND WHATEVER YOU'RE DOING IS NOT IT.
THEN WHAT IS?
SOMETHING A LITTLE MORE UNPREDICTABLE.

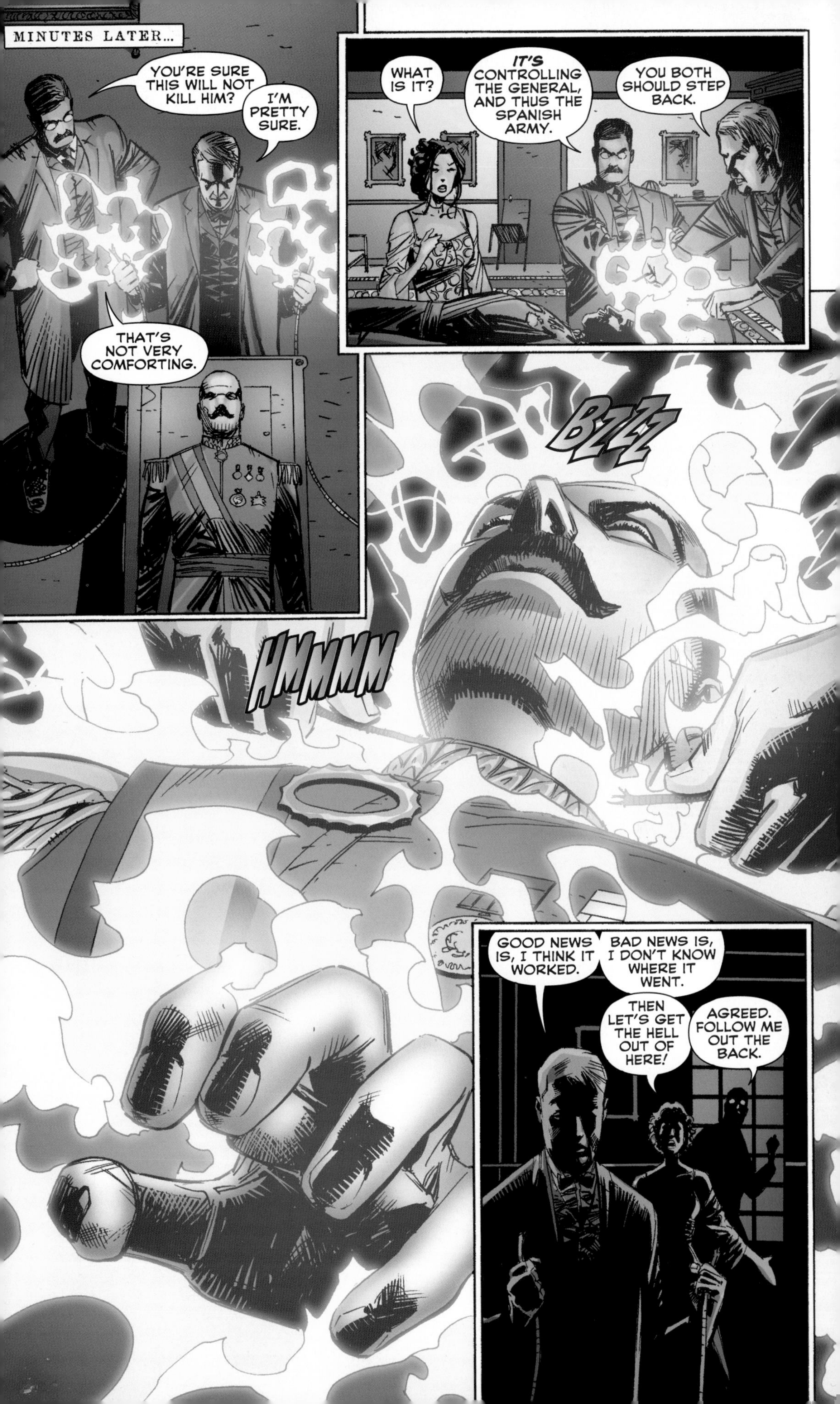

MINUTES LATER...
YOU'RE SURE THIS WILL NOT KILL HIM?
I'M PRETTY SURE.
THAT'S NOT VERY COMFORTING.
WHAT IS IT?
IT'S CONTROLLING THE GENERAL, AND THUS THE SPANISH ARMY.
YOU BOTH SHOULD STEP BACK.
BZZZ
HMMMM
GOOD NEWS IS, I THINK IT WORKED.
BAD NEWS IS, I DON'T KNOW WHERE IT WENT.
THEN LET'S GET THE HELL OUT OF HERE!
AGREED. FOLLOW ME OUT THE BACK.

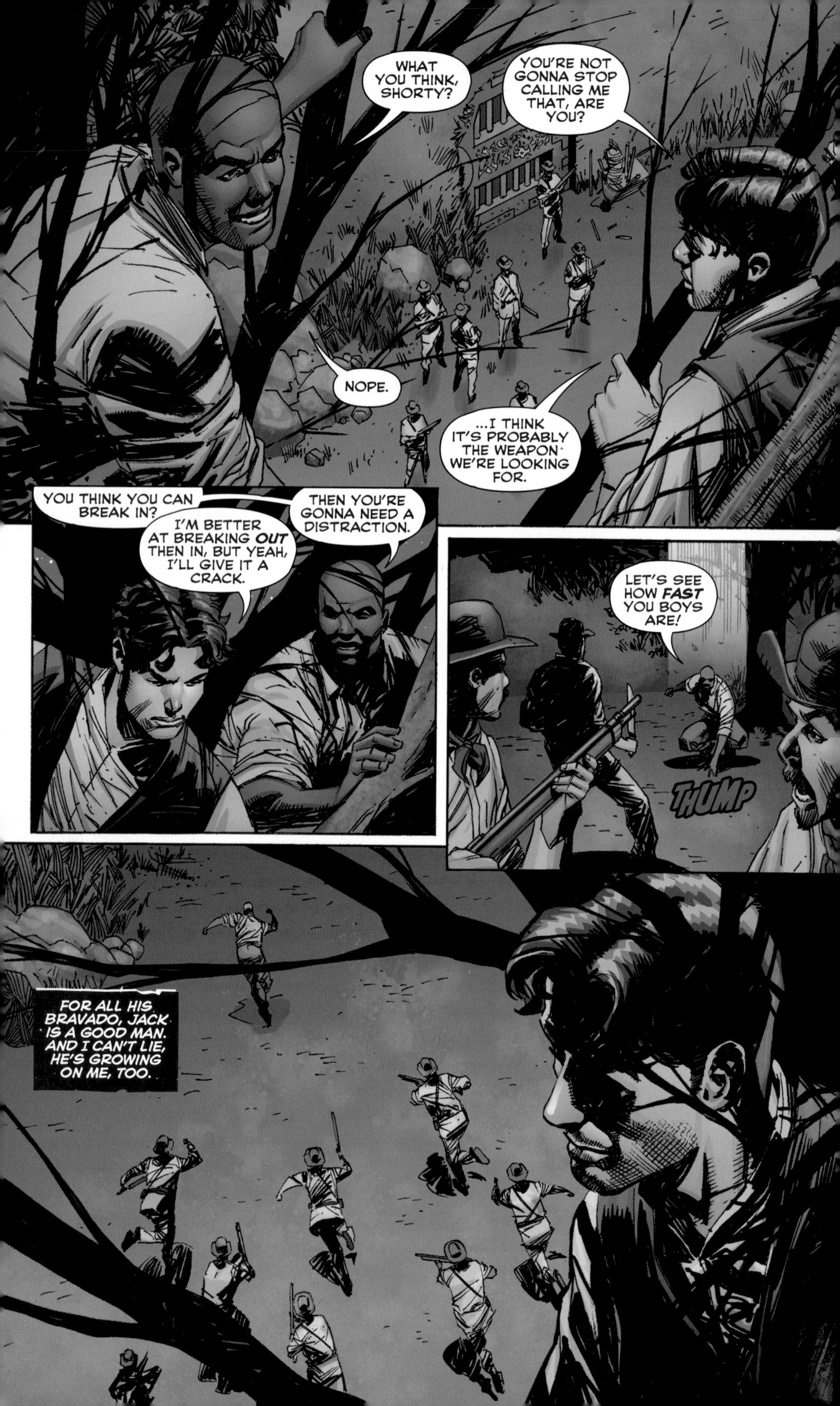
WHAT YOU THINK, SHORTY?
YOU'RE NOT GONNA STOP CALLING ME THAT, ARE YOU?
NOPE.
...I THINK IT'S PROBABLY THE WEAPON WE'RE LOOKING FOR.
YOU THINK YOU CAN BREAK IN?
I'M BETTER AT BREAKING OUT THEN IN, BUT YEAH, I'LL GIVE IT A CRACK.
THEN YOU'RE GONNA NEED A DISTRACTION.
LET'S SEE HOW FAST YOU BOYS ARE!
THUMP
FOR ALL HIS BRAVADO, JACK IS A GOOD MAN. AND I CAN'T LIE, HE'S GROWING ON ME, TOO.

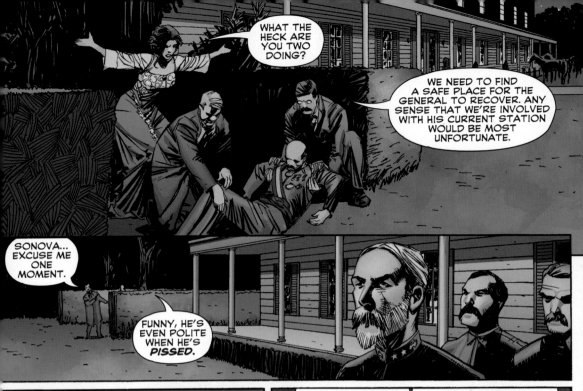

WHAT THE HECK ARE YOU TWO DOING?

WE NEED TO FIND A SAFE PLACE FOR THE GENERAL TO RECOVER. ANY SENSE THAT WE'RE INVOLVED WITH HIS CURRENT STATION WOULD BE MOST UNFORTUNATE.

SONOVA... EXCUSE ME ONE MOMENT.

FUNNY, HE'S EVEN POLITE WHEN HE'S *PISSED*.

ROOSEVELT, WHERE HAVE YOU BEEN?

SORRY, BUT THE FOOD HAS NOT EXACTLY BEEN WELCOMING.

I APOLOGIZE FOR MY ABSENCE, BUT I WANTED TO INQUIRE ABOUT YOUR CONVERSATION WITH GENERAL LINARES.

THERE WAS NONE. HIS ACTIONS WERE CLEARLY STATED WHEN HE SNUCK OUT A BACKDOOR AND NEVER SPOKE TO ME. SPAIN WANTS *WAR*, AND WAR WE SHALL *GIVE* THEM.

NO DISRESPECT, SIR, BUT WHAT IF WE'RE JUMPING THE GUN HERE. IF YOU'D ALLOW ME TO TRY AND CREATE A *BRIDGE* TO--

I DON'T LIKE YOU, ROOSEVELT! YOU'RE AN *OPPORTUNIST*.

A POLITICIAN AND AN ELITIST PLAYING A SOLDIER.

I'M DEALING WITH YOU BECAUSE I HAVE *NO CHOICE*, BUT IT DOESN'T MEAN THAT I HAVE TO LIKE IT. OR *YOU*.

YOU WILL REPORT BACK TO BASE AND AWAIT FURTHER ORDERS.

YES, SIR.

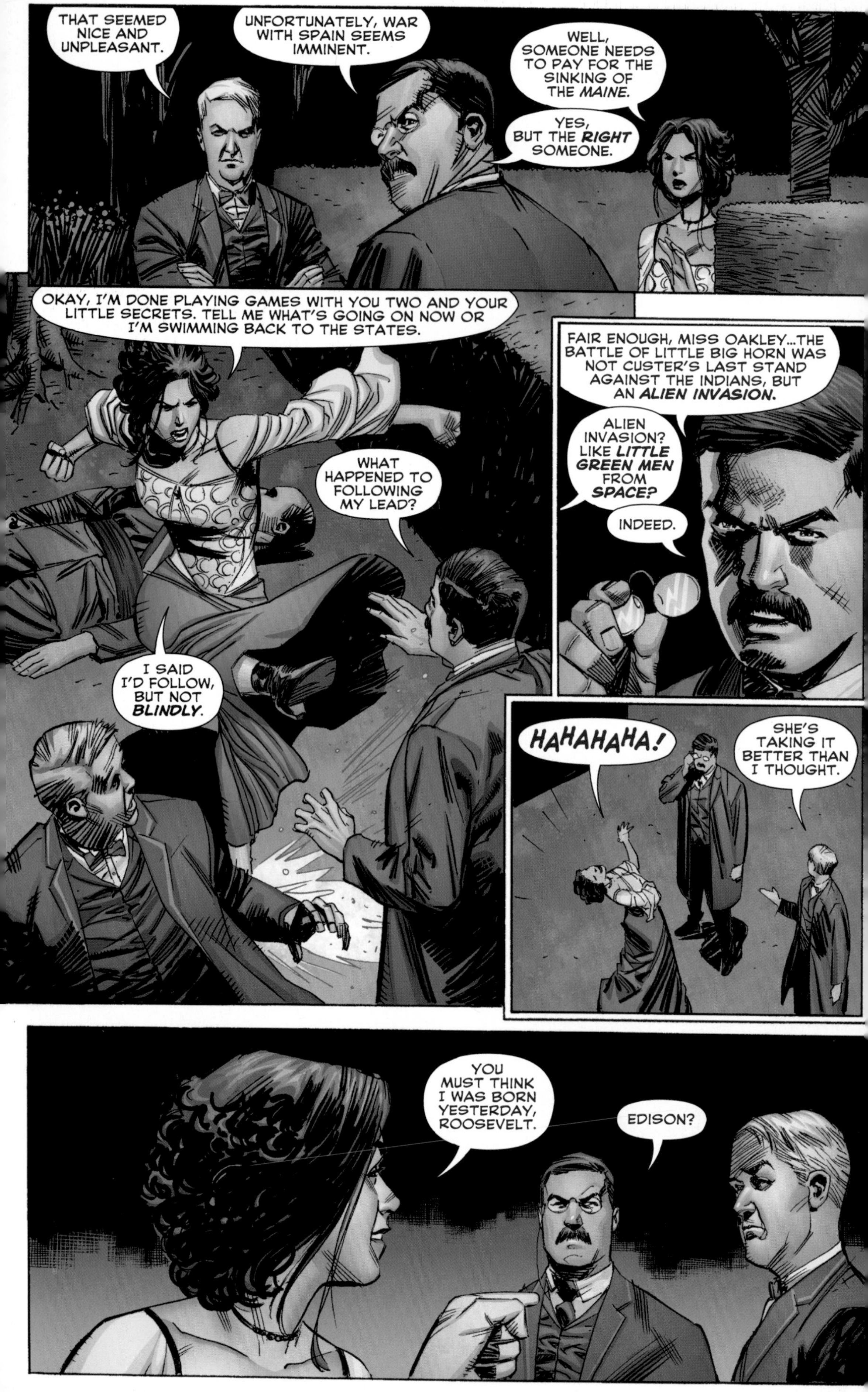
THAT SEEMED NICE AND UNPLEASANT.
UNFORTUNATELY, WAR WITH SPAIN SEEMS IMMINENT.
WELL, SOMEONE NEEDS TO PAY FOR THE SINKING OF THE *MAINE*.
YES, BUT THE ***RIGHT*** SOMEONE.
OKAY, I'M DONE PLAYING GAMES WITH YOU TWO AND YOUR LITTLE SECRETS. TELL ME WHAT'S GOING ON NOW OR I'M SWIMMING BACK TO THE STATES.
WHAT HAPPENED TO FOLLOWING MY LEAD?
I SAID I'D FOLLOW, BUT NOT ***BLINDLY***.
FAIR ENOUGH, MISS OAKLEY...THE BATTLE OF LITTLE BIG HORN WAS NOT CUSTER'S LAST STAND AGAINST THE INDIANS, BUT AN ***ALIEN INVASION***.
ALIEN INVASION? LIKE ***LITTLE GREEN MEN*** FROM ***SPACE?***
INDEED.
HAHAHAHA!
SHE'S TAKING IT BETTER THAN I THOUGHT.
YOU MUST THINK I WAS BORN YESTERDAY, ROOSEVELT.
EDISON?

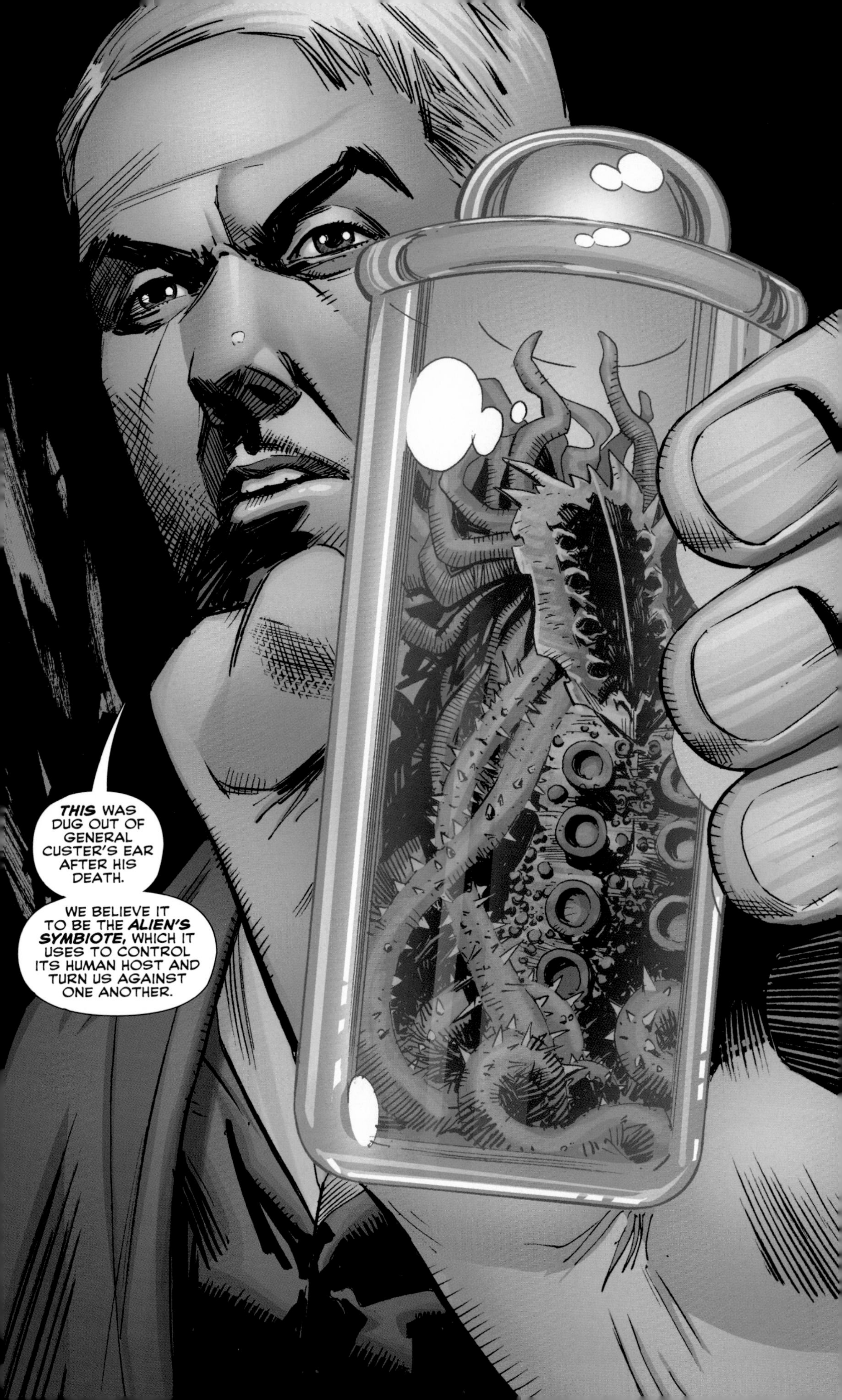
THIS WAS DUG OUT OF GENERAL CUSTER'S EAR AFTER HIS DEATH.
WE BELIEVE IT TO BE THE ALIEN'S SYMBIOTE, WHICH IT USES TO CONTROL ITS HUMAN HOST AND TURN US AGAINST ONE ANOTHER.

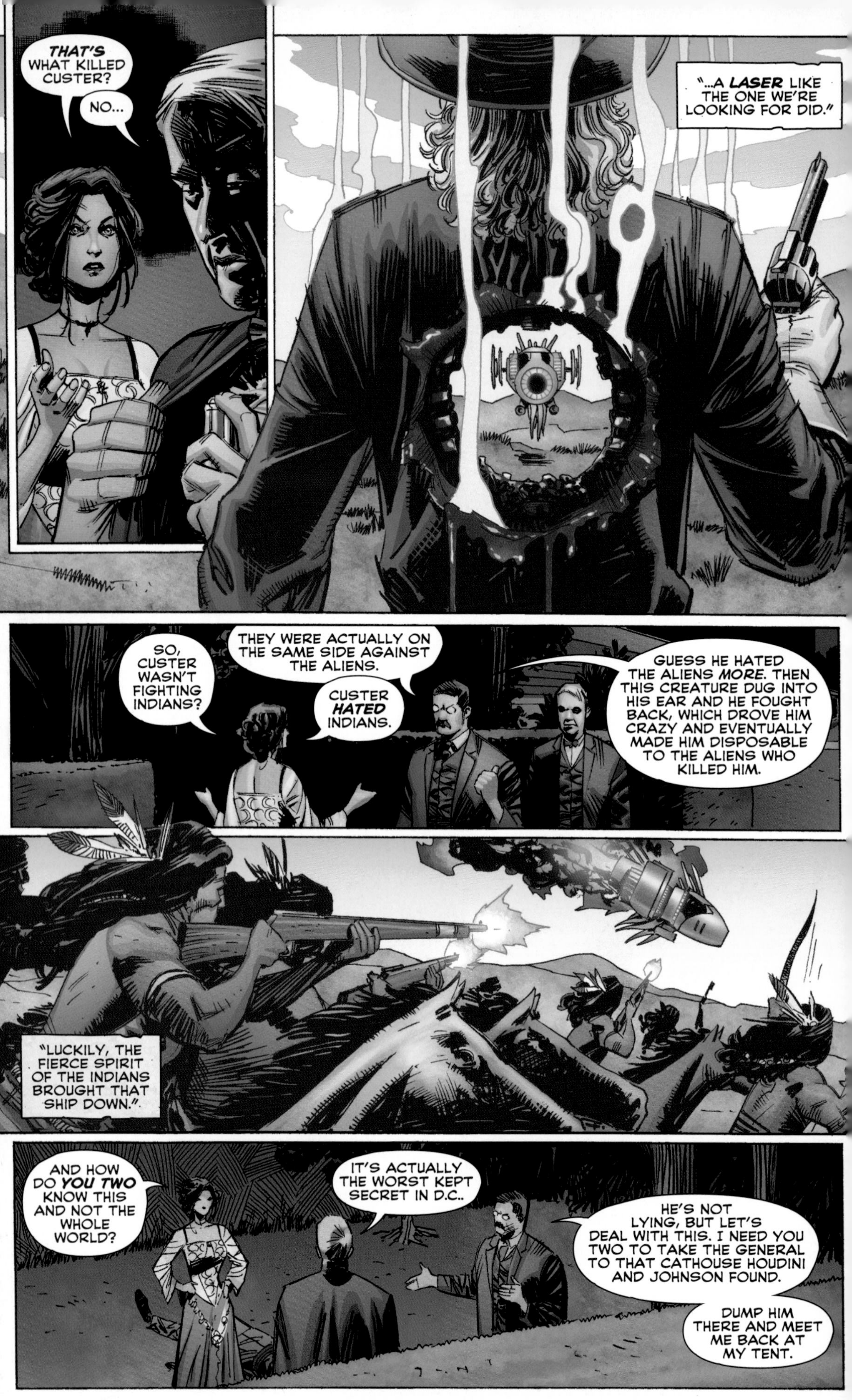
THAT'S WHAT KILLED CUSTER?
NO...
"...A LASER LIKE THE ONE WE'RE LOOKING FOR DID."
SO, CUSTER WASN'T FIGHTING INDIANS?
THEY WERE ACTUALLY ON THE SAME SIDE AGAINST THE ALIENS.
CUSTER HATED INDIANS.
GUESS HE HATED THE ALIENS MORE. THEN THIS CREATURE DUG INTO HIS EAR AND HE FOUGHT BACK, WHICH DROVE HIM CRAZY AND EVENTUALLY MADE HIM DISPOSABLE TO THE ALIENS WHO KILLED HIM.
"LUCKILY, THE FIERCE SPIRIT OF THE INDIANS BROUGHT THAT SHIP DOWN."
AND HOW DO YOU TWO KNOW THIS AND NOT THE WHOLE WORLD?
IT'S ACTUALLY THE WORST KEPT SECRET IN D.C..
HE'S NOT LYING, BUT LET'S DEAL WITH THIS. I NEED YOU TWO TO TAKE THE GENERAL TO THAT CATHOUSE HOUDINI AND JOHNSON FOUND.
DUMP HIM THERE AND MEET ME BACK AT MY TENT.

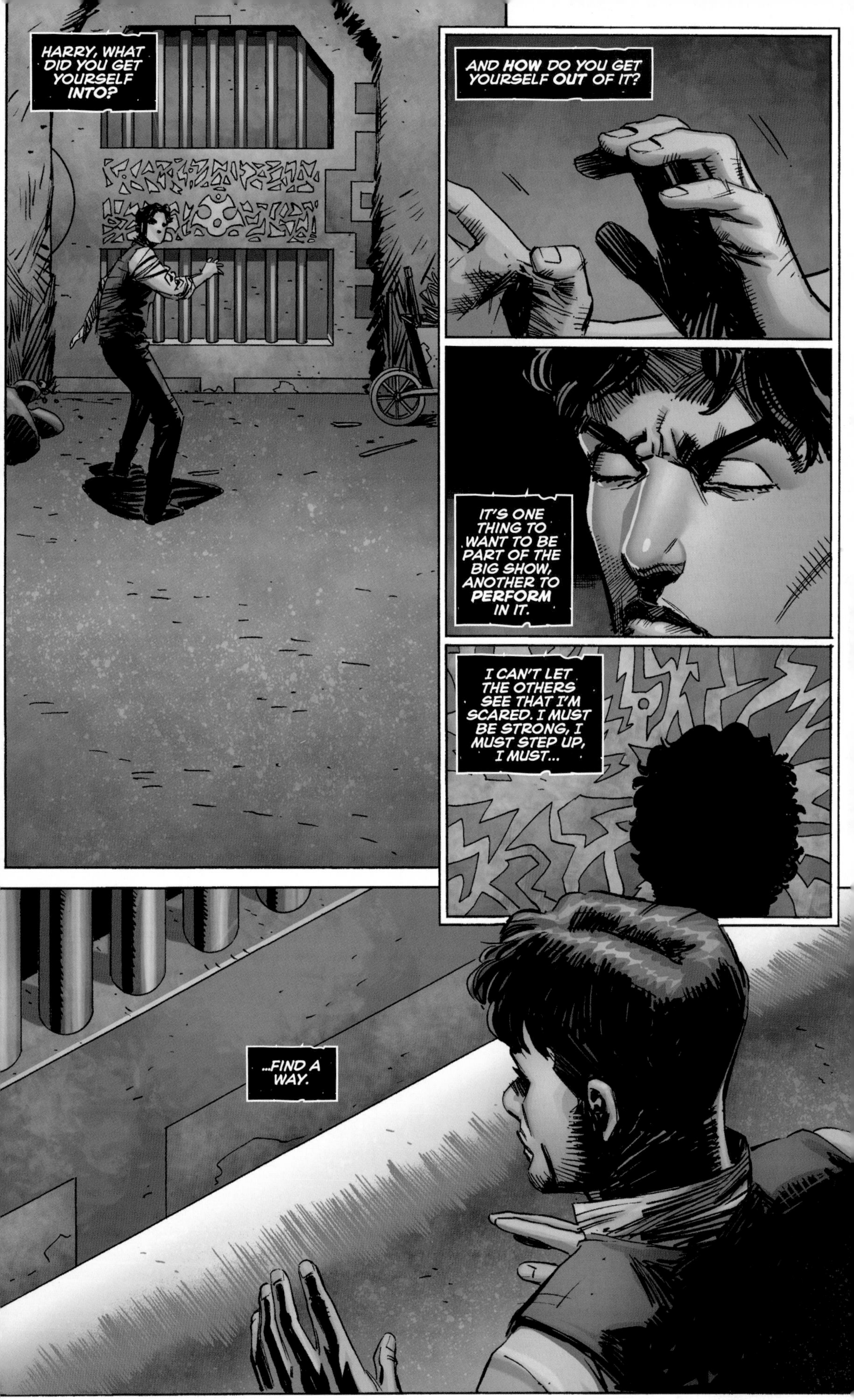
HARRY, WHAT DID YOU GET YOURSELF INTO?
AND HOW DO YOU GET YOURSELF OUT OF IT?
IT'S ONE THING TO WANT TO BE PART OF THE BIG SHOW, ANOTHER TO PERFORM IN IT.
I CAN'T LET THE OTHERS SEE THAT I'M SCARED. I MUST BE STRONG, I MUST STEP UP, I MUST...
...FIND A WAY.

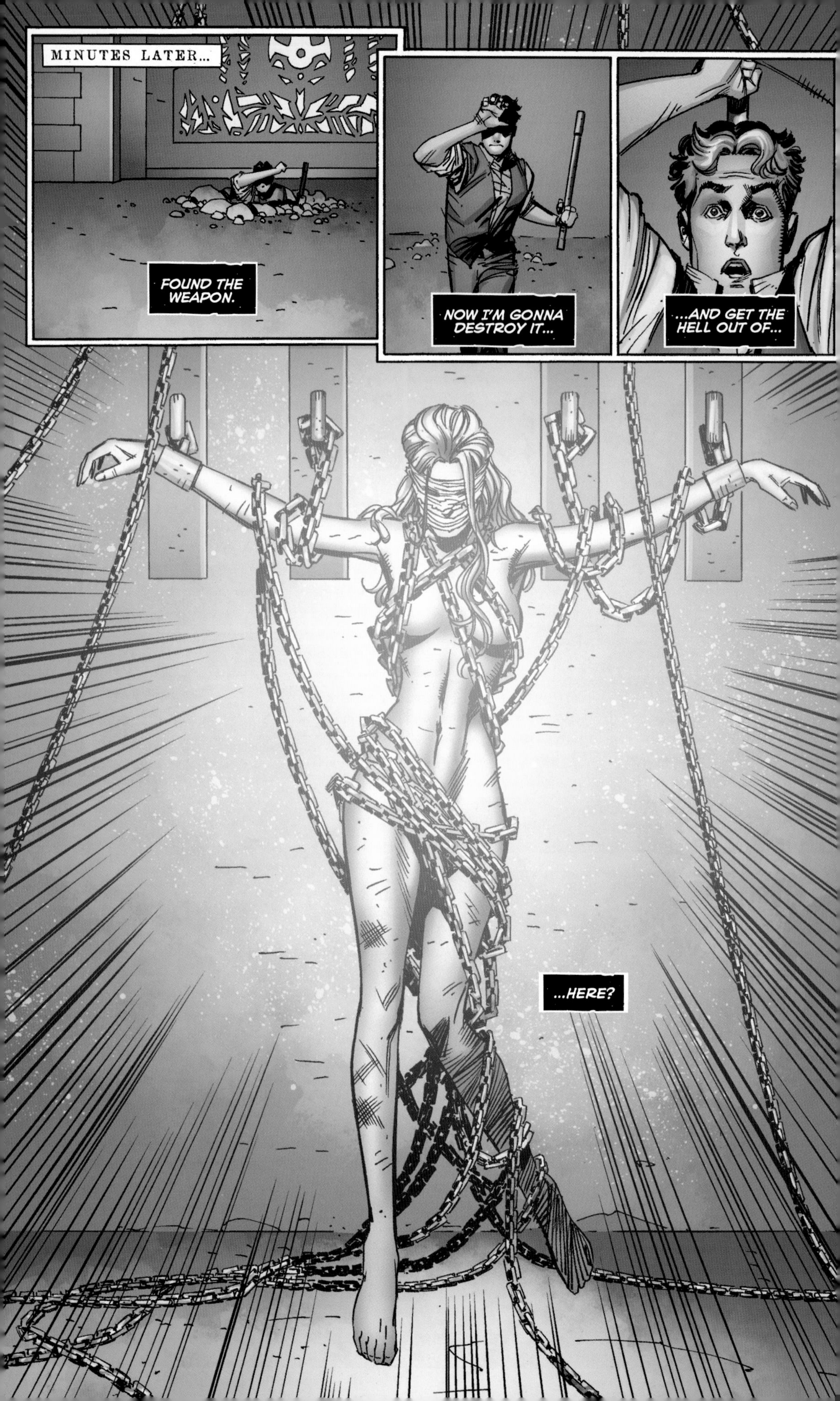
MINUTES LATER...
FOUND THE WEAPON.
NOW I'M GONNA DESTROY IT...
...AND GET THE HELL OUT OF...
...HERE?

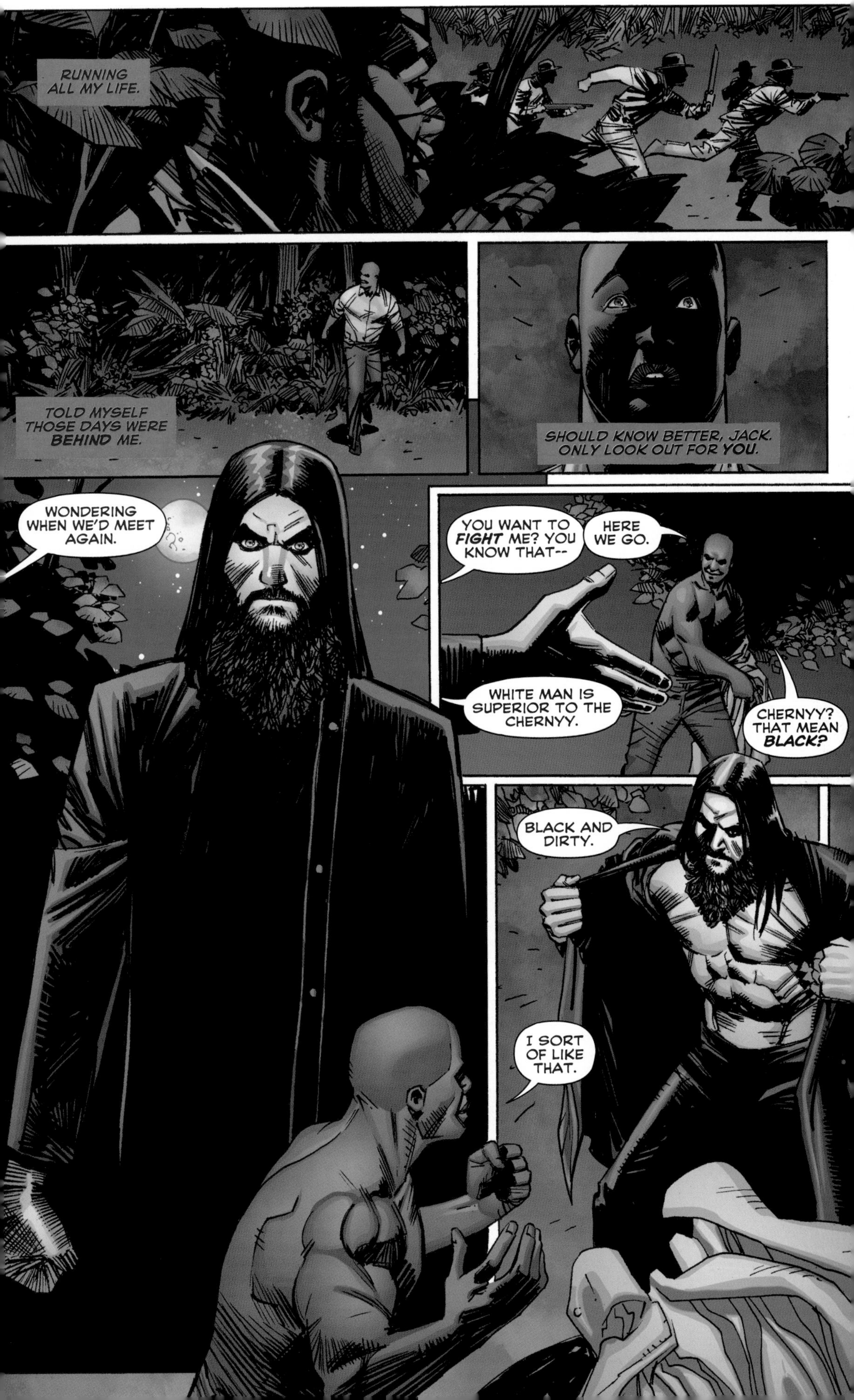
RUNNING ALL MY LIFE.
TOLD MYSELF THOSE DAYS WERE BEHIND ME.
SHOULD KNOW BETTER, JACK. ONLY LOOK OUT FOR YOU.
WONDERING WHEN WE'D MEET AGAIN.
YOU WANT TO FIGHT ME? YOU KNOW THAT--
HERE WE GO.
WHITE MAN IS SUPERIOR TO THE CHERNYY.
CHERNYY? THAT MEAN BLACK?
BLACK AND DIRTY.
I SORT OF LIKE THAT.

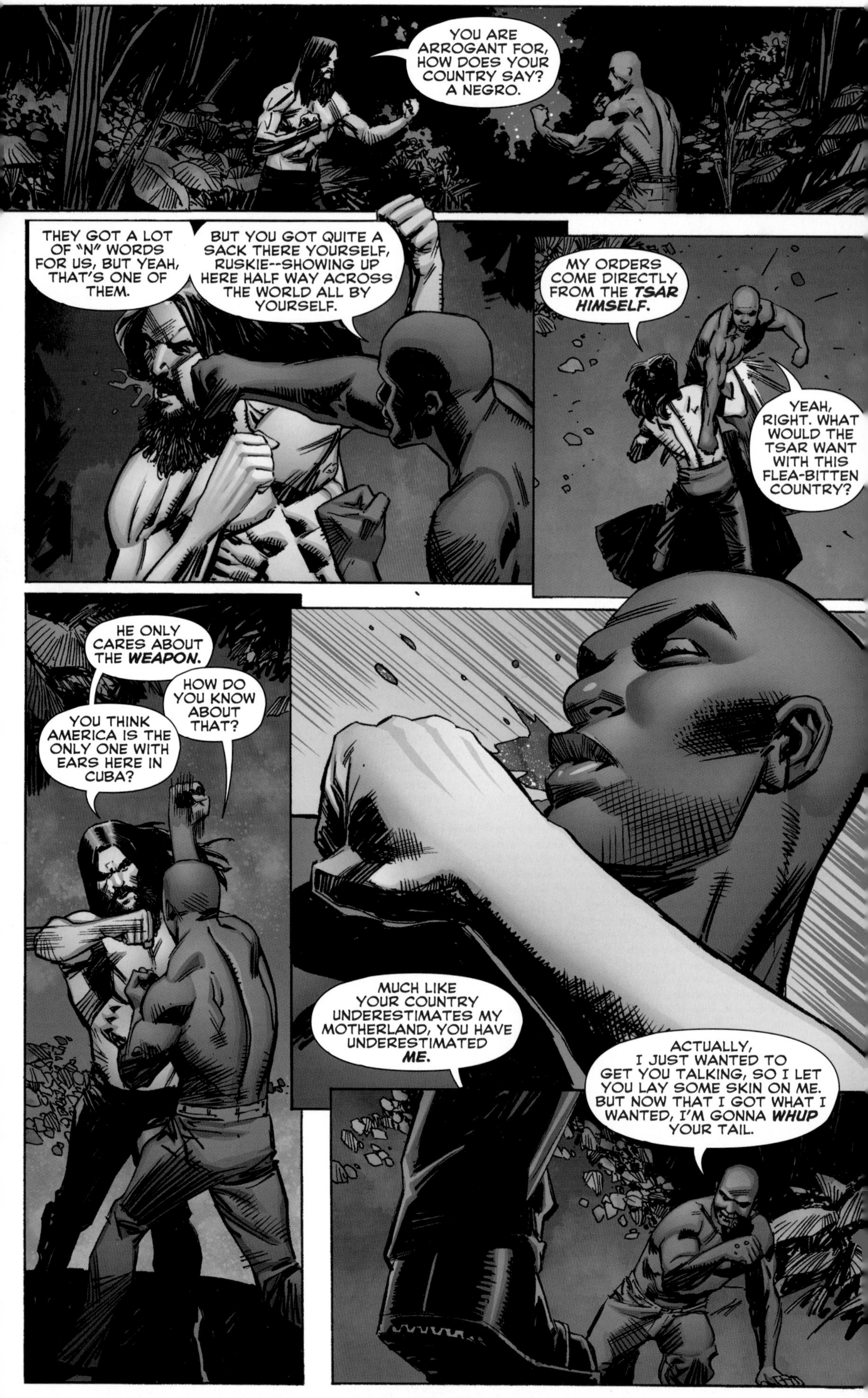
YOU ARE ARROGANT FOR, HOW DOES YOUR COUNTRY SAY? A NEGRO.
THEY GOT A LOT OF "N" WORDS FOR US, BUT YEAH, THAT'S ONE OF THEM.
BUT YOU GOT QUITE A SACK THERE YOURSELF, RUSKIE--SHOWING UP HERE HALF WAY ACROSS THE WORLD ALL BY YOURSELF.
MY ORDERS COME DIRECTLY FROM THE ***TSAR HIMSELF.***
YEAH, RIGHT. WHAT WOULD THE TSAR WANT WITH THIS FLEA-BITTEN COUNTRY?
HE ONLY CARES ABOUT THE ***WEAPON.***
HOW DO YOU KNOW ABOUT THAT?
YOU THINK AMERICA IS THE ONLY ONE WITH EARS HERE IN CUBA?
MUCH LIKE YOUR COUNTRY UNDERESTIMATES MY MOTHERLAND, YOU HAVE UNDERESTIMATED ***ME.***
ACTUALLY, I JUST WANTED TO GET YOU TALKING, SO I LET YOU LAY SOME SKIN ON ME. BUT NOW THAT I GOT WHAT I WANTED, I'M GONNA ***WHUP*** YOUR TAIL.

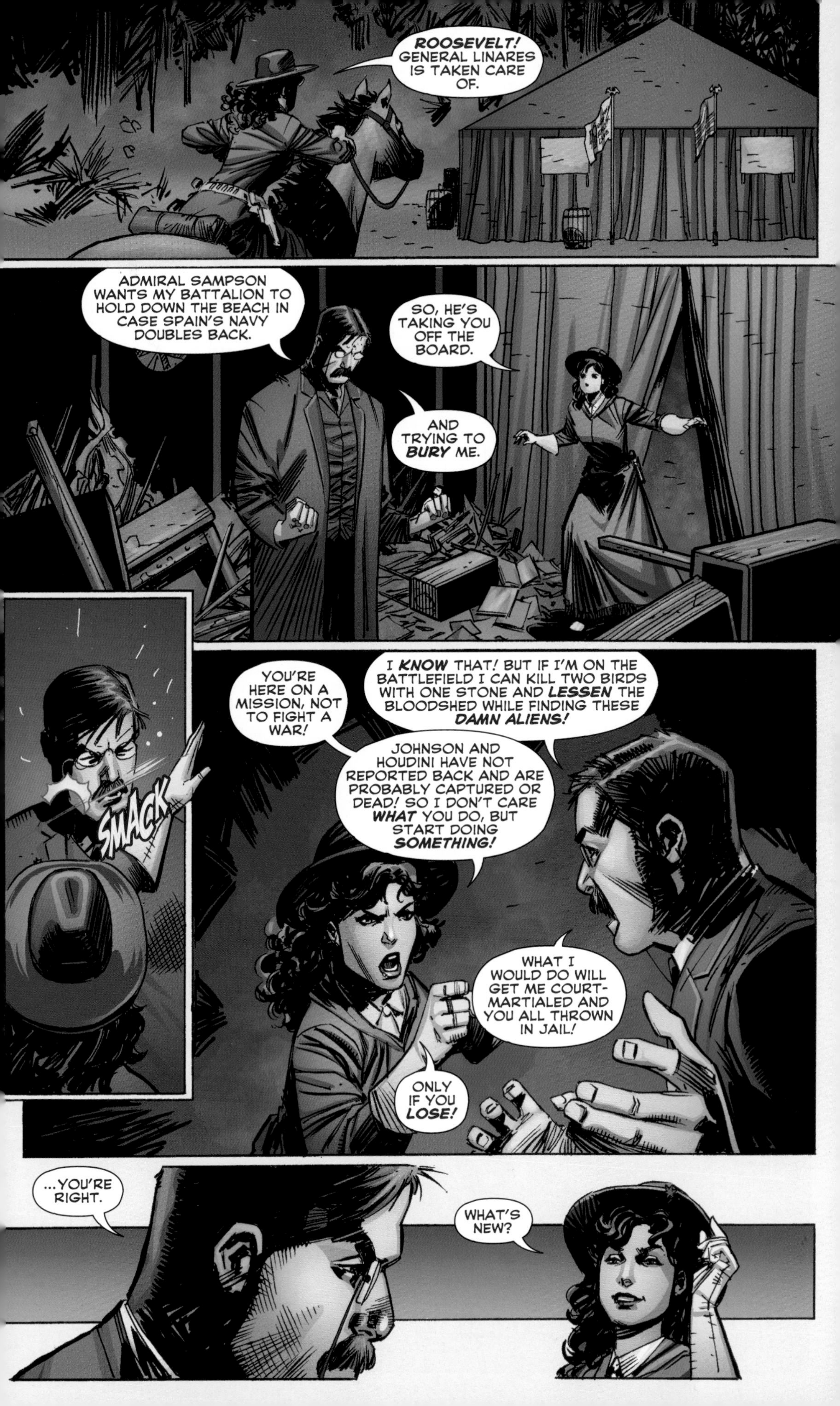
ROOSEVELT! GENERAL LINARES IS TAKEN CARE OF.
ADMIRAL SAMPSON WANTS MY BATTALION TO HOLD DOWN THE BEACH IN CASE SPAIN'S NAVY DOUBLES BACK.
SO, HE'S TAKING YOU OFF THE BOARD.
AND TRYING TO BURY ME.
SMACK
YOU'RE HERE ON A MISSION, NOT TO FIGHT A WAR!
I KNOW THAT! BUT IF I'M ON THE BATTLEFIELD I CAN KILL TWO BIRDS WITH ONE STONE AND LESSEN THE BLOODSHED WHILE FINDING THESE DAMN ALIENS!
JOHNSON AND HOUDINI HAVE NOT REPORTED BACK AND ARE PROBABLY CAPTURED OR DEAD! SO I DON'T CARE WHAT YOU DO, BUT START DOING SOMETHING!
WHAT I WOULD DO WILL GET ME COURT-MARTIALED AND YOU ALL THROWN IN JAIL!
ONLY IF YOU LOSE!
...YOU'RE RIGHT.
WHAT'S NEW?

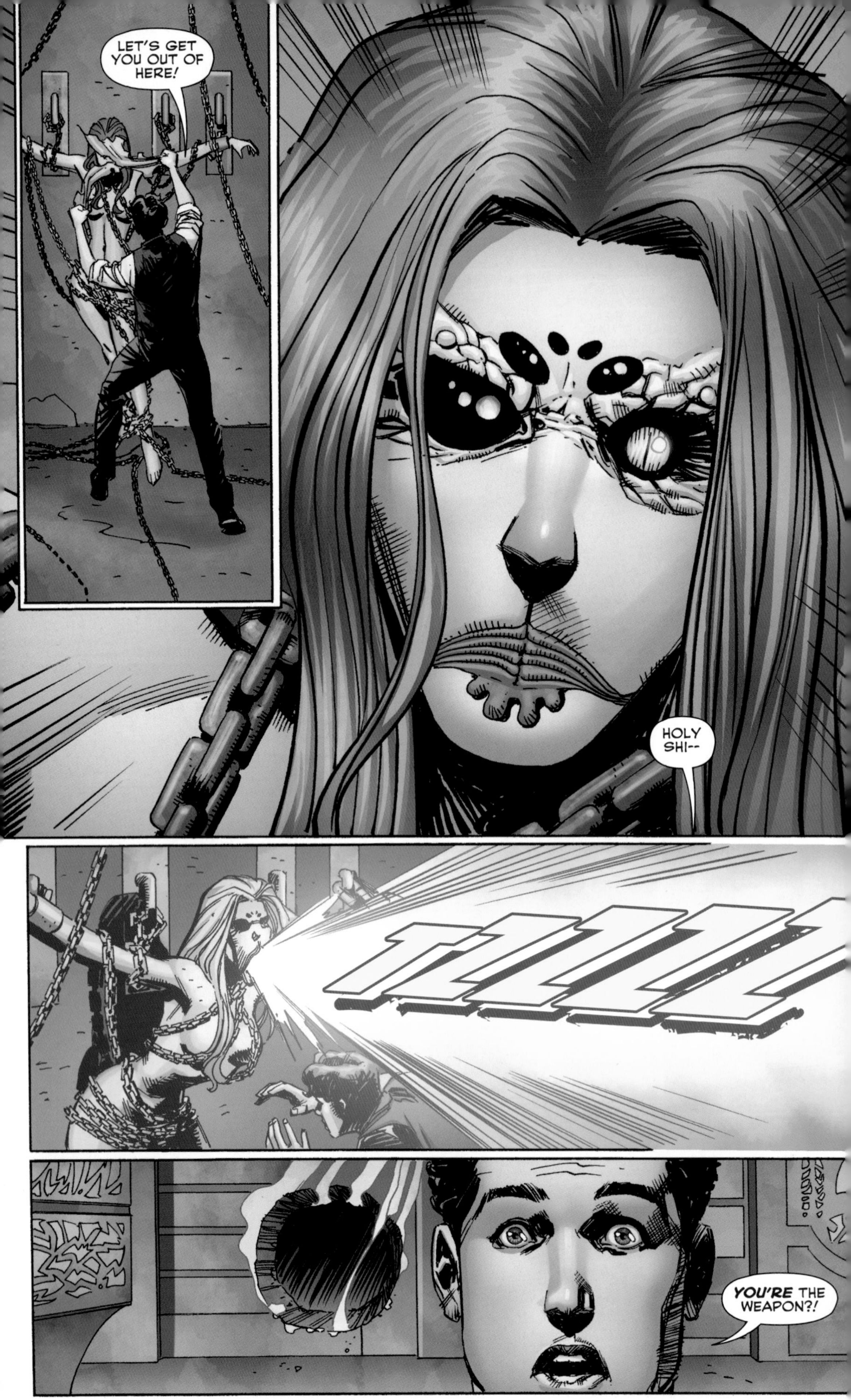
LET'S GET YOU OUT OF HERE!
HOLY SHI--
TZZZZ
YOU'RE THE WEAPON?!

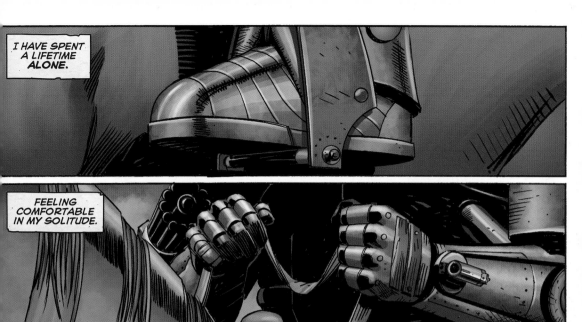

I HAVE SPENT A LIFETIME ALONE.

FEELING COMFORTABLE IN MY SOLITUDE.

FOR THERE I ANSWER TO NO ONE BUT MYSELF.

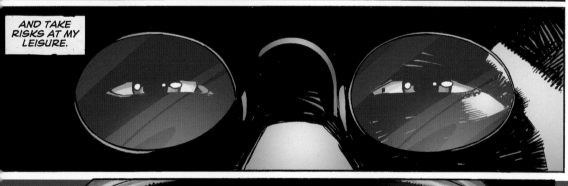

AND TAKE RISKS AT MY LEISURE.

BUT ANNIE IS RIGHT. IT IS TIME TO COME OUT OF THE SHADOWS AND RUFFLE A FEW FEATHERS...

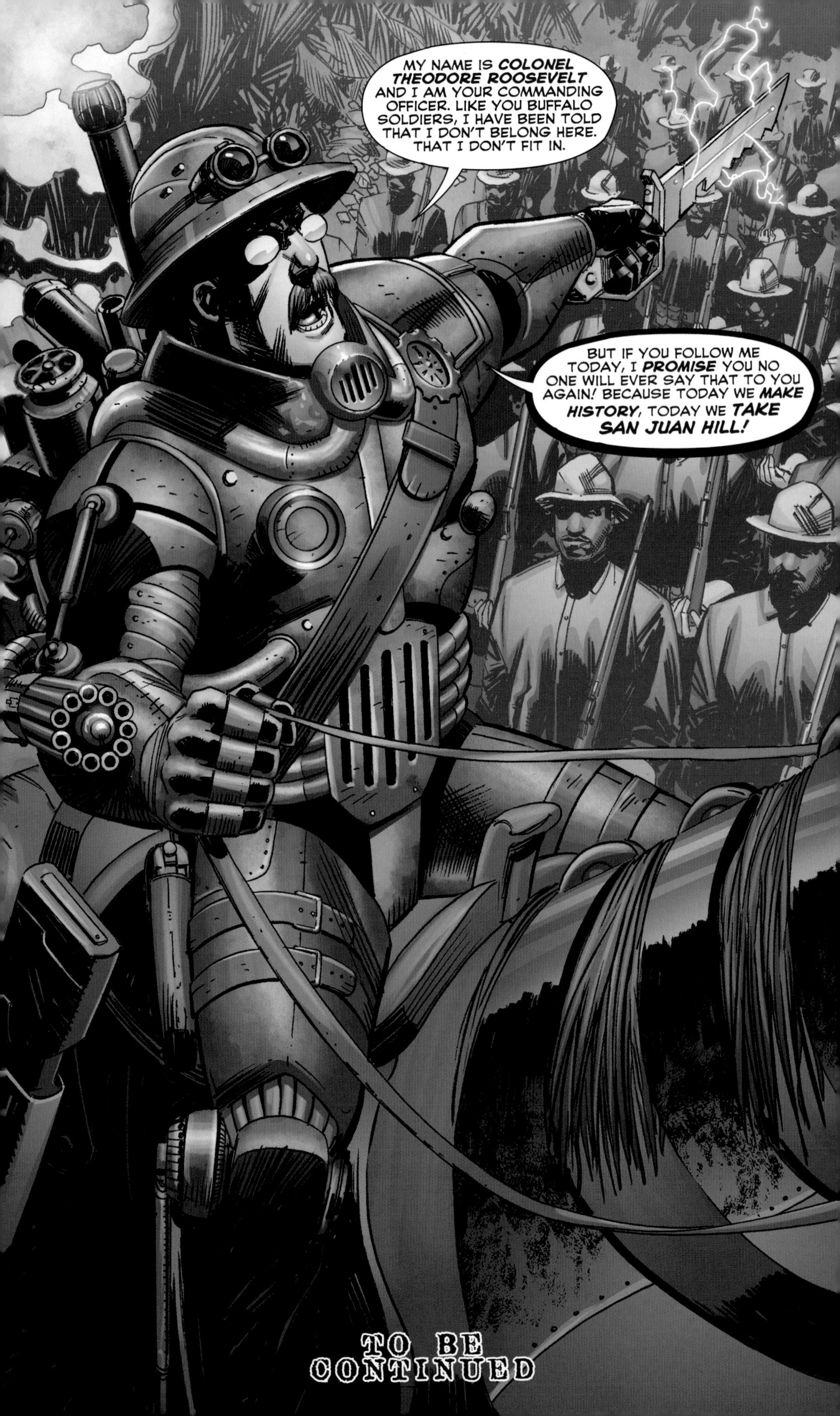
MY NAME IS COLONEL THEODORE ROOSEVELT AND I AM YOUR COMMANDING OFFICER. LIKE YOU BUFFALO SOLDIERS, I HAVE BEEN TOLD THAT I DON'T BELONG HERE. THAT I DON'T FIT IN.
BUT IF YOU FOLLOW ME TODAY, I PROMISE YOU NO ONE WILL EVER SAY THAT TO YOU AGAIN! BECAUSE TODAY WE MAKE HISTORY, TODAY WE TAKE SAN JUAN HILL!
TO BE CONTINUED

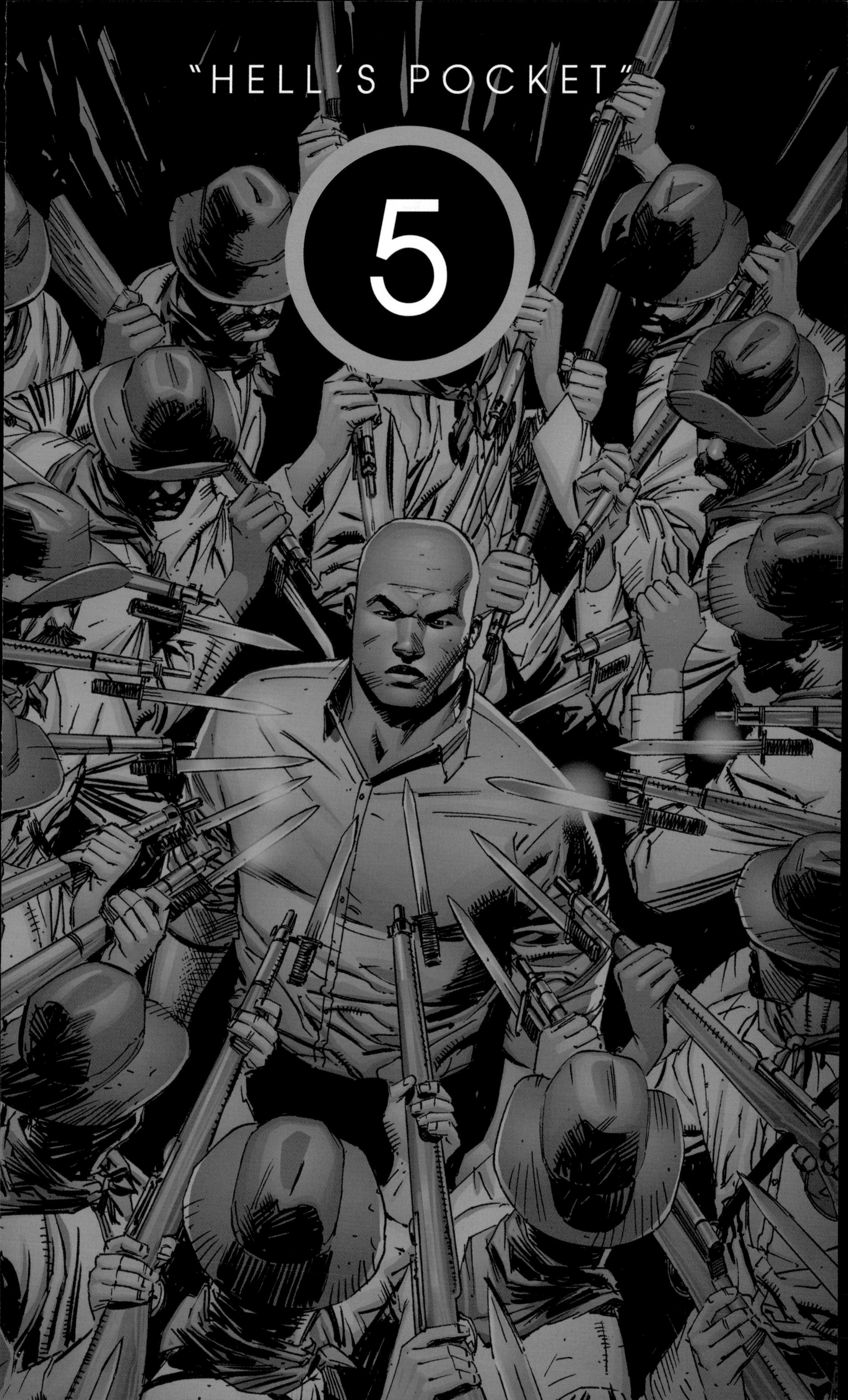
"HELL'S POCKET"
5

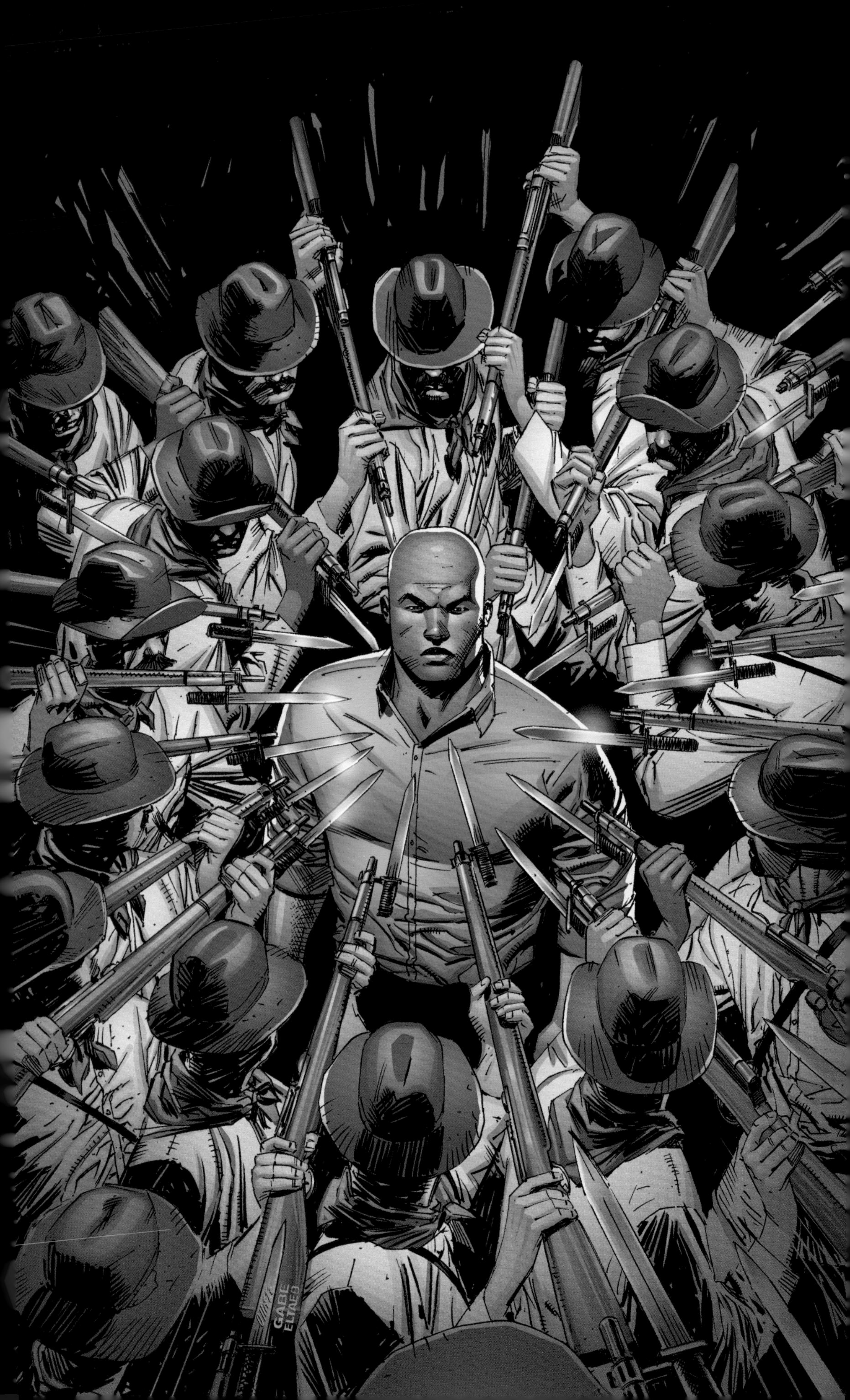
GABE
ELTAEB

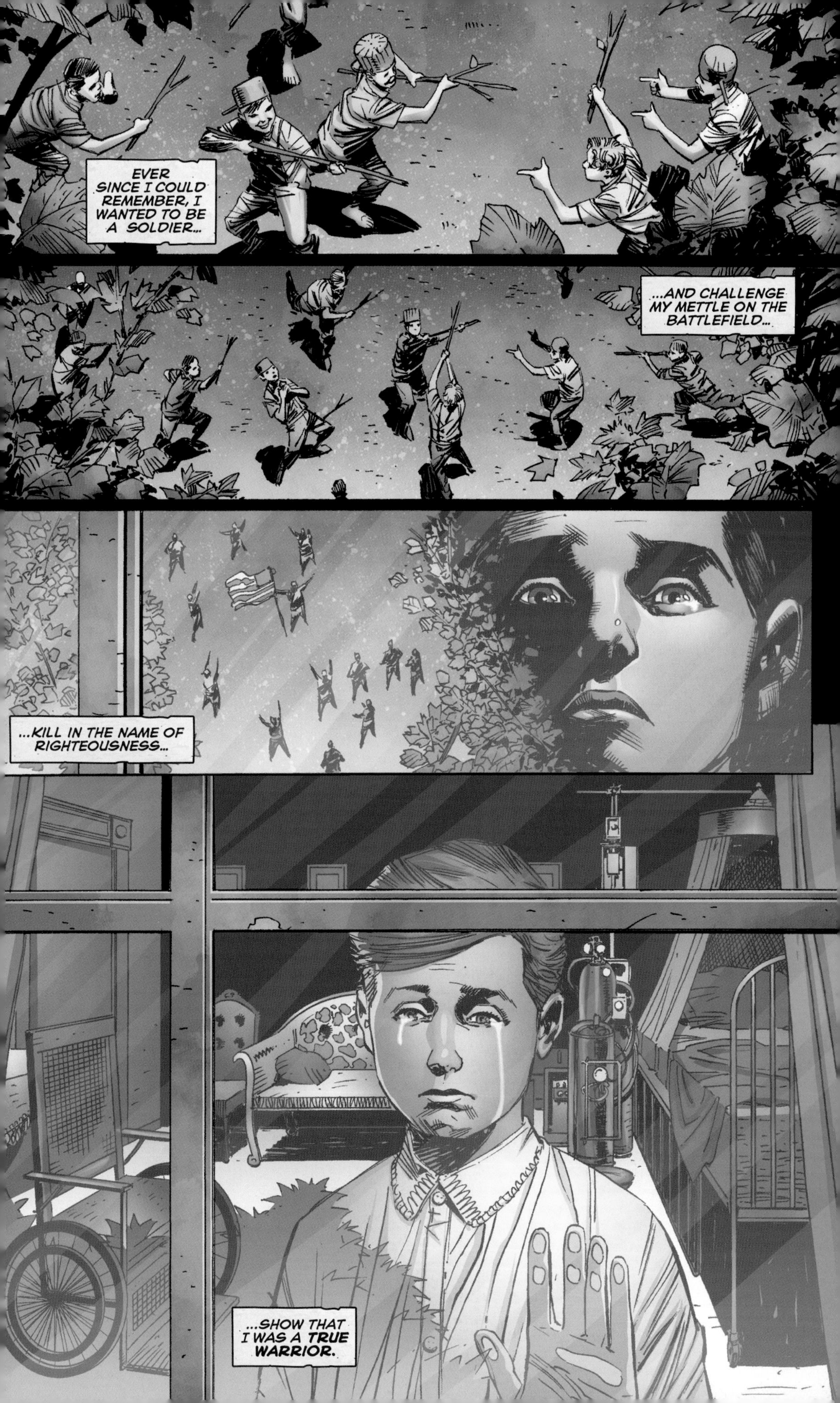
EVER SINCE I COULD REMEMBER, I WANTED TO BE A SOLDIER...
...AND CHALLENGE MY METTLE ON THE BATTLEFIELD...
...KILL IN THE NAME OF RIGHTEOUSNESS...
...SHOW THAT I WAS A TRUE WARRIOR.

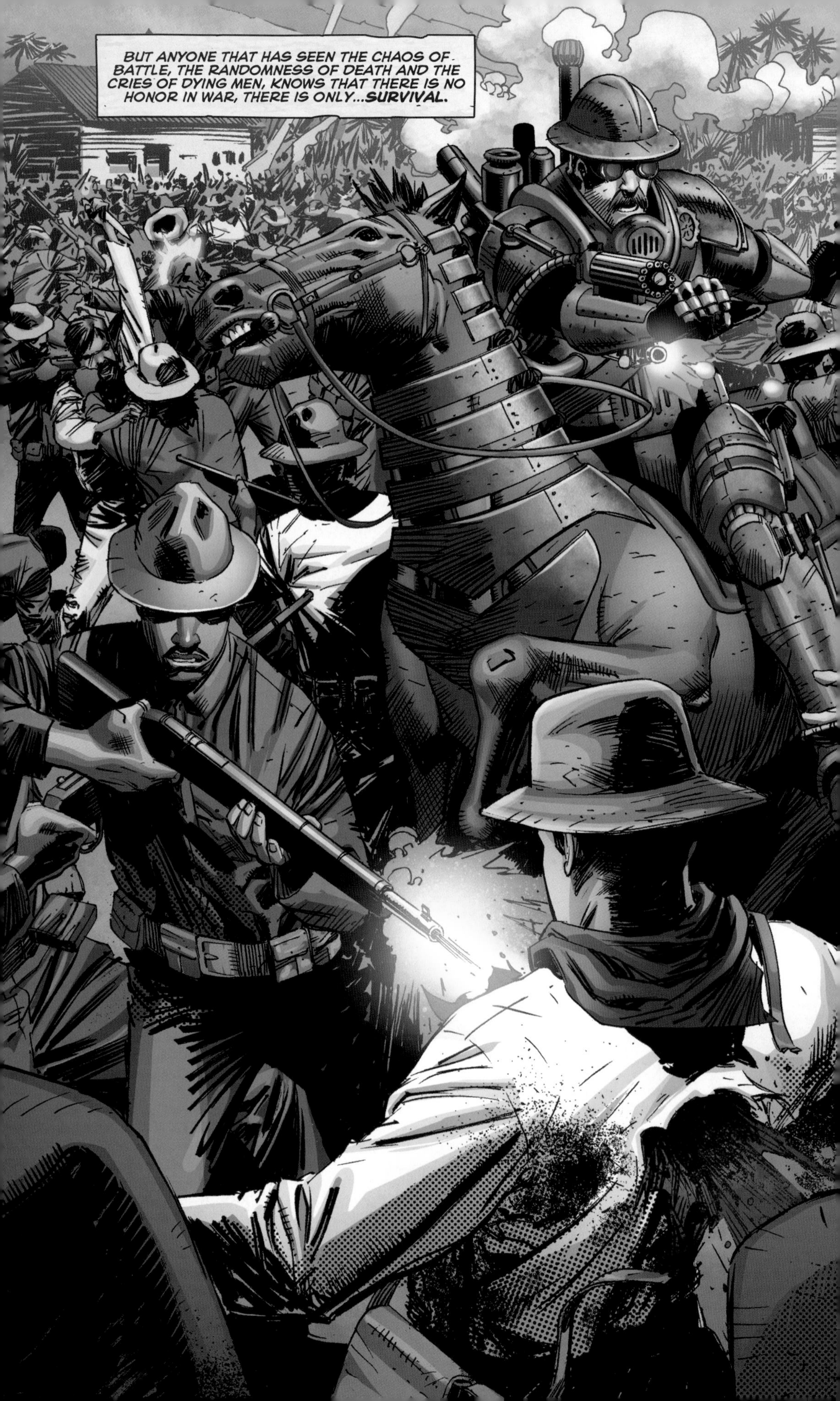
BUT ANYONE THAT HAS SEEN THE CHAOS OF BATTLE, THE RANDOMNESS OF DEATH AND THE CRIES OF DYING MEN, KNOWS THAT THERE IS NO HONOR IN WAR, THERE IS ONLY...SURVIVAL.

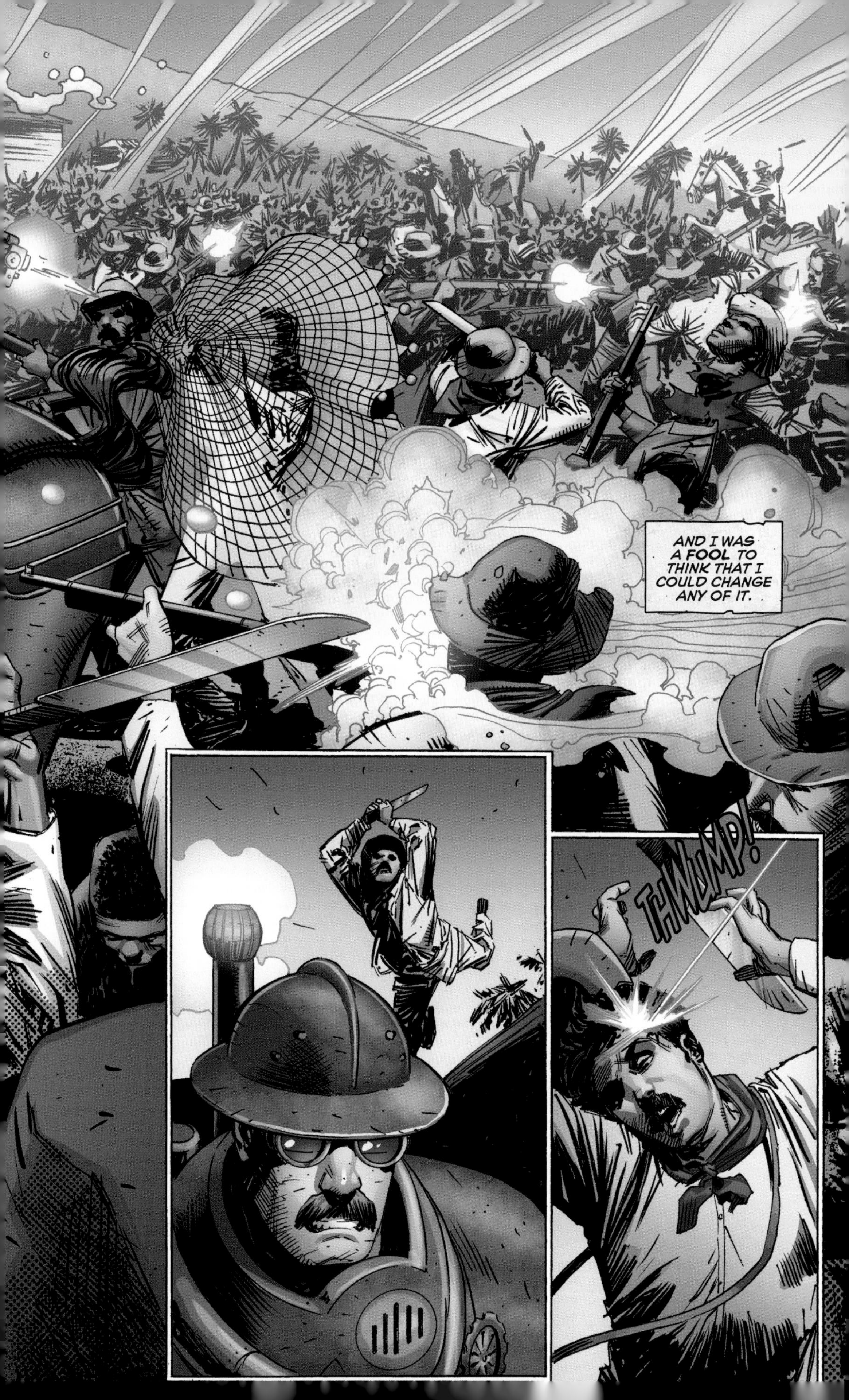
AND I WAS A FOOL TO THINK THAT I COULD CHANGE ANY OF IT.
THWUMP!

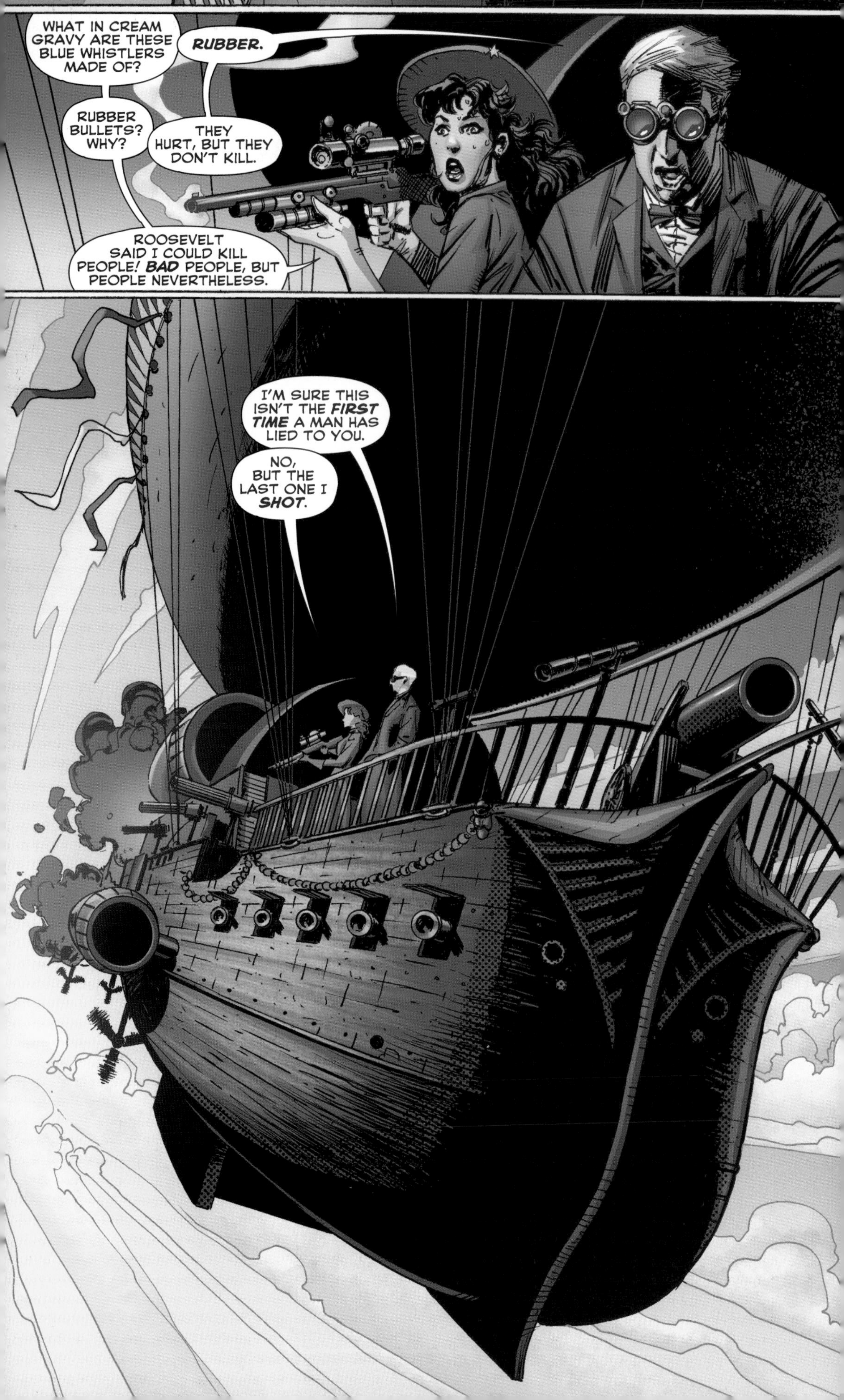
WHAT IN CREAM GRAVY ARE THESE BLUE WHISTLERS MADE OF?
RUBBER.
RUBBER BULLETS? WHY?
THEY HURT, BUT THEY DON'T KILL.
ROOSEVELT SAID I COULD KILL PEOPLE! BAD PEOPLE, BUT PEOPLE NEVERTHELESS.
I'M SURE THIS ISN'T THE FIRST TIME A MAN HAS LIED TO YOU.
NO, BUT THE LAST ONE I SHOT.

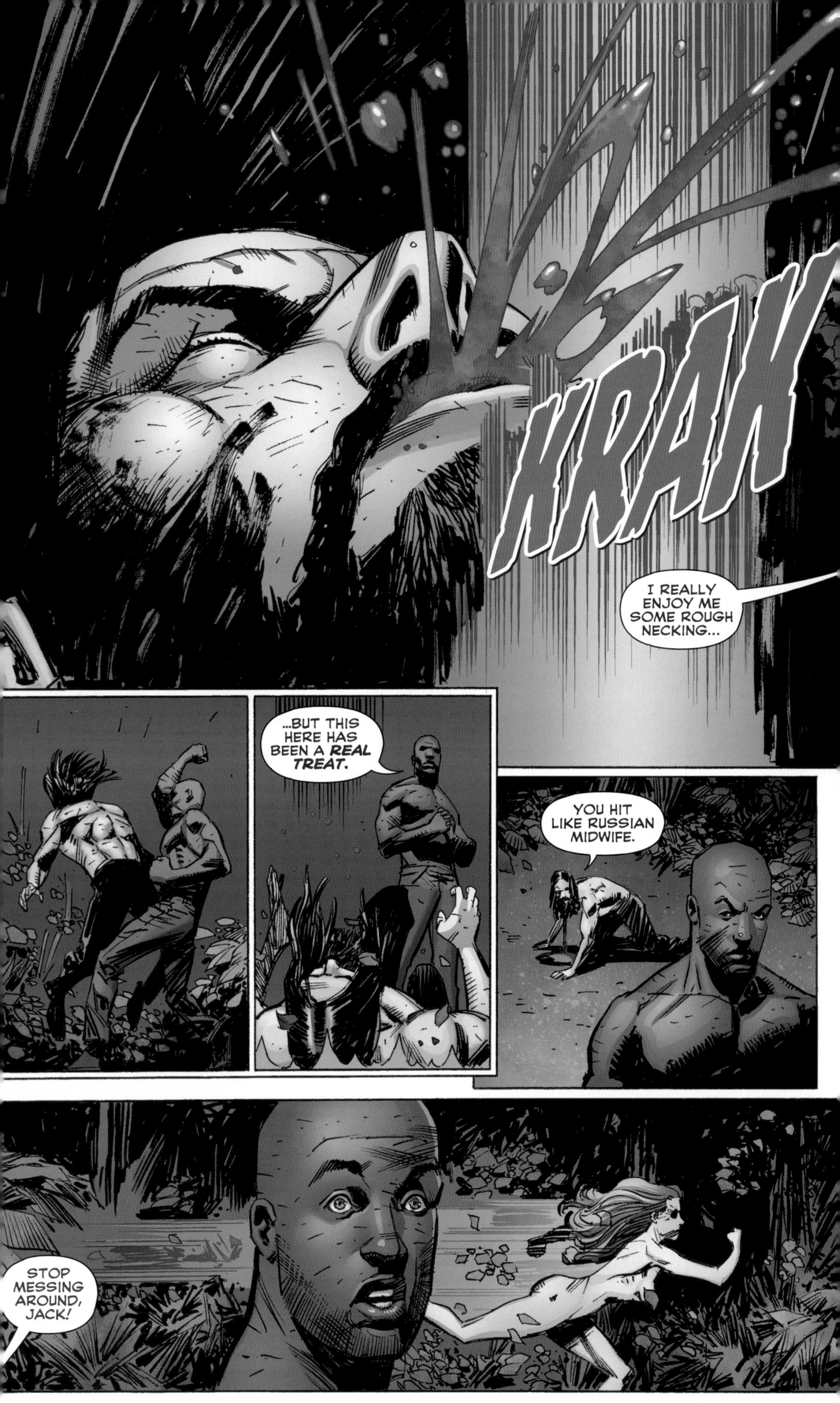
KRAK
I REALLY ENJOY ME SOME ROUGH NECKING...
...BUT THIS HERE HAS BEEN A *REAL TREAT*.
YOU HIT LIKE RUSSIAN MIDWIFE.
STOP MESSING AROUND, JACK!

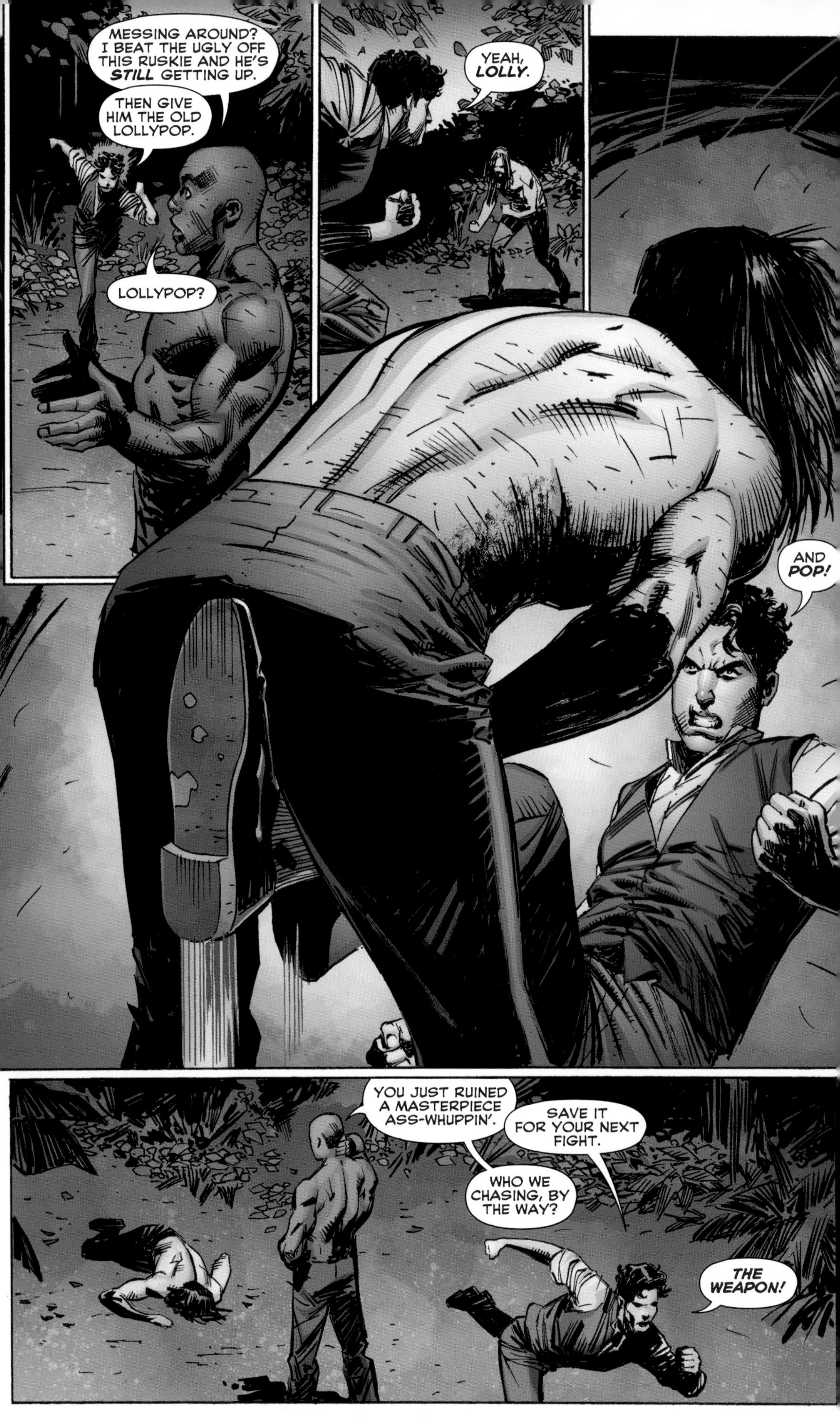

MESSING AROUND? I BEAT THE UGLY OFF THIS RUSKIE AND HE'S *STILL* GETTING UP.
THEN GIVE HIM THE OLD LOLLYPOP.
LOLLYPOP?
YEAH, *LOLLY*.
AND *POP!*
YOU JUST RUINED A MASTERPIECE ASS-WHUPPIN'.
WHO WE CHASING, BY THE WAY?
SAVE IT FOR YOUR NEXT FIGHT.
THE WEAPON!

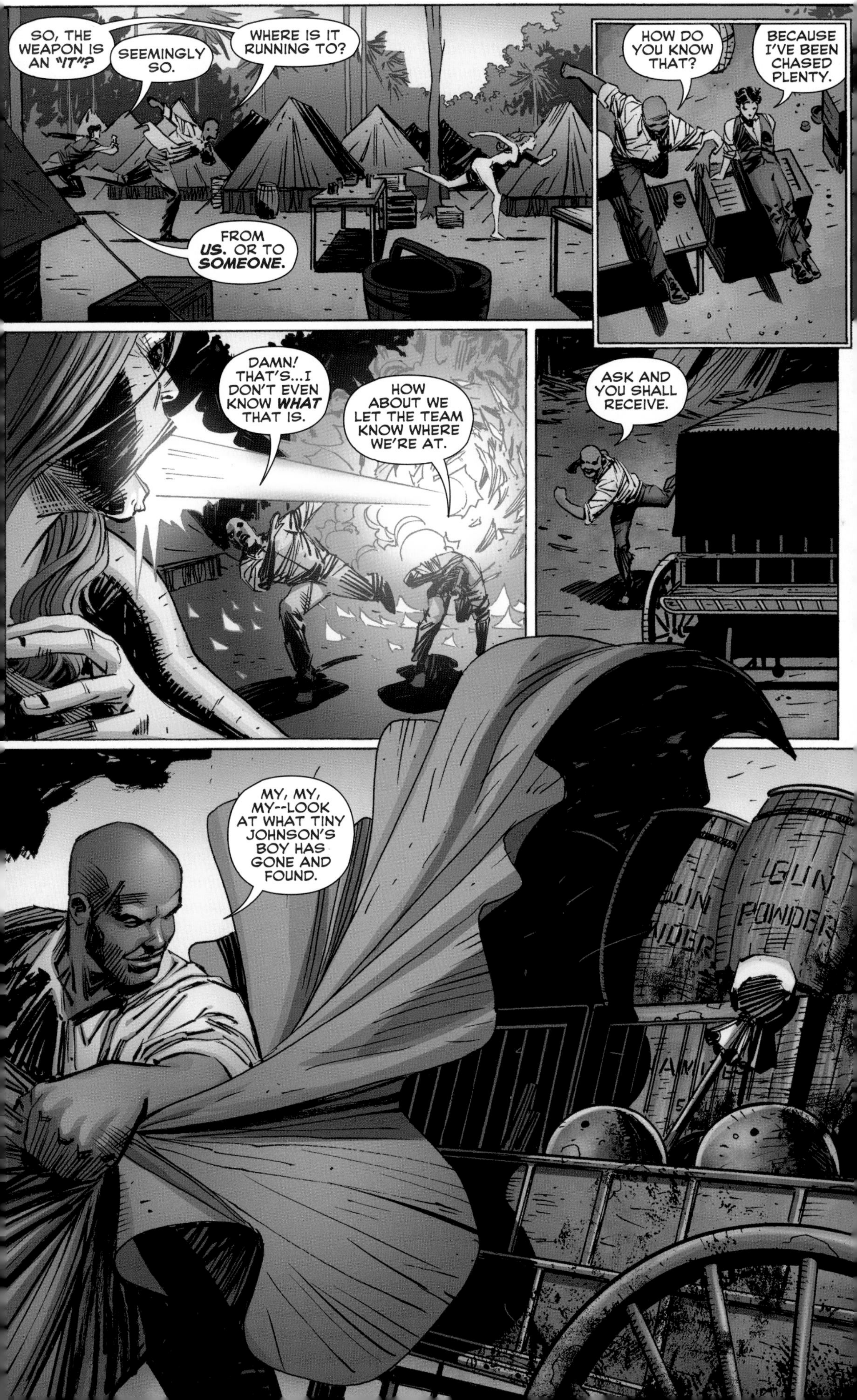

SO, THE WEAPON IS AN "IT"?
SEEMINGLY SO.
WHERE IS IT RUNNING TO?
FROM US. OR TO SOMEONE.
HOW DO YOU KNOW THAT?
BECAUSE I'VE BEEN CHASED PLENTY.
DAMN! THAT'S...I DON'T EVEN KNOW WHAT THAT IS.
HOW ABOUT WE LET THE TEAM KNOW WHERE WE'RE AT.
ASK AND YOU SHALL RECEIVE.
MY, MY, MY--LOOK AT WHAT TINY JOHNSON'S BOY HAS GONE AND FOUND.
GUN POWDER

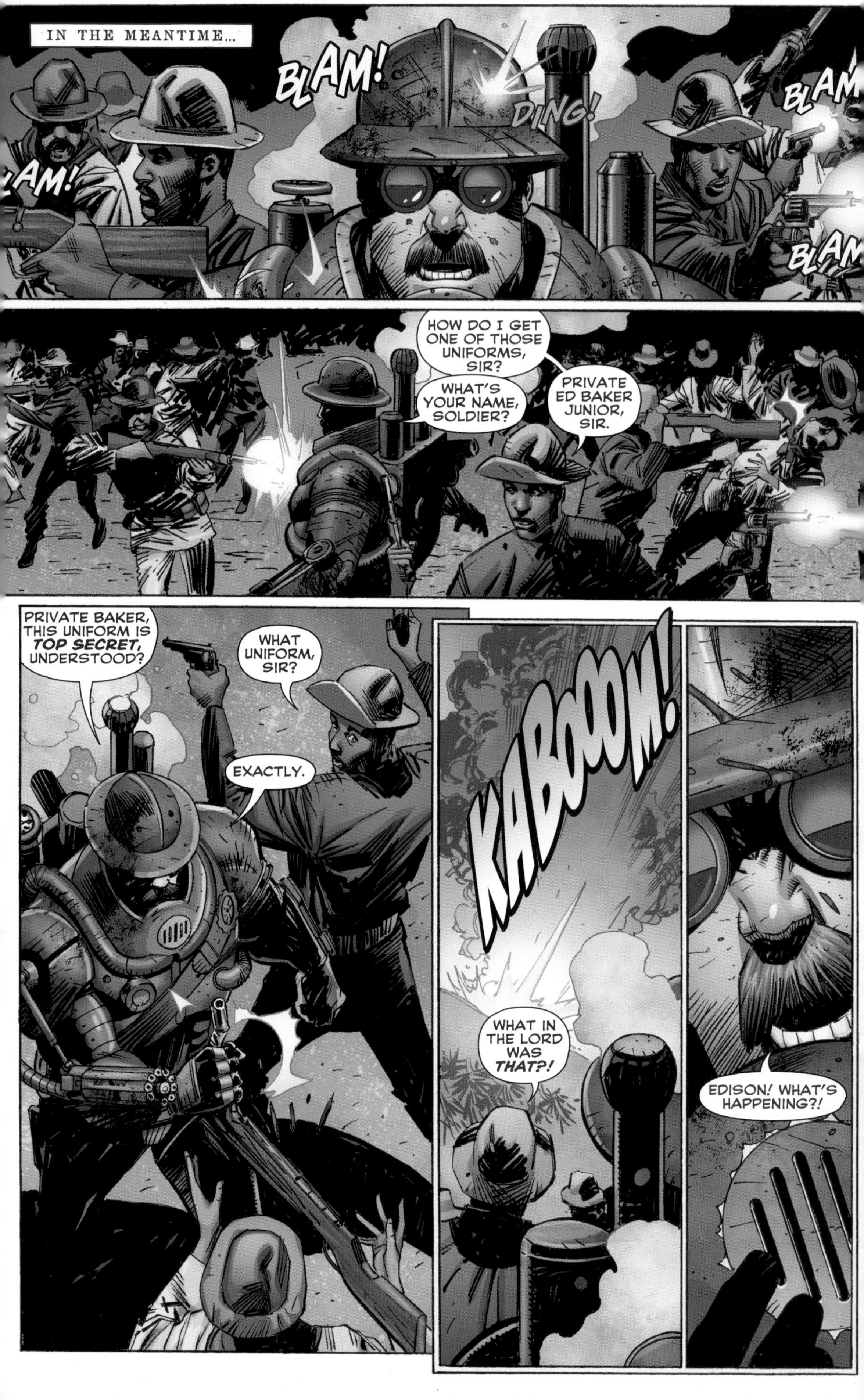
IN THE MEANTIME...
BLAM!
AM!
DING!
BLAM
BLAM
HOW DO I GET ONE OF THOSE UNIFORMS, SIR?
WHAT'S YOUR NAME, SOLDIER?
PRIVATE ED BAKER JUNIOR, SIR.
PRIVATE BAKER, THIS UNIFORM IS *TOP SECRET*, UNDERSTOOD?
WHAT UNIFORM, SIR?
EXACTLY.
KABOOOM!
WHAT IN THE LORD WAS *THAT?!*
EDISON! WHAT'S HAPPENING?!

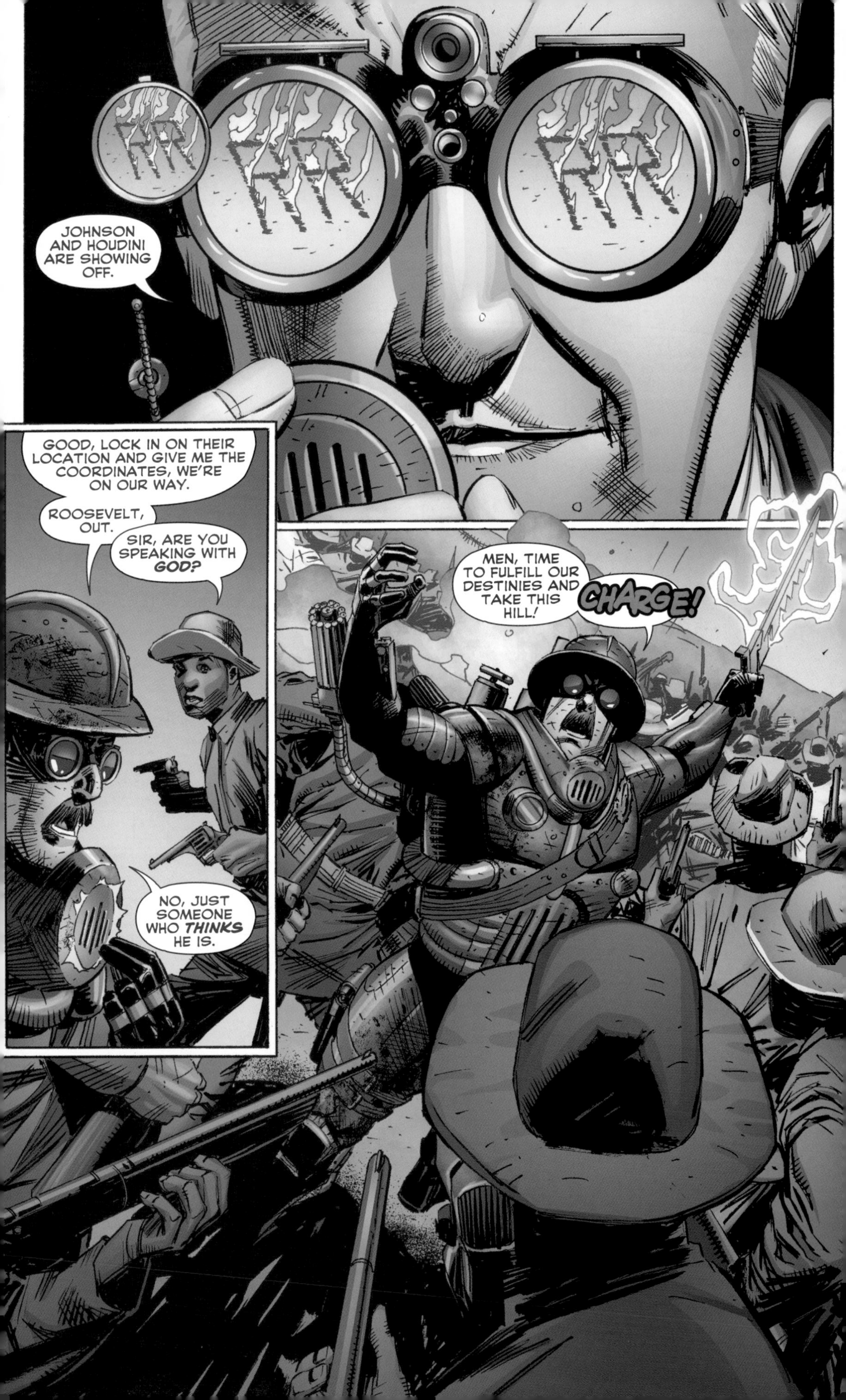
JOHNSON AND HOUDINI ARE SHOWING OFF.
GOOD, LOCK IN ON THEIR LOCATION AND GIVE ME THE COORDINATES, WE'RE ON OUR WAY.
ROOSEVELT, OUT.
SIR, ARE YOU SPEAKING WITH *GOD?*
NO, JUST SOMEONE WHO *THINKS* HE IS.
MEN, TIME TO FULFILL OUR DESTINIES AND TAKE THIS HILL!
CHARGE!

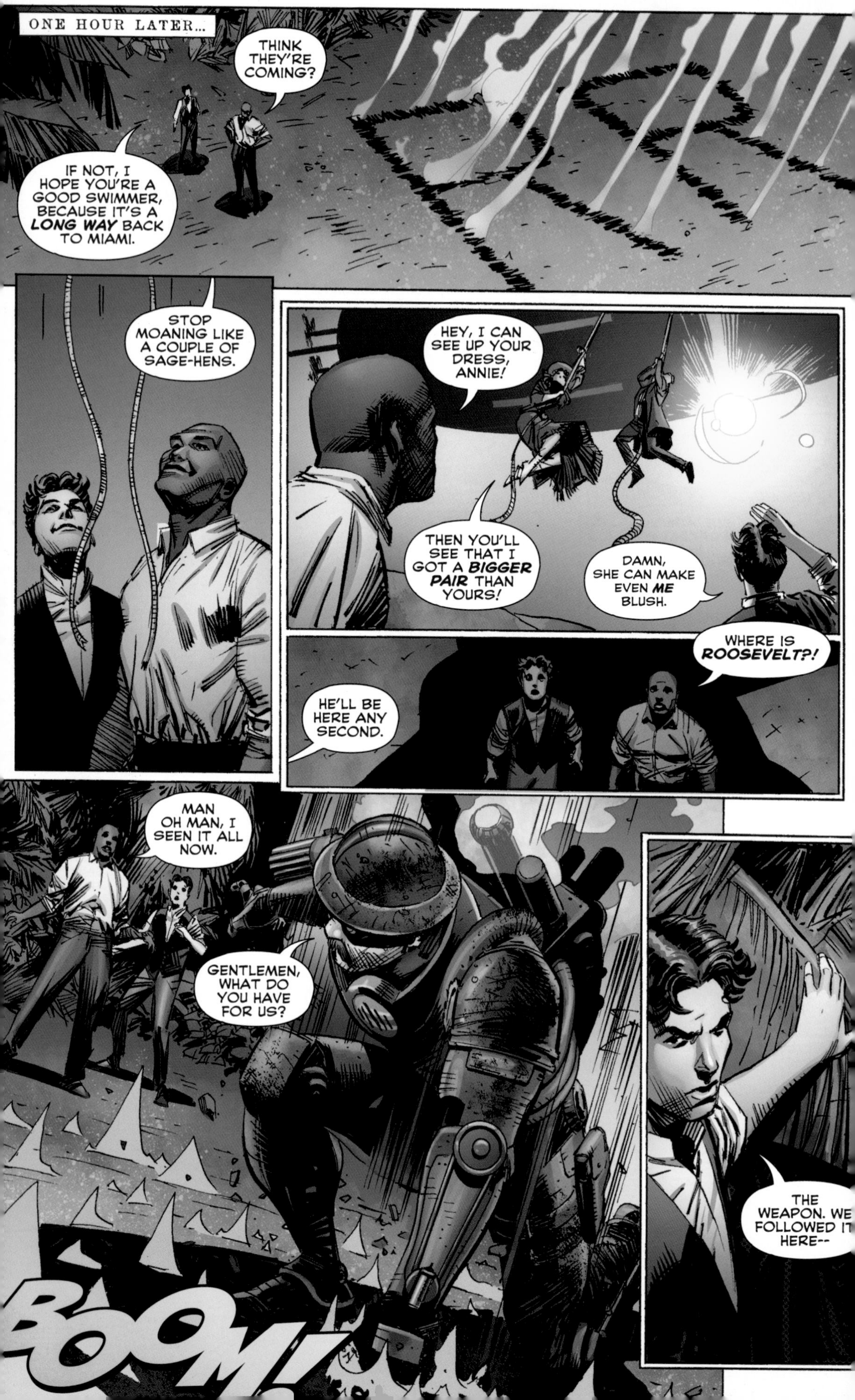

ONE HOUR LATER...
THINK THEY'RE COMING?
IF NOT, I HOPE YOU'RE A GOOD SWIMMER, BECAUSE IT'S A LONG WAY BACK TO MIAMI.
STOP MOANING LIKE A COUPLE OF SAGE-HENS.
HEY, I CAN SEE UP YOUR DRESS, ANNIE!
THEN YOU'LL SEE THAT I GOT A BIGGER PAIR THAN YOURS!
DAMN, SHE CAN MAKE EVEN ME BLUSH.
WHERE IS ROOSEVELT?!
HE'LL BE HERE ANY SECOND.
MAN OH MAN, I SEEN IT ALL NOW.
GENTLEMEN, WHAT DO YOU HAVE FOR US?
THE WEAPON. WE FOLLOWED IT HERE--
BOOM!

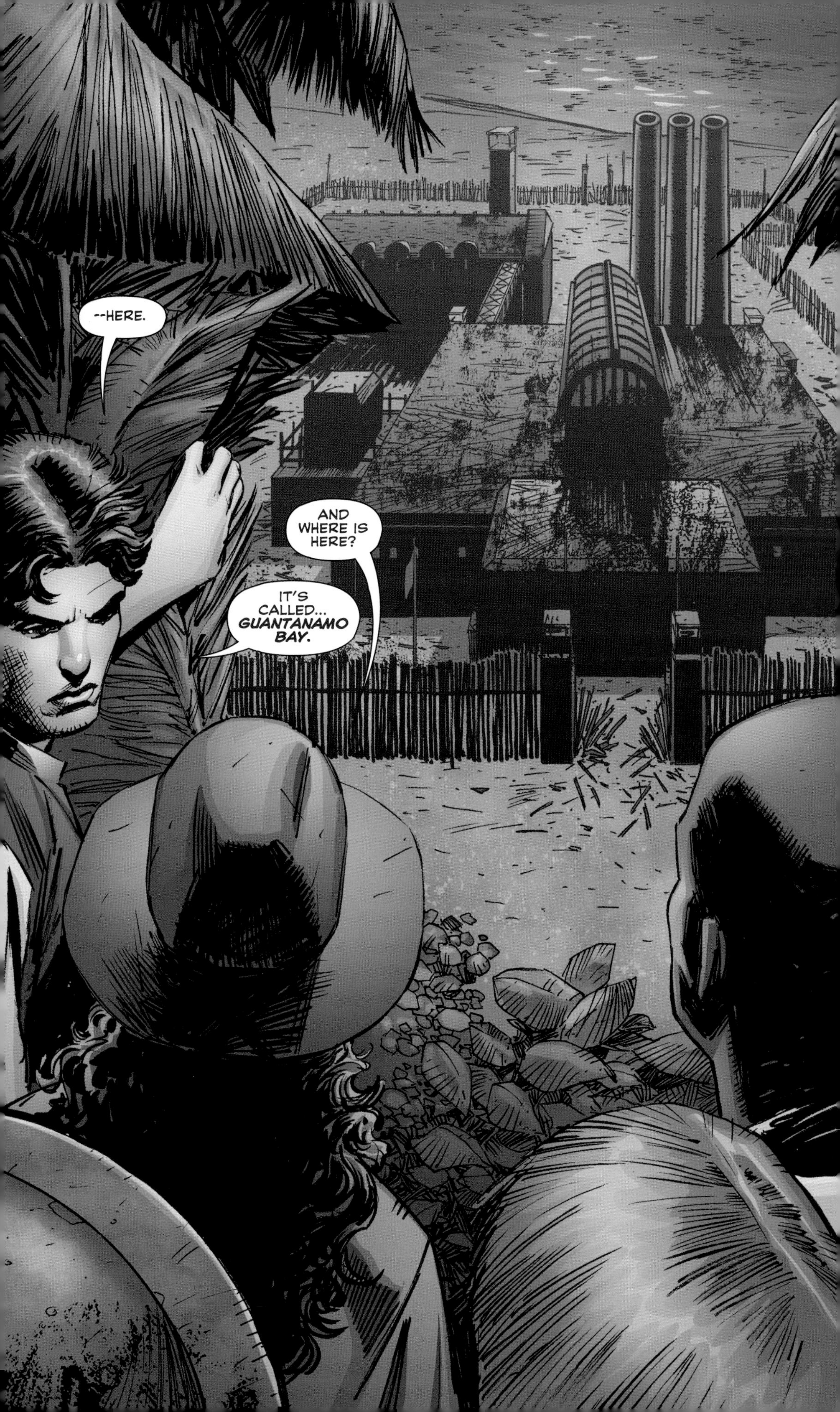
--HERE.
AND WHERE IS HERE?
IT'S CALLED... GUANTANAMO BAY.

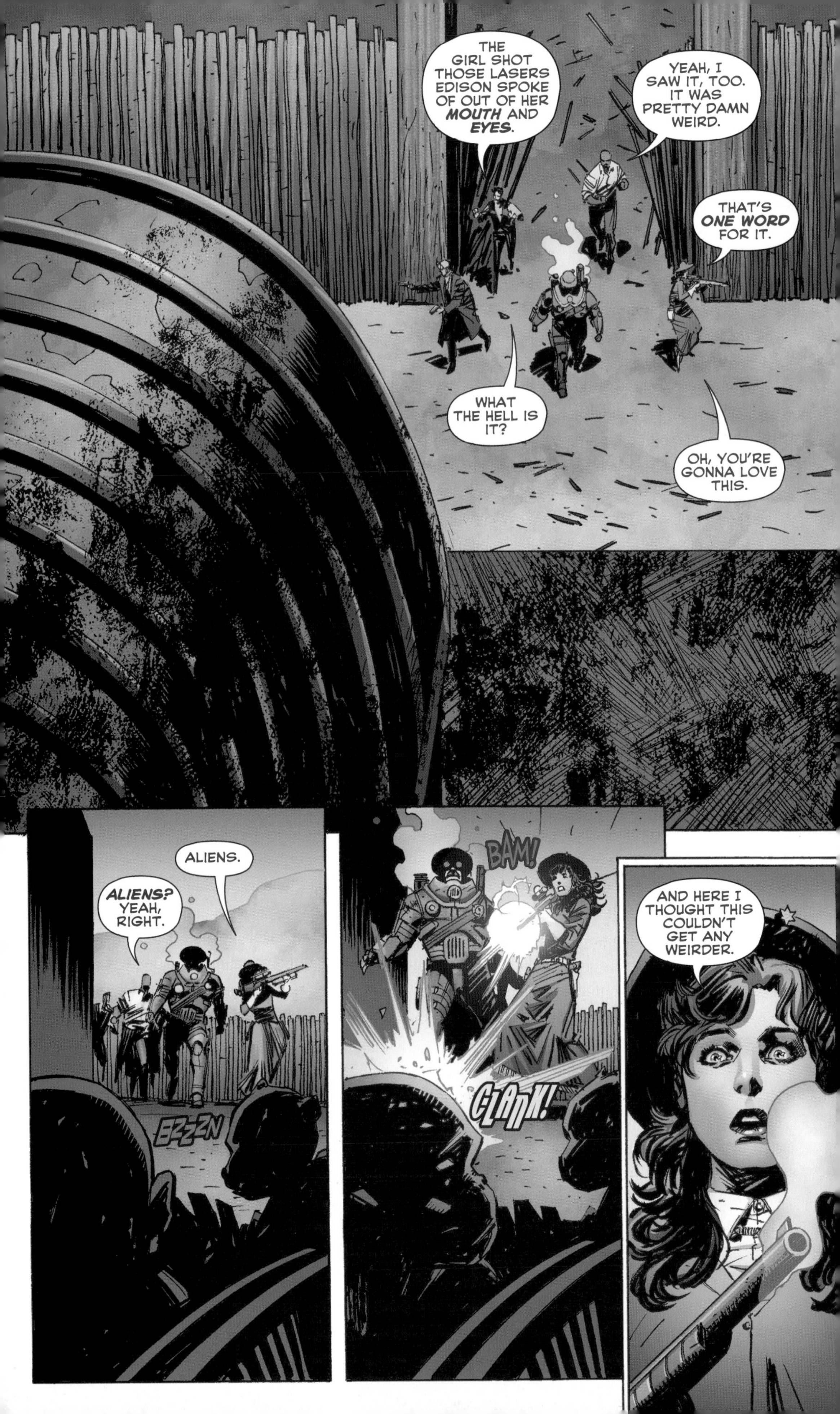
THE GIRL SHOT THOSE LASERS EDISON SPOKE OF OUT OF HER *MOUTH* AND *EYES*.
YEAH, I SAW IT, TOO. IT WAS PRETTY DAMN WEIRD.
THAT'S *ONE WORD* FOR IT.
WHAT THE HELL IS IT?
OH, YOU'RE GONNA LOVE THIS.
ALIENS.
ALIENS? YEAH, RIGHT.
BZZZN
BAM!
CLANK!
AND HERE I THOUGHT THIS COULDN'T GET ANY WEIRDER.

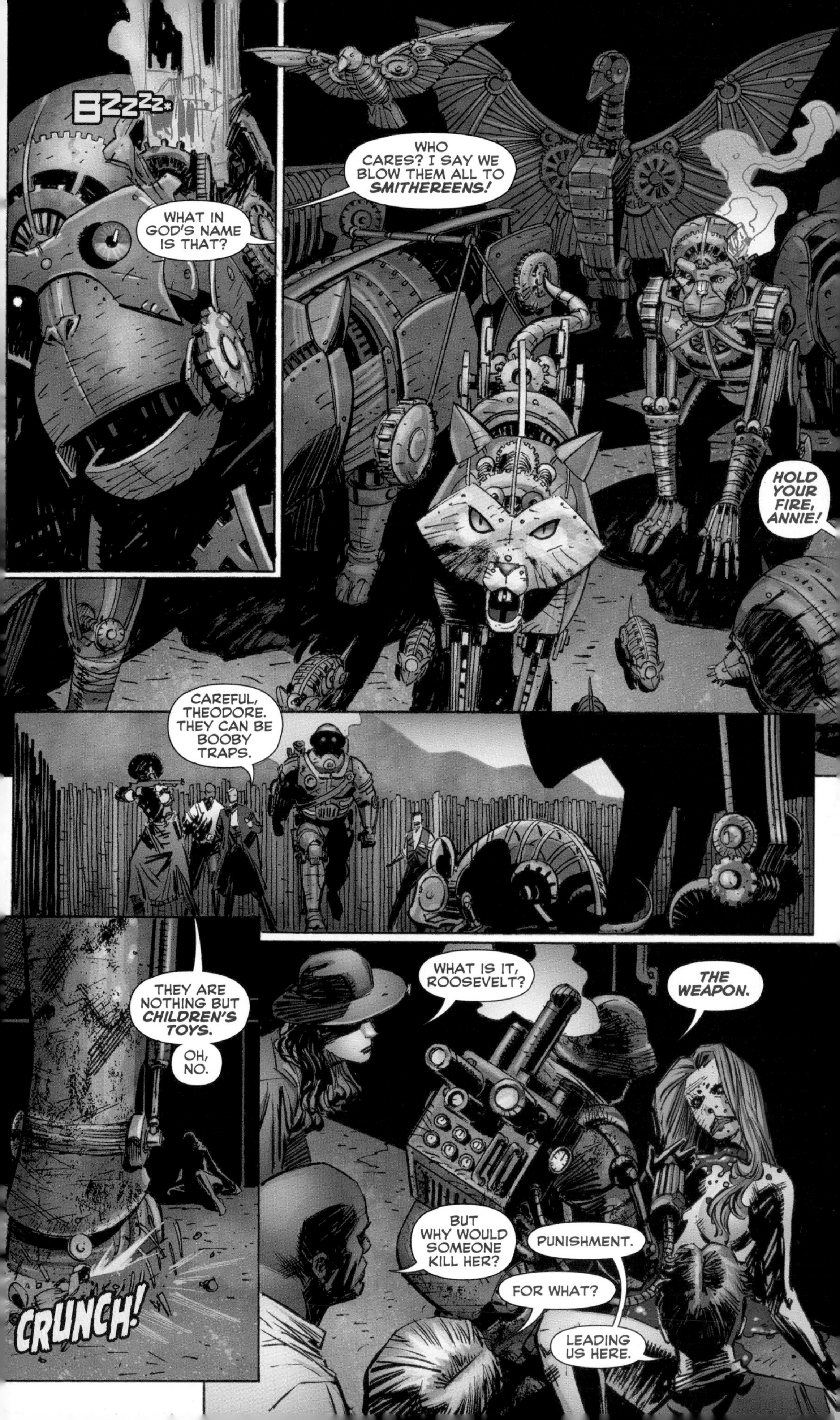

BZZZZ*
WHAT IN GOD'S NAME IS THAT?
WHO CARES? I SAY WE BLOW THEM ALL TO SMITHEREENS!
HOLD YOUR FIRE, ANNIE!
CAREFUL, THEODORE. THEY CAN BE BOOBY TRAPS.
THEY ARE NOTHING BUT CHILDREN'S TOYS.
OH, NO.
CRUNCH!
WHAT IS IT, ROOSEVELT?
THE WEAPON.
BUT WHY WOULD SOMEONE KILL HER?
PUNISHMENT.
FOR WHAT?
LEADING US HERE.

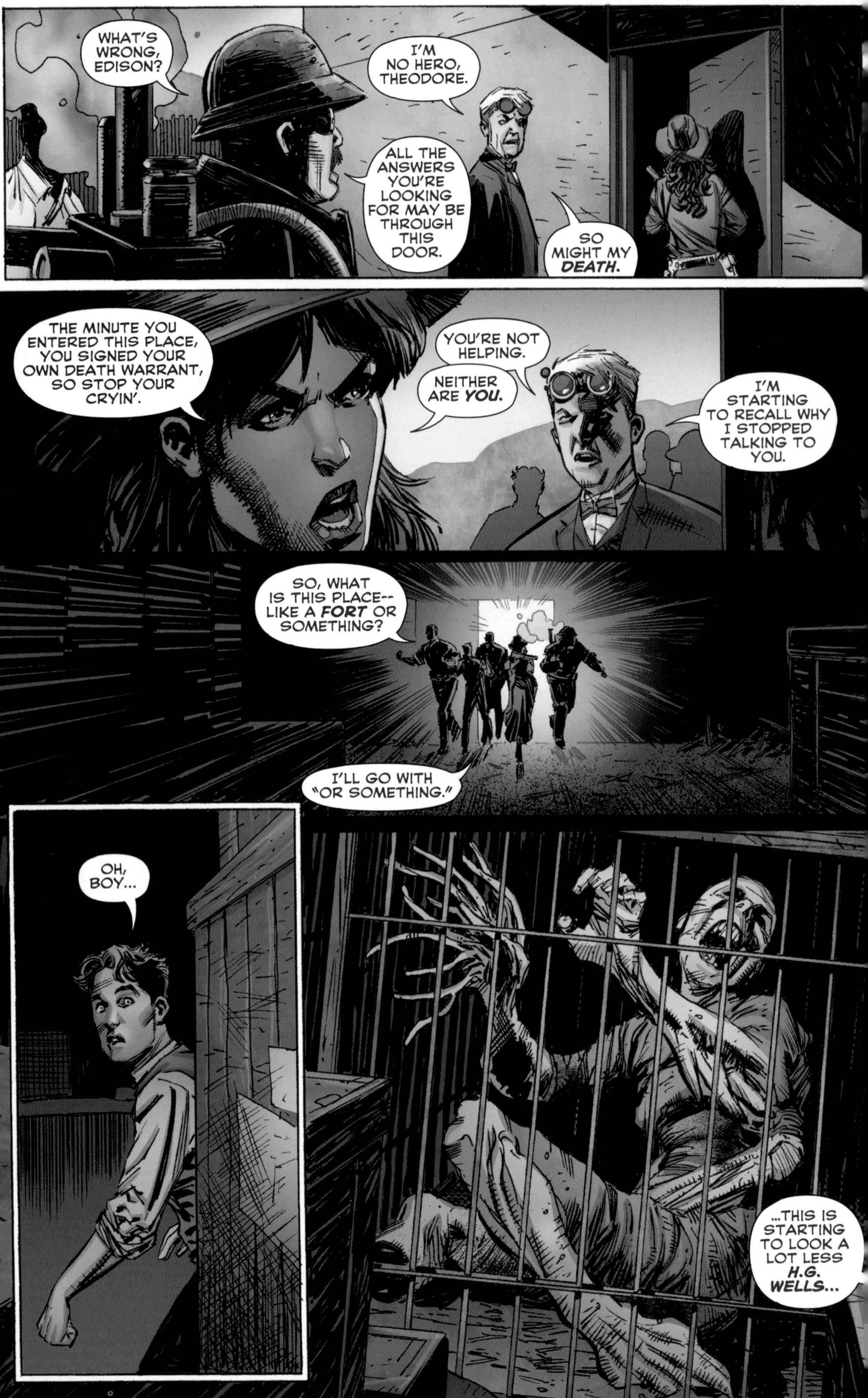
WHAT'S WRONG, EDISON?
I'M NO HERO, THEODORE.
ALL THE ANSWERS YOU'RE LOOKING FOR MAY BE THROUGH THIS DOOR.
SO MIGHT MY *DEATH.*
THE MINUTE YOU ENTERED THIS PLACE, YOU SIGNED YOUR OWN DEATH WARRANT, SO STOP YOUR CRYIN'.
YOU'RE NOT HELPING.
NEITHER ARE *YOU.*
I'M STARTING TO RECALL WHY I STOPPED TALKING TO YOU.
SO, WHAT IS THIS PLACE-- LIKE A *FORT* OR SOMETHING?
I'LL GO WITH "OR SOMETHING."
OH, BOY...
...THIS IS STARTING TO LOOK A LOT LESS *H.G. WELLS...*

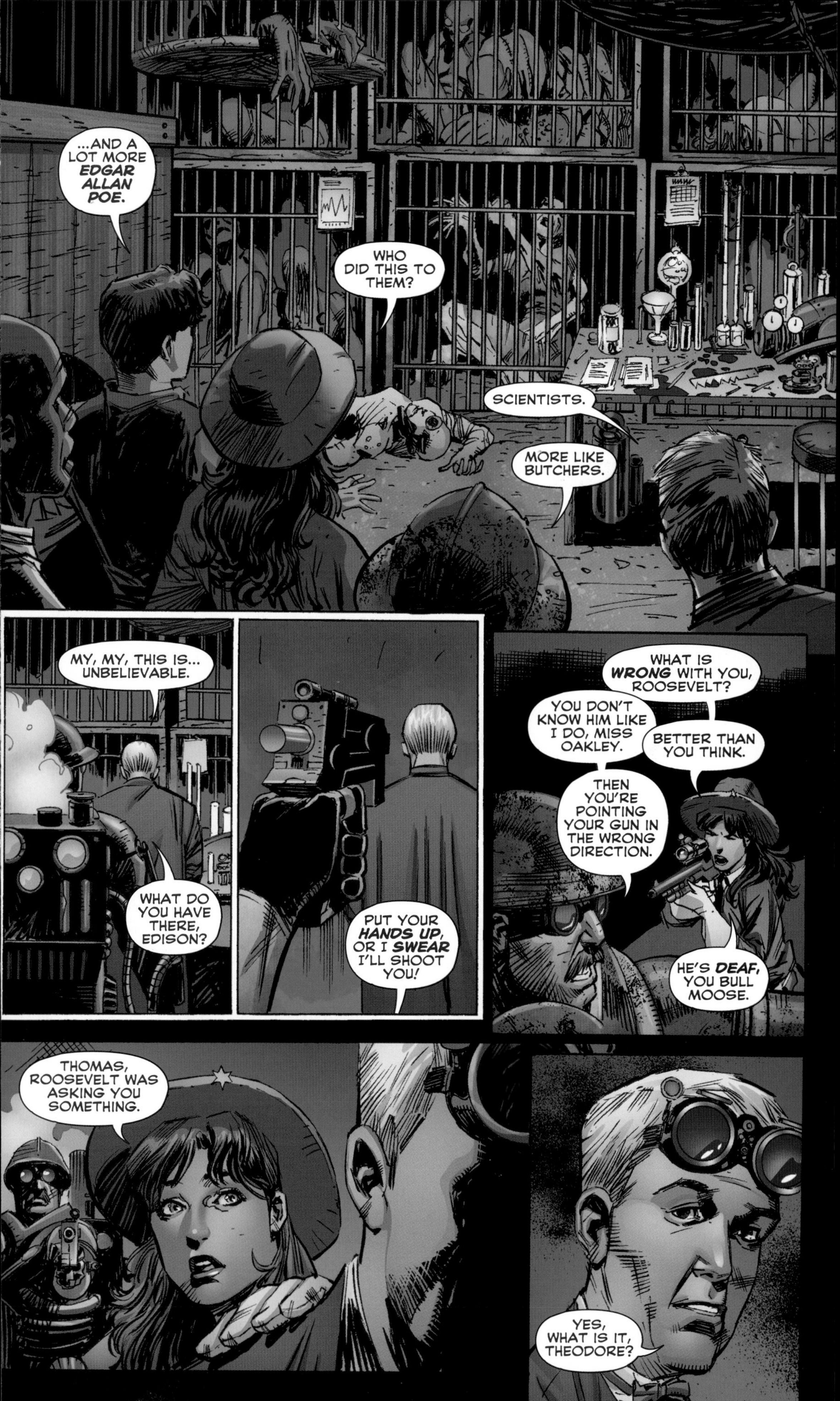
...AND A LOT MORE EDGAR ALLAN POE.
WHO DID THIS TO THEM?
SCIENTISTS.
MORE LIKE BUTCHERS.
MY, MY, THIS IS... UNBELIEVABLE.
WHAT DO YOU HAVE THERE, EDISON?
PUT YOUR HANDS UP, OR I SWEAR I'LL SHOOT YOU!
WHAT IS WRONG WITH YOU, ROOSEVELT?
YOU DON'T KNOW HIM LIKE I DO, MISS OAKLEY.
BETTER THAN YOU THINK.
THEN YOU'RE POINTING YOUR GUN IN THE WRONG DIRECTION.
HE'S DEAF, YOU BULL MOOSE.
THOMAS, ROOSEVELT WAS ASKING YOU SOMETHING.
YES, WHAT IS IT, THEODORE?

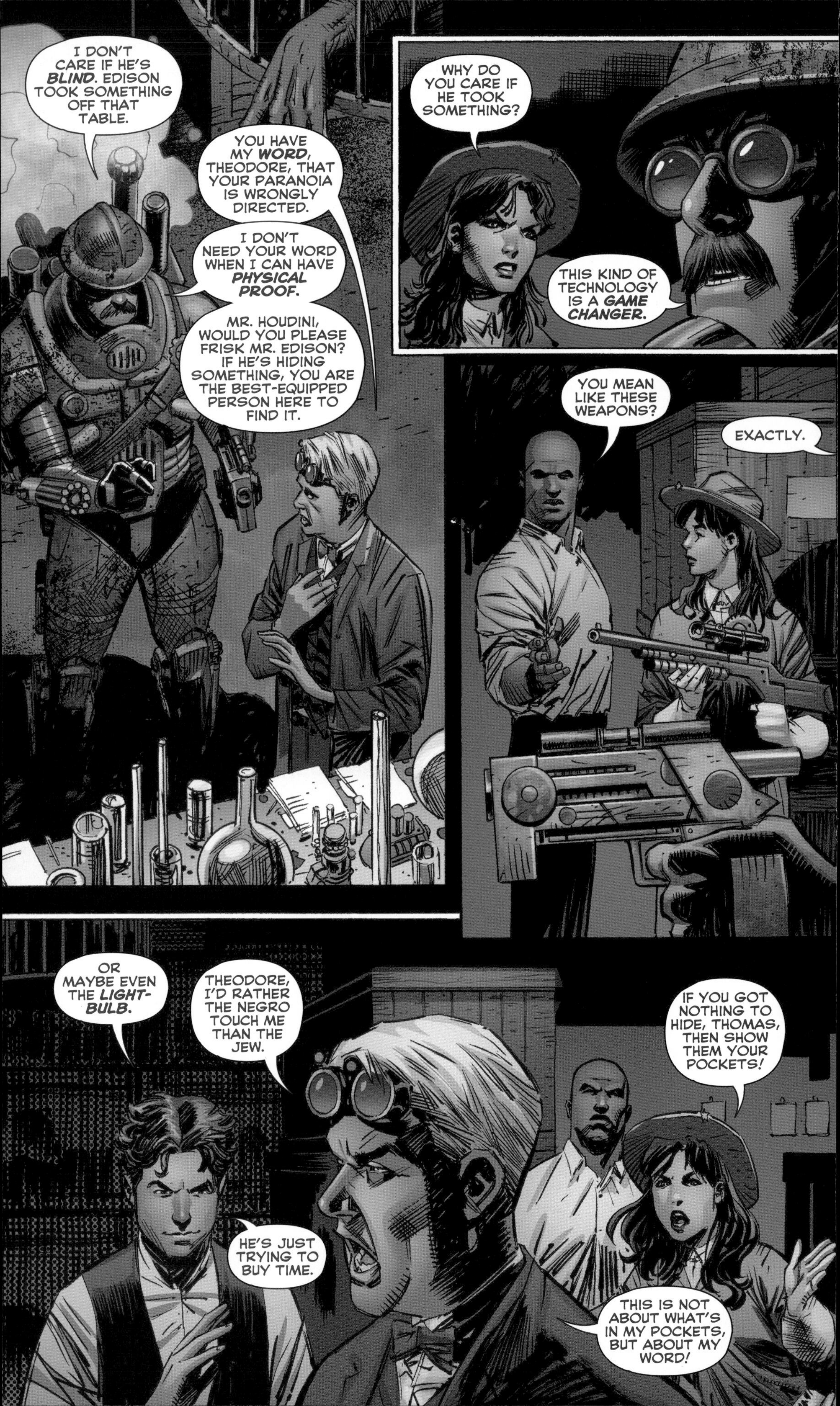
I DON'T CARE IF HE'S *BLIND*. EDISON TOOK SOMETHING OFF THAT TABLE.
YOU HAVE MY *WORD*, THEODORE, THAT YOUR PARANOIA IS WRONGLY DIRECTED.
I DON'T NEED YOUR WORD WHEN I CAN HAVE *PHYSICAL PROOF*.
MR. HOUDINI, WOULD YOU PLEASE FRISK MR. EDISON? IF HE'S HIDING SOMETHING, YOU ARE THE BEST-EQUIPPED PERSON HERE TO FIND IT.
WHY DO YOU CARE IF HE TOOK SOMETHING?
THIS KIND OF TECHNOLOGY IS A *GAME CHANGER*.
YOU MEAN LIKE THESE WEAPONS?
EXACTLY.
OR MAYBE EVEN THE *LIGHT-BULB*.
THEODORE, I'D RATHER THE NEGRO TOUCH ME THAN THE JEW.
HE'S JUST TRYING TO BUY TIME.
IF YOU GOT NOTHING TO HIDE, THOMAS, THEN SHOW THEM YOUR POCKETS!
THIS IS NOT ABOUT WHAT'S IN MY POCKETS, BUT ABOUT MY *WORD*!

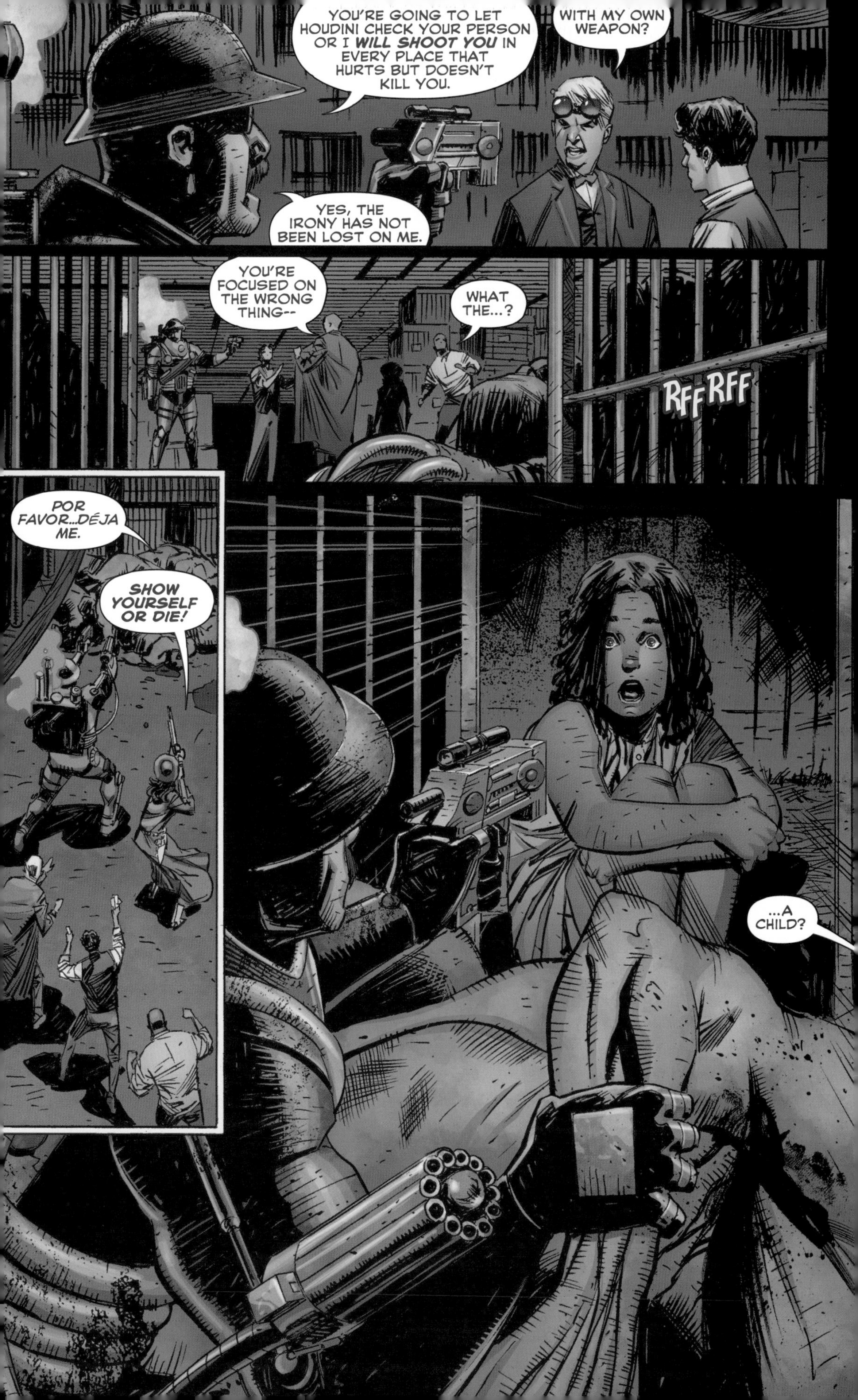
YOU'RE GOING TO LET HOUDINI CHECK YOUR PERSON OR I WILL SHOOT YOU IN EVERY PLACE THAT HURTS BUT DOESN'T KILL YOU.
WITH MY OWN WEAPON?
YES, THE IRONY HAS NOT BEEN LOST ON ME.
YOU'RE FOCUSED ON THE WRONG THING--
WHAT THE...?
RFF RFF
POR FAVOR...DÉJA ME.
SHOW YOURSELF OR DIE!
...A CHILD?

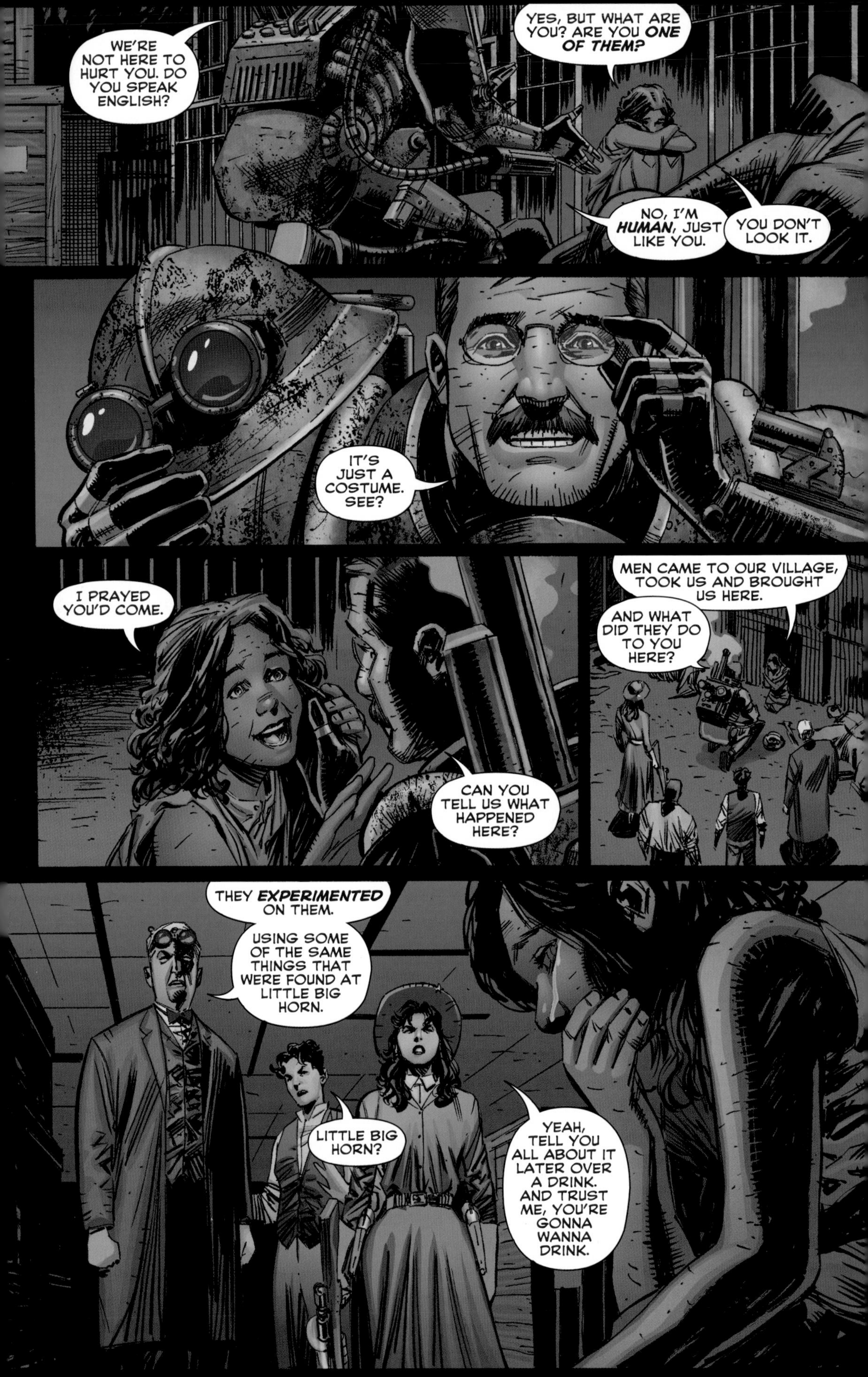
WE'RE NOT HERE TO HURT YOU. DO YOU SPEAK ENGLISH?
YES, BUT WHAT ARE YOU? ARE YOU ONE OF THEM?
NO, I'M HUMAN, JUST LIKE YOU.
YOU DON'T LOOK IT.
IT'S JUST A COSTUME. SEE?
I PRAYED YOU'D COME.
CAN YOU TELL US WHAT HAPPENED HERE?
MEN CAME TO OUR VILLAGE, TOOK US AND BROUGHT US HERE.
AND WHAT DID THEY DO TO YOU HERE?
THEY EXPERIMENTED ON THEM.
USING SOME OF THE SAME THINGS THAT WERE FOUND AT LITTLE BIG HORN.
LITTLE BIG HORN?
YEAH, TELL YOU ALL ABOUT IT LATER OVER A DRINK. AND TRUST ME, YOU'RE GONNA WANNA DRINK.

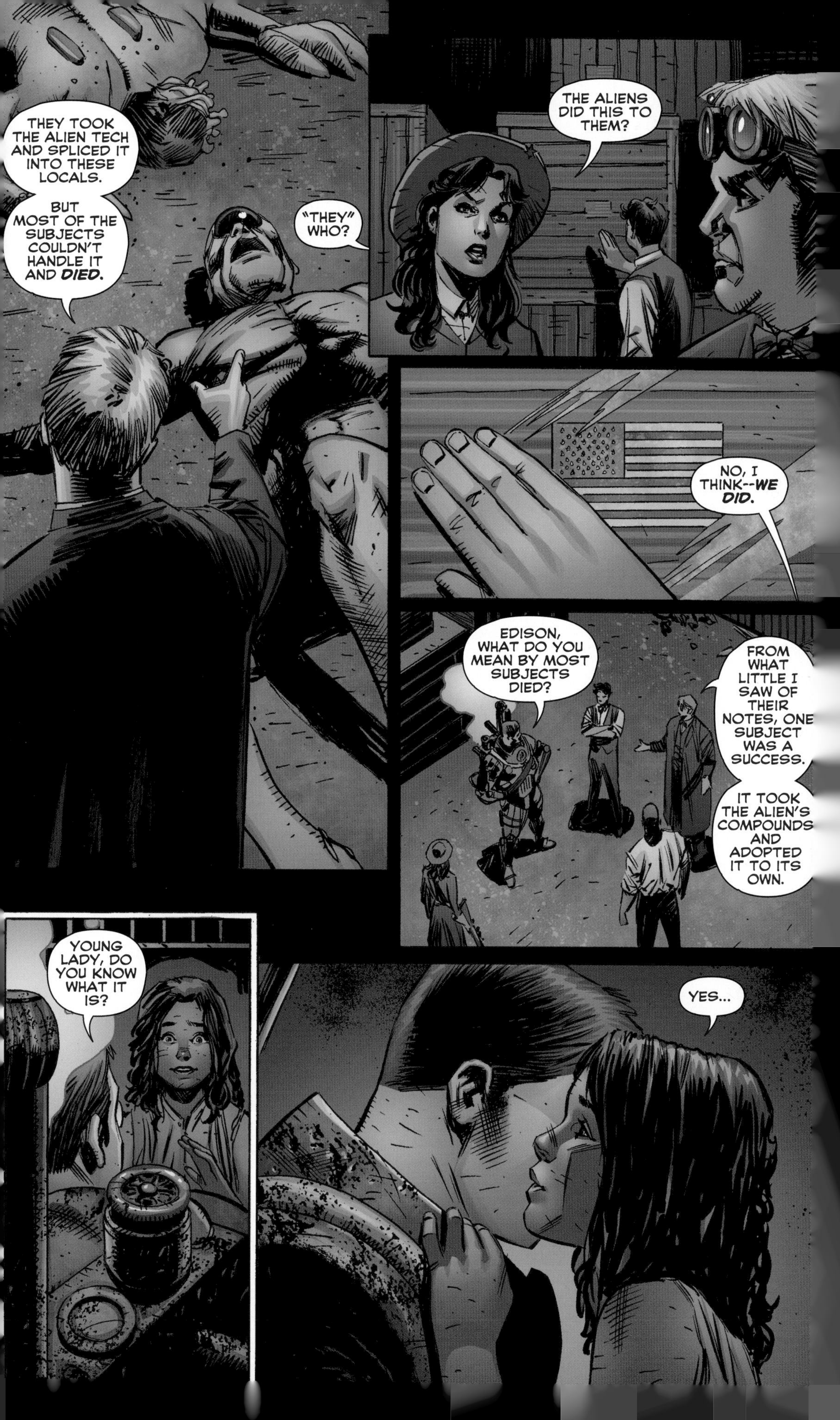

THEY TOOK THE ALIEN TECH AND SPLICED IT INTO THESE LOCALS.
BUT MOST OF THE SUBJECTS COULDN'T HANDLE IT AND *DIED.*
"THEY" WHO?
THE ALIENS DID THIS TO THEM?
NO, I THINK--*WE DID.*
EDISON, WHAT DO YOU MEAN BY MOST SUBJECTS DIED?
FROM WHAT LITTLE I SAW OF THEIR NOTES, ONE SUBJECT WAS A SUCCESS.
IT TOOK THE ALIEN'S COMPOUNDS AND ADOPTED IT TO ITS OWN.
YOUNG LADY, DO YOU KNOW WHAT IT IS?
YES...

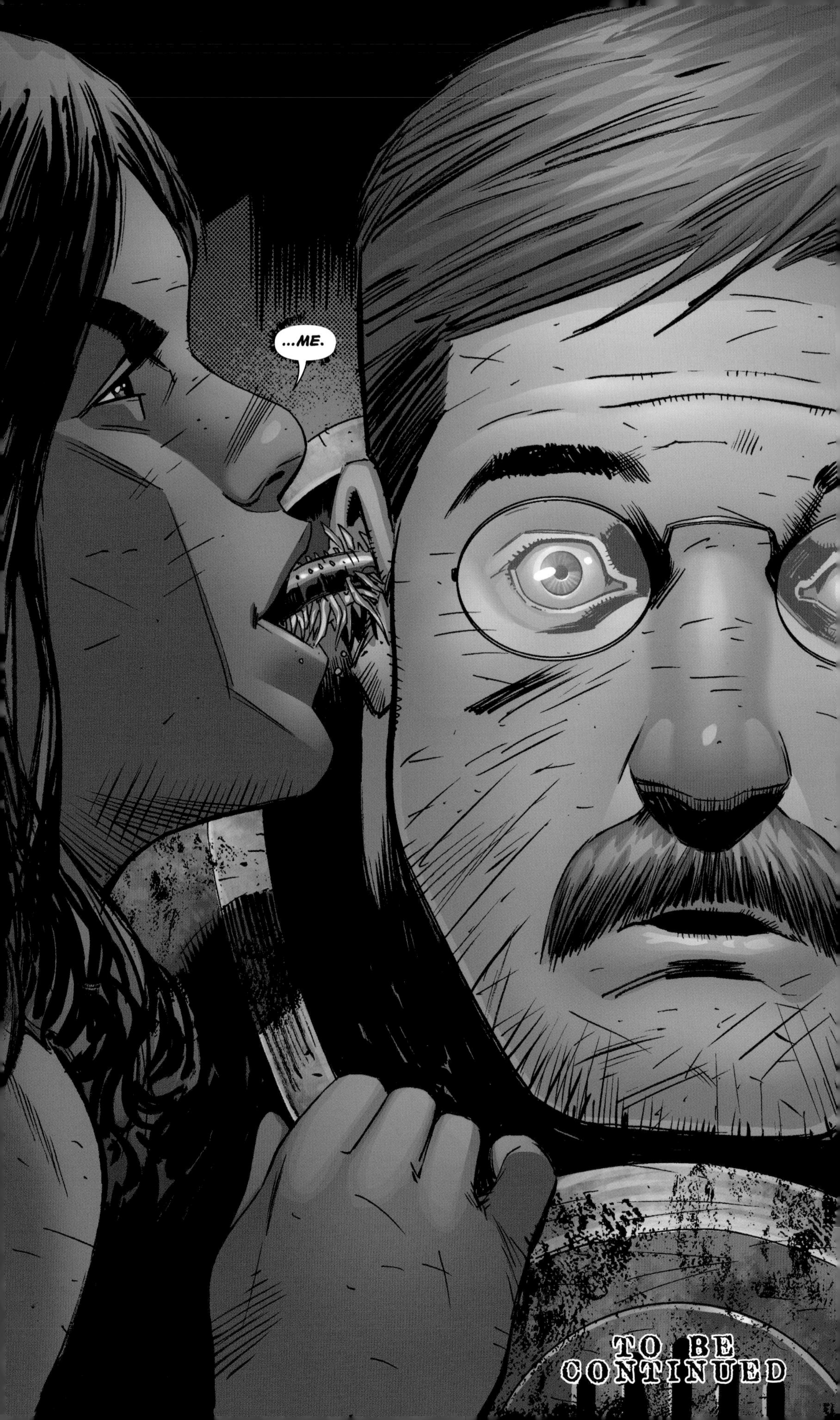
...ME.
TO BE CONTINUED

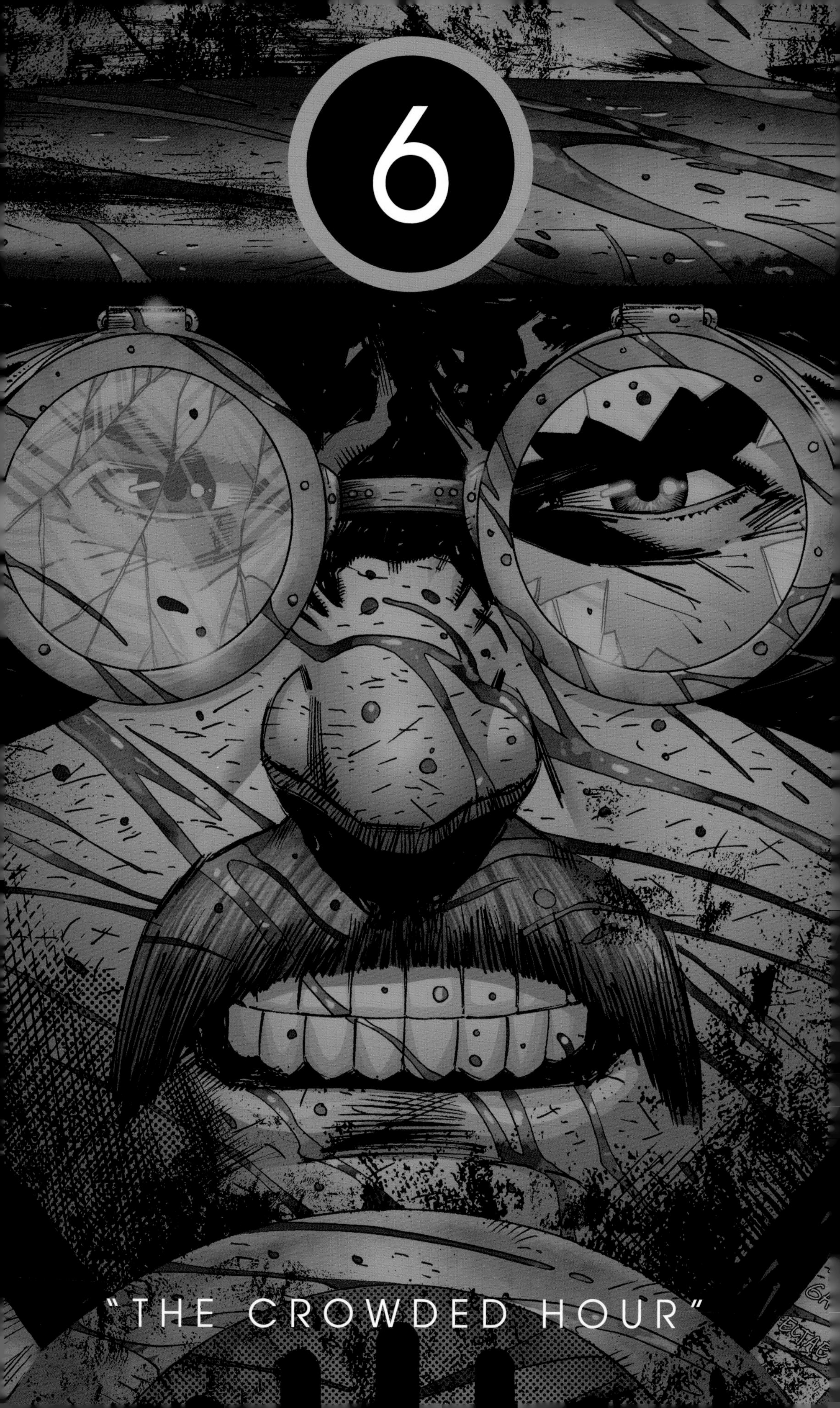
6
"THE CROWDED HOUR"

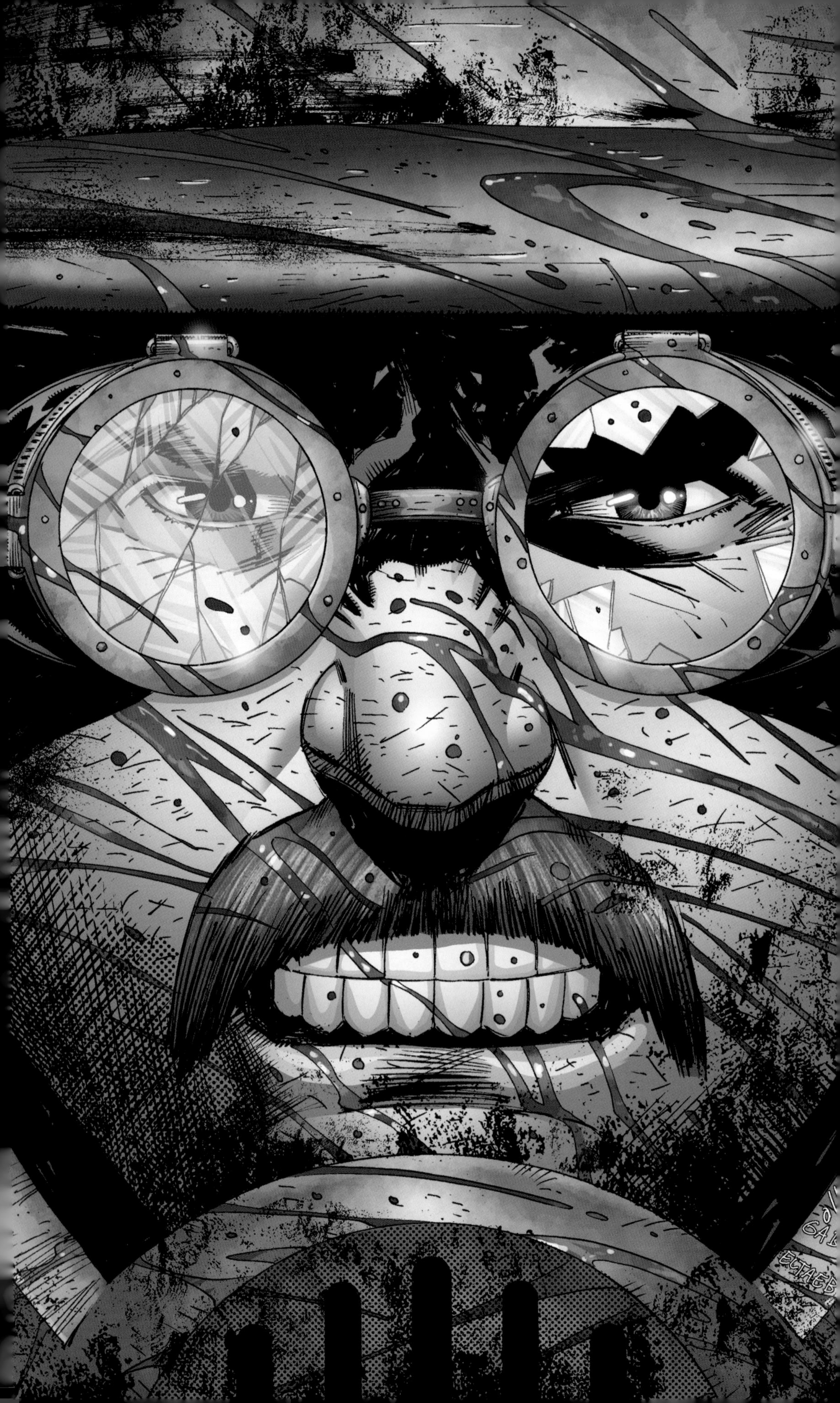

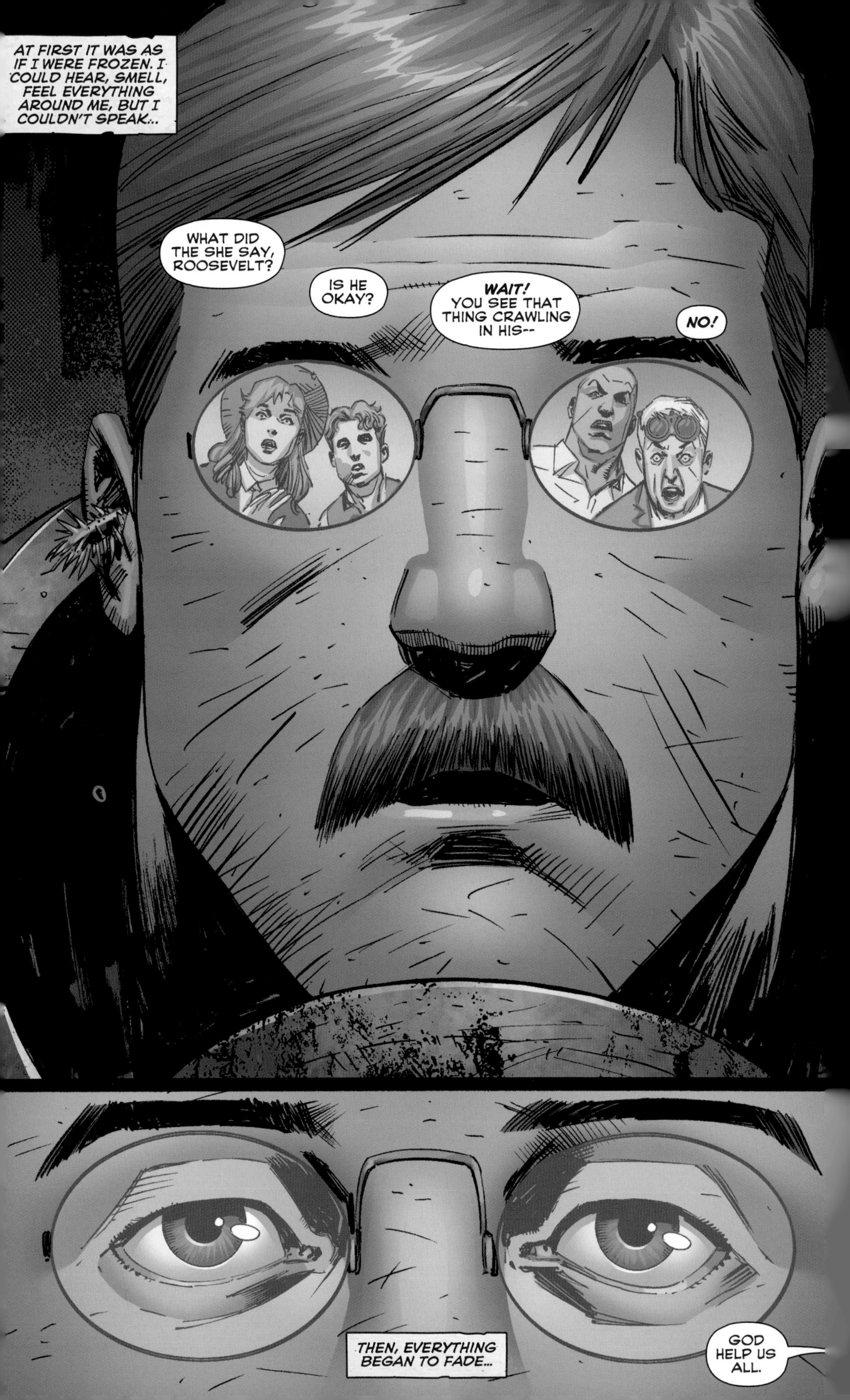
AT FIRST IT WAS AS IF I WERE FROZEN. I COULD HEAR, SMELL, FEEL EVERYTHING AROUND ME, BUT I COULDN'T SPEAK...
WHAT DID THE SHE SAY, ROOSEVELT?
IS HE OKAY?
WAIT! YOU SEE THAT THING CRAWLING IN HIS--
NO!
THEN, EVERYTHING BEGAN TO FADE...
GOD HELP US ALL.

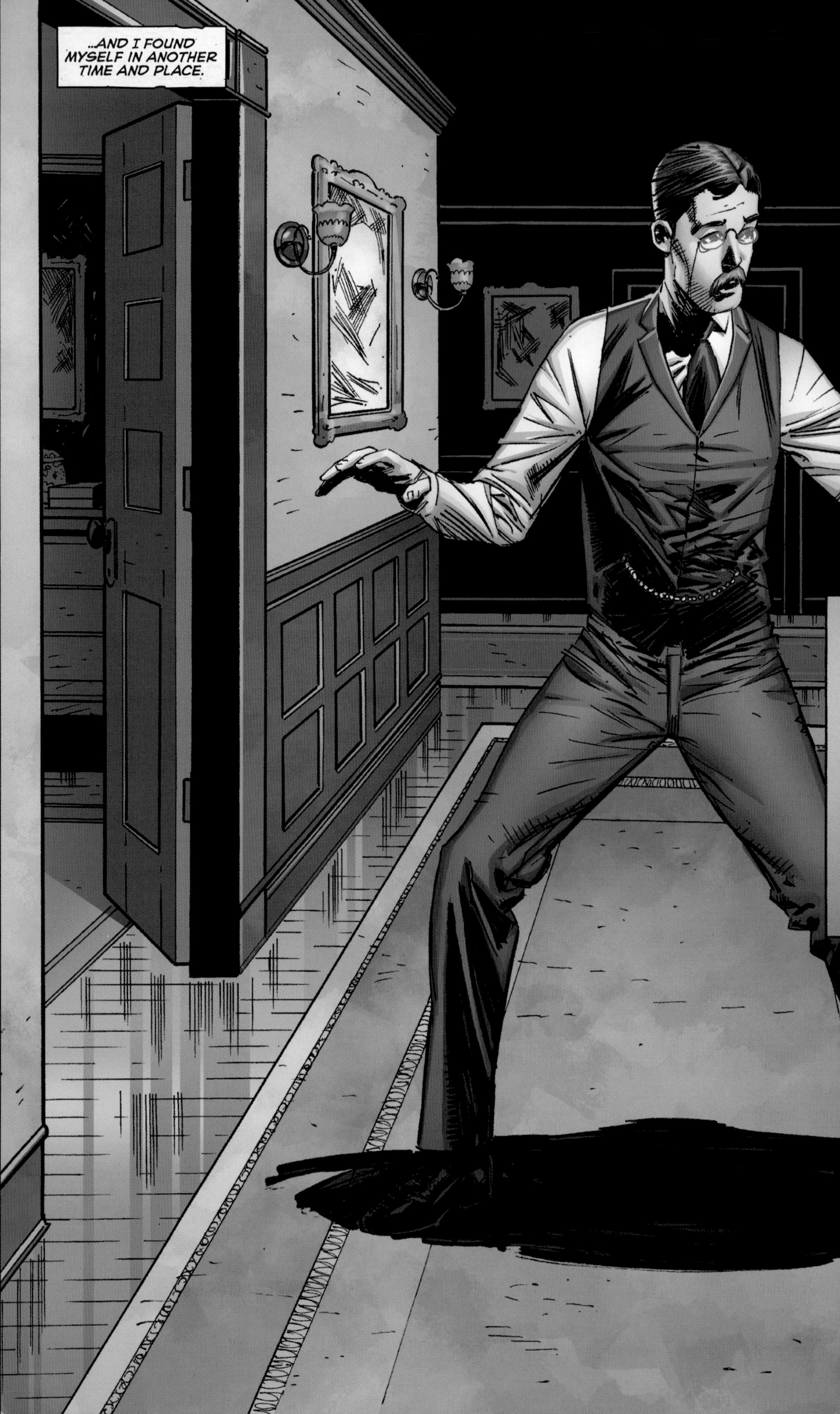
...AND I FOUND MYSELF IN ANOTHER TIME AND PLACE.

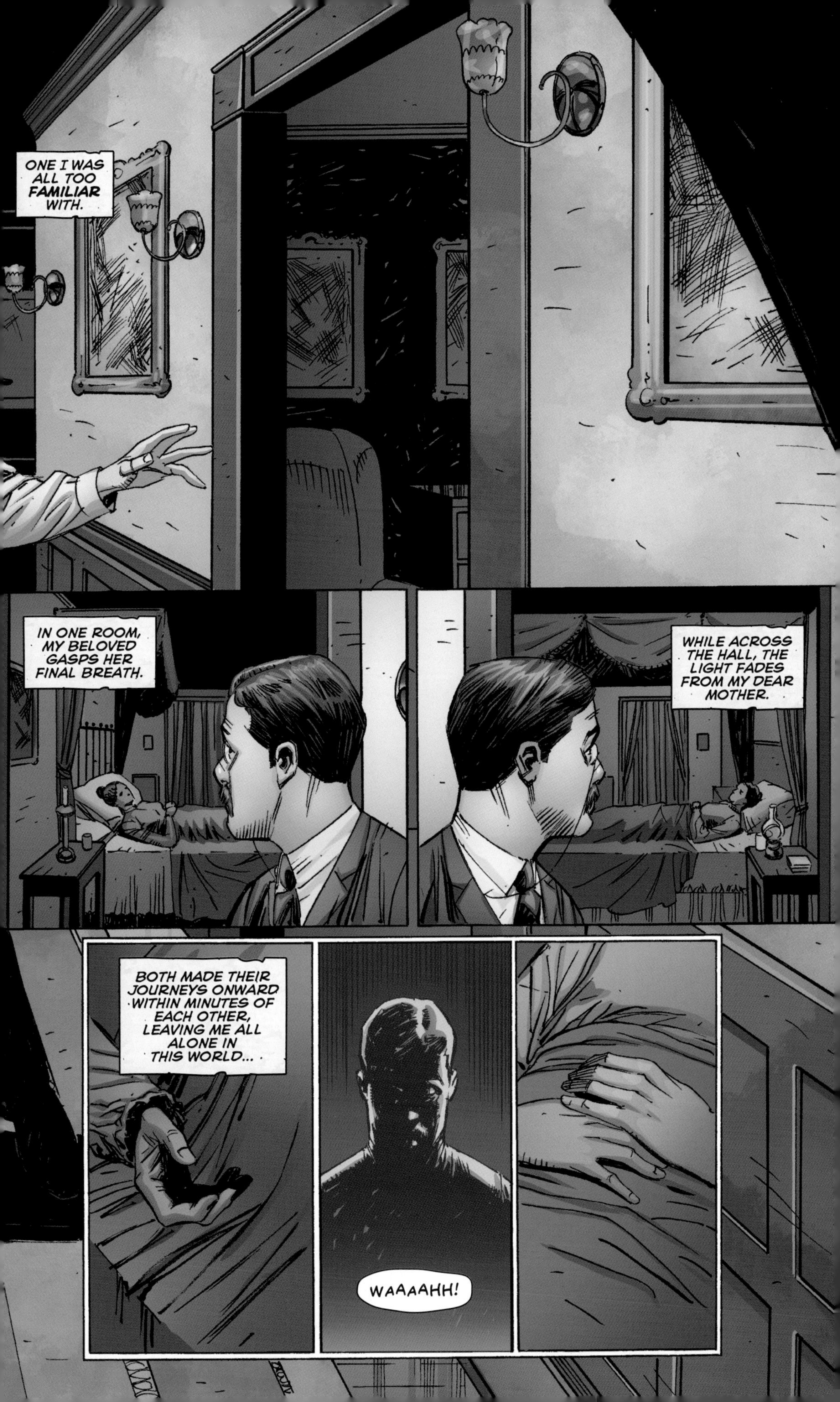
ONE I WAS ALL TOO FAMILIAR WITH.
IN ONE ROOM, MY BELOVED GASPS HER FINAL BREATH.
WHILE ACROSS THE HALL, THE LIGHT FADES FROM MY DEAR MOTHER.
BOTH MADE THEIR JOURNEYS ONWARD WITHIN MINUTES OF EACH OTHER, LEAVING ME ALL ALONE IN THIS WORLD...
WAAAAHH!

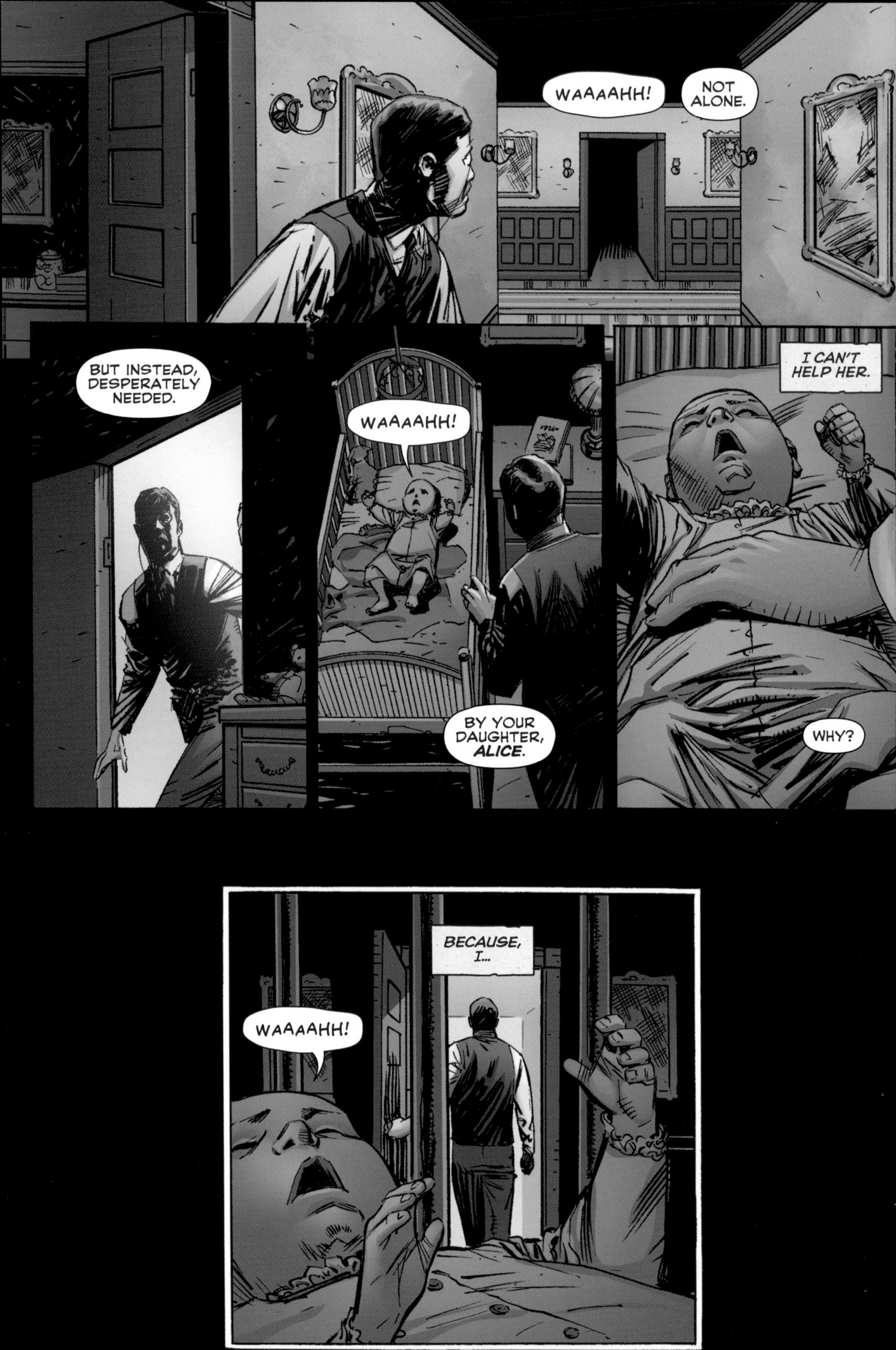
WAAAAHH!
NOT ALONE.
BUT INSTEAD, DESPERATELY NEEDED.
WAAAAHH!
BY YOUR DAUGHTER, ALICE.
I CAN'T HELP HER.
WHY?
BECAUSE, I...
WAAAAHH!

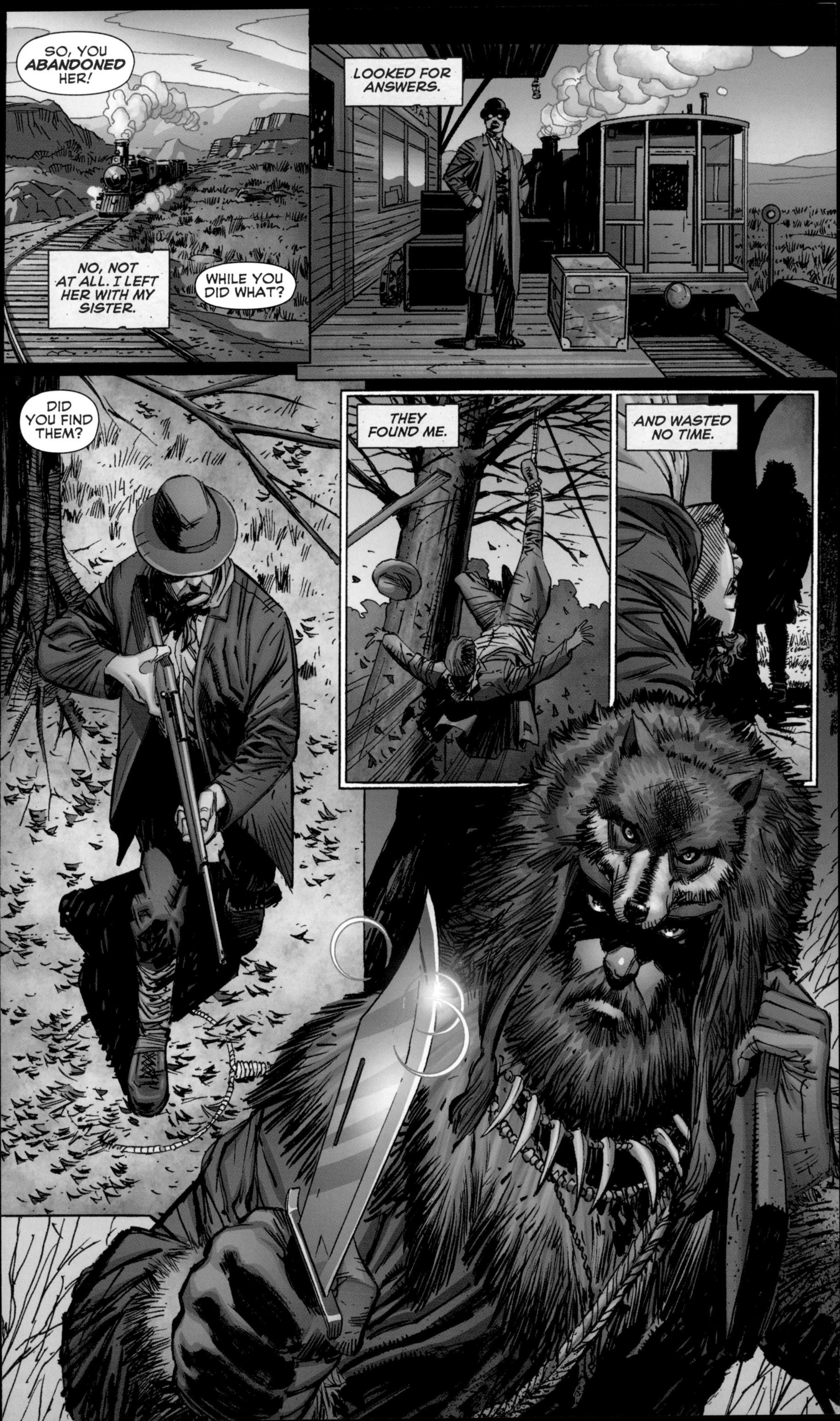
SO, YOU ABANDONED HER!
NO, NOT AT ALL. I LEFT HER WITH MY SISTER.
WHILE YOU DID WHAT?
LOOKED FOR ANSWERS.
DID YOU FIND THEM?
THEY FOUND ME.
AND WASTED NO TIME.

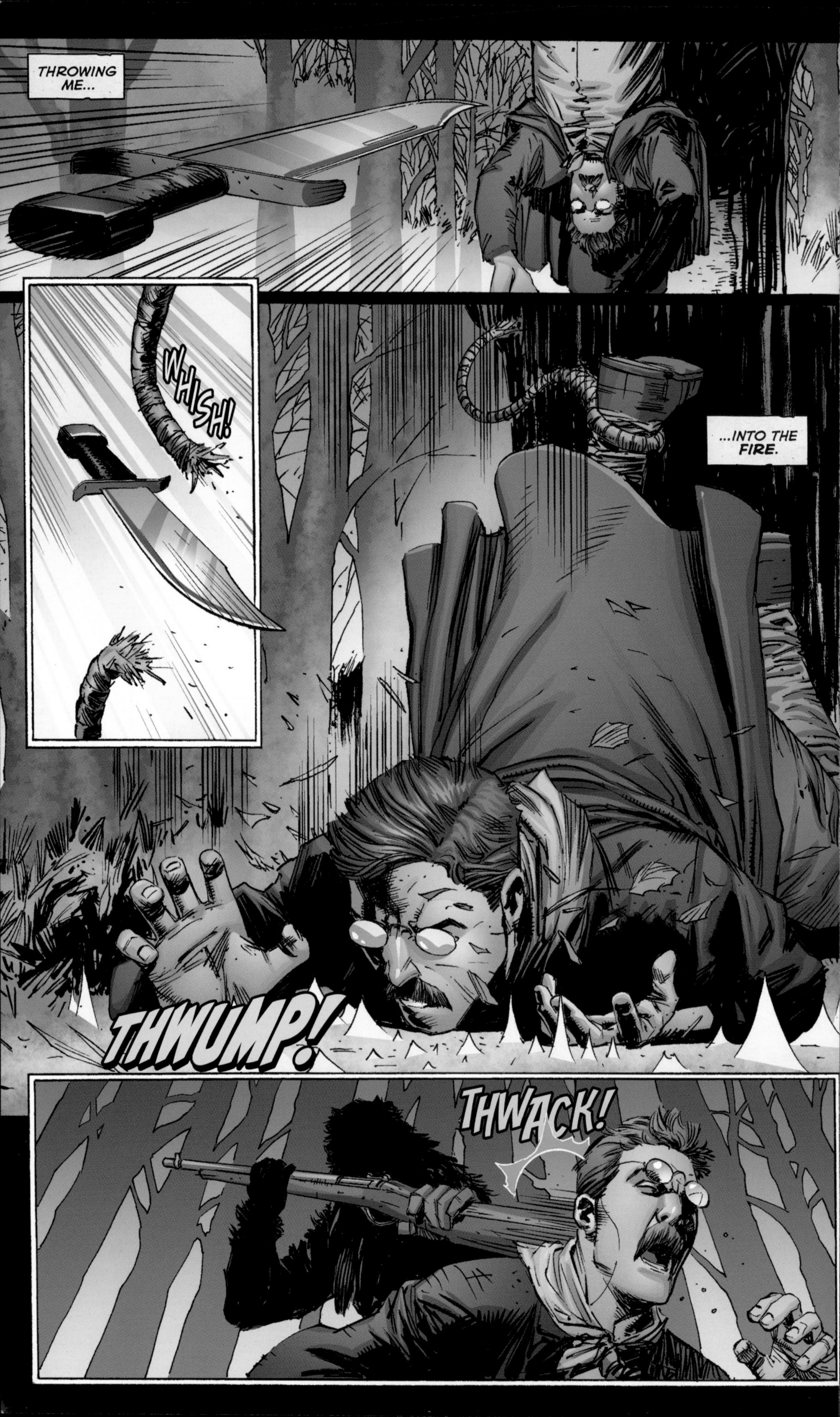
THROWING ME...
WHISH!
...INTO THE FIRE.
THWUMP!
THWACK!

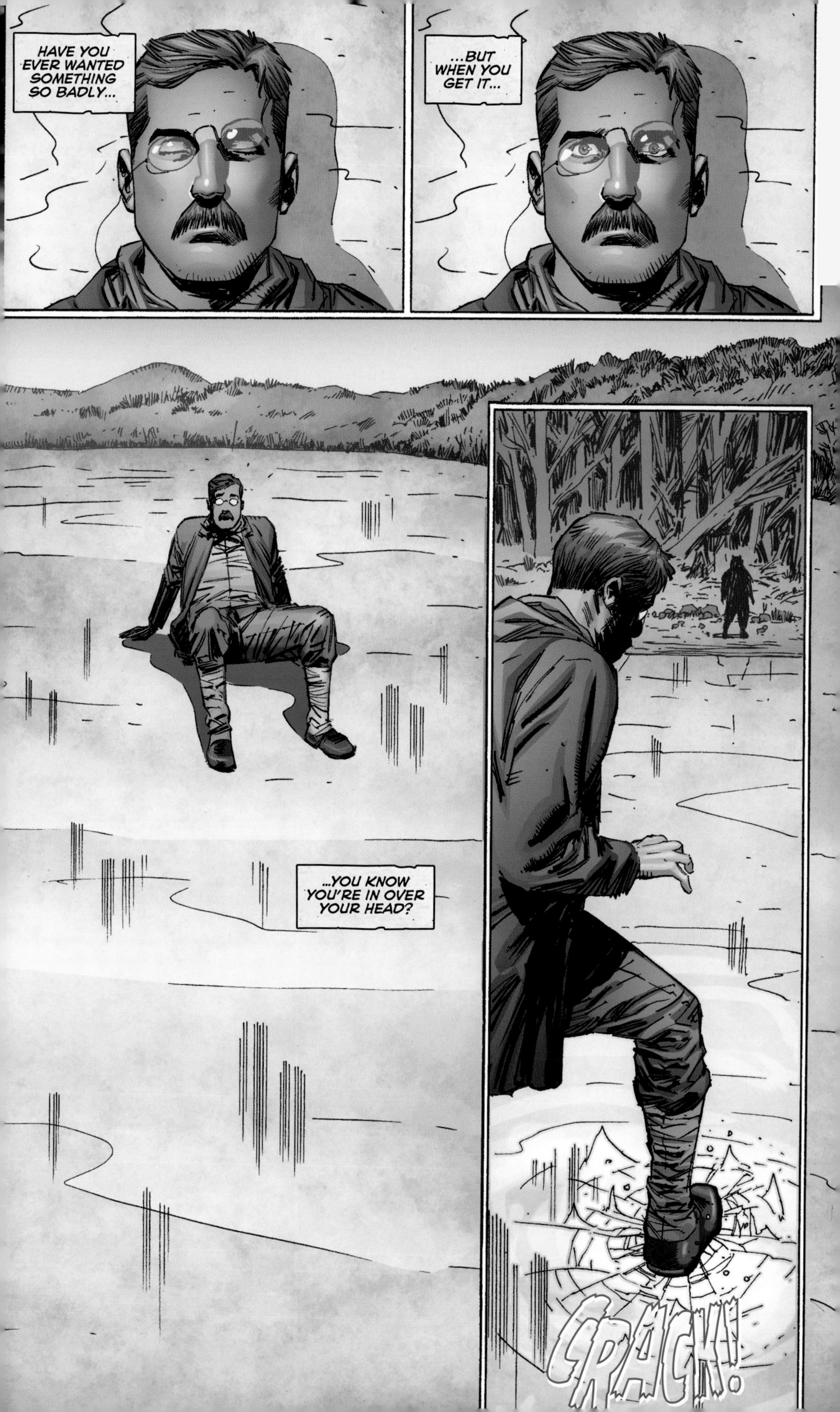
HAVE YOU EVER WANTED SOMETHING SO BADLY...
...BUT WHEN YOU GET IT...
...YOU KNOW YOU'RE IN OVER YOUR HEAD?
CRACK!

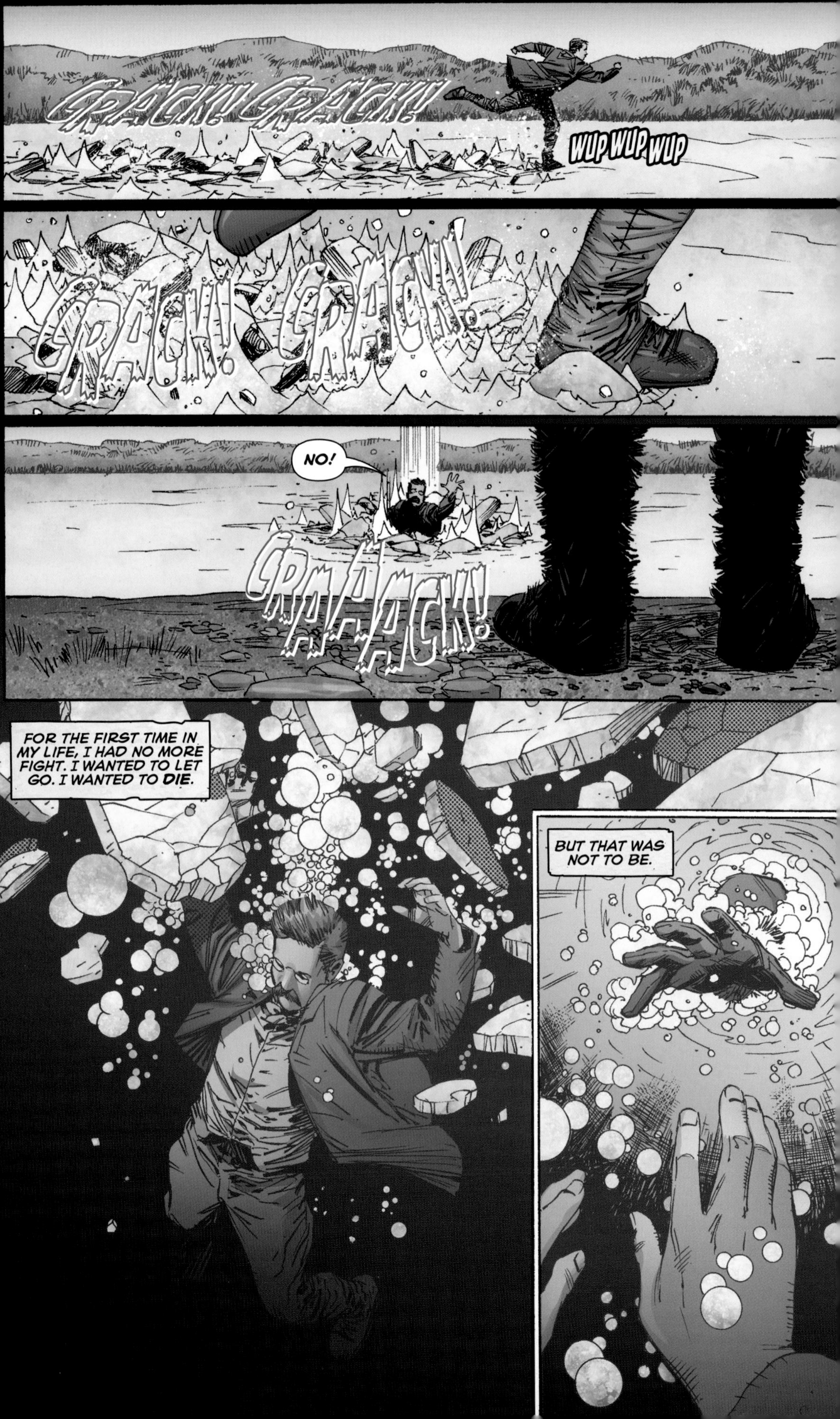
CRACK! CRACK!
WUP WUP WUP
CRACK! CRACK!
NO!
CRAAACK!
FOR THE FIRST TIME IN MY LIFE, I HAD NO MORE FIGHT. I WANTED TO LET GO. I WANTED TO DIE.
BUT THAT WAS NOT TO BE.

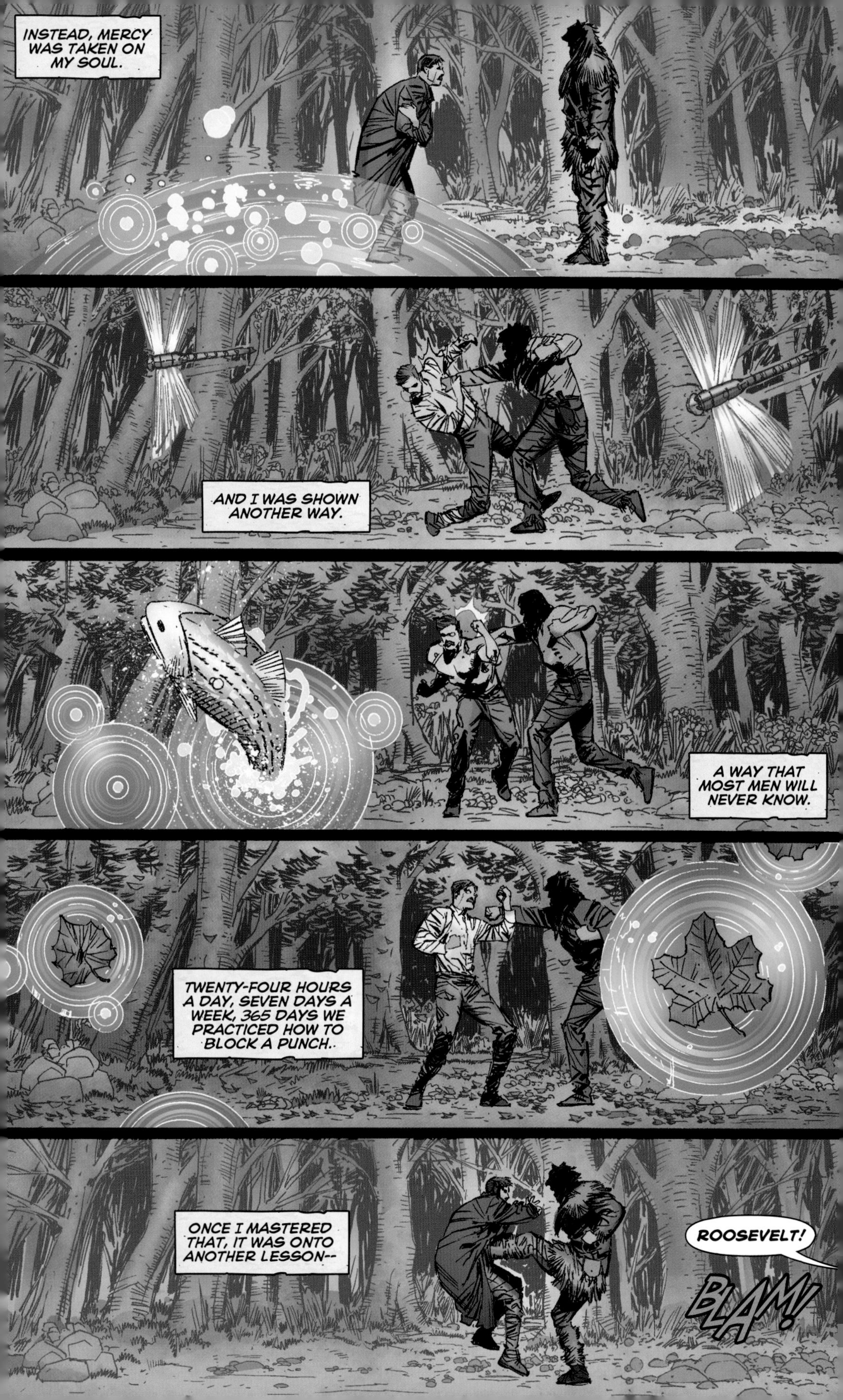
INSTEAD, MERCY WAS TAKEN ON MY SOUL.
AND I WAS SHOWN ANOTHER WAY.
A WAY THAT MOST MEN WILL NEVER KNOW.
TWENTY-FOUR HOURS A DAY, SEVEN DAYS A WEEK, 365 DAYS WE PRACTICED HOW TO BLOCK A PUNCH.
ONCE I MASTERED THAT, IT WAS ONTO ANOTHER LESSON--
ROOSEVELT!
BLAM!

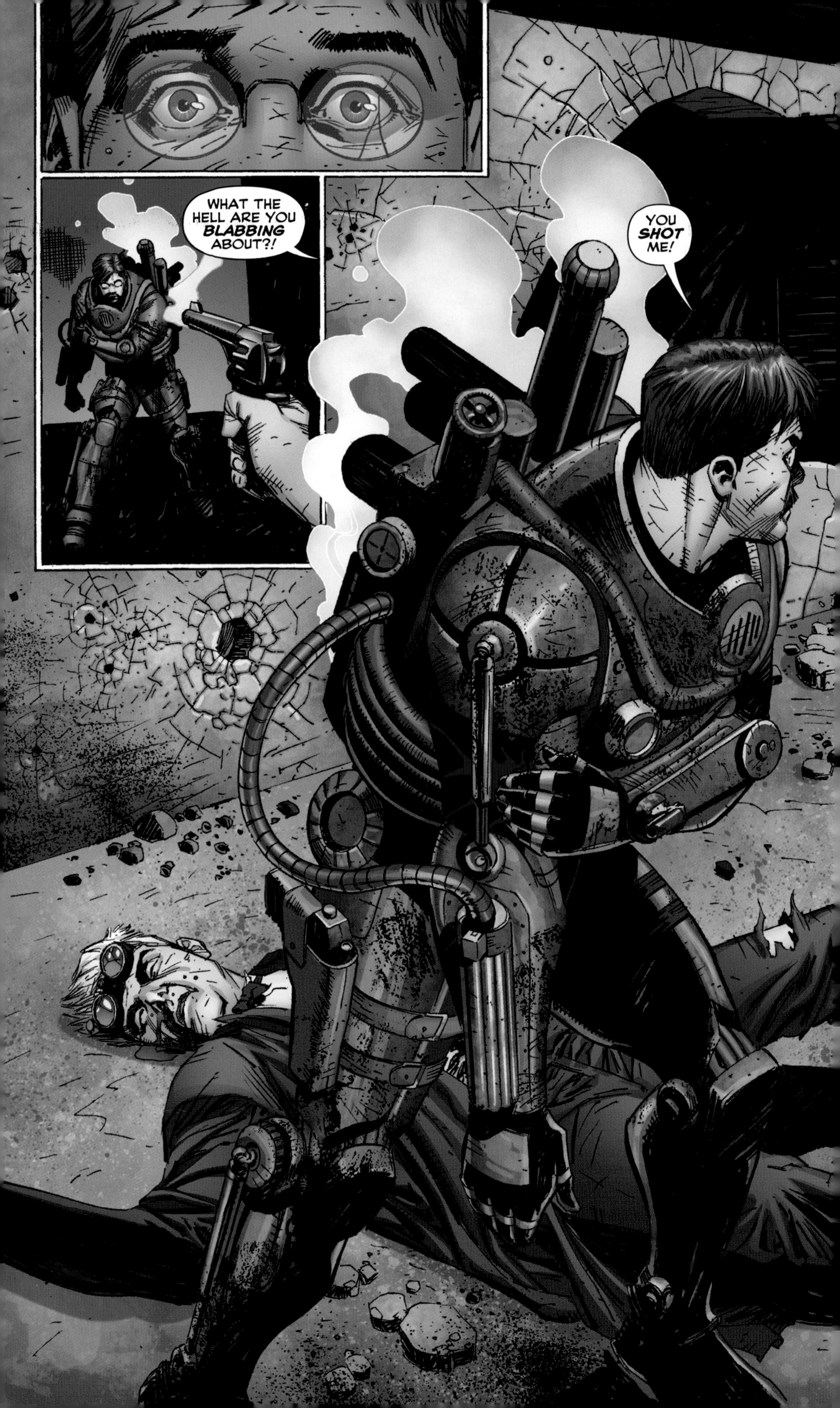

WHAT THE HELL ARE YOU BLABBING ABOUT?!
YOU SHOT ME!

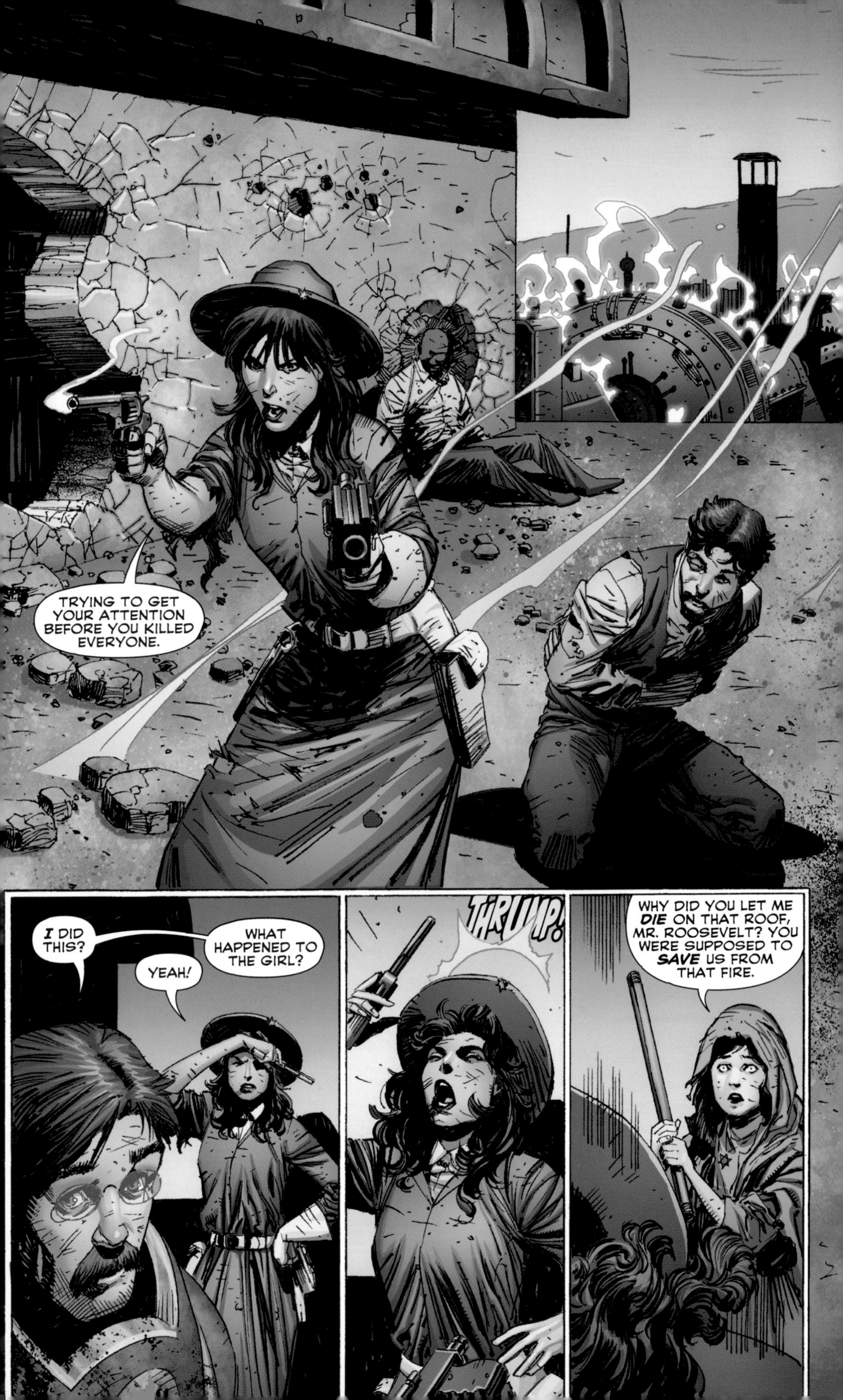
TRYING TO GET YOUR ATTENTION BEFORE YOU KILLED EVERYONE.
I DID THIS?
YEAH!
WHAT HAPPENED TO THE GIRL?
THRUMP!
WHY DID YOU LET ME DIE ON THAT ROOF, MR. ROOSEVELT? YOU WERE SUPPOSED TO SAVE US FROM THAT FIRE.

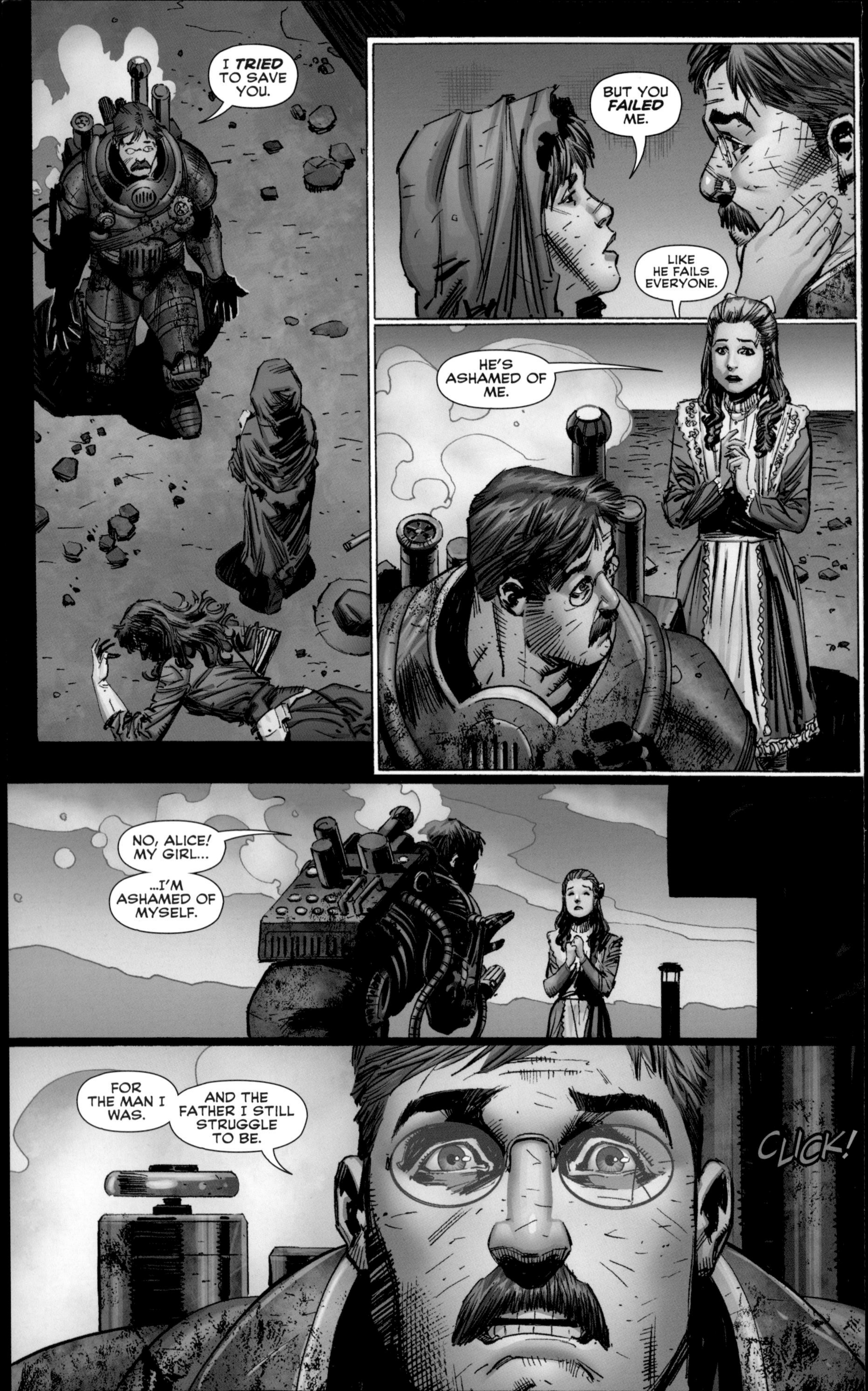
I TRIED TO SAVE YOU.
BUT YOU FAILED ME.
LIKE HE FAILS EVERYONE.
HE'S ASHAMED OF ME.
NO, ALICE! MY GIRL...
...I'M ASHAMED OF MYSELF.
FOR THE MAN I WAS.
AND THE FATHER I STILL STRUGGLE TO BE.
CLICK!

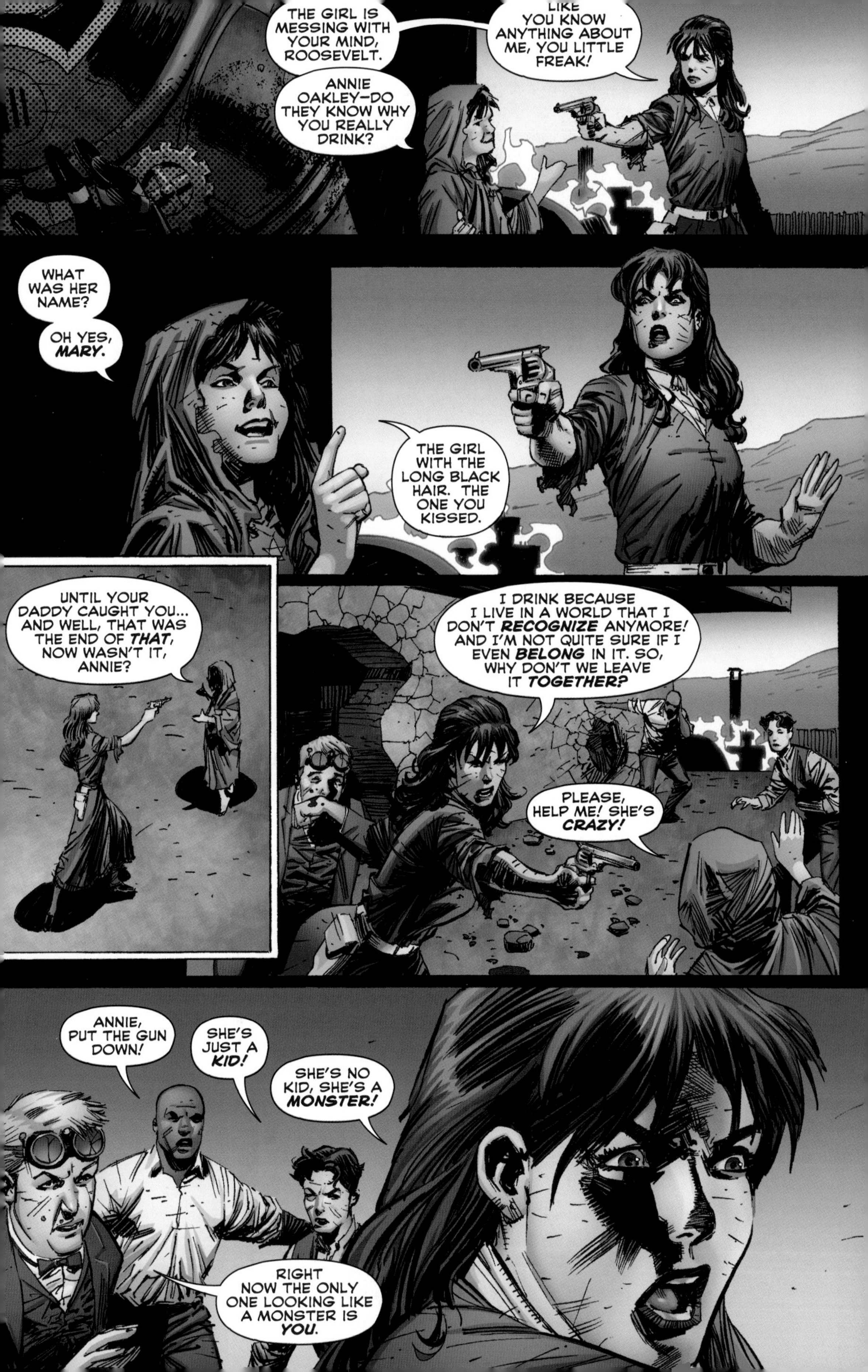
THE GIRL IS MESSING WITH YOUR MIND, ROOSEVELT.
LIKE YOU KNOW ANYTHING ABOUT ME, YOU LITTLE FREAK!
ANNIE OAKLEY—DO THEY KNOW WHY YOU REALLY DRINK?
WHAT WAS HER NAME?
OH YES, *MARY*.
THE GIRL WITH THE LONG BLACK HAIR. THE ONE YOU KISSED.
UNTIL YOUR DADDY CAUGHT YOU... AND WELL, THAT WAS THE END OF *THAT*, NOW WASN'T IT, ANNIE?
I DRINK BECAUSE I LIVE IN A WORLD THAT I DON'T *RECOGNIZE* ANYMORE! AND I'M NOT QUITE SURE IF I EVEN *BELONG* IN IT. SO, WHY DON'T WE LEAVE IT *TOGETHER?*
PLEASE, HELP ME! SHE'S *CRAZY!*
ANNIE, PUT THE GUN DOWN!
SHE'S JUST A *KID!*
SHE'S NO KID, SHE'S A *MONSTER!*
RIGHT NOW THE ONLY ONE LOOKING LIKE A MONSTER IS *YOU*.

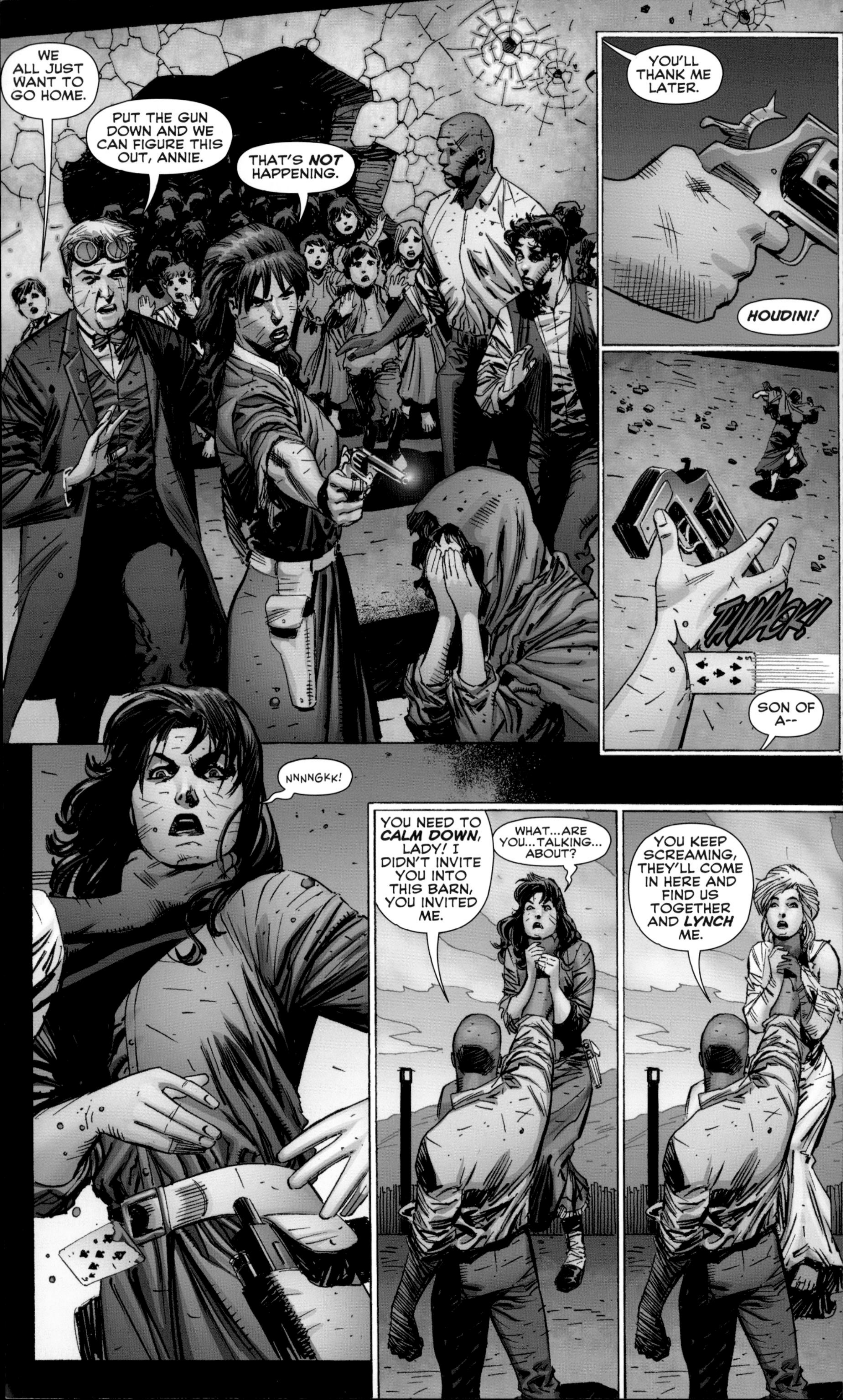

WE ALL JUST WANT TO GO HOME.
PUT THE GUN DOWN AND WE CAN FIGURE THIS OUT, ANNIE.
THAT'S NOT HAPPENING.
YOU'LL THANK ME LATER.
HOUDINI!
THWACK!
SON OF A--
NNNNGKK!
YOU NEED TO CALM DOWN, LADY! I DIDN'T INVITE YOU INTO THIS BARN, YOU INVITED ME.
WHAT...ARE YOU...TALKING... ABOUT?
YOU KEEP SCREAMING, THEY'LL COME IN HERE AND FIND US TOGETHER AND LYNCH ME.

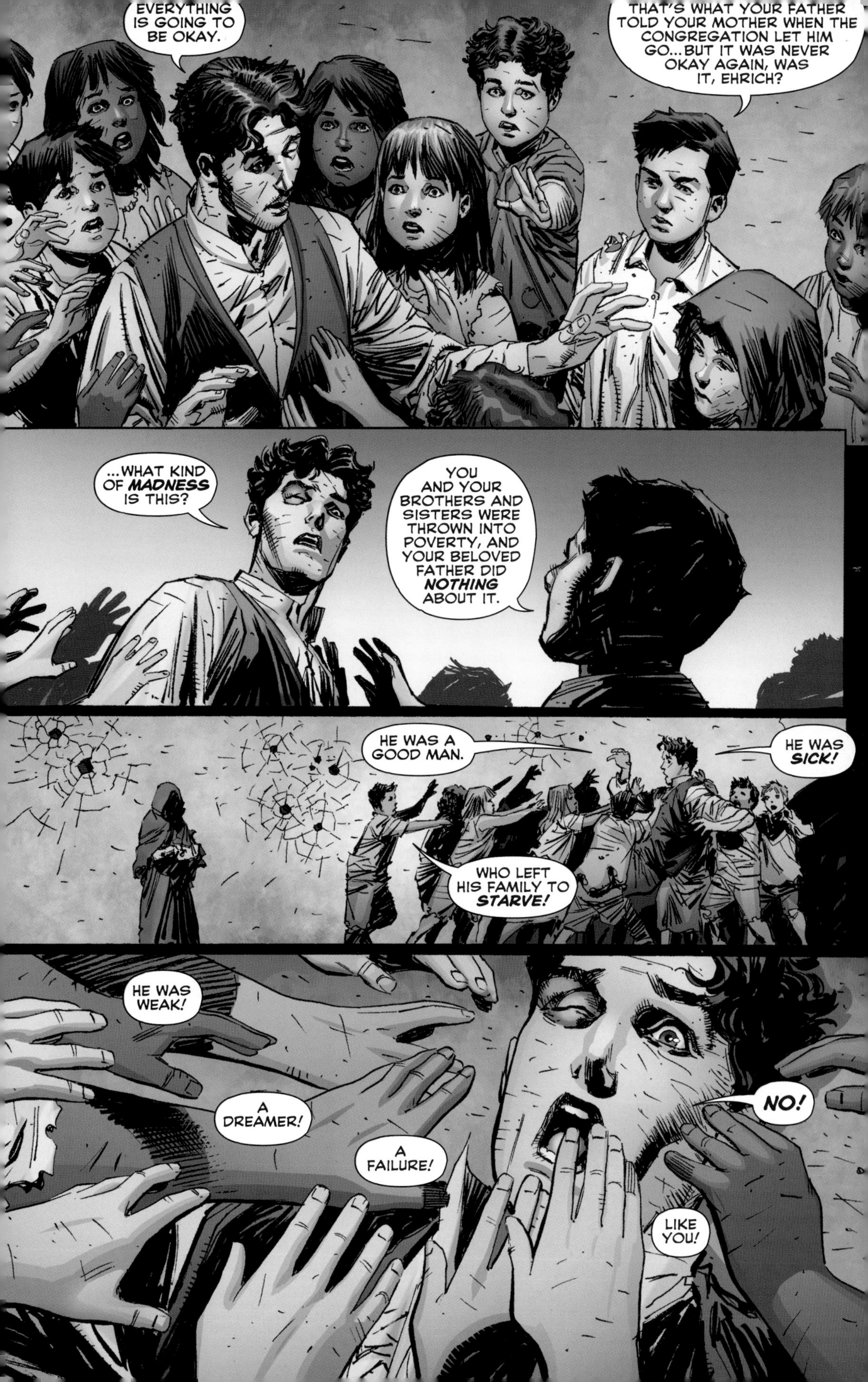
EVERYTHING IS GOING TO BE OKAY.
THAT'S WHAT YOUR FATHER TOLD YOUR MOTHER WHEN THE CONGREGATION LET HIM GO...BUT IT WAS NEVER OKAY AGAIN, WAS IT, EHRICH?
...WHAT KIND OF MADNESS IS THIS?
YOU AND YOUR BROTHERS AND SISTERS WERE THROWN INTO POVERTY, AND YOUR BELOVED FATHER DID NOTHING ABOUT IT.
HE WAS A GOOD MAN.
HE WAS SICK!
WHO LEFT HIS FAMILY TO STARVE!
HE WAS WEAK!
A DREAMER!
A FAILURE!
NO!
LIKE YOU!

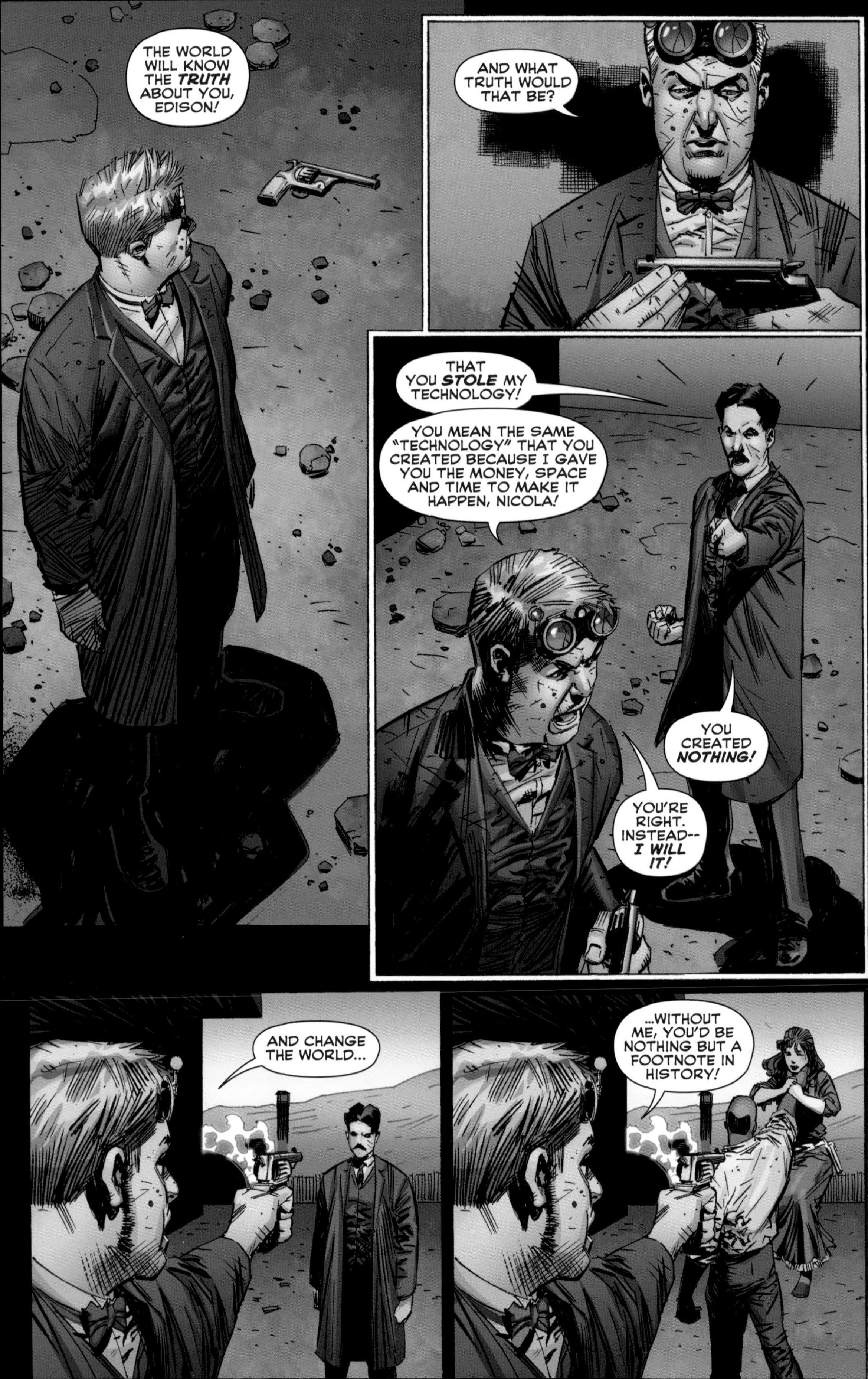
THE WORLD WILL KNOW THE *TRUTH* ABOUT YOU, EDISON!
AND WHAT TRUTH WOULD THAT BE?
THAT YOU *STOLE* MY TECHNOLOGY!
YOU MEAN THE SAME "TECHNOLOGY" THAT YOU CREATED BECAUSE I GAVE YOU THE MONEY, SPACE AND TIME TO MAKE IT HAPPEN, NICOLA!
YOU CREATED *NOTHING!*
YOU'RE RIGHT. INSTEAD-- *I WILL IT!*
AND CHANGE THE WORLD...
...WITHOUT ME, YOU'D BE NOTHING BUT A FOOTNOTE IN HISTORY!

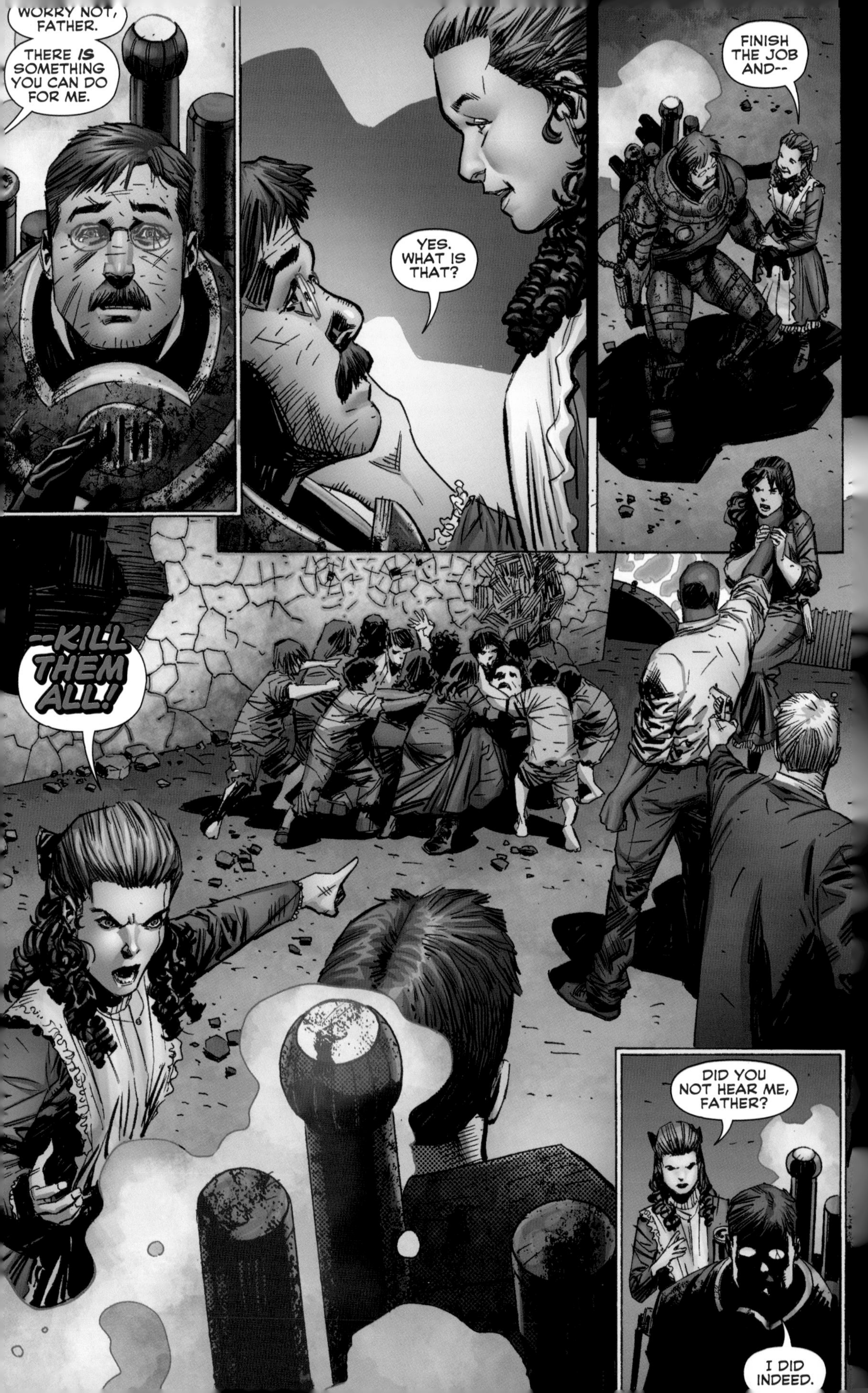
WORRY NOT, FATHER.
THERE IS SOMETHING YOU CAN DO FOR ME.
YES. WHAT IS THAT?
FINISH THE JOB AND--
--KILL THEM ALL!
DID YOU NOT HEAR ME, FATHER?
I DID INDEED.

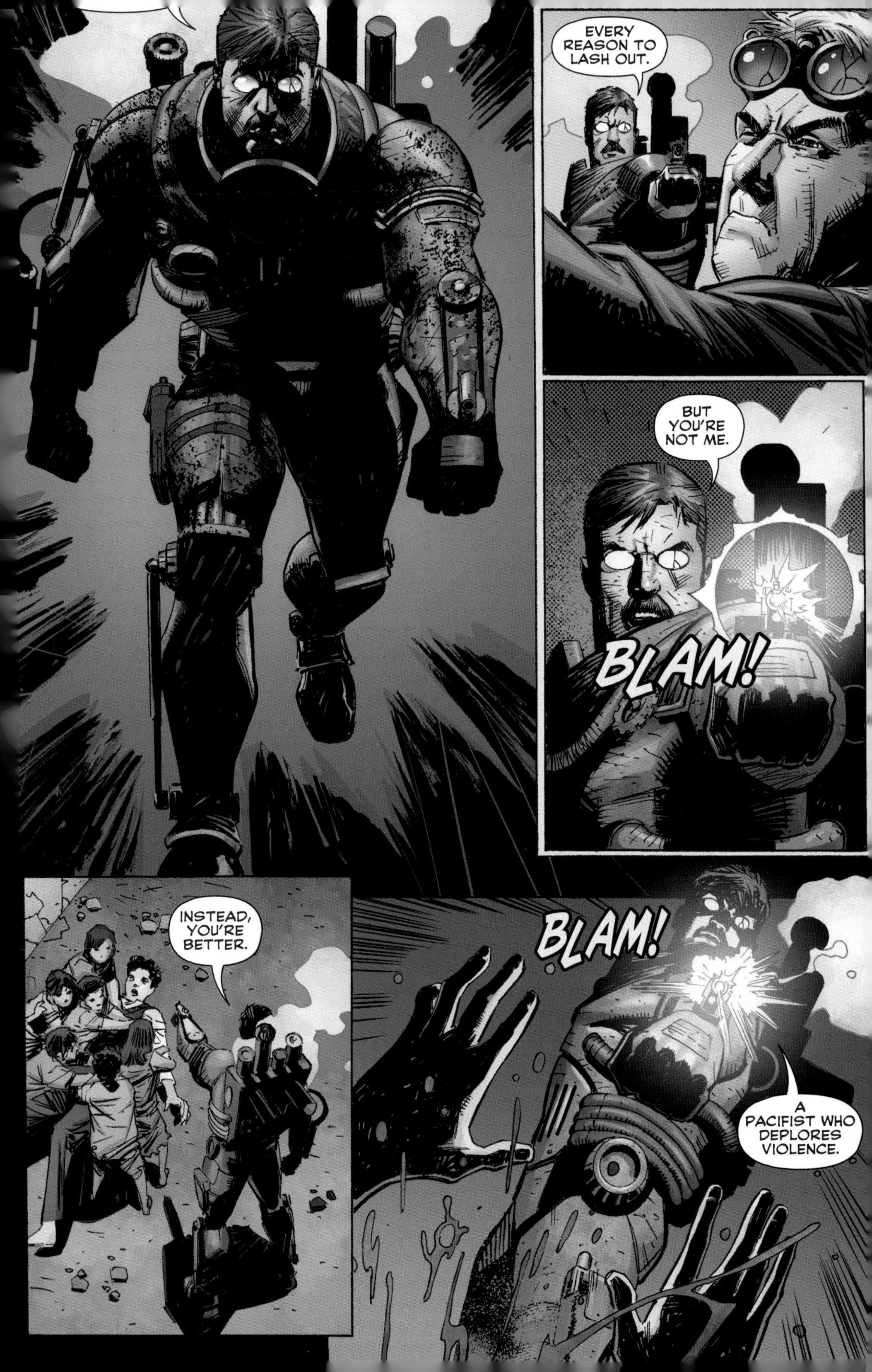
EVERY REASON TO LASH OUT.
BUT YOU'RE NOT ME.
BLAM!
INSTEAD, YOU'RE BETTER.
BLAM!
A PACIFIST WHO DEPLORES VIOLENCE.

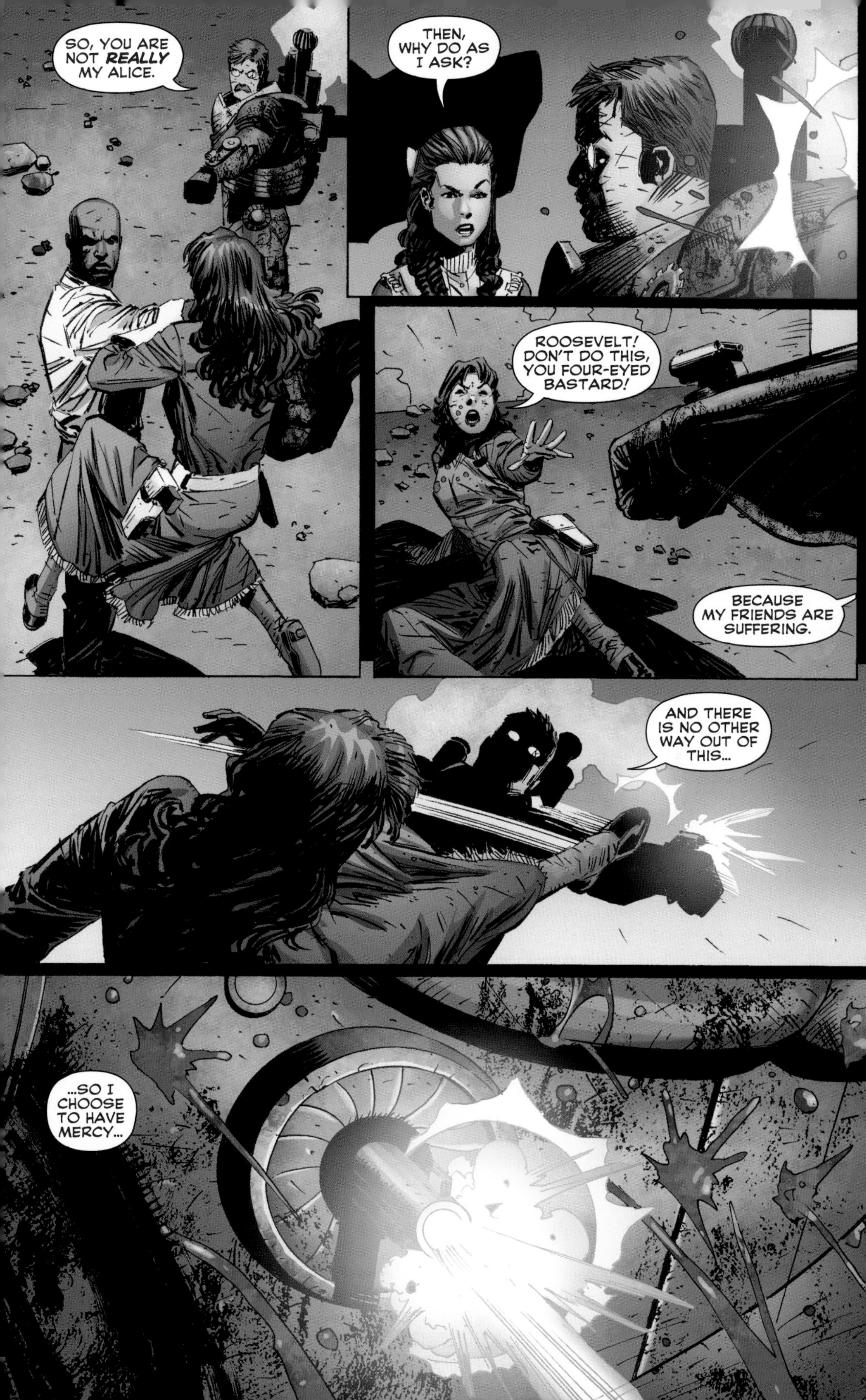
SO, YOU ARE NOT REALLY MY ALICE.
THEN, WHY DO AS I ASK?
ROOSEVELT! DON'T DO THIS, YOU FOUR-EYED BASTARD!
BECAUSE MY FRIENDS ARE SUFFERING.
AND THERE IS NO OTHER WAY OUT OF THIS...
...SO I CHOOSE TO HAVE MERCY...

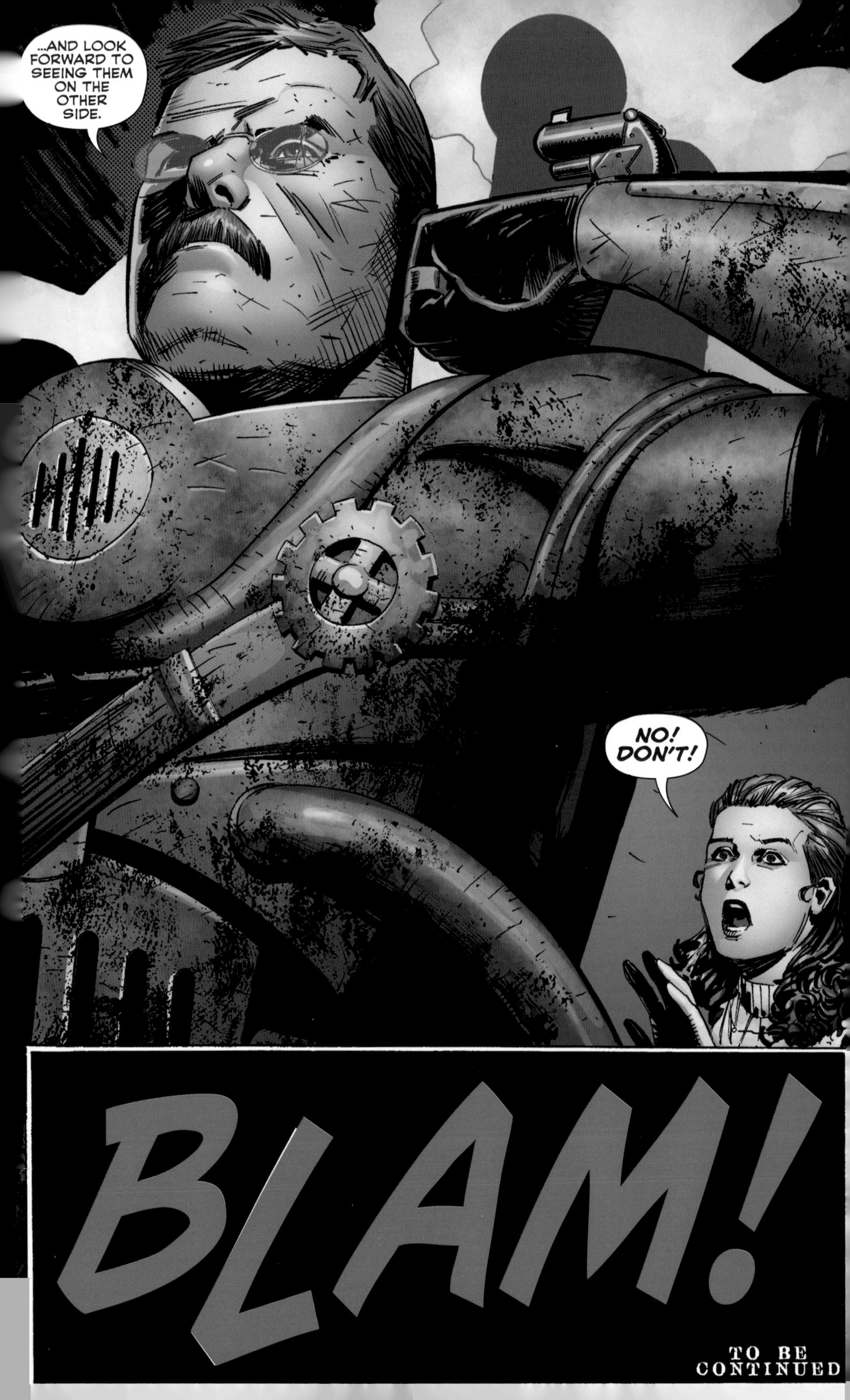
...AND LOOK FORWARD TO SEEING THEM ON THE OTHER SIDE.
NO! DON'T!
BLAM!
TO BE CONTINUED

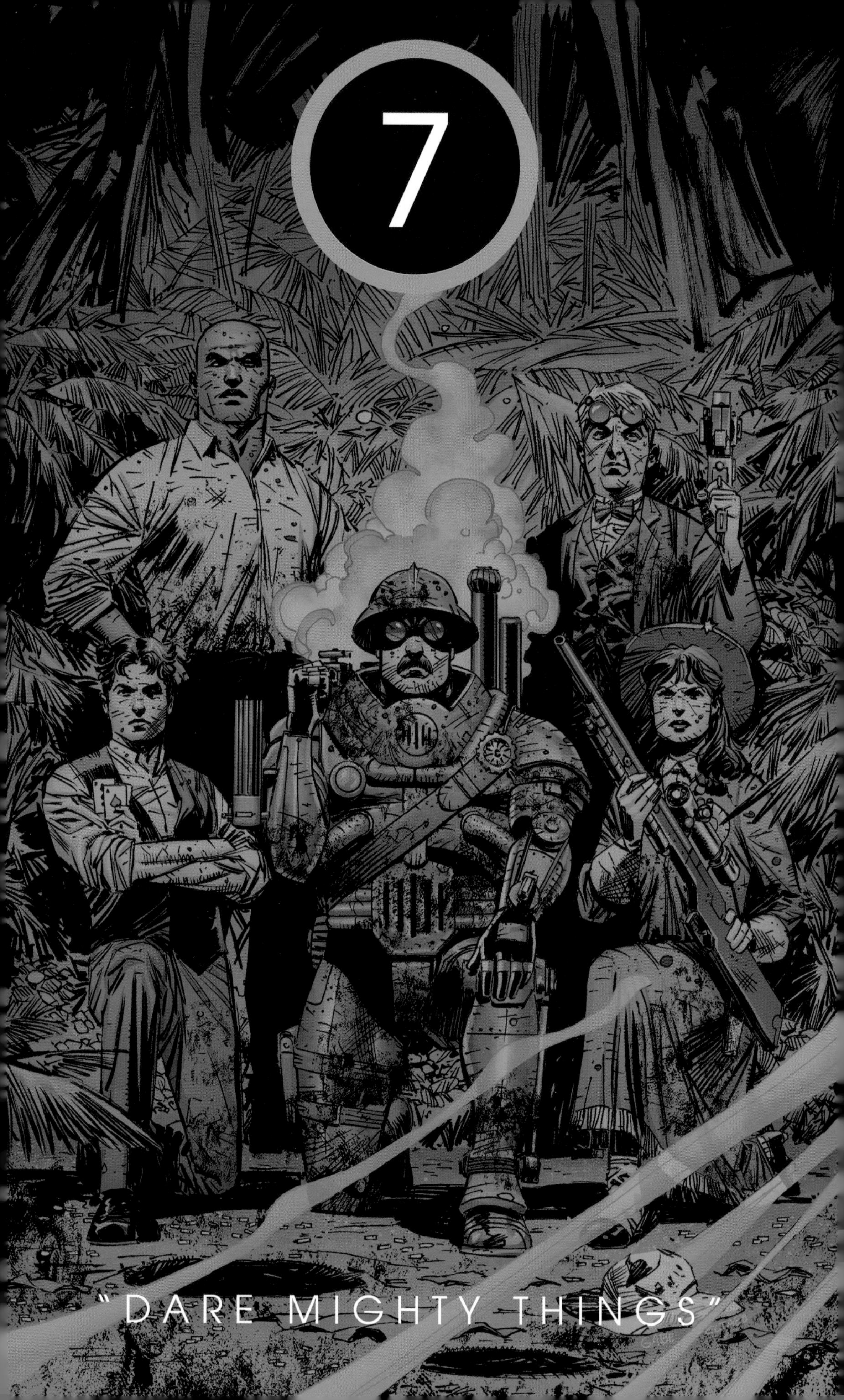
7
"DARE MIGHTY THINGS"

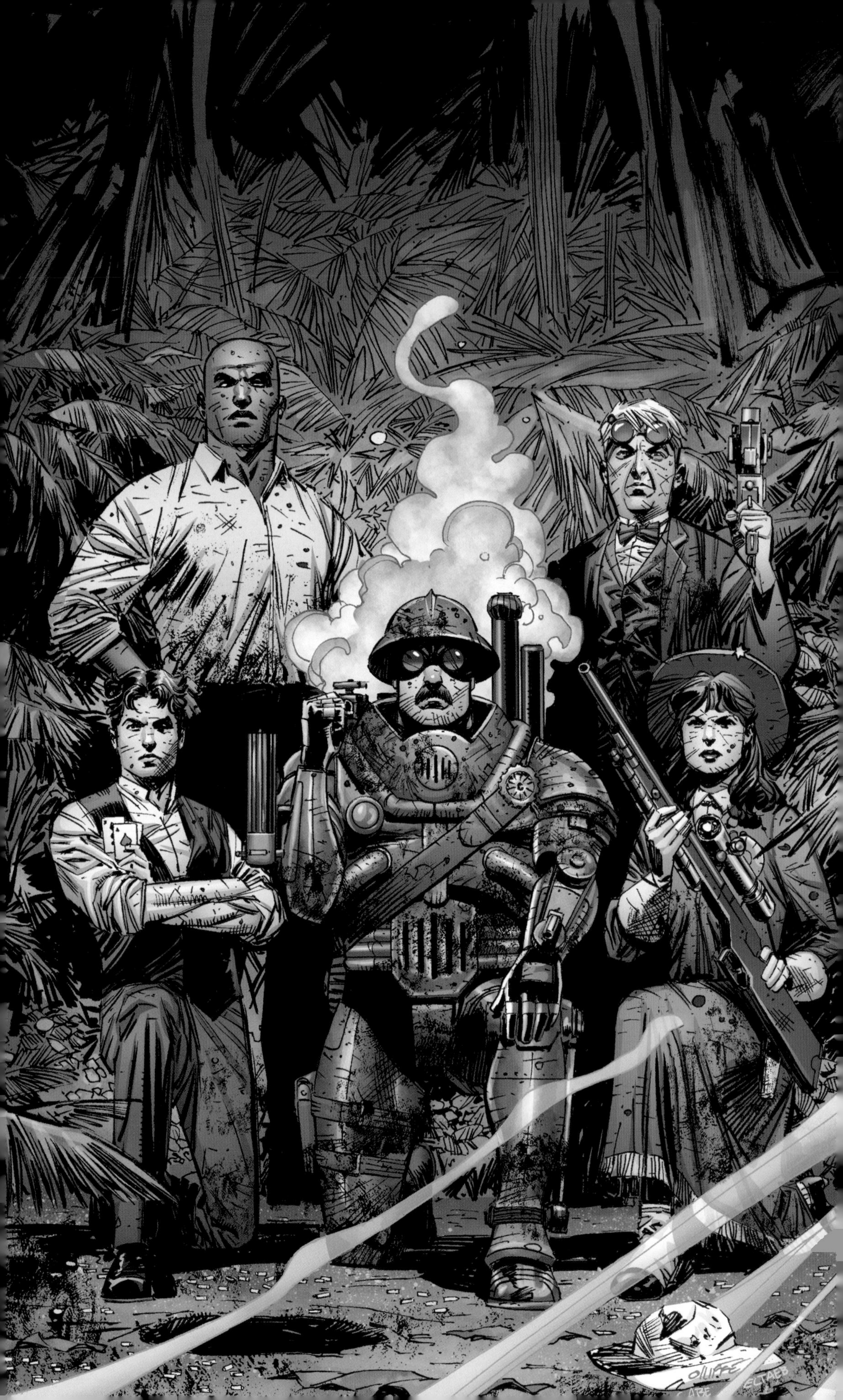

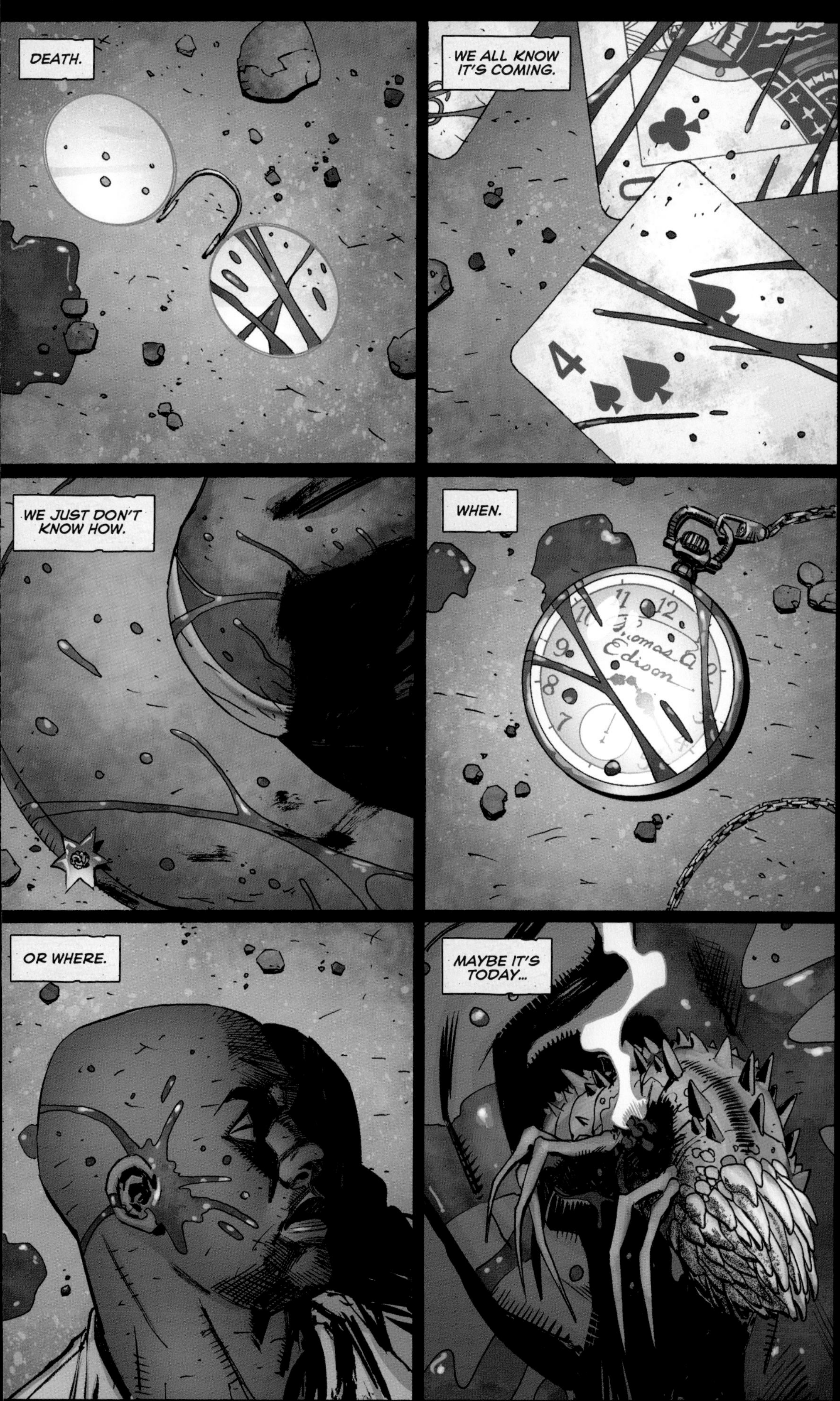
DEATH.
WE ALL KNOW IT'S COMING.
WE JUST DON'T KNOW HOW.
WHEN.
OR WHERE.
MAYBE IT'S TODAY...

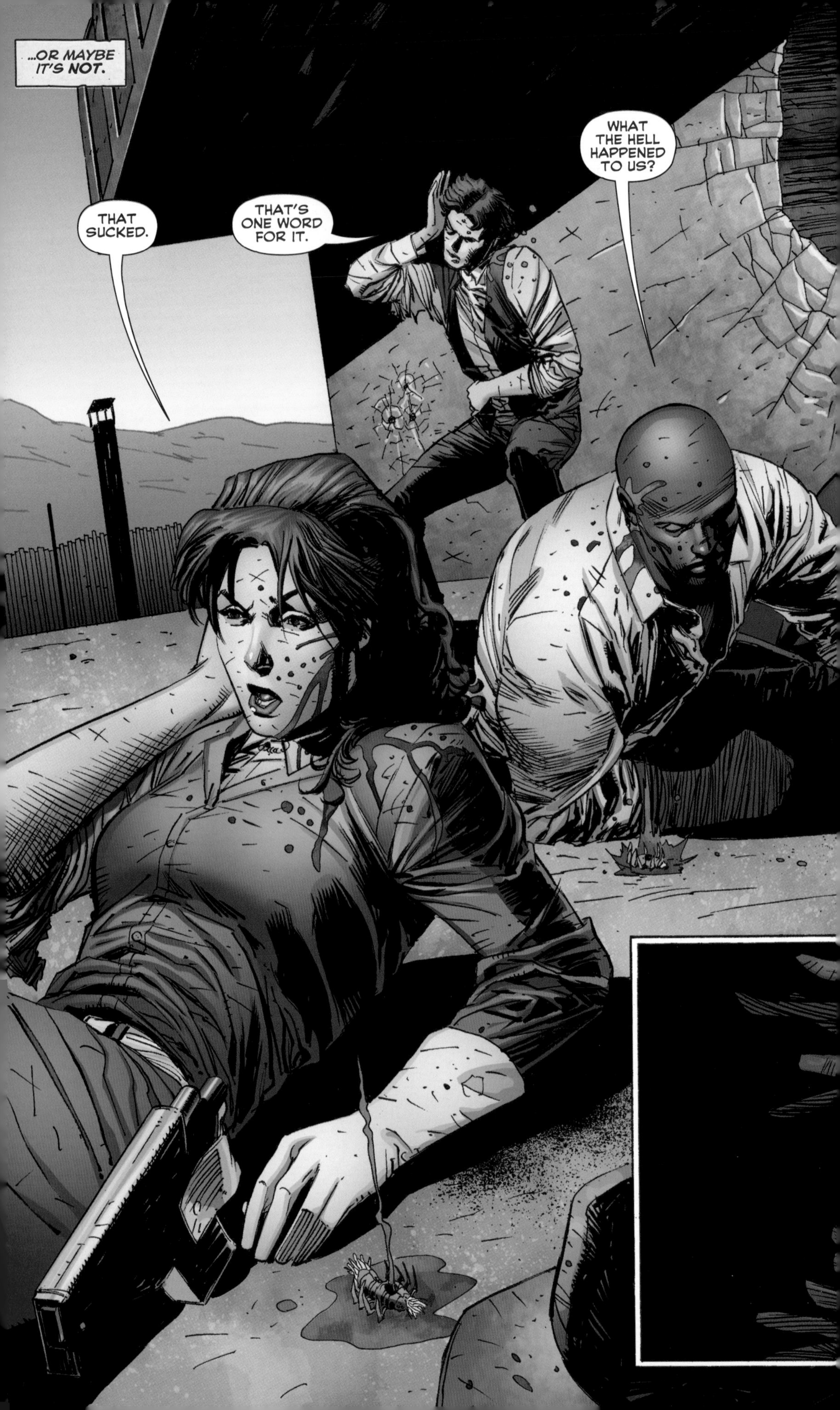
...OR MAYBE IT'S NOT.
THAT SUCKED.
THAT'S ONE WORD FOR IT.
WHAT THE HELL HAPPENED TO US?

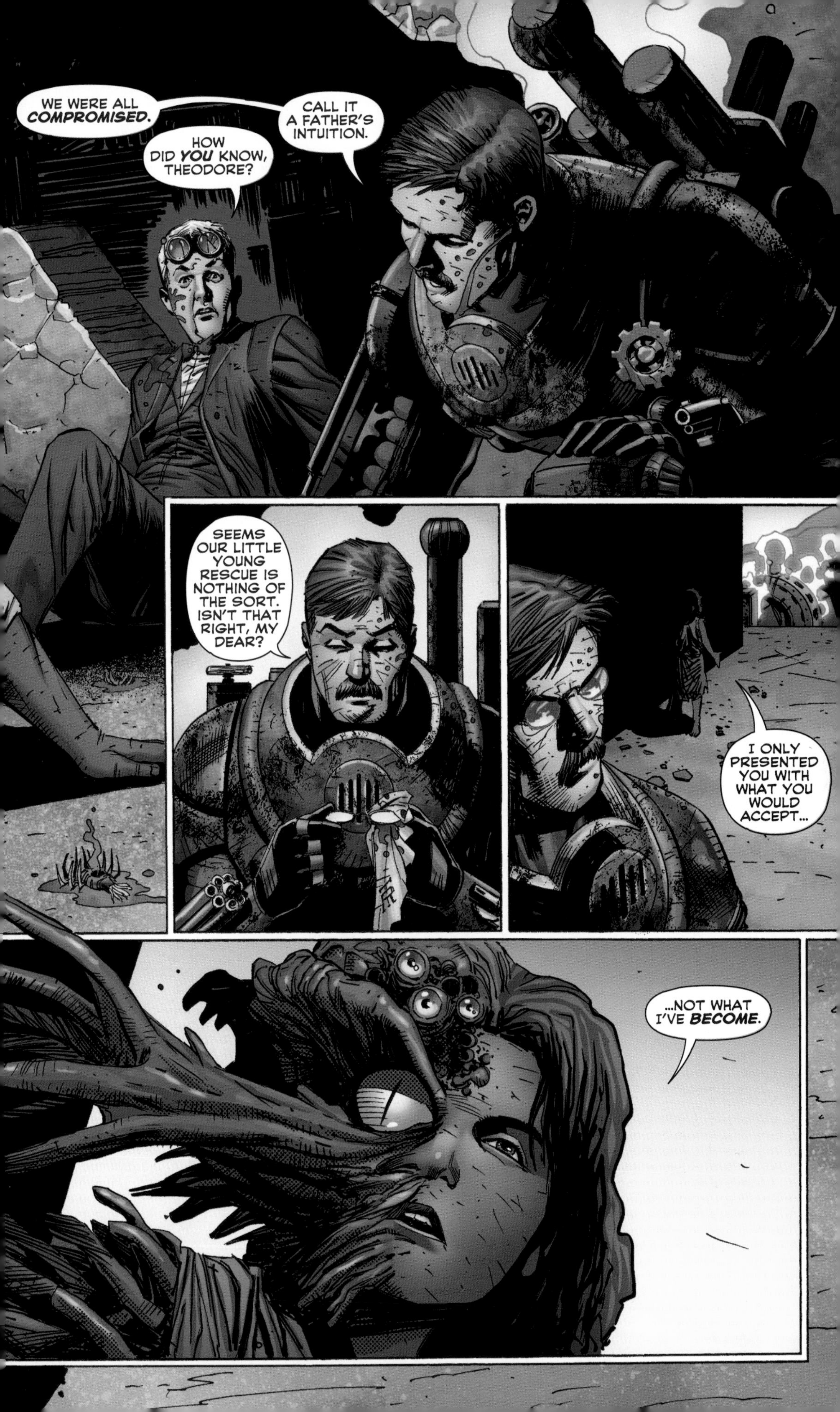
WE WERE ALL COMPROMISED.
HOW DID YOU KNOW, THEODORE?
CALL IT A FATHER'S INTUITION.
SEEMS OUR LITTLE YOUNG RESCUE IS NOTHING OF THE SORT. ISN'T THAT RIGHT, MY DEAR?
I ONLY PRESENTED YOU WITH WHAT YOU WOULD ACCEPT...
...NOT WHAT I'VE BECOME.

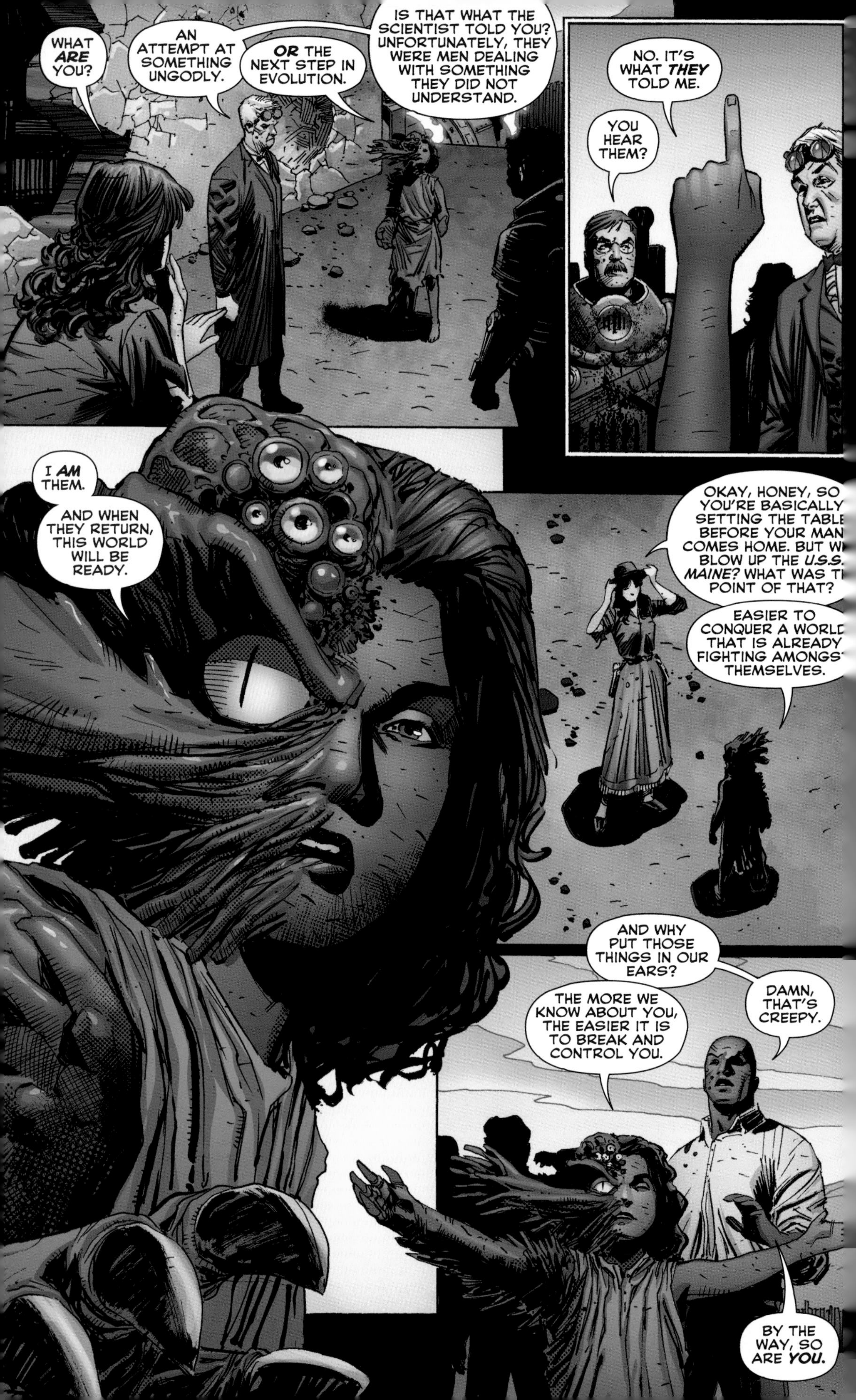
WHAT *ARE* YOU?
AN ATTEMPT AT SOMETHING UNGODLY.
OR THE NEXT STEP IN EVOLUTION.
IS THAT WHAT THE SCIENTIST TOLD YOU? UNFORTUNATELY, THEY WERE MEN DEALING WITH SOMETHING THEY DID NOT UNDERSTAND.
NO. IT'S WHAT *THEY* TOLD ME.
YOU HEAR THEM?
I *AM* THEM.
AND WHEN THEY RETURN, THIS WORLD WILL BE READY.
OKAY, HONEY, SO YOU'RE BASICALLY SETTING THE TABLE BEFORE YOUR MAN COMES HOME. BUT WHY BLOW UP THE *U.S.S. MAINE?* WHAT WAS THE POINT OF THAT?
EASIER TO CONQUER A WORLD THAT IS ALREADY FIGHTING AMONGST THEMSELVES.
AND WHY PUT THOSE THINGS IN OUR EARS?
THE MORE WE KNOW ABOUT YOU, THE EASIER IT IS TO BREAK AND CONTROL YOU.
DAMN, THAT'S CREEPY.
BY THE WAY, SO ARE *YOU.*

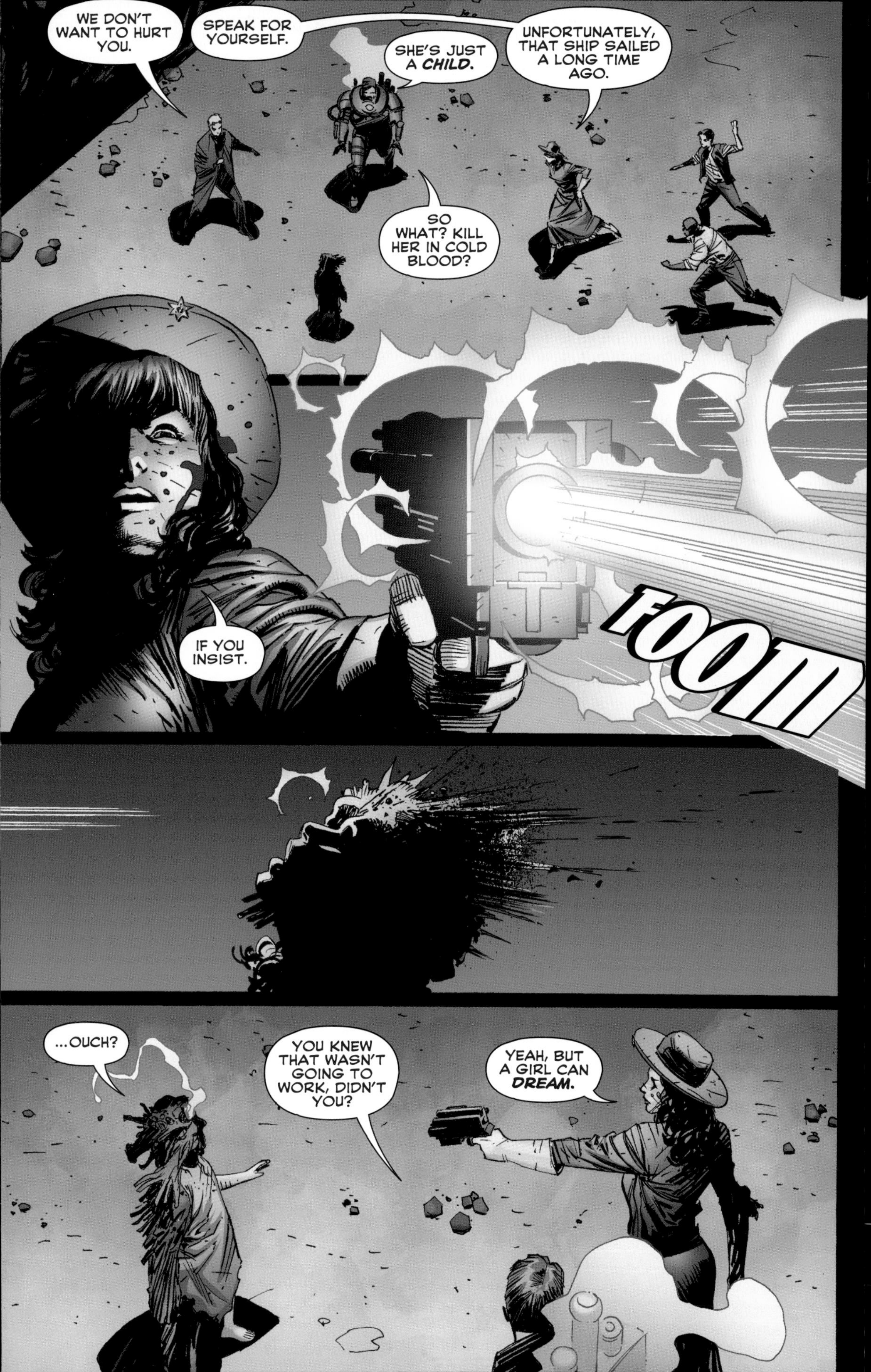
WE DON'T WANT TO HURT YOU.
SPEAK FOR YOURSELF.
SHE'S JUST A CHILD.
UNFORTUNATELY, THAT SHIP SAILED A LONG TIME AGO.
SO WHAT? KILL HER IN COLD BLOOD?
IF YOU INSIST.
FOOM
...OUCH?
YOU KNEW THAT WASN'T GOING TO WORK, DIDN'T YOU?
YEAH, BUT A GIRL CAN DREAM.

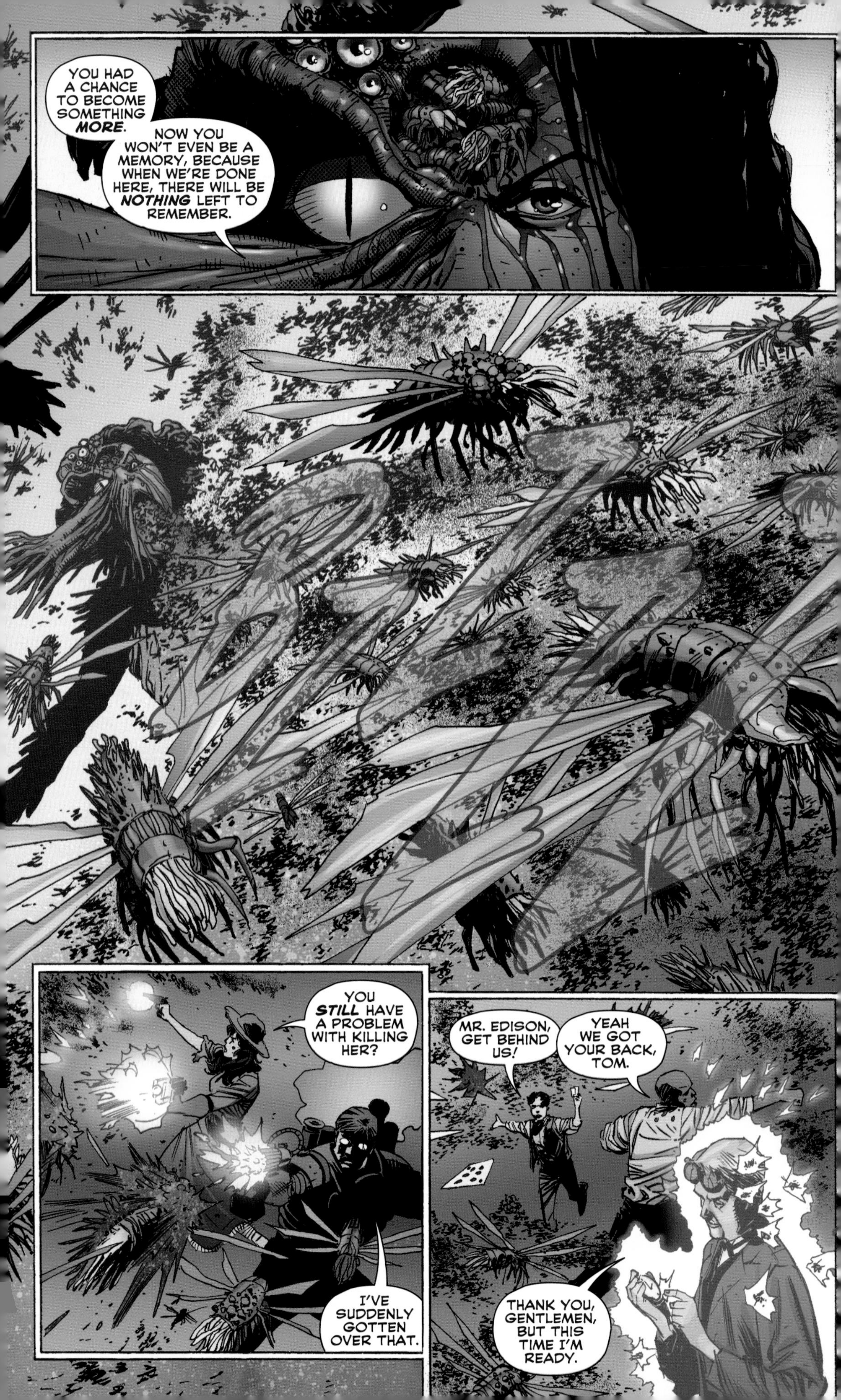
YOU HAD A CHANCE TO BECOME SOMETHING MORE.
NOW YOU WON'T EVEN BE A MEMORY, BECAUSE WHEN WE'RE DONE HERE, THERE WILL BE NOTHING LEFT TO REMEMBER.
YOU STILL HAVE A PROBLEM WITH KILLING HER?
I'VE SUDDENLY GOTTEN OVER THAT.
MR. EDISON, GET BEHIND US!
YEAH WE GOT YOUR BACK, TOM.
THANK YOU, GENTLEMEN, BUT THIS TIME I'M READY.

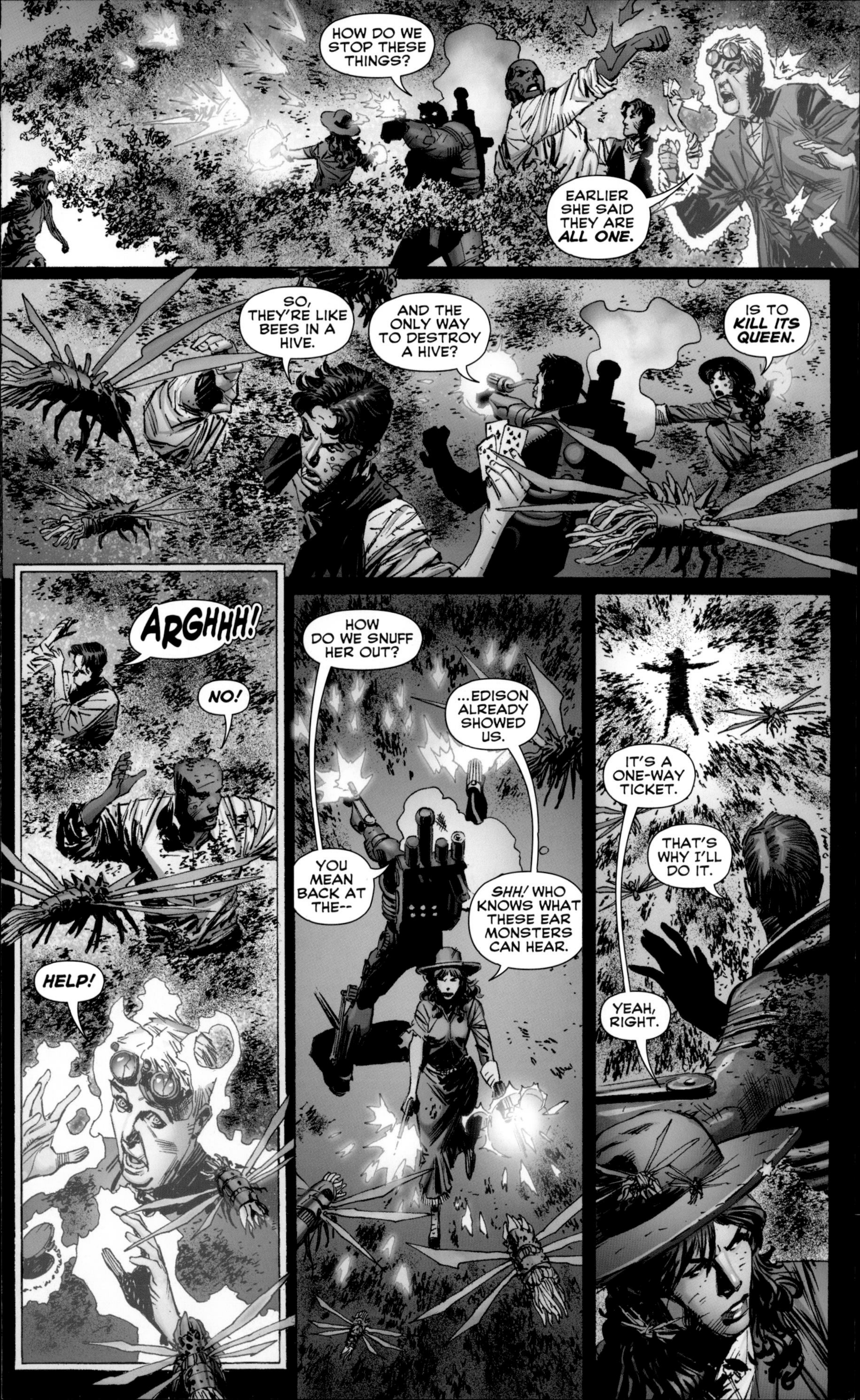
HOW DO WE STOP THESE THINGS?
EARLIER SHE SAID THEY ARE ALL ONE.
SO, THEY'RE LIKE BEES IN A HIVE.
AND THE ONLY WAY TO DESTROY A HIVE?
IS TO KILL ITS QUEEN.
ARGHHH!
NO!
HELP!
HOW DO WE SNUFF HER OUT?
...EDISON ALREADY SHOWED US.
YOU MEAN BACK AT THE--
SHH! WHO KNOWS WHAT THESE EAR MONSTERS CAN HEAR.
IT'S A ONE-WAY TICKET.
THAT'S WHY I'LL DO IT.
YEAH, RIGHT.

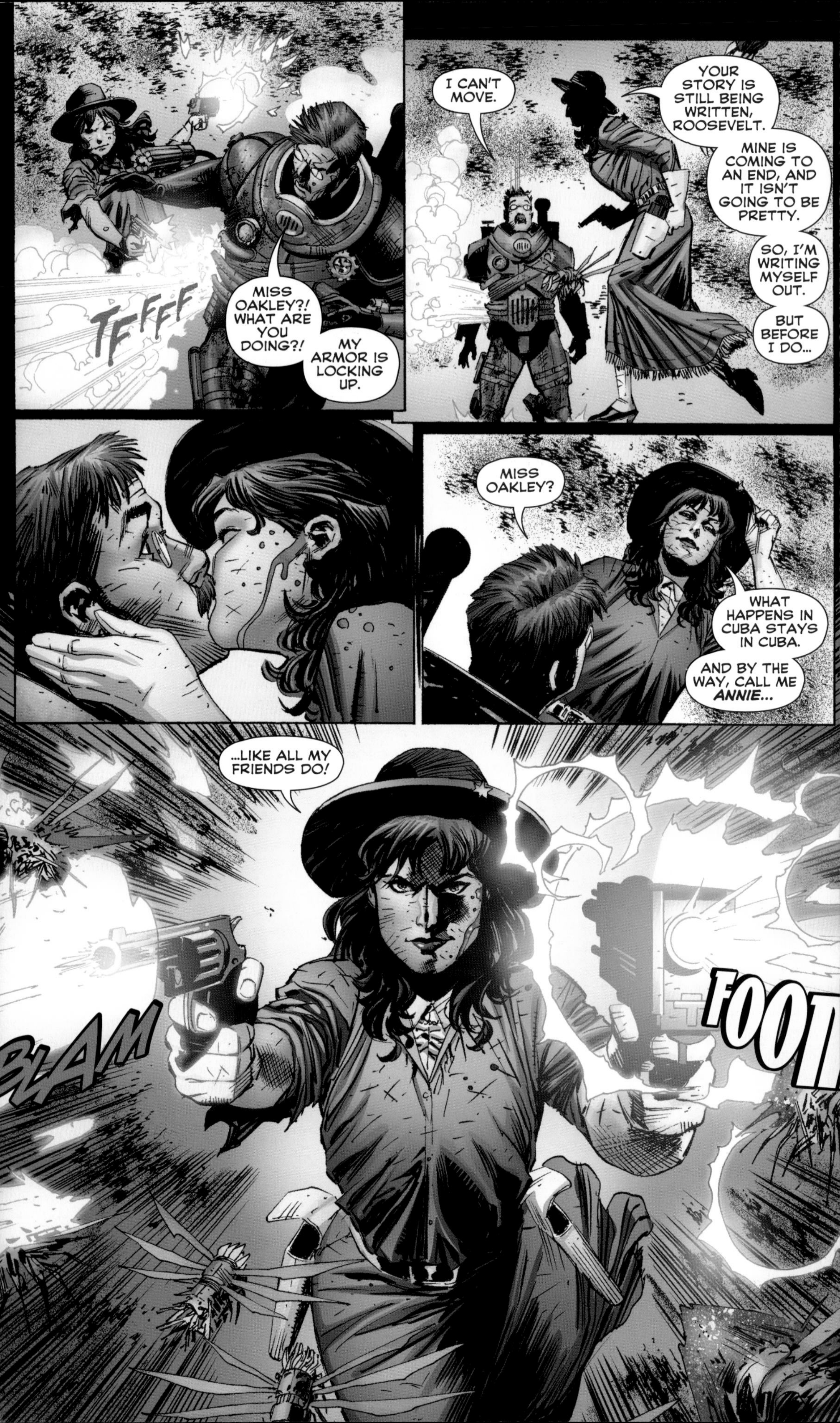
TFFFF
MISS OAKLEY?! WHAT ARE YOU DOING?!
MY ARMOR IS LOCKING UP.
I CAN'T MOVE.
YOUR STORY IS STILL BEING WRITTEN, ROOSEVELT.
MINE IS COMING TO AN END, AND IT ISN'T GOING TO BE PRETTY.
SO, I'M WRITING MYSELF OUT.
BUT BEFORE I DO...
MISS OAKLEY?
WHAT HAPPENS IN CUBA STAYS IN CUBA.
AND BY THE WAY, CALL ME *ANNIE*...
...LIKE ALL MY FRIENDS DO!
BLAM
FOOT

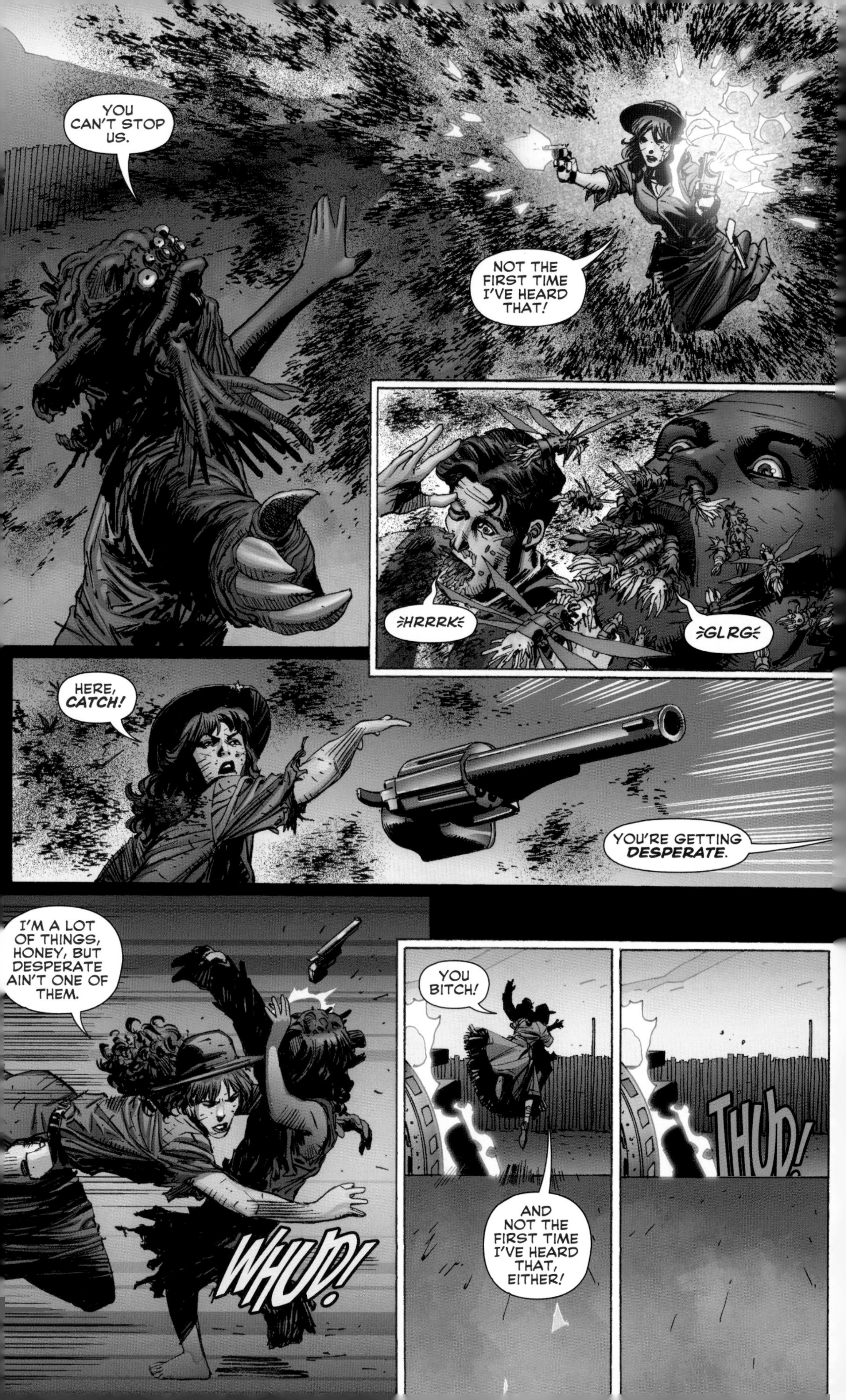
YOU CAN'T STOP US.
NOT THE FIRST TIME I'VE HEARD THAT!
HRRRK
GLRG
HERE, CATCH!
YOU'RE GETTING DESPERATE.
I'M A LOT OF THINGS, HONEY, BUT DESPERATE AIN'T ONE OF THEM.
WHUD!
YOU BITCH!
AND NOT THE FIRST TIME I'VE HEARD THAT, EITHER!
THUD!

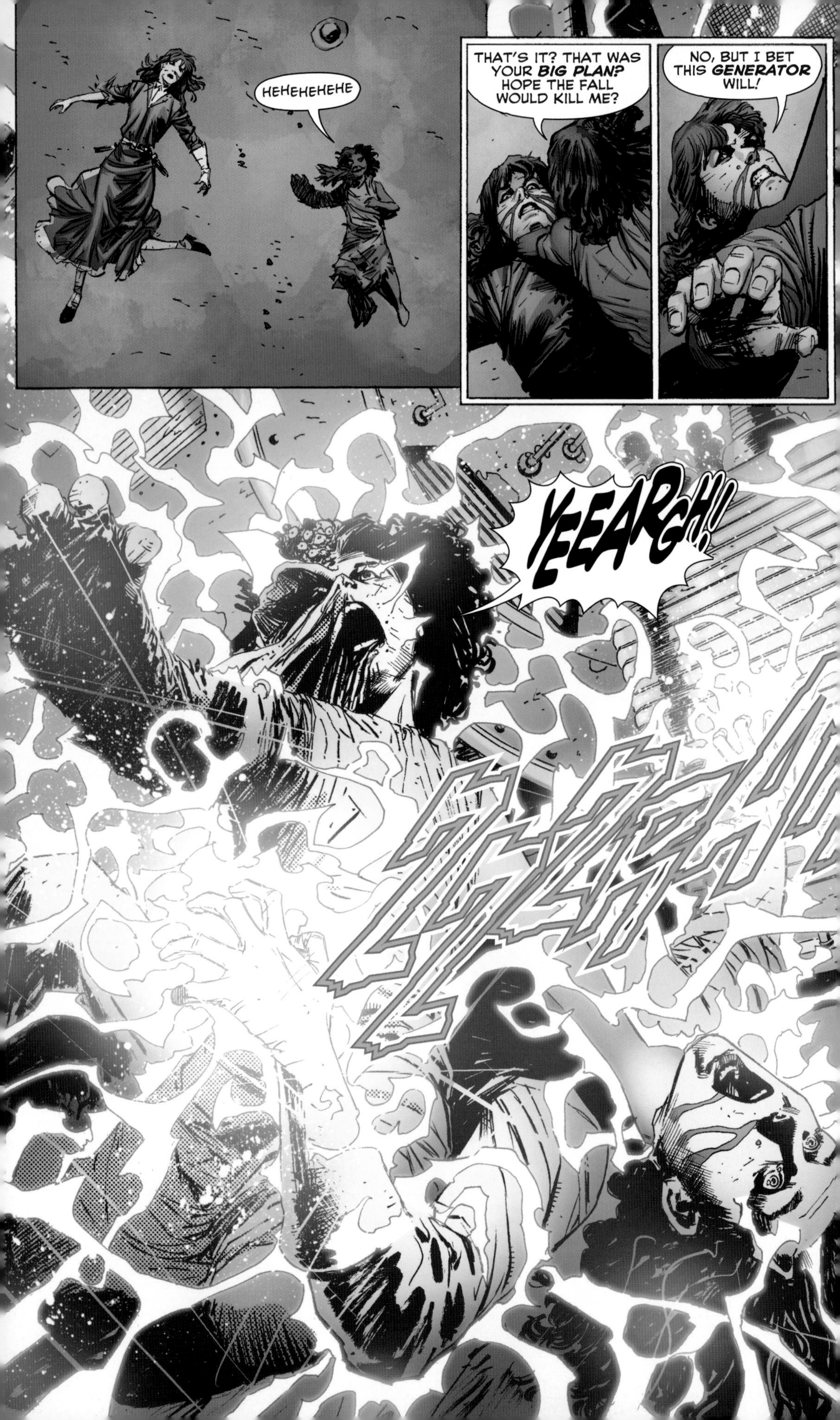
HEHEHEHEHE
THAT'S IT? THAT WAS YOUR **BIG PLAN?** HOPE THE FALL WOULD KILL ME?
NO, BUT I BET THIS **GENERATOR** WILL!
YEEARGH!

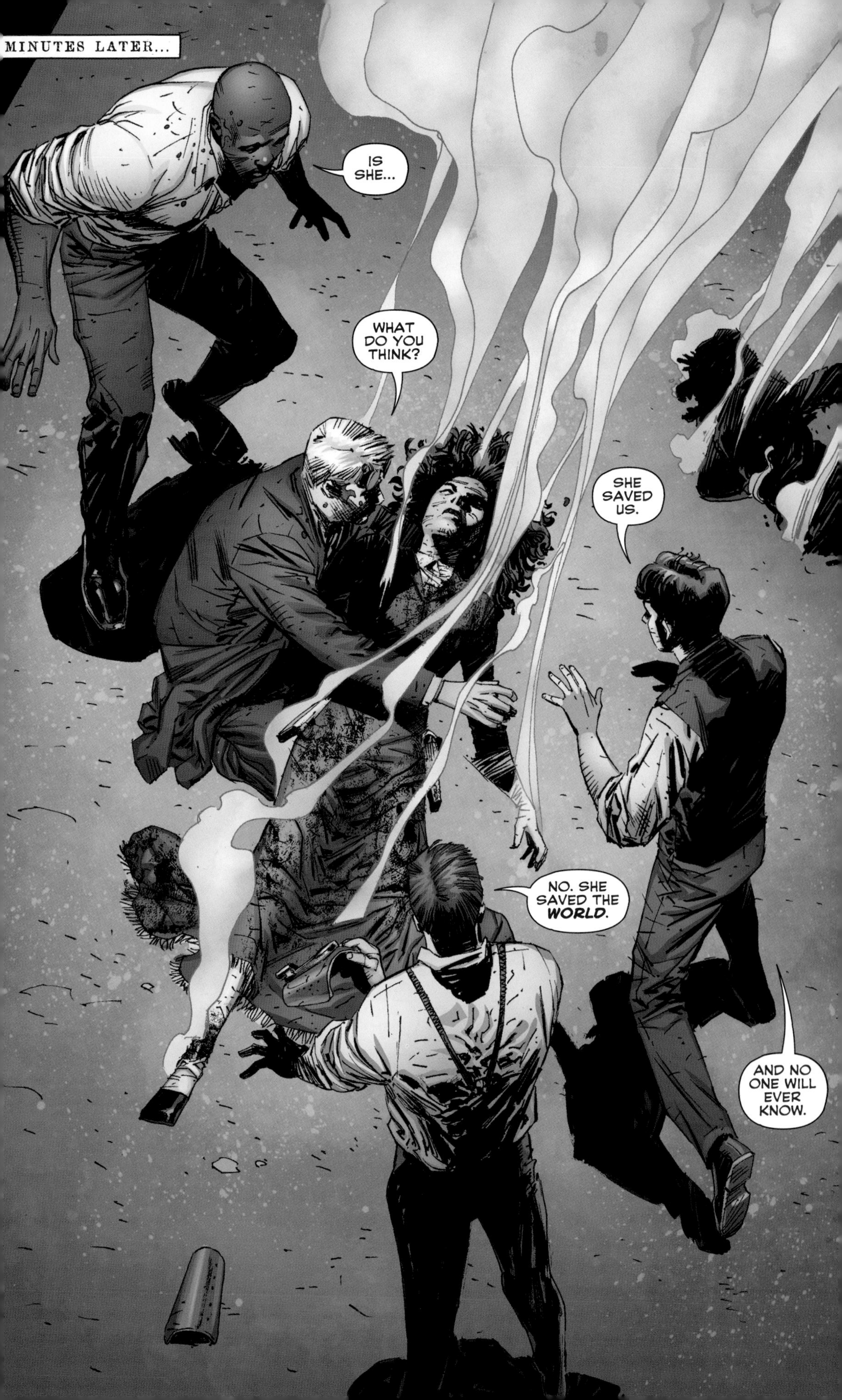
MINUTES LATER...
IS SHE...
WHAT DO YOU THINK?
SHE SAVED US.
NO. SHE SAVED THE WORLD.
AND NO ONE WILL EVER KNOW.

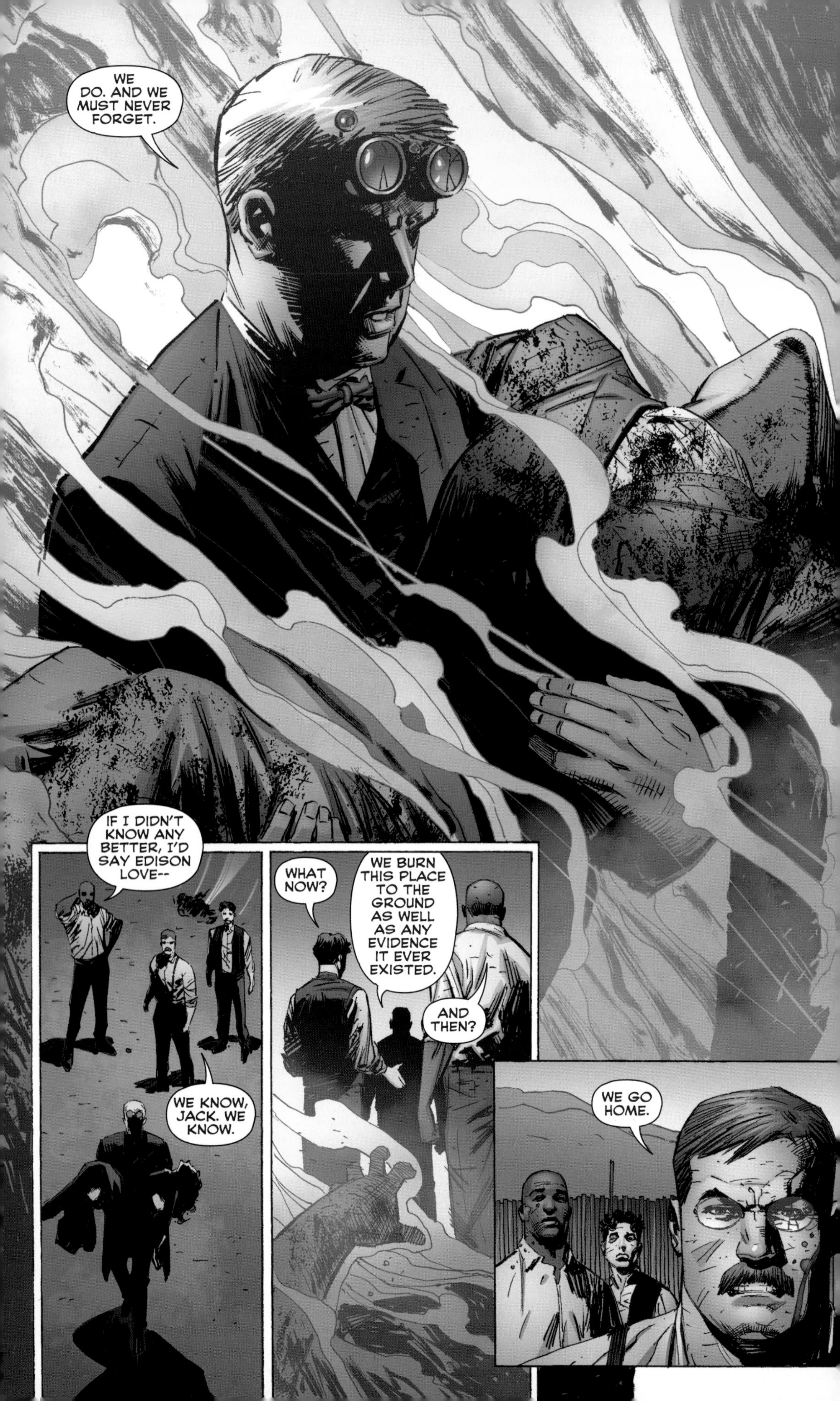
WE DO. AND WE MUST NEVER FORGET.
IF I DIDN'T KNOW ANY BETTER, I'D SAY EDISON LOVE--
WE KNOW, JACK. WE KNOW.
WHAT NOW?
WE BURN THIS PLACE TO THE GROUND AS WELL AS ANY EVIDENCE IT EVER EXISTED.
AND THEN?
WE GO HOME.

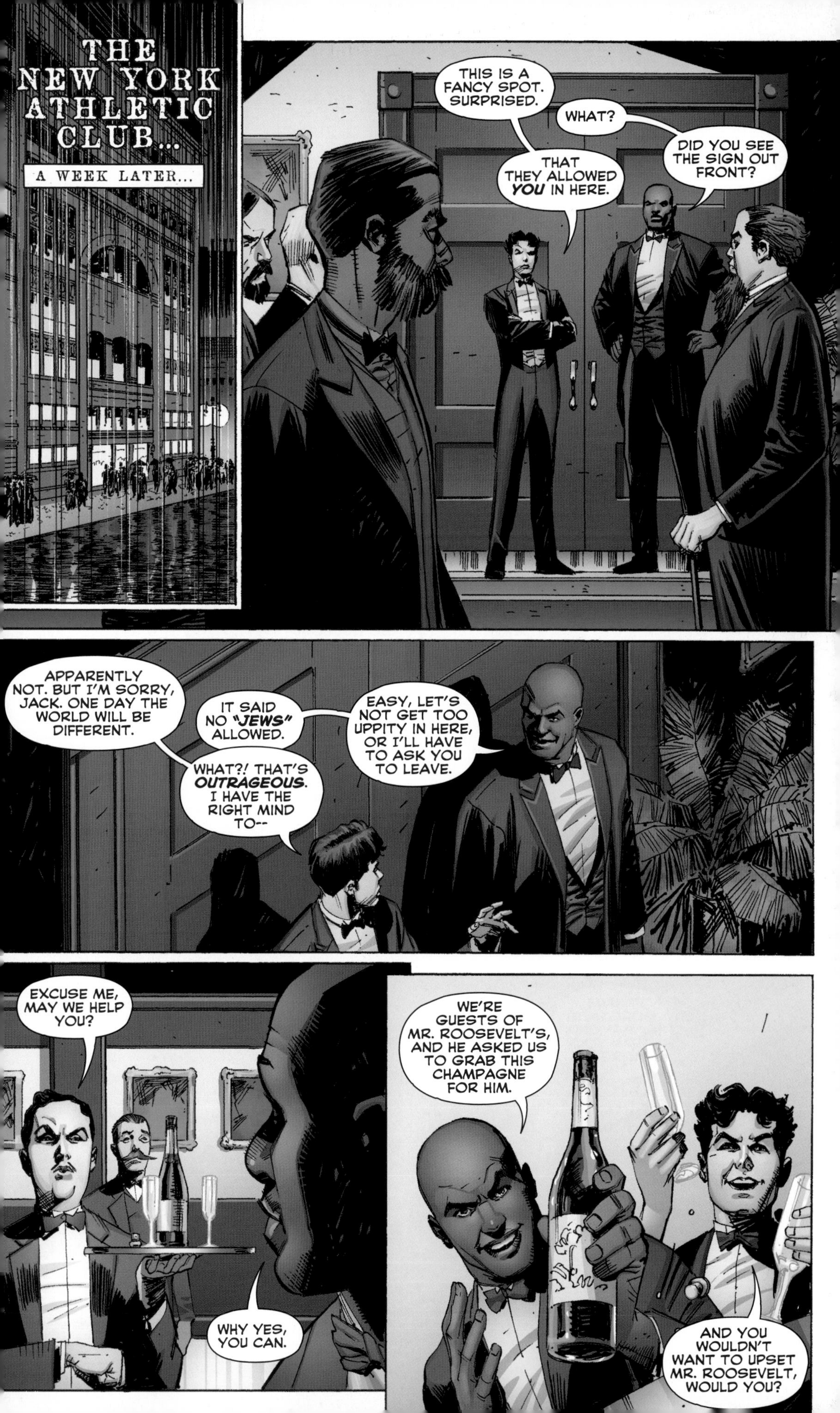
THE NEW YORK ATHLETIC CLUB...
A WEEK LATER...
THIS IS A FANCY SPOT. SURPRISED.
WHAT?
THAT THEY ALLOWED *YOU* IN HERE.
DID YOU SEE THE SIGN OUT FRONT?
APPARENTLY NOT. BUT I'M SORRY, JACK. ONE DAY THE WORLD WILL BE DIFFERENT.
IT SAID NO *"JEWS"* ALLOWED.
WHAT?! THAT'S ***OUTRAGEOUS***. I HAVE THE RIGHT MIND TO--
EASY, LET'S NOT GET TOO UPPITY IN HERE, OR I'LL HAVE TO ASK YOU TO LEAVE.
EXCUSE ME, MAY WE HELP YOU?
WHY YES, YOU CAN.
WE'RE GUESTS OF MR. ROOSEVELT'S, AND HE ASKED US TO GRAB THIS CHAMPAGNE FOR HIM.
AND YOU WOULDN'T WANT TO UPSET MR. ROOSEVELT, WOULD YOU?

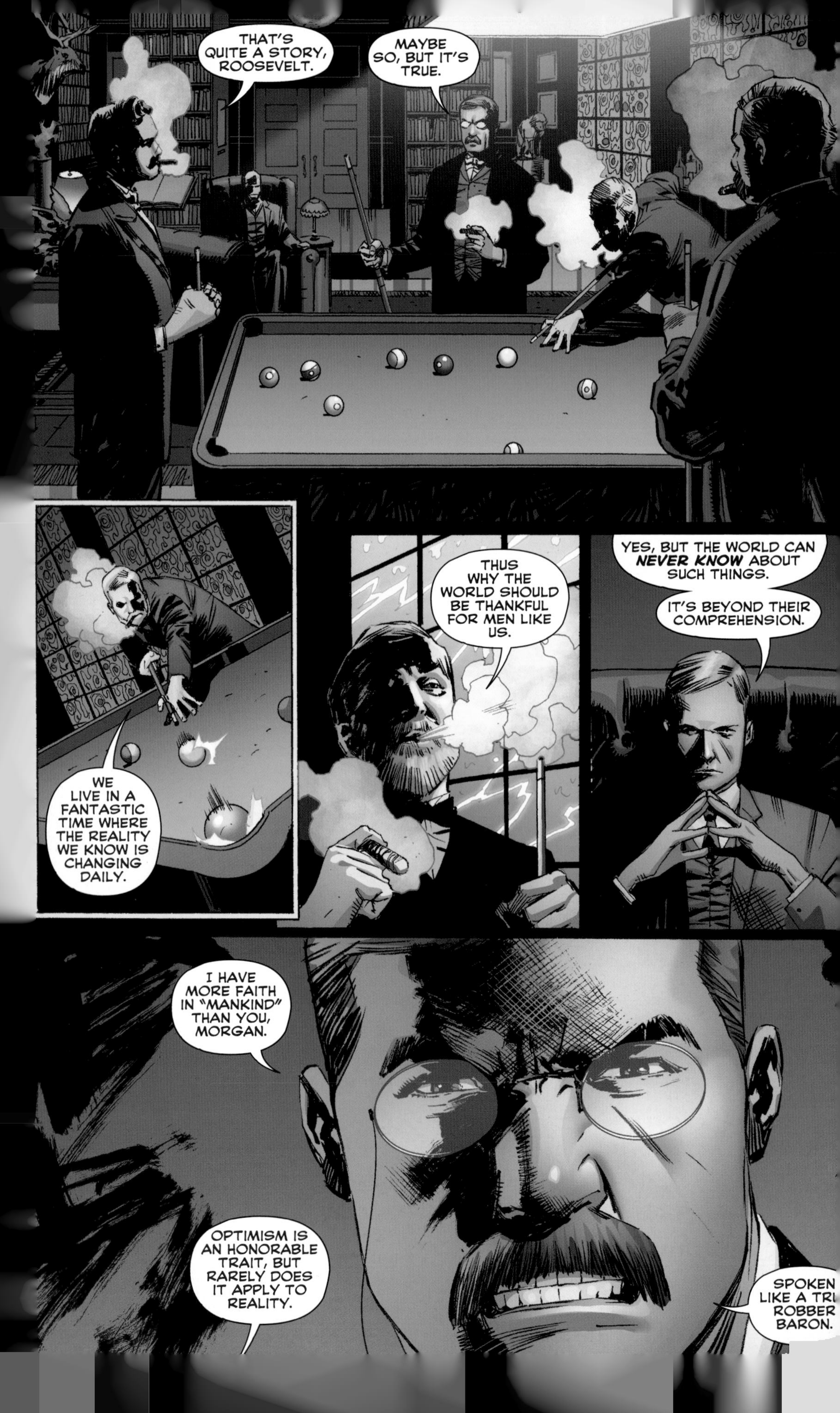
THAT'S QUITE A STORY, ROOSEVELT.
MAYBE SO, BUT IT'S TRUE.
WE LIVE IN A FANTASTIC TIME WHERE THE REALITY WE KNOW IS CHANGING DAILY.
THUS WHY THE WORLD SHOULD BE THANKFUL FOR MEN LIKE US.
YES, BUT THE WORLD CAN NEVER KNOW ABOUT SUCH THINGS.
IT'S BEYOND THEIR COMPREHENSION.
I HAVE MORE FAITH IN "MANKIND" THAN YOU, MORGAN.
OPTIMISM IS AN HONORABLE TRAIT, BUT RARELY DOES IT APPLY TO REALITY.
SPOKEN LIKE A TR
ROBBER BARON.

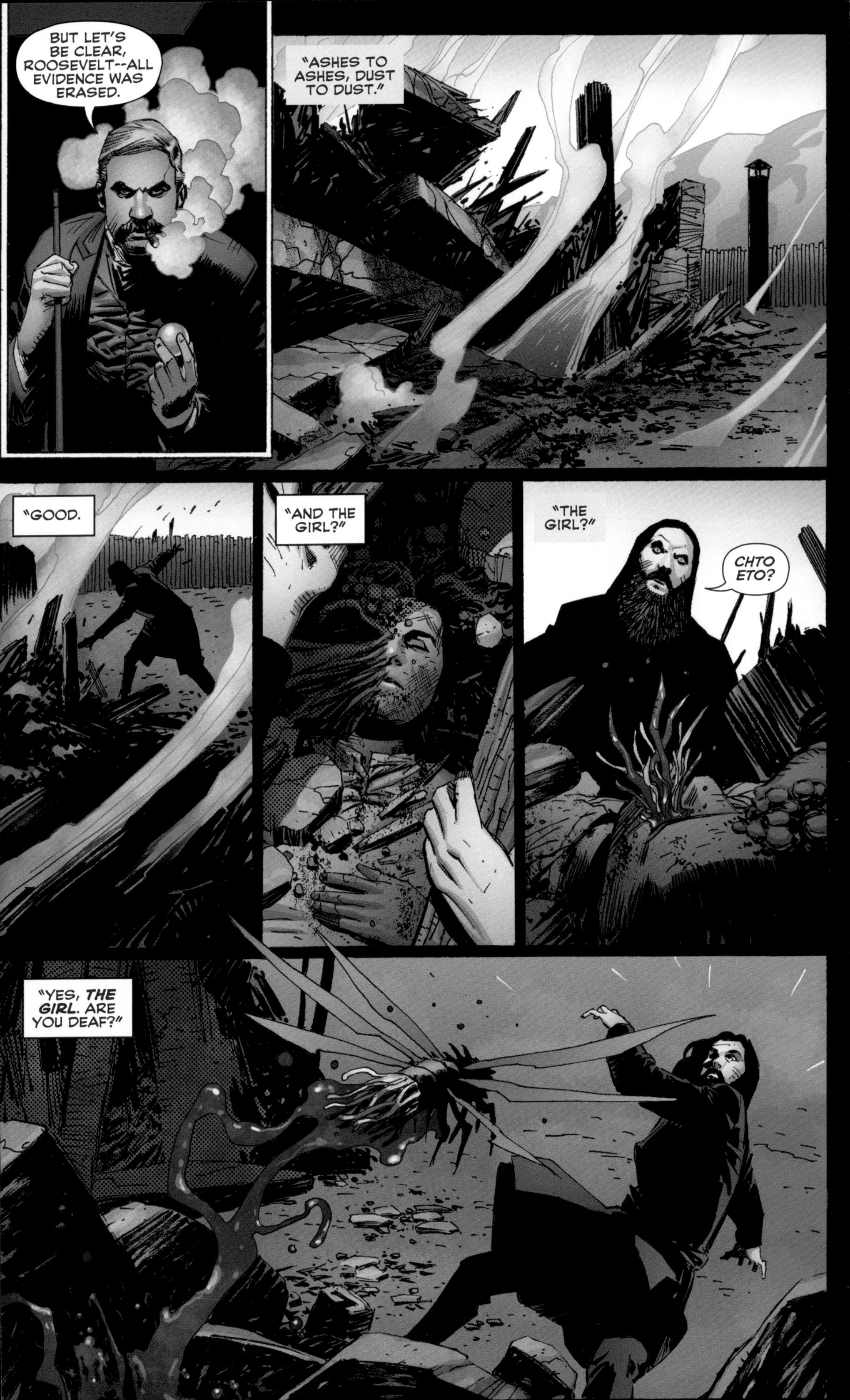
BUT LET'S BE CLEAR, ROOSEVELT--ALL EVIDENCE WAS ERASED.
"ASHES TO ASHES, DUST TO DUST."
"GOOD.
"AND THE GIRL?"
"THE GIRL?"
CHTO ETO?
"YES, THE GIRL. ARE YOU DEAF?"

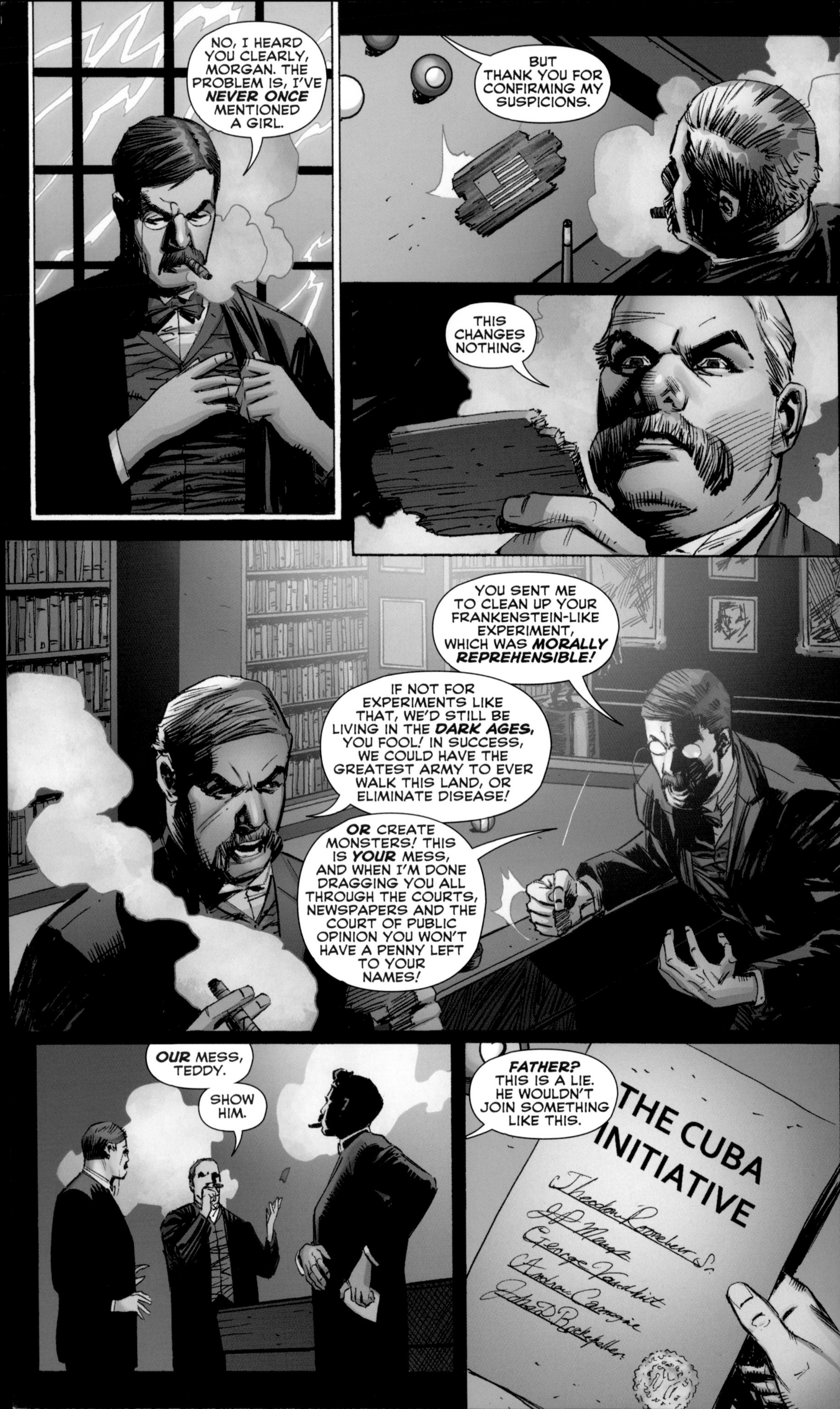
NO, I HEARD YOU CLEARLY, MORGAN. THE PROBLEM IS, I'VE **NEVER ONCE** MENTIONED A GIRL.
BUT THANK YOU FOR CONFIRMING MY SUSPICIONS.
THIS CHANGES NOTHING.
YOU SENT ME TO CLEAN UP YOUR FRANKENSTEIN-LIKE EXPERIMENT, WHICH WAS **MORALLY REPREHENSIBLE!**
IF NOT FOR EXPERIMENTS LIKE THAT, WE'D STILL BE LIVING IN THE **DARK AGES,** YOU FOOL! IN SUCCESS, WE COULD HAVE THE GREATEST ARMY TO EVER WALK THIS LAND, OR ELIMINATE DISEASE!
OR CREATE MONSTERS! THIS IS **YOUR** MESS, AND WHEN I'M DONE DRAGGING YOU ALL THROUGH THE COURTS, NEWSPAPERS AND THE COURT OF PUBLIC OPINION YOU WON'T HAVE A PENNY LEFT TO YOUR NAMES!
OUR MESS, TEDDY.
SHOW HIM.
FATHER? THIS IS A LIE. HE WOULDN'T JOIN SOMETHING LIKE THIS.
THE CUBA INITIATIVE

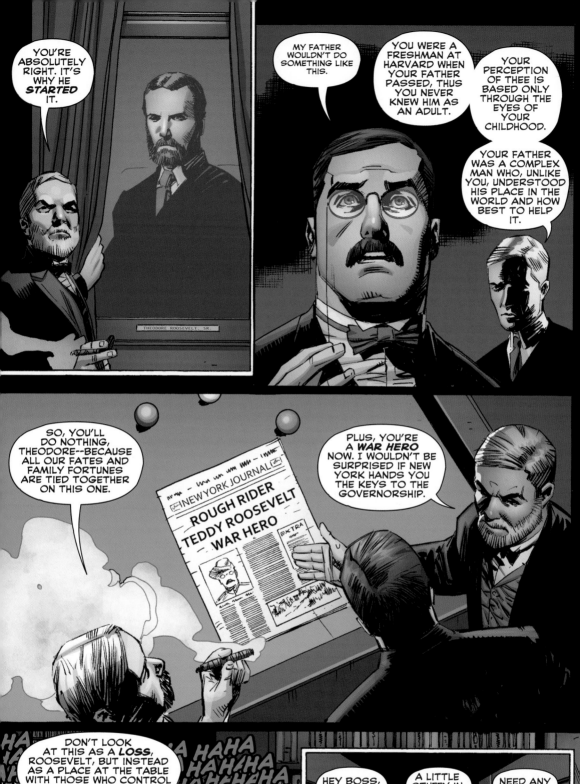

YOU'RE ABSOLUTELY RIGHT. IT'S WHY HE **STARTED** IT.

THEODORE ROOSEVELT, SR.

MY FATHER WOULDN'T DO SOMETHING LIKE THIS.

YOU WERE A FRESHMAN AT HARVARD WHEN YOUR FATHER PASSED, THUS YOU NEVER KNEW HIM AS AN ADULT.

YOUR PERCEPTION OF THEE IS BASED ONLY THROUGH THE EYES OF YOUR CHILDHOOD.

YOUR FATHER WAS A COMPLEX MAN WHO, UNLIKE YOU, UNDERSTOOD HIS PLACE IN THE WORLD AND HOW BEST TO HELP IT.

SO, YOU'LL DO NOTHING, THEODORE--BECAUSE ALL OUR FATES AND FAMILY FORTUNES ARE TIED TOGETHER ON THIS ONE.

NEW YORK JOURNAL
ROUGH RIDER TEDDY ROOSEVELT WAR HERO
EXTRA

PLUS, YOU'RE A **WAR HERO** NOW. I WOULDN'T BE SURPRISED IF NEW YORK HANDS YOU THE KEYS TO THE GOVERNORSHIP.

DON'T LOOK AT THIS AS A **LOSS**, ROOSEVELT, BUT INSTEAD AS A PLACE AT THE TABLE WITH THOSE WHO CONTROL THE DESTINY OF THE WORLD.

HEY BOSS, HOW GOES IT?

A LITTLE STUFFY IN THERE.

NEED ANY HELP?

YES, WHATEVER YOU DO, WHATEVER YOU HEAR, MAKE SURE **NO ONE** COMES IN OR OUT.

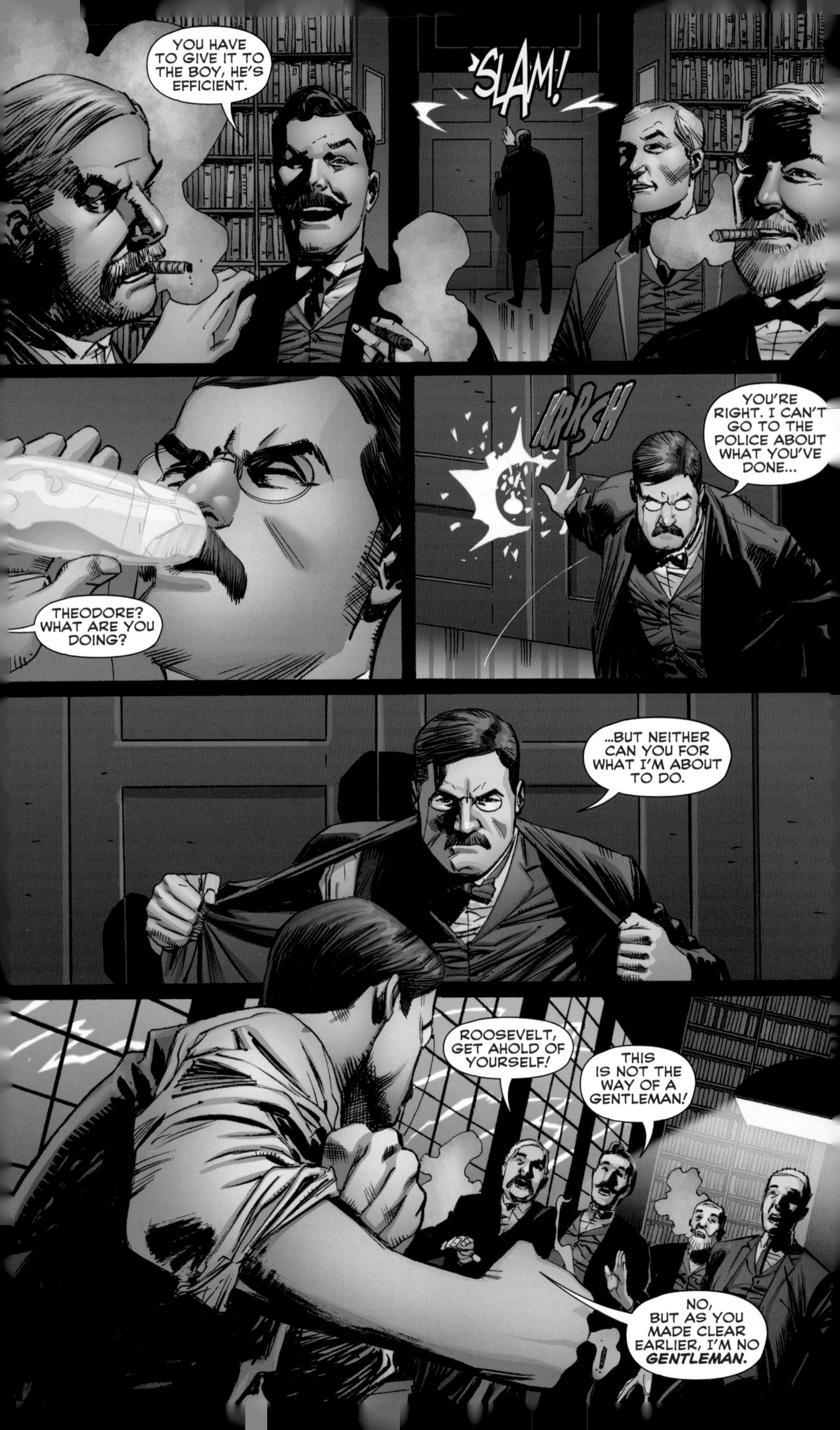
YOU HAVE TO GIVE IT TO THE BOY, HE'S EFFICIENT.
'SLAM!
THEODORE? WHAT ARE YOU DOING?
KRRSH
YOU'RE RIGHT. I CAN'T GO TO THE POLICE ABOUT WHAT YOU'VE DONE...
...BUT NEITHER CAN YOU FOR WHAT I'M ABOUT TO DO.
ROOSEVELT, GET AHOLD OF YOURSELF!
THIS IS NOT THE WAY OF A GENTLEMAN!
NO, BUT AS YOU MADE CLEAR EARLIER, I'M NO ***GENTLEMAN***.

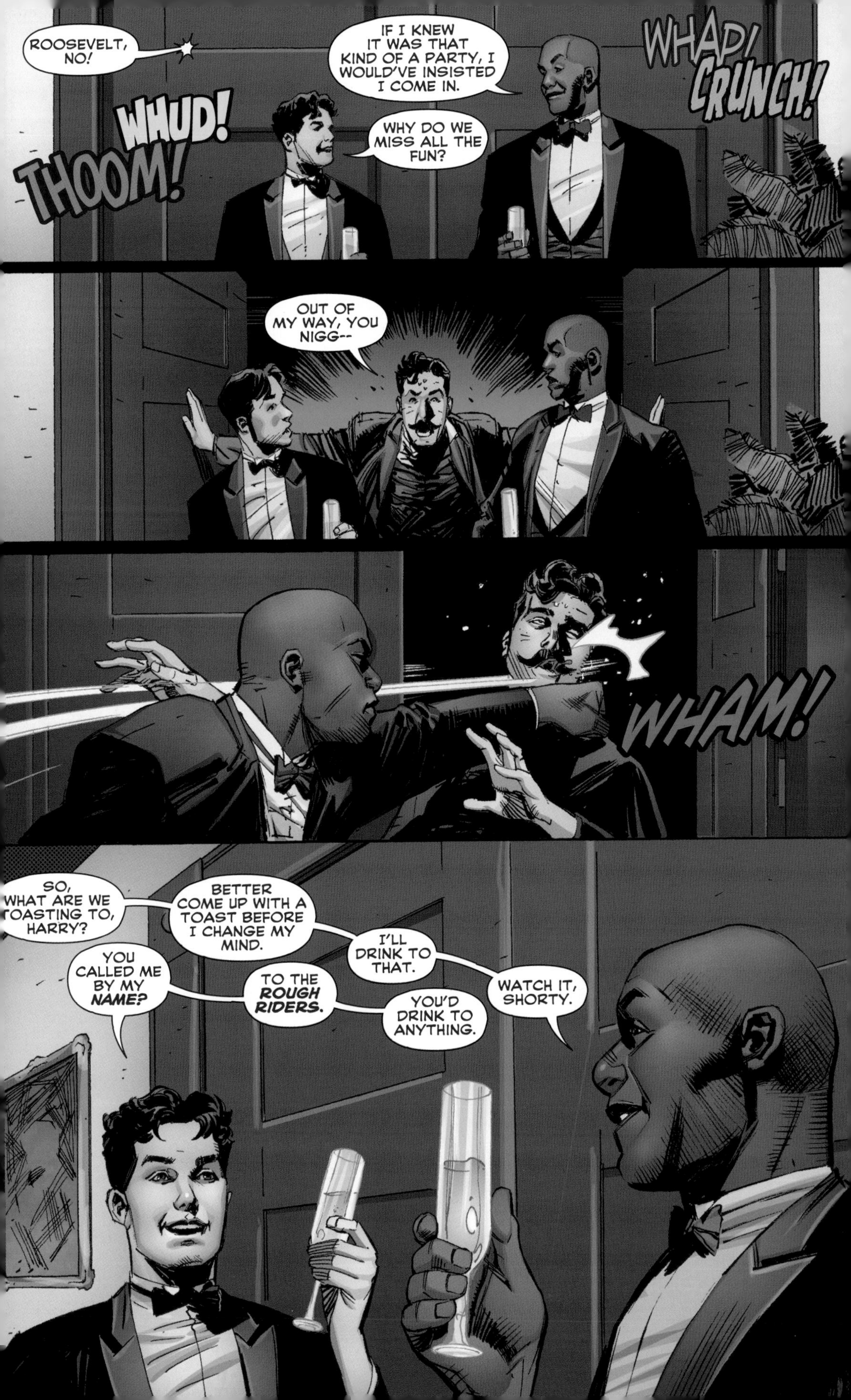

ROOSEVELT, NO!
IF I KNEW IT WAS THAT KIND OF A PARTY, I WOULD'VE INSISTED I COME IN.
WHY DO WE MISS ALL THE FUN?
WHUD!
THOOM!
WHAP!
CRUNCH!
OUT OF MY WAY, YOU NIGG--
WHAM!
SO, WHAT ARE WE TOASTING TO, HARRY?
YOU CALLED ME BY MY *NAME?*
BETTER COME UP WITH A TOAST BEFORE I CHANGE MY MIND.
TO THE ***ROUGH RIDERS.***
I'LL DRINK TO THAT.
YOU'D DRINK TO ANYTHING.
WATCH IT, SHORTY.

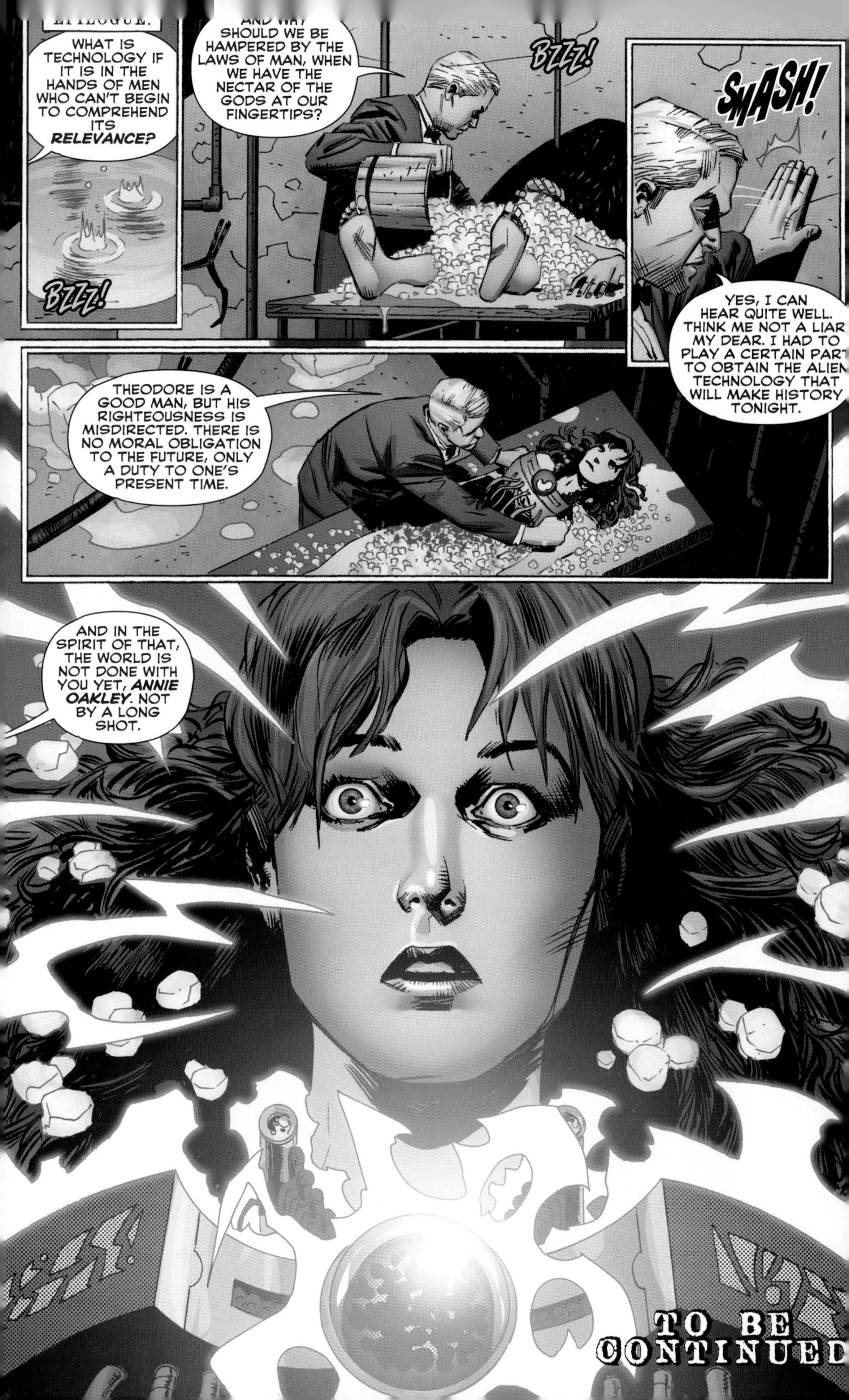
EPILOGUE.
WHAT IS TECHNOLOGY IF IT IS IN THE HANDS OF MEN WHO CAN'T BEGIN TO COMPREHEND ITS RELEVANCE?
BZZZ!
AND WHY SHOULD WE BE HAMPERED BY THE LAWS OF MAN, WHEN WE HAVE THE NECTAR OF THE GODS AT OUR FINGERTIPS?
BZZZ!
SMASH!
YES, I CAN HEAR QUITE WELL. THINK ME NOT A LIAR MY DEAR. I HAD TO PLAY A CERTAIN PAR TO OBTAIN THE ALIE TECHNOLOGY THAT WILL MAKE HISTORY TONIGHT.
THEODORE IS A GOOD MAN, BUT HIS RIGHTEOUSNESS IS MISDIRECTED. THERE IS NO MORAL OBLIGATION TO THE FUTURE, ONLY A DUTY TO ONE'S PRESENT TIME.
AND IN THE SPIRIT OF THAT, THE WORLD IS NOT DONE WITH YOU YET, ANNIE OAKLEY. NOT BY A LONG SHOT.
TO BE CONTINUED

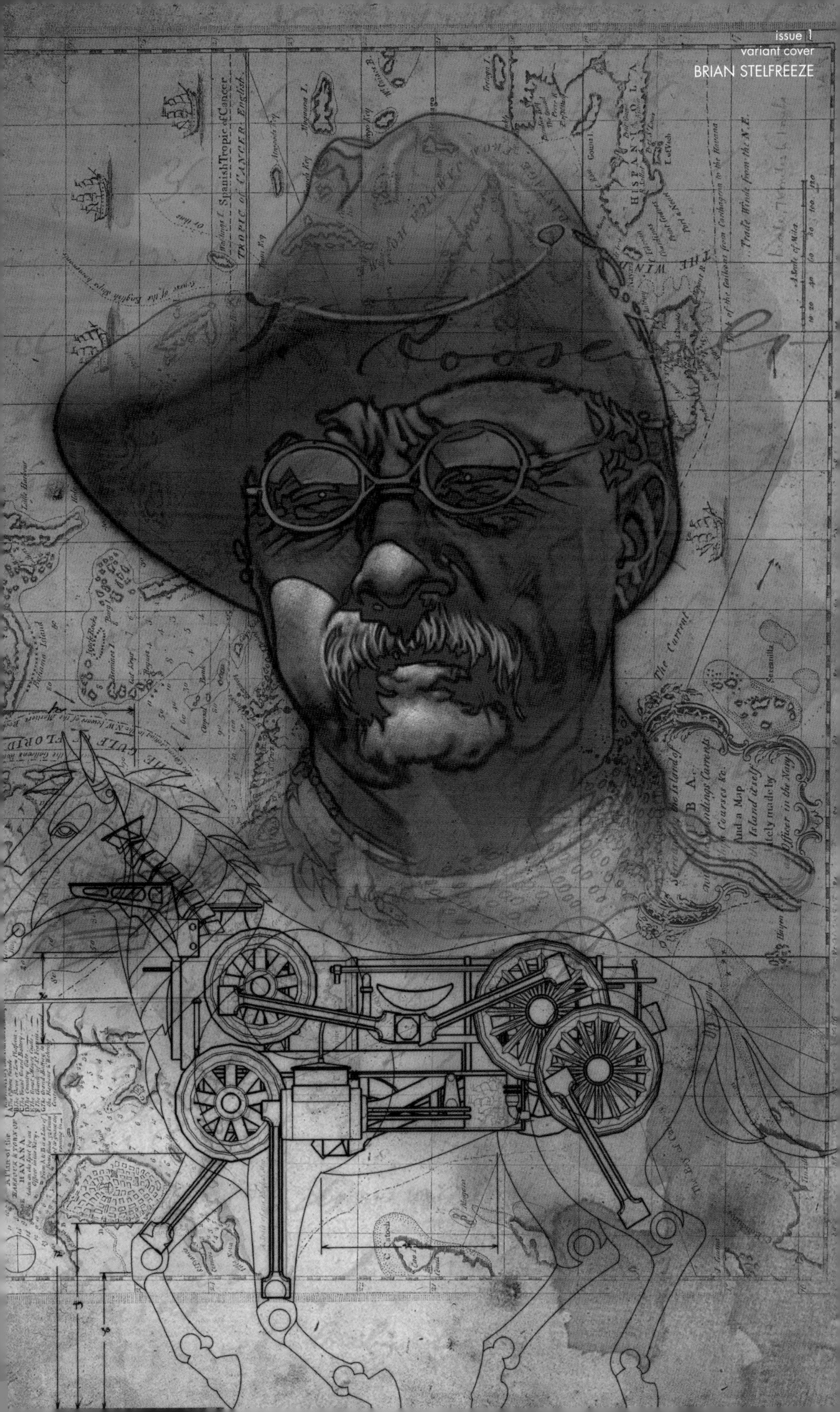

issue 1
variant cover
BRIAN STELFREEZE

issue 1
variant cover
FRANCESCO FRANCAVILLA

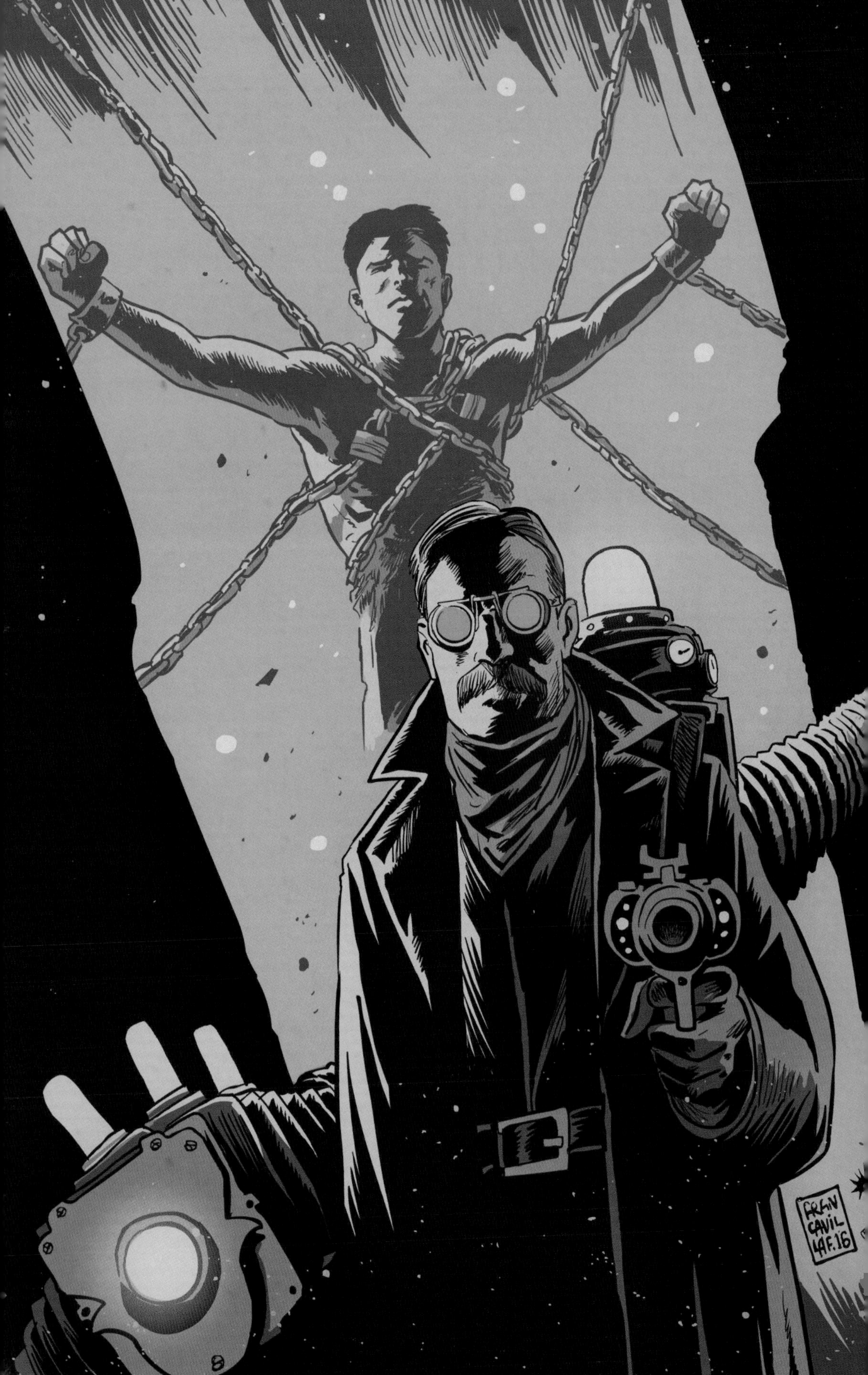
FRAN
CAVIL
14F.16

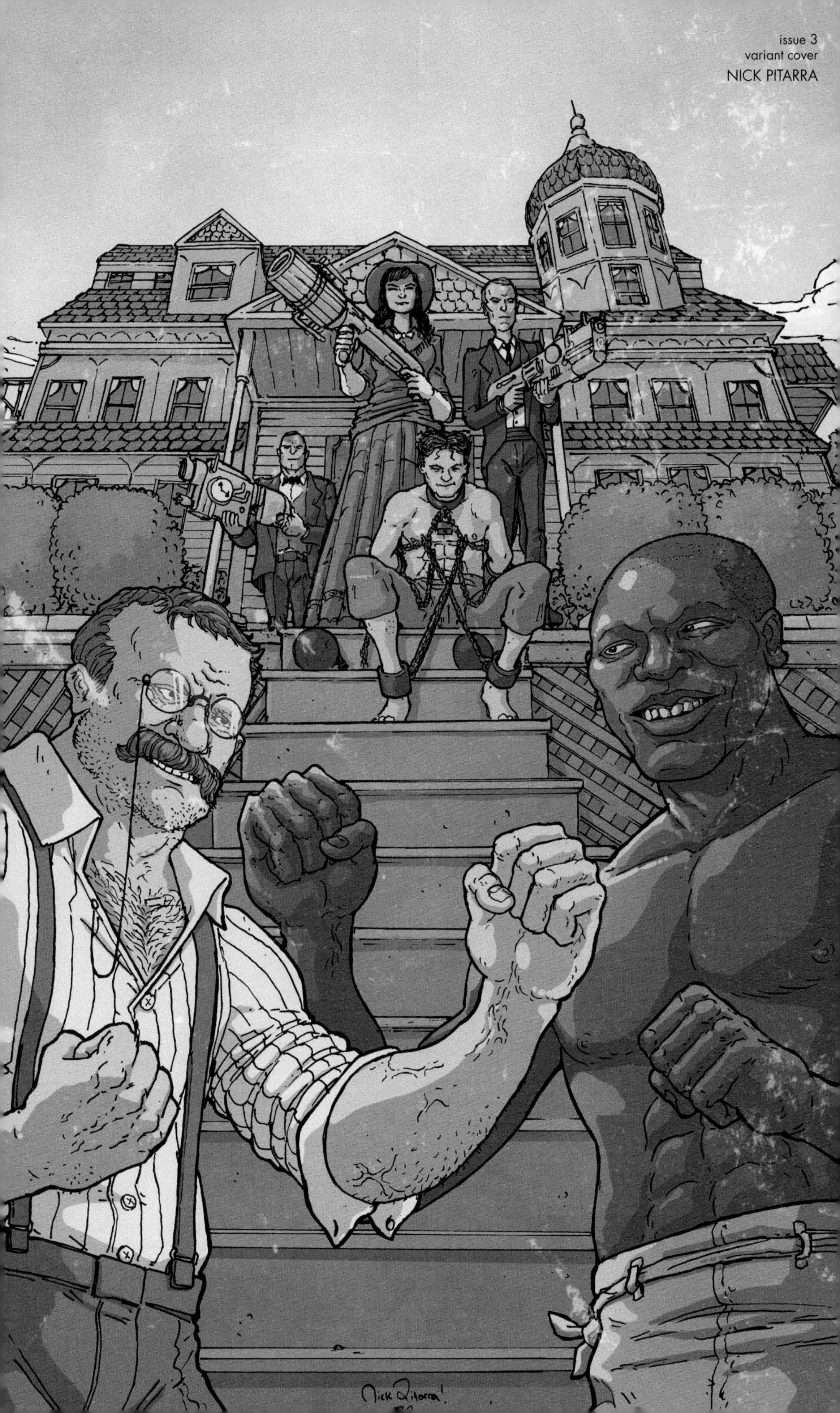
Nick Pitarra!

issue 3
variant cover
NICK PITARRA

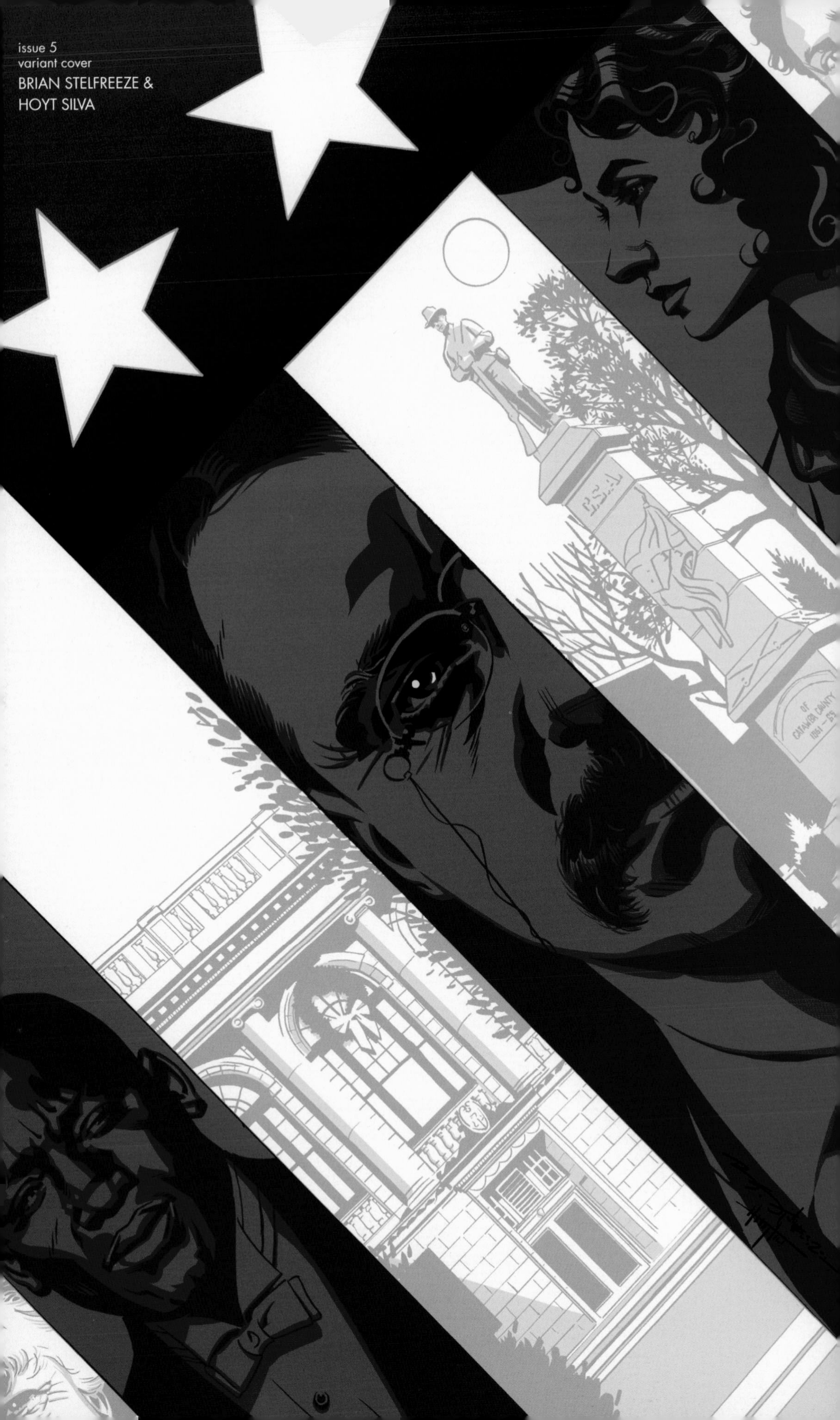
C.S.A.
OF CATAWBA COUNTY 1861 — 65

issue 5
variant cover
BRIAN STELFREEZE &
HOYT SILVA

issue 6
variant cover
ANDREW ROBINSON

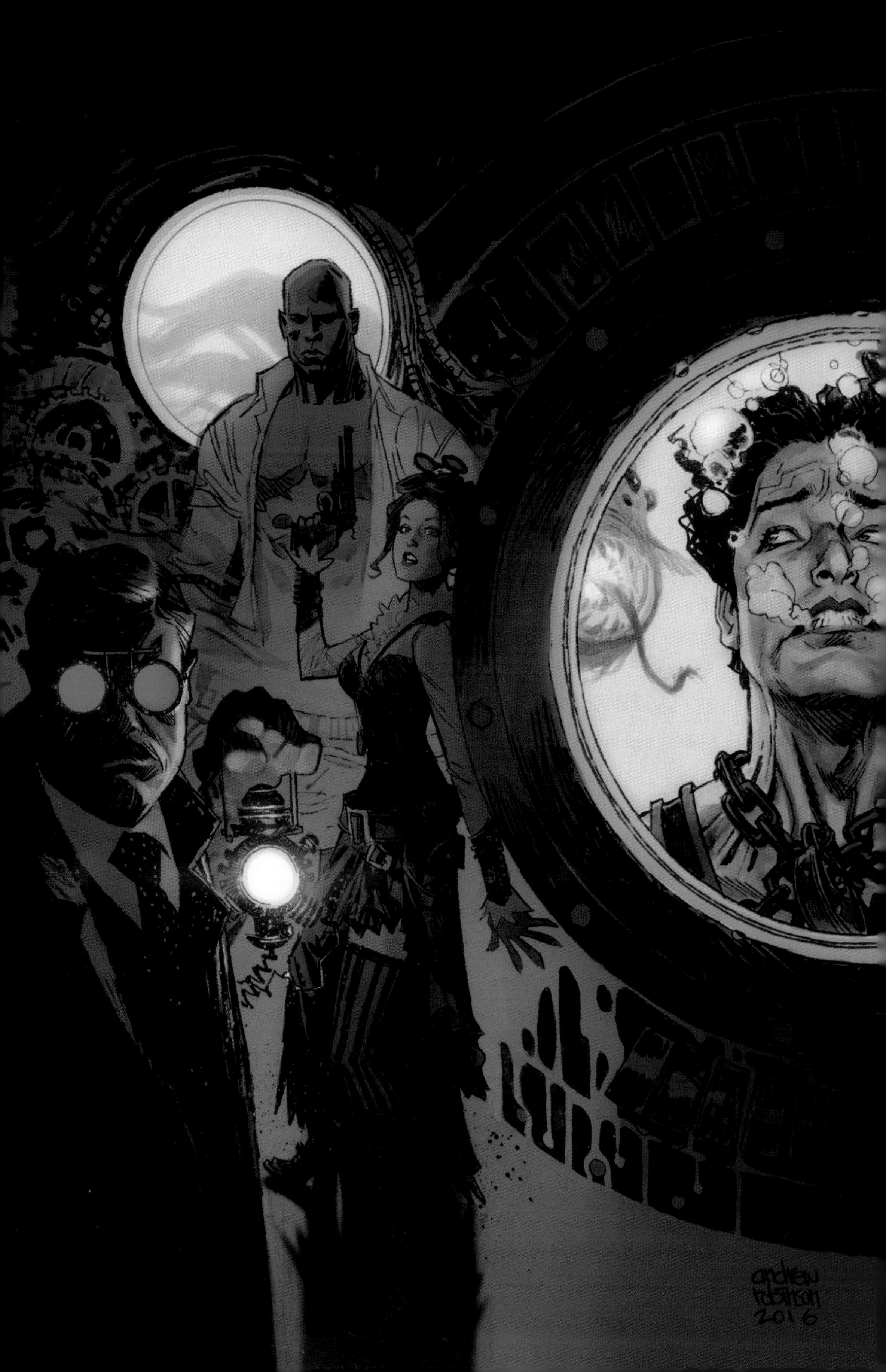

issue 6
variant cover
ANDREW ROBINSON

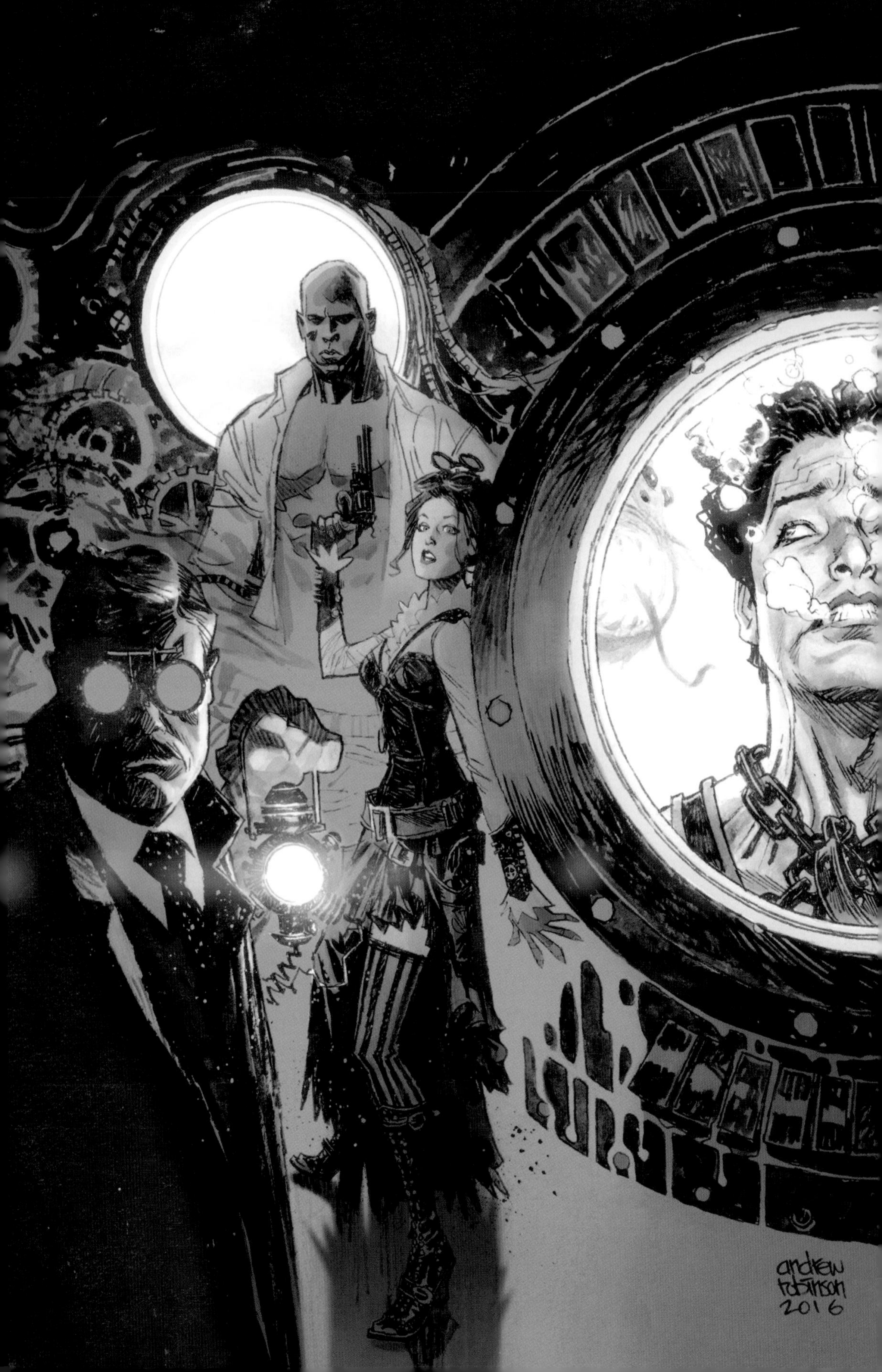
andrew robinson 2016

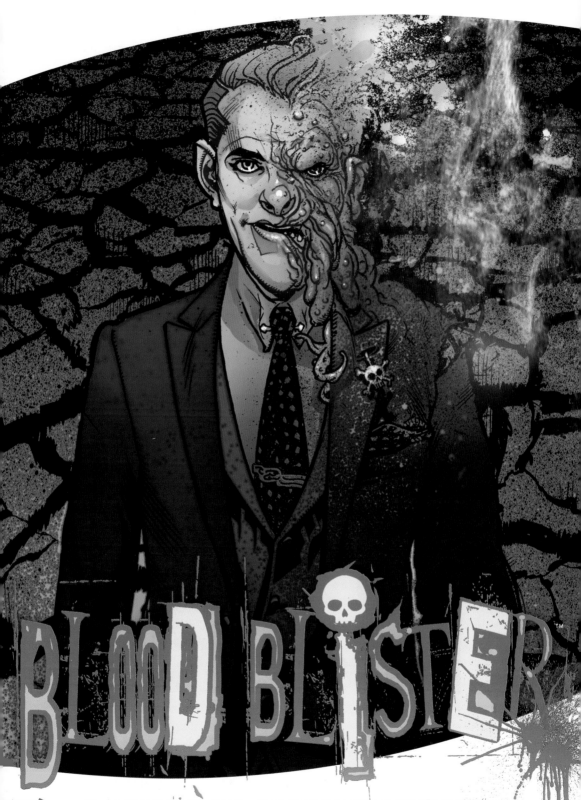

YOU DON'T HAVE TO DIE TO GO TO HELL...
FROM PHIL HESTER (SHIPWRECK, GREEN ARROW)
& TONY HARRIS (STARMAN, EX-MACHINA)

BLOOD BLISTER

COMING IN JANUARY 2017!
THE CREATIVE REVOLUTION STARTS HERE

BLOOD BLISTER Copyright © 2016 by Phil Hester & Tony Harris. All rights reserved. AfterShock Comics and its logos are trademarks of AfterShock Comics, LLC.

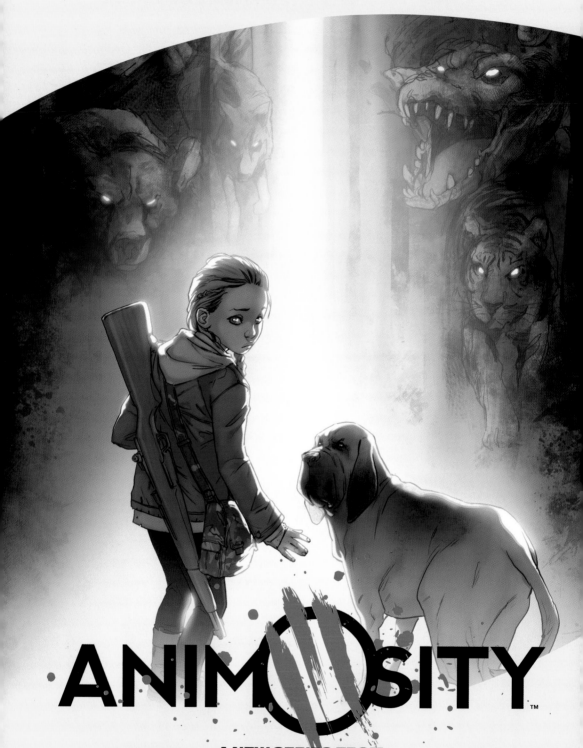

One day, for no damn reason, the Animals woke up.
They started thinking. They started talking.
They started taking revenge.

ANIM(O)SITY ™

A NEW SERIES FROM
MARGUERITE BENNETT (INSEXTS)
AND **RAFAEL DE LATORRE** (SUPERZERO)

ON SALE NOW!
RESERVE THIS AFTERSHOCK SERIES TODAY!

ANIMOSITY Copyright © 2016 by Marguerite Bennett. All rights reserved. AfterShock Comics and its logos are trademarks of AfterShock Comics, LLC.

AFTERSHOCK

SERIES COLLECTIONS

The **ugliest side** of humanity may be humanity's **only hope.**

"Absolutely gorgeous and striking artwork..."
Chris Beveridge
FANDOMPOST.COM

"Epic is not a word I like to throw around, but two issues in you can sense a palpable significance to AMERICAN MONSTER."
Andrew McGlinn
BIGCOMICPAGE.COM

AMERICAN MONSTER

VOLUME 1

COLLECTING THE FIRST FIVE ISSUES FROM
BRIAN AZZARELLO & JUAN DOE

ON SALE NOW!

ALSO AVAILABLE:

AMERICAN MONSTER, REPLICA, SUPERZERO, INSEXTS, BLACK-EYED KIDS & DREAMING EAGLES (including all prominent characters featured herein), logos and all character likenesses are ™ and © 2016 of their respective creators, unless otherwise noted. All rights reserved. AfterShock Comics and its logos are trademarks of AfterShock Comics, LLC.

ADAMN GLASS writer

@AdamGlass44

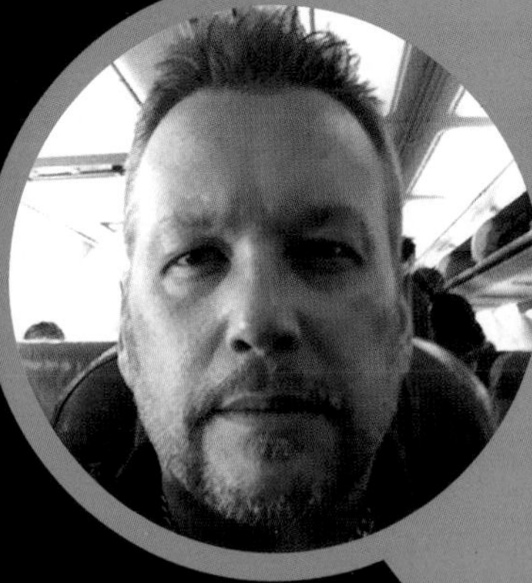

Though NYC will always be home, Adam resides in Los Angeles and is a TV Writer/Executive Producer of such shows as *SUPERNATURAL, COLD CASE* and currently *CRIMINAL MINDS: BEYOND BORDERS* on CBS. When Adam is not writing for TV or films, he's writing graphic novels. Some of these titles include: Marvel's *Deadpool: Suicide Kings* and DC Comics' *Suicide Squad* — both of which were NY Times bestsellers. Other books Adam has written or co-written for Marvel are *Deadpool: Pulp, Luke Cage: Noir, Deadpool Team-Up* and *Luke Cage: Origins.* And for DC, *JLA Annual* and the *Flashpoint* series *Legion of Doom.* Most recently, Adam finished an original graphic novel for Oni Press called *Brick.*

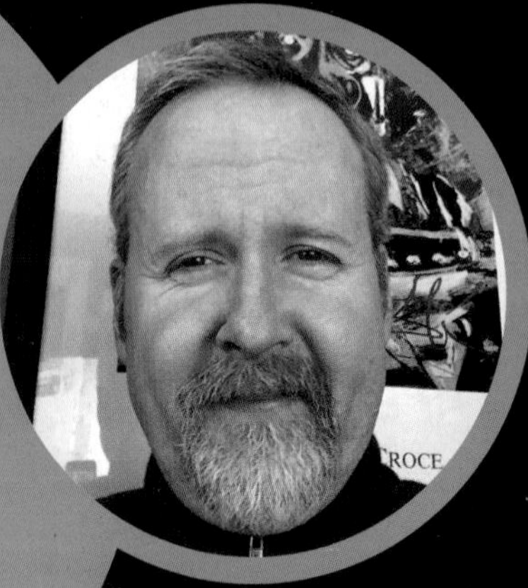

PATRICK OLLIFFE artist

Patrick is a veteran comic book illustrator with over twenty-five years of experience, working for such publishers as Marvel, DC Comics, Dark Horse and Disney. His long list of credits include *Untold Tales of Spider-Man, Spider-Girl, Thor, Captain Marvel, X-Men Gold, 52, The Atom, Superman, Batman, Wonder Woman: 52 Aftermath The Four Horsemen, Catwoman, Barb Wire, Avengers, Captain America Joins The Avengers* and *The X-Men* for Disney's Marvel Press. He is thrilled to be working with Adam Glass on Aftershock's *Rough Riders!*

GABE ELTAEB colorist

@gabeeltaeb

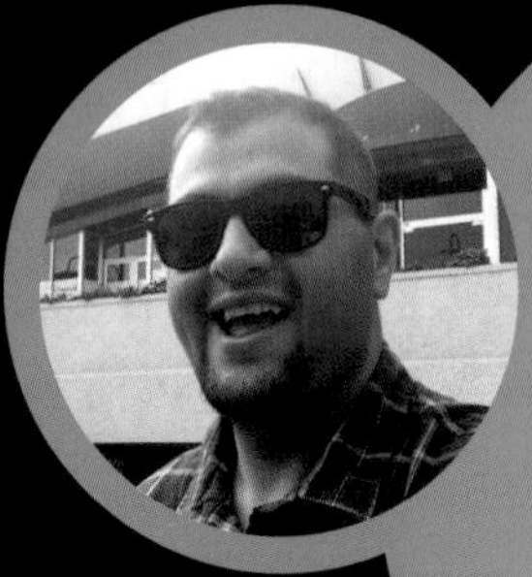

Sharing his hometown of Greeley, Colorado with DC comic's Jonah Hex, colorist Gabe Eltaeb was compelled to work in comics after seeing Jim Lee's cover for *X-Men* #1 in middle school. Gabe grew up in San Diego, married his high school sweetheart, Adrienne, and has three kids. Coming full circle, Gabe was hired by Jim Lee in late 2007 to work as a colorist at Wildstorm. He has colored hundreds of books for DC Comics, Dark Horse, Image and IDW since going pro in 2004. Notable titles include: *Justice League, Star Wars, Green Lantern, Green Arrow, Batman and Robin Eternal* and now *Rough Riders.* Gabe loves the Denver Broncos more than anyone ever could.

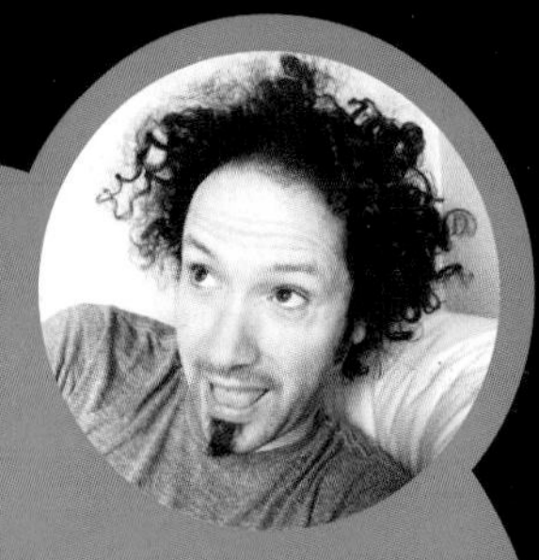

SAL CIPRIANO letterer

@salcipriano

Brooklyn-born/coffee-addicted Sal Cipriano is a freelance letterer and the former Lettering Supervisor for DC Comics. His previous position at DC coupled with experience in writing, drawing, coloring, editing, designing, and publishing comics gives him unique vision as a freelancer. Sal is currently working with — amongst others — DC, Skybound, Lion Forge, Stela, and now AfterShock! Better fire up another fresh pot!